The
Garland
CLASSICS OF
FILM LITERATURE

REPRINTED IN PHOTO-FACSIMILE
IN 32 VOLUMES

Thought Control in the U.S.A.

edited by
Harold J. Salemson

GARLAND PUBLISHING, INC. ● NEW YORK & LONDON ● 1977

Library of Congress Cataloging in Publication Data

Conference on Thought Control in the U. S.,
    Beverly Hills, Calif., 1947.
    Thought control in the U.S.A.

    (The Garland classics of film literature ; 30)
    Reprint of the ed. published by Hollywood
A.S.P. Council, PCA, Hollywood, Calif., under
title: Thought control in U. S. A.
    Includes index.
    1. Liberty--Congresses. 2. Censorship--
United States--Congresses. I. Salemson, Harold J.
II. Progressive Citizens of America. Hollywood
Arts, Sciences, and Professions Council. III. Ti-
tle. IV. Series.
JC599.U5C6 1947a   323.44'0973   76-52131
ISBN 0-8240-2895-3

THOUGHT CONTROL IN U.S.A.

● ● ● ● ● ● ● ● ●

No. 1

the
CONFERENCE

the opening session
the legal aspects

THOUGHT CONTROL IN THE U. S. A.
The collected proceedings of the
Conference on the Subject of Thought Control in the U. S.,
called by the Hollywood Arts, Sciences & Professions Council, PCA,
July 9-13, 1947

Edited by Harold J. Salemson
Designed by Herbert D. Klynn
Published by Hollywood A. S. P. Council, P. C. A.,
1515 Crossroads of the World, Hollywood 28, Calif.

Printed in the U. S. A. by union labor
Aldine Printing Co., Los Angeles, Calif.

(111)

INTRODUCTION

In the comparatively short time that history has been recorded, man's adaptation to the physical world seems to me a remarkable achievement. The bare fact of his survival on an enigmatic and sometimes obstreperous planet is testimony of his resourcefulness and tenacity. It even carries an implicit suggestion that he has some business in being here.

However, in the field of human relations his record has unfortunately been somewhat less creditable. On the whole, he appears to have made a better adjustment to volcanos and tidal waves than to his fellow-creatures. Perhaps because of his precarious footing on this spinning globe—or for whatever economic and psychological reasons,—he too often finds it necessary to dominate rather than adjust on any equalitarian basis. Being of an inventive nature, he has thought up all sorts of ways to maintain supposed or real advantages over other people. Demons, tabus, witches, kings and priests with self-proclaimed divine rights, racial supremacy, manifest destiny—what an imaginative assortment of devices to induce his fellow-men to think along profitable lines—profitable lines to him!

Of course, there have always been those in every generation who spoke up for a rational and humanitarian approach to the problems of their society. By the manipulation of opinion through one or another device like the above, the entrenched authorities of the time usually managed to still their voices with a cup of poison or a cross or an assassin's bullet or a concentration camp. A few generations later, these same martyrs are enshrined while the then authorities are busy persecuting their spiritual successors. In our own day, we watch the same men place wreaths on the grave of Lincoln who are the first to shout "subversive" at anyone whose political precepts even remotely resemble those of the Emancipator.

If this seems a cynical perspective from which to view our past and present, let me now assert my long-range optimism. All over the world people show signs of beginning to think for themselves, of rejecting the fear-words and shibboleths of those whose purpose is to confuse and manipulate rather than nourish the minds of men.

A small but significant manifestation of this growing awareness was the calling of a Conference on the Subject of Thought Control,

1

which we believe was the first of its kind in history. Sponsored by the Arts, Sciences and Professions Council of the Progressive Citizens of America, its participants were representative West Coast scientists, educators, lawyers, doctors, writers, actors, directors, musicians, artists and other cultural workers, who examined the extent of thought control in their respective fields, reporting them to the Conference as a whole.

The sessions were held at the Beverly Hills Hotel, July 9 - 13 of this year, and the audiences that attended overflowed the facilities of the hotel. The conclusions of the reports were of overwhelming unanimity that there is an alarming trend to control the cultural life of the American people in accordance with reactionary conceptions of our national interest. We felt it our obligation to record this evidence in printed form and to make it available to all those who regard freedom of thought as our primary right as Americans and as human beings.

We respectfully dedicate these collected papers of the Conference to the memory of a man who believed in people and gave them the courage, while he lived, to believe in themselves—Franklin Delano Roosevelt.

> HOWARD KOCH,
> *Chairman, Thought Control Conference.*

the opening session

Wednesday, July 9, 1947, 8:00-10:30 P. M.

Howard Koch, Chairman

Speakers: John Cromwell, John Howard Lawson, Bernard Smith, Norman Corwin

Messages from: Roy Harris, Henry A. Wallace, Harlow Shapley, Frank Kingdon, Abraham L. Pomerantz

John Cromwell
Noted film director of Abe Lincoln in Illinois, etc.

INTRODUCTORY ADDRESS

As chairman of the Arts, Sciences and Professions Council of the Progressive Citizens of America, I bid you welcome to this conference on the subject of thought control. When first I heard of the conference, I thought it was going to be one of those cozy, intimate affairs, where a handful or two would gather. Look around and see how wrong I was and know that I was never happier to have been wrong. Again, welcome!

On May 10, 1939, the Museum of Modern Art opened the doors of its new building in New York City, Franklin Delano Roosevelt sent a message to the trustees. In this message I find two paragraphs so rich in understanding, so prophetic in regard to the problem that faces the artist, that I am going to read them to you.

"As in our democracy we enjoy the rights to believe in different religions or in none, so can American artists express themselves in complete freedom from the strictures of a dead artistic tradition or

3

political ideology. While American artists have discovered a new obligation to the society in which they live, they have no compulsion to be limited in method or manner of expression.

"The arts cannot survive except where men are free to be themselves and to be in charge of the discipline of their own energies and ardors. The conditions for democracy and for art are one and the same. What we call liberty in politics resulted in freedom of the arts."

If freedom for the artist can result only from liberty in politics, then freedom for the scientist, the educator, the lawyer and the other professions can result only from liberty in politics. This liberty was ever the profound concern of our late president. This liberty we intend to preserve!

American men and women of the cultural world have played an honorable role in their country's politics, throughout our history, but it has not been made easy for them. Every conceivable type of pressure, from the threat of loss of a job, to adverse publicity, to open intimidation, was used to silence their far-reaching voices.

But the artist, scientist and the professional realized that culture and creative expression could not exist in a vacuum—realized that his right to express his creative thoughts was closely connected with his right to express his political thoughts—and that his means of protecting that right went further than the ballot box. He learned that through working with his fellow artists he could draw strength—and even greater talents. The scientists could give factual knowledge to the writer; the writer could give real inspiration to the actor; the actor could dramatically bring to the people the meaning behind the problems they faced daily—and an answer to those problems. This was the responsibility of the artist, scientist and professional.

As a member of a community that includes some of the finest representatives of the creative fields, I am proud to have been part of the growing awareness of this responsibility. Here in Hollywood, many of us remember the open intimidation of those in the industry who dared to support Upton Sinclair in his fight for better government. We remember the attacks on the Hollywood Democratic Committee, when it so ably campaigned for Franklin Roosevelt. We remember, too, how that sturdy group grew rapidly in membership and influence and became the Hollywood Independent Citizens' Committee of the Arts, Sciences and Professions.

Day by day, leading figures in every cultural field found in this organization the answer to their need to express themselves politically

4

as well as artistically.

Today those needs are being met even more capably by the Arts, Sciences and Professions Council of PCA. In this council the artist not only reaches vast numbers of people with his message, but he works with fellow artists on problems directly affecting his field.

Those who recognize the power of the artist, the scientist and the educator to awaken the people to their dangers, have never hesitated to use every means at their command to stifle these gifted and articulate voices using the great powers of the press, legislative committees—and, of course, name-calling.

Those of us who have been in the fight for many years do not doubt that these attacks were and are political, birthed by politicians and the men behind the politicians. Tonight we are here to examine the current trends toward even greater intimidation of the artist, scientist and professional. If this trend is evident, then we of the arts, sciences and professions must wield political weapons to defeat any and all attempts at thought control whether they be instigated locally, statewide or nationally. Let us learn from the defeats of the past and resolve to stay together and to fight together.

The calling of this conference on the subject of thought control sets a precedent. It's a hopeful precedent, and I know that here we shall set the pattern for such conferences in other cultural centers in our country.

In closing, I would like to read a message to the conference which expresses its spirit and intent: A message from one of the most distinguished composers in the world of music, Roy Harris:

"As I sit here on the afternoon of Independence Day thinking about your thought control conference, I am surrounded by the explosion of fireworks, which is supposed to be in celebration of the winning of America's freedom from England. The independence for which our forefathers fought so desperately was not only economic and political, it was independence of being, independence of thinking and acting. Democracy was conceived in the conviction that the independent thoughts and actions of free citizens would yield a better life than any form of government in which the thoughts and actions of the body politic were controlled by a centralized group.

"Experience has taught us that the control of the thoughts and actions of the many by the few makes for quick decisions and quick actions at the great risk of losing a mutually protective civilization. Experience has also taught us that if we wish the benefit of a broadly

5

canvassed democratic point of view to precede economic and political action, decisions will come slowly, but final actions will be powerfully effective. In fact, the world today stands at a crossroads where one direction is well paved to destruction, and the other direction must be laboriously charted to freedom. We know all too well how straight and sure and swift is the road to annihilation which we could be led down by those who prefer to play the professional game of international politics rather than face the difficult task of finding the way to international understanding, justice and mutual trust and aid.

"We know the road of progress is now, as it always has been, uncharted; we must find each step of the way into the fertile, waiting future, and, strange as it may seem, we must find it against the old ways of thinking, acting and being which have thus far not yielded any nation of people the good life.

"You are quite right in thinking that the old ways have yielded outward circumstances of the good life to those who have been able to take it for themselves—those who were strong enough to take it in whatever way it had to be taken—but those of us who have taken what we needed find small solace in the bulwark of our possessions, because there are always hungry eyes, sad hearts and puzzled minds surrounding us. We human beings seem to be able to master time and space, and the elements of chemistry and the principles of physics, we seem to be able to create the stage properties of a powerfully-humanistic world, but we, ourselves, who have to play the parts in this terrible world-drama, have not as much control over ourselves as we have over the forces which surround us.

"Our whole problem then is not one of creating a more facile mechanism of civilization; our problem is one of learning to be better human beings—as individuals and as groups. This problem can never be solved without progressive thinking towards the solution of human relationships, individually and in groups.

"So, we come directly to the basic problem of thought control. As far back as we have records of human activity, we find that small, organized groups were very effective in controlling the thoughts of unorganized humanity at large. As far back as we can go we find the ruling class arbitrarily taking on to themselves the power of forbidding people to think. Now, of course, actually this is ridiculous, because nobody can control another's thought. It is very difficult for us to control our own thoughts. And so, the ruling groups, whether they were military, political, ecclesiastic, educational or economic,

6

have had to content themselves with controlling the expression of people's thoughts and hoping to condition their thinking by various forms of propaganda. It seems to me, therefore, the purpose of a thought control conference should be that of examining: (1) the means of conditioning people's minds through propaganda; and (2) the machinery whereby the expression of people's thoughts is silenced.

"I am sure that all of us will agree that we cannot have a good civilization without thoughtful citizens. It seems almost axiomatic that the effectiveness of any political, economic system depends directly upon the ability of its citizens to think; that is, if we are to have a society of free citizens. As Nietzsche pointed out, if we wish to have slaves, we must not educate them. The complement of this thought is that if we wish to have free men, we must encourage them to think and protect their rights to express their thoughts. To encourage people to think and to deny them the right of expressing their thoughts would be equivalent to encouraging our farmers to plant and forcing them to allow their harvest to rot.

"I cannot refrain from stating, before closing my letter to this important conference, that anyone who hopes to curtail thought and freedom to express thought is historically a damned fool. One might as well try to keep the sun from shining by raising his umbrella! It might conceivably be done if one could go a step further and remove the brain from all people except those whom they wish to include in their minority group.

"And now, in closing, may I send you my sincere regrets that I cannot be there with you people? I am sure, whether I know you all individually or not, the very fact that you are there makes you my fellow workers towards a better world."

I believe these eloquent words are a fitting introduction to our conference and should be of inspiration to us all.

MESSAGES FROM

Henry A. Wallace

"I was delighted to learn that you have arranged an important conference to discuss thoroughly the ways and means of stopping the dangerous trend towards restriction of basic civil liberties. It is heartening to know that the artists, actors, writers, scientists and professional people of one of our most important cultural centers are not easily intimidated. A specific program of action from your conference will be a genuine contribution in the fight to preserve and extend our civil liberties."

Dr. Harlow Shapley

"This is not the moment to run to cover because of a noisy, inane, dishonest spasm of witch-hunting. To abandon our principles of freedom of speech, and to give up our proper rights of peaceful assembly would be civic cowardice. If Americans do not at this time stand resolutely against the studied crusades of defamation, they will soon be in the helpless cowering position of Fascism's slaves of ten years ago. Both ancient and recent dictatorships have shown the tragic price of submission.

"The situation is frankly incredible. It could scarcely happen under the stress of war hysteria. But now in peacetime we experience persecution and defamation, not because it is needed, or is legal, or is effective, but as a tawdry by-product of political maneuvering. Certainly it is a low stage in American politics when witch-hunting, and the attempt to terrorize progressive thinking and speaking, is used as a transparent device for vote-catching in a presidential election eighteen months away.

"The most un-American activity I know of in America is the performance of the Un-American Activities Committee itself. Its tactics of probe and smear, with misleading reports, are deplored both in Congress and out. The Committee's extra-legal operations have recently brought censure and vigorous protest from sixty-nine leading citizens of Massachusetts—jurors, educators, scientists, and industrial leaders.

"In America we have always had some extreme reactionaries and extreme radicals in our spectrum of political thought. Probably it is healthy that we have them both. But, however we deplore radicals and reactionaries, we can in no way under good law or good conscience stoop to civic persecution. There are no dangers either from extreme left or extreme right that are commensurate with the peril of losing our constitutional freedoms."

Frank Kingdon

"In the name of Americanism the errand boys of reaction are on the most un-American of witch hunts. They are substituting Salem for Monticello as the shrine of their tradition and pillorying free men in the name of security. The president insists that no employee of the government shall be exposed to any group or idea which does not fit the orthodoxy of a man from Texas. The Un-American Affairs Committee would drive from all employment any individual guilty of going beyond the Congressional Record for a fact or a philosophy. They are blind to the truth that there is no security for a free country to compare with that assured by free minds and free speech. They have become enemies of liberty and saboteurs of genuine Americanism. We have no alternative but to meet them on this ground and fight the fight for freedom on all fronts. Thought control is a weapon borrowed from the arsenal of Fascism. Let us bury it once and for all beneath the soil of a free America".

Abraham L. Pomerantz

"Greetings on your magnificent fight to stem the tidal wave of Nazi-like laws which are engulfing California, Michigan, New York, Washington and our entire land. As in Germany, so here, all efforts to resist this destruction of our most sacred heritage, our civil liberties, are being met with a vicious smear campaign. There are two kinds of people in America today: those who, having forgotten the lessons of Nazi Germany, are surrendering without contest to the Fascists out of fear of personal contamination, and those like yourselves who are courageously marching to meet the enemy. May your ranks grow and your courage never falter."

John Howard Lawson

Author, *Theory & Technique of Playwriting,* many plays, screenplays; now making a study of U. S. culture and history

THE HISTORICAL SETTING

ERIC JOHNSTON, speaking recently before the Belgium-American Society in Brussels, assured his audience that Henry Wallace is giving a false impression of American foreign policy and the internal situation in the United States. According to press reports, Mr. Johnston said that "the spirit of imperialism simply does not exist in my country", and asked: "How can you call reactionary a nation so fanatical in its devotion to the ideal of individual liberties?"

One cannot disagree with the statement that we as a people hate imperialism and are devoted to the ideal of individual liberty. Yet Mr. Johnston's optimism, taken in the context of present American policy, seems to many of us, and must have seemed to many of his foreign listeners, a mockery of the ideals and beliefs to which the speaker declared his allegiance.

How does it happen that such common words as liberty and democracy—words which supposedly describe a common American heritage and belief—can be used today in such contradictory ways as to convert our civilization into a tower of Babel, a shining edifice whose builders can no longer understand each other? It is not merely a matter of semantics. It is our future that is being built; it is our house that is jeopardized by the confusion of tongues.

To a considerable extent, the problem is one of historical interpretation. The words that we use, and the beliefs that underlie these words, are derived from our experience as a nation and our understanding of that experience. It may therefore be of value to examine the points mentioned by Mr. Johnston—"the spirit of imperialism" and "the ideal of individual liberties"—in their relationship to the political and cultural development of our country. This may provide us with an over-all pattern, an historical frame of reference, which will aid us in defining the forces that tend to control thought and enforce propaganda-stereotypes in our contemporary society.

10

The conflict between an expanding democratic culture and restrictive or repressive tendencies is as old as our history. It began with the settlement of Jamestown; it originated in England in the struggle between the Court Party and the Popular Party regarding the rights to be exercised under the Virginia charter.

Since the terms of the charter determined the form of colonial government, the struggle was transferred to Virginia, and shortly thereafter to New England. Even in the first year of the settlement of Massachusetts Bay, the outlying villages protested against the authoritarian regime in Boston; a few years later, the defenders of controlled thought scored a temporary triumph with the banishment of Roger Williams, Anne Hutchinson and others, whose insistence on the right to speak was regarded as subversive.

But banishments did not solve the problem. Protests continued. Quakers defied the death penalty to visit Massachusetts Bay, and in the last decade of the Seventeenth Century, the rulers of the colony organized a witch-hunt, which is distinguished from later events of a similar character in that the victims were frankly accused of being witches. American historiography has given us a one-sided impression of the New England witchcraft cases, treating them as a spontaneous outbreak of religious zeal and superstition. The stereotype concerning the Puritanical fanaticism of our New England ancestors is so generally accepted that it comes as something of a shock to discover that the majority of Seventeenth Century New Englanders were not religious at all. Not one in five of the adult population of Massachusetts Bay were church-members, even though those who did not join the church were deprived of the franchise.* It hardly seems reasonable to suppose that the four-fifths of the people who were not even church-members were swept into a religious frenzy by the charge that their neighbors were possessed of devils.

An examination of the political situation at the end of the Seventeenth Century throws considerable light on Cotton Mather's sudden outcry against witches. The coming of William and Mary to the throne of England and the adoption of the English Bill of Rights in 1689 caused a democratic ferment throughout the colonies. In New York, shopkeepers, craftsmen and small farmers seized the government under the leadership of Jacob Leisler; the wealthy landholders fled from New York and a Committee of Safety was elected in the

* James Truslow Adams, *The Founding of New England*, Boston, 1921, p. 121.

11

first genuinely democratic election ever held on the American continent. The Leisler revolution had an exhilarating effect upon the other colonies; delegates from Massachusetts went to New York to attend the first inter-colonial congress, called by Leisler in 1690. The forces that would eventually lead to colonial unity and independence were already in motion.

The situation was tense in Massachusetts. The people suffered seriously from the economic dislocations brought about by the war with France. Popular pressure was responsible for the granting of a new charter in 1691, substituting a property qualification for the religious qualification that had formerly determined the franchise. But the people were not satisfied with this partial victory. The first newspaper printed in the United States appeared in Boston in 1690, and was promptly suppressed, with a statement of "high resentment and disallowance" from the Governor and Council.* The first governor under the new charter, Sir William Phips, was under the influence of the theocracy, which was determined to retain its power.

The trials and executions of witches were designed to consolidate the theocratic control, dramatize the danger of heresy, and divert public attention from political issues. The course of the witchcraft cases parallels the political struggle, beginning in 1688, and reaching a climax with the introduction of the new charter in 1692. By this time, the power of the theocracy was seriously undermined, and drastic measures were required to reinforce the authority of the ruling clergy. Within a short time in 1692, two hundred persons were accused. Of these, one hundred and fifty were imprisoned, nineteen were hanged and one pressed to death. Far from being a matter of public hysteria, the popular opposition was so strong that on several occasions its was necessary to call out the militia to prevent angry crowds from rescuing the victims. As the opposition grew and became organized, the whole scheme of persecution was abandoned. Its abandonment was a decisive political defeat for the theocracy, and marked the end of its power. It also was a milestone on the road to the American Revolution.

The witchcraft trials, like later attempts at legal suppression, were accompanied by an elaborate propaganda, designed to silence opposition and justify the unusual court procedure. In order to prove that there was actually what he described as a "stupendious growth of

*Clyde Augustus Duniway, *Freedom of the Press in Massachusetts*, New York, 1906, p. 69.

12

witches among us",* Cotton Mather had to construct a theoretical base: he had to show that devils habitually enter human bodies and control the actions and words of the unfortunate persons who are thus possessed. He denounced Sadducees; the term was applied to anyone who refused to believe in witches. "No man but a Sadducee", he thundered, "doubts of the ill will of devils".** Rigid censorship of the press prevented the Sadducees from communicating their doubts. But the common sense of the people triumphed over the propaganda. It turned out that the great majority of them were Sadducees. They were not afraid to doubt authority, or to test the truth by their own experience.

Let us move across the years to another crisis in American history—another witch hunt, which occurred almost a century later, when the young Republic was attempting to protect and extend its newly-won freedom. At the end of the Eighteenth Century, the wholesale suppression of free speech under the Alien and Sedition Laws was accompanied by a propaganda campaign as fantastic as Cotton Mather's denunciation of witches. In this case, the Sadducees were allegedly members of an organization called the *Order of the Illuminati*. The international campaign against the *Illuminati* is of special interest because it is the foundation upon which has been built the whole structure of Nineteenth and Twentieth Century propaganda justifying the suppression of free communication and control of "dangerous thoughts". A careful study of the accusations against the *Illuminati* is essential for those who would understand the mechanism of the witch-hunt.

Democratic aspirations stirred the peoples of the world in the years following the American and French Revolutions. The rulers of the British Empire and the monarchs of Europe knew that their thrones were insecure. The old structure of power and privilege was crumbling. In 1797, a book written by John Robison was published in Edinburgh. It charged that all the woes of the world were due to the pernicious influence of the *Illuminati*. According to Robison, the *Illuminati* circulated "doctrines subversive of all notions of morality—of all confidence in the moral order of the universe . . . AN ASSOCIATION HAS BEEN FORMED for the express purpose of ROOTING OUT ALL THE RELIGIOUS ESTABLISHMENTS, AND OVERTURNING

---

*Cotton Mather, *The Wonders of the Invisible World*, London, 1862, p. 97.
** *Ibid.*, p. 237.

ALL THE EXISTING GOVERNMENTS OF EUROPE".* It was asserted that this association was connected with the Free Masons, and functioned through Masonic Lodges.

There really was a society of the *Illuminati.* It was formed in Bavaria in 1776, devoted to moral and intellectual improvement; its membership included Duke Ferdinand of Brunswick, the philosopher Herder, the poet Goethe, the educator Pestalozzi. One need hardly point out that the only crime of which these individuals might be guilty was a penchant for rational speculation and the application of science and philosophy to social problems. However, the American Federalists, closely allied with British reaction, seized upon the yarn about the *Illuminati* as proof that the Jeffersonian political clubs were part of a world conspiracy to destroy all morality and religion. Robison's book was rushed to America and printed simultaneously in New York and Philadelphia; the Philadelphia edition was manufactured and on the market in the unbelievably short time of three weeks. Another similar book about the *Illuminati,* by Augustin Barruel, was published at New York, Hartford, Connecticut, and Elizabethtown, N. J.

The flood-gates of propaganda were let loose. Sermons, leaflets, hysterical appeals, swept the country. While William Cobbett denounced the Jeffersonians as "frog-eating, man-eating, blood-drinking cannibals",** the Reverend Jedediah Morse preached a sermon, which was immediately printed, in which he described the *Illuminati* as approving of promiscuous intercourse between the sexes, condemning the principles of patriotism and the right to accumulate private property; he said the *Illuminati* were seeking to get control of cultural agencies, schools, literary societies, newspapers, writers, booksellers, and postmasters; they were bent on insinuating their members into all positions of distinction and influence, whether literary, civil or religious.*** Shortly afterward, on July 4, 1798, Timothy Dwight, President of Yale University, preached a sermon on *The Duty of Americans in the Present Crisis,* repeating all the charges against the *Illuminati,* tracing their pernicious philosophy to Voltaire and the French Encyclopedists: "In these hot beds were sown the seeds of that astonishing Revolution, and all its dreadful appendages, which now spreads dismay and horror throughout the globe."****

---

*Cited, Vernon Stauffer, *New England and the Bavarian Illuminati,* New York, 1918, pp. 202-203.
**Cited, Charles Warren, *Jacobin and Junto,* Cambridge, Mass., 1931, p. 90.
***Stauffer, *opus cit.,* p. 234.   ****Cited, *ibid.,* p. 249.

14

The scope and force of the social pressure that was exerted in support of these absurdities may be judged from the fact that even George Washington was involved. When the Reverend G. W. Snyder sent Washington a copy of Robison's book, the former President replied that he had heard about the "nefarious and dangerous plan and doctrines of the *Illuminati*", but that he hardly believed that Masonic Lodges in the United States were contaminated. Snyder addressed him angrily, saying that he was surprised that Washington took the danger so lightly. Washington felt constrained to reply that he had not intended to give the impression "that the doctrines of the *Illuminati* and the principles of Jacobinism had not spread in the United States."*

In spite of this high-pressure campaign, and in spite of the reign of terror, the suppression of newspapers and the arrest of editors under the Alien and Sedition Laws, the good sense and democratic will of the American people triumphed. The *Illuminati* scare failed; the discredited Federalists disappeared from the American political scene.

It is not sufficient merely to smile at the imbecilities of the *Illuminati* campaign. We must ask a further question: What were the social forces that directed the campaign of lies? What interests were served by the monstrous distortion of truth?

The Hamiltonian party was engaged in an attempt to exploit and degrade the people which could be successful only through the destruction of the democratic process. The propaganda went to extremes, because the political purpose also went to extremes. American historiography has given a one-sided and misleading impression of the struggle between Jefferson and Hamilton, and has thus concealed the issues that were at stake. An historical stereotype is substituted for the complex reality. We are told that, although Hamilton and Jefferson were diametrically opposed to each other, they were somehow both right. According to James Truslow Adams, "Without Jefferson the new nation might have lost its soul. Without Hamilton it would assuredly have been killed in body".** Allan Nevins and Henry Steele Commager use almost identical phraseology: "Hamilton's aim was to give the country a more efficient organization. Jefferson's great aim was to give individual men a wider liberty. The United States needed both influences.***

This is an assertion that the nation needed democracy, but it also

*Cited, *ibid.*, p. 342.   ***Hamiltonian Principles*, Boston, 1928, p. XVII.
***Pocket History of the United States*, New York, 1943, p. 147.

15

needed its opposite—dictatorship by a financial oligarchy, which Hamilton openly advocated. We can recognize Hamilton's brilliance, the fascinating contradictions in his personality and conduct; but this need not lead us to misunderstand or condone his policies. When the farmers of western Pennsylvania rebelled against the discriminatory taxes that deprived them of the means of livelihood, Hamilton personally led the Army against the rebels, and brought back his prisoners to march in captivity through the streets of Philadelphia. These men placed on exhibition as captives were frontiersmen, tillers of the soil, men who loved independence and had fought in the revolution; they bowed their heads in shame as they were led through the streets.* It was the climax of Hamilton's power. It was also the guarantee of his doom.

The American people were "fanatical", to use Eric Johnston's term, about their newly-won liberties. After that march of captive frontiersmen and veterans through the Philadelphia streets, it seemed as if there could be no question that the issue was joined; there was a clear choice between democracy and suppression. But there were many men at that time who talked of liberty and advocated suppression. The question of human rights was also a question of wages and taxes, homes and living standards. And it was at the same time an urgent question of foreign policy.

American historical thought has tended to assume that, at least as far as the past is concerned, internal problems have no connection with foreign policy, and that our geographical isolation has kept us from being involved in European and world events. The study of our history does not support this assumption, but rather indicates that we have moved in a web of world relationships from our beginnings as a nation—and, indeed, from the first days of colonial settlement. Furthermore, domestic policy has always interacted upon and determined foreign policy. Attempts at exploitation and the impoverishment of the people have invariably been accompanied by a foreign policy contrary to the nation's welfare and the interests of the people. Hamilton's plan for vesting power in the hands of a financial oligarchy necessarily involved subservience to England and abandonment of many of the privileges of trade and commerce achieved through the revolution. In order to exploit American resources, Hamilton and his friends had to mortgage the nation and its liberties to the British Empire.

*Claude Bowers, *Jefferson and Hamilton,* Boston and New York (1925), p. 256.

16

Hamilton's subservience to England brought him tragically close to treason when he conveyed secret information to the British government at a crucial point in the English negotiations with John Jay, in 1794. Hamilton bears a measure of respsonsibility for the dangerous concessions which the United States accepted in the Jay treaty—concessions which prepared the way for the war of 1812.

Hamilton's conduct also verged on treason when he entered into secret correspondence with the Latin-American adventurer, Francesco do Miranda, discussing grandiose schemes for South American conquest. Without the knowledge of the President, John Adams, or of George Washington, Hamilton encouraged Miranda to seek English aid for an American seizure of Florida and Cuba. "Through all this period", as Bowers observes, "Hamilton had visions of himself on horseback, at the head of troops in South America, with England as an ally".*

Thus, imperialism was an urgent question even at this early stage of our history. The men who wished to exploit and degrade the American people also dreamed of foreign aggression and the exploitation of subject populations. The program was a betrayal of democracy. It was also a betrayal of our national interest. Instead of the development of free commerce which Jefferson advocated, we would enter upon military adventures which would necessarily require English financial aid and bind us to British power.

At the height of the *Illuminati* campaign in 1798, the traitor Benedict Arnold wrote that he rejoiced "to hear that so many of my countrymen have shaken off their delusion, as I predicted they would eighteen years ago".** Benedict Arnold was wrong about the people whom he dared to refer to as his countrymen. They had not shaken off their preference for liberty. But he was right in recognizing that there was a link between his own offer to sell West Point to England during the war and the attempt of the Federalists to abandon the achievements of the Revolution and return to a semi-colonial status.

It is to Hamilton's credit that he accepted the popular verdict, retiring from public life with the bitter comment: "Every day proves to me more and more that this American world is not for me".***

But the forces that Hamilton represented were not eliminated from our national life. The remnants of the Federalist party moved

*Ibid., p. 428.
**Cited, ibid., p. 372.
***Cited, ibid., p. 510.

to actual treason in the Hartford Convention in 1814. Greed and privilege assumed new forms and achieved new positions of power, and developed new forms of propaganda.

When Irish immigrants arrived in large numbers to labor in our factories and fields, the special exploitation of these newcomers was aided by a brutal propaganda campaign against Catholics and foreigners. The Catholics were now accused of precisely the same worldwide conspiracy against decency and civil government formerly attributed to the *Illuminati*. The circulation of anti-Catholic falsehoods produced the "normal" results—the burning of the Ursuline Convent at Charlestown, Mass., in 1834, and riots that destroyed houses, schools and churches in Philadelphia a decade later. Books written specifically for this political purpose, such as *Six Months in a Convent*, and the *Awful Disclosure of Maria Monk*, propagated the blatant falsehoods that brought these disturbances—and kept the wages of immigrants at a level which was satisfactory to their employers.

How did these anti-democratic tendencies in the decades preceding the Civil War relate to the question of imperialism, and foreign policy? The bankers and speculators who were the most determined enemies of Jacksonian democracy were closely allied with the Southern plantation-owners. The same bankers and speculators were also entangled with the British financiers and industrialists who purchased the Southern cotton crop.

A three-cornered web of cotton threads was woven between the Eastern seaboard of the United States, Manchester cotton mills and the slave plantations. Nicholas Biddle, of the Bank of the United States, was so deeply involved in the plantation system and its English connections that, during the panic of 1837, he found it necessary to extend heavy unsecured loans to Southern banks even when the position of his own bank was desperate.* These credits were an important contributing factor in the failure of the Bank of the United States.

This complex of power explains the dominant role that the slaveholders assumed in national politics in the decades preceding the Civil War. Southern aims were frankly imperialistic. Slavery involved the wasteful exhaustion of the soil and the exclusion of industrial development. The slave system could not exist without

*Readings in the Economic and Social History of the United States, edited by Felix Flugel and Harold U. Faulkner, New York, 1929, p. 233.

territorial expansion. The rulers of the South inherited the Hamiltonian dream of conquest in Central and Southern America. W. H. Holcombe wrote:

> "We anticipate no terminus to the institution of slavery. It is the means whereby the white man is to subdue the tropics all around the globe to order and beauty, and to the wants and interests of an ever expanding civilization."*

Langdon Cheves called on Southerners to

> "unite, and you shall form one of the most splendid empires on which the sun ever shone, of the most homongeneous population, all of the same blood and lineage.**

Theories of white supremacy and *Lebensraum* for a "homogeneous population" (which obviously did not include the slaves whose labors were the economic basis for the plan) constituted the structure of propaganda that concealed the poverty and degradation of the majority of the white population of the slave states. The enslavement of human beings necessitated the enslavement of the mind. In *The Impending Crisis,* published in 1857, Clinton Rowan Helper wrote that "the South can never have a literature of her own until after slavery shall have been abolished" * * * . . . .

> "Where a system of enforced slavery prevails a fearful degree of ignorance prevails also, as its necessary accompaniment. The enslaved masses, of course, are thrust back from the fountains of knowledge by the strong arm of the law, while the poor non-slaveholding classes are almost as effectually excluded from the institutions of learning by their poverty."* * * *

So the exploitation of human beings, and dreams of empire that would bring limitless wealth to a small privileged group through further exploitation, coupled with enforced ignorance and the degradation of culture, led to treason, and plunged the nation into four years of bloody warfare.

Yes, Mr. Johnston, there has been imperialism and denial of the ideal of individual liberties in our past. The free people of our country fought and died to preserve the Union and create a new birth of freedom. Even in the last year of the Civil War, when Lee's armies were on the verge of surrender, the South tried to stave off disaster by offering to join the North in an imperial adventure. Francis

*Cited, William Sumner Jenkins, *Pro-Slavery Thought in the Old South,* Chapel Hill, N. C., 1935, p. 147.
**Cited, *Cambridge History of American Literature,* New York, 1936, V. III, p. 341.
***Sixtieth edition, New York, 1860, p. 361.
*****Ibid,* p. 398.

P. Blair, Sr., who went to Richmond for a secret interview with Jefferson Davis, reported to Lincoln that Davis offered to lead an invasion of Mexico: Davis suggested "that no circumstance would have a greater effect than to see the arms of countrymen from the North and the South united in a war upon a foreign power".*

One can imagine the sorrowful wonder in Lincoln's eyes when he heard this fantastic proposal. It was not for this that our young men had died at Gettysburg and stormed the heights of Missionary Ridge.

But, as we know, there were many men in the North, including men in positions of great power, who favored the Southern cause. Paradoxically enough, the industrial and financial interests that derived major benefits from the Northern victory found it to their advantage to prevent the full unfolding of the logic of the victory. They were afraid that the emancipation of all labor, from the bondage of poverty as well as from the chains of slavery, which Lincoln had profoundly recognized as the aim of the war, might be carried to a point that would endanger the profits of industrial expansion.

So the weapon of propaganda, the white supremacy myth that had inspired the South, was not abandoned when the Confederate armies laid down their arms. A campaign of distortion and prejudice that has seldom been equalled in history was launched to discredit the democratic Reconstruction of the South. With the abandonment of Reconstruction in 1876, the old alliance of Northern business interests and Southern plantation-owners was reestablished. The Northern captains of industry were now the senior partners in the alliance. They found the ideology of white supremacy extremely useful in implementing their domestic and foreign policy. As immigrants entered the country in increasing numbers to serve the needs of our vast industrial machine, suspicion of foreigners and prejudice against radical agitators who urged the organization of labor were fitted into the existent propaganda structure. Anglo-Saxon superiority justified an aggressive foreign policy and the subjection of lesser breeds.

The propaganda of Manifest Destiny was an extension of the earlier Southern demand for territorial expansion.

Josiah Strong wrote in 1885:

> "This race of unequaled energy . . . the representative, let us hope, of the largest liberty, the purest Christianity, the highest civilization—having developed peculiarly aggressive traits calculated to impress

*John G. Nicolay and John Hay, *Abraham Lincoln, A History*, New York, 1908, Vol. X, pp. 101-104.

its institutions upon mankind, will spread itself over the earth. If I read not amiss, this powerful race will move down upon Mexico, down upon Central and South America, out upon the islands of the sea, over Africa and beyond".*

And John W. Burgess, most eminent historian of the period, advocated an autocratic state and pointed to the manifest superiority of the Teutonic race. He opposed "participation of other ethnical elements in the exercise of political power" . . . He said the Teutonic nations were "called to carry the political civilization of the modern world into those parts of the world inhabited by unpolitical and barbaric races; *i.e.,* they must have a colonial policy".**

The suppression of the strike movement in the 1890's and the defeat of the Populists were related to the development of an aggressive foreign policy. The authoritarian trends manifested in the treatment of American workers at Pullman and Homestead and Coeur d'Alene were also manifested, for the accomplishment of identical ends, in Hawaii and the Philippines.

Eric Johnston may never have heard of American imperialism, but it was a fateful issue to thousands of Americans who formed the Anti-Imperialist League in 1899 to protest the further development of an un-democratic and dangerous foreign policy. The League soon had a hundred branches. Thought control was invoked to interfere with its activities, and an attempt was made to bar its pamphlets from the mails.

During the years preceding the First World War, American investments in foreign lands, and especially in the Western Hemisphere and the Pacific area, increased rapidly. We undertook direct and forcible interference in the affairs of Colombia, Nicaragua, and Mexico. The change in the whole pattern of international relationships that followed the First World War brought a major crisis in American domestic and foreign policy.

In 1919, the most sweeping attempt at thought control since the Alien and Sedition Laws was instituted in the United States. During the witch-hunt conducted by A. Mitchell Palmer, Attorney General of the United States, more than four thousand people were arrested and there were 505 deportations. Workers' meetings were lawlessly broken up; private homes were entered and innocent persons were

*Cited, Julius W. Pratt, *Expansionists of* 1898, Baltimore, 1936, p. 6.
**Political Science and Comparative Constitutional Law, New York, etc., 1890, pp. 44-45. It is only fair to note that Burgess opposed American war with Spain, and joined in protest against the imperialist policy that followed it.

21

dragged to jail. What was the purpose of the deportation delirium? It was designed to crush the steel strike and other efforts of workers to raise their wages to meet the spiralling prices that followed the war. Louis F. Post, who was Assistant Secretary of Labor at the time, speaks of the event as "a nightmare" creating "a collection of lawless precedents".* He also observes that "the whole 'red' crusade seems to have been saturated with 'labor spy' interests."**

There is no secret of the benefits that Big Business derived from the Palmer raids. With their usual patriotism, the employers of labor formed organizations to foster *The American Plan,* which was simply the Open Shop. In 1920, fifty organizations pledged to the Open Shop were formed in New York State alone, and in January 1921 a convention of manufacturers in Chicago developed the plan on a national scale.

The drive against American wages and living standards instituted by the Palmer raids was accompanied by an increasingly reactionary foreign policy. American historians have failed to note the interrelationship between the Palmer raids and the defeat of Wilson's proposal for American membership in the League of Nations. An examination of the Hearst and other papers at the time will show what excellent propaganda use they made of the hysterical attacks on Communists, radicals and alleged foreign agents. Scare headlines day after day warned that membership in a world organization for peace would place us at the mercy of the dangerous foreigners whose agents were already in our midst. Embittered and divided by the attacks on labor, the people voted against the League.

But refusal to join the League did not mean our abandonment of participation in world affairs. On the contrary, we by-passed the League of Nations in order to pursue an independently aggressive policy of economic domination and control of foreign markets. We continued active interference in Mexico, Central and South America, support of reactionary European regimes, suppression of the democratic movement that emerged under Sun-Yat-Sen's leadership in China, and the economic blockade of the Soviet Union. All of these policies disrupted normal trade activities and contributed to the severity of the approaching economic catastrophe.

So the United States moved into the profiteering and corruption of the Roaring Twenties. The sacred rights of the individual were

*The Deportation Delirium of Nineteen-Twenty, Chicago, 1923, pp. 89-90.
**Ibid., p. 56.

safeguarded by the Open Shop and political gangsterism. When Harry M. Daugherty, Harding's Attorney General, was implicated in the Teapot Dome scandal, he blamed it all on the reds:

> "I was the first public official that was thrown to the wolves by orders of the Red borers of America."*

Al Capone was another of the defenders of American ideals:

> "We must keep the worker away from Red literature and Red ruses; we must see that his mind remains healthy".**

Concluding his great work on American culture in the last years of the Twenties, Vernon Louis Parrington described American history as a "ceaseless conflict between the man, and the dollar, between democracy and property".*** It seemed to Parrington that the power of privilege, centered in huge aggregations of wealth, moved toward greater triumphs. He could not know the changes that would come with the great depression—a depression that was guaranteed by the policies inaugurated by the Palmer raids and continued by the Harding, Coolidge and Hoover administrations. Parrington could not foresee the flowering of democratic action that would meet the crisis and bring Franklin Delano Roosevelt to the Presidency in 1933. The vast creative power of the people, which has been demonstrated at repeated crises in our history, was mobilized under Roosevelt's inspiring leadership, to restore prosperity and unite us against the most dangerous attack that the nation had ever been called upon to meet.

It seems evident that there is a pattern and direction in the whole course of our history; Americans have hated imperialism and loved liberty. But imperialism and exploitation are also a continuous part of our history. We have preserved our rights, and advanced our economic interests only to the degree that we have consciously recognized and opposed those who would betray the nation and degrade its people. Are these forces of power and privilege stronger or weaker, today, than they have been in the past? It takes very little pondering upon the lessons of history to answer the question. The enormous concentration of economic power in the past half-century, the national and international organization of trusts and cartels, has created a political and economic force which controls a technological potential and means of propaganda that no previous epoch in history has known.

---

*Cited, W. E. Woodward, *A New American History*, New York, 1938, p. 826-827.
**Cited, *ibid.*, p. 827.
***Main Currents in American Thought*, 3 vols., New York, 1927-1930, Vol. III, p. 410.

But the people also have increasing strength, deeper experience, greater capacities for democratic organization. In order to realize these capacities, we must know our history and recognize the forces that seek to limit and destroy our liberties.

The purposes of privileged groups seeking autocratic control follow a recognizable pattern. Historical thought, as I have had occasion to note in the foregoing discussion, has tended to obscure this pattern, to veil the essential issues in the long conflict "between man and the dollar". Historical literature is an integral part of our culture and reflects the pressures which affect other branches of literature, as well as art, science and education. These pressures have resulted in a systematic underestimation of the role of the people as a creative force in history, and this in turn is responsible for much of the confusion and outright cynicism that becloud our faith in democracy today.

The attempt to divide the people and prevent the full functioning of the democratic process has led to the use of certain propaganda-structures which have a remarkable continuity. The only significant new development from the days of the *Illuminati* campaign is the increasing emphasis on Anglo-Saxon superiority and the systematic appeal to religious and racial prejudice. We have noted that this began with the influx of foreign labor into the United States in the early Nineteenth Century, and merged with the propaganda against the Negro that originated in the slave South. The purposes of this propaganda are self-evident: it divides labor, disfranchises an important part of the population, helps to maintain a special area of intensified exploitation in the South, enables politicians who are not elected by the people to sit in Congress and make our laws, and justifies American participation in the exploitation of colonial peoples.

The whole structure and function of this propaganda were revealed in 1919. Along with the Palmer raids and the attack on trade unions, went the revival of the Ku Klux Klan. From 1920 to 1921, and as the direct accompaniment of the propaganda that implemented the Palmer raids, the Klan increased its membership from 2,000 to 700,000; and in 1925, it was said to have nearly nine million members. The figure is hardly believable, but it may be explained in part by the flood of expensive propaganda attacking Communists, Jews, Catholics, Negroes and foreigners that was spread across the country. The *Protocols of Zion,* a forged document purporting to prove a Jewish conspiracy to control the world, was printed by the *Dearborn Independent,* a periodical wholly controlled by Henry Ford, and circulated in millions of copies in a dozen languages. Respectable historians and philosophers contributed arguments as irrational as those presented by Cotton Mather to prove the existence of witches. Lothrop Stoddard wrote *The Revolt Against Civilization: The Menace of the Underman,* devoted to an attack on the barbarous Russians, and purporting to show that "civilization depends upon superior racial stocks",* . . . "the idea of 'natural equality' is one of the most pernicious illusions that ever afflicted mankind".**

It was fairly customary at this period to link the *Protocols of Zion* with the *Illuminati* as the basis for the Red conspiracy that was supposed to threaten mankind. Nesta H. Webster, in a volume, *World Revolution,* published in 1921, traced the trouble to the French Revolution, the *Illuminati* and the Freemasons: "If the Protocols are genuine, they are the revised programme of illuminized Freemasonry formulated by a Jewish lodge of the order.***

Today the old propaganda machine is again grinding out its lies. The imebecilities of the *Illuminati* campaign are repeated in our press and on the radio. The Klan rides again. I. F. Stone reports in *PM* that Washington is "living under the shadow of terror". Medieval superstition degrades our colleges. Professors are urged to take thought that the plague of non-conformity is a communicable disease. As they brood in their studies, scholars may seem to feel a spectral presence, and to hear the ghostly voice of Cotton Mather:

"May not the devil make me, though ignorantly and unwillingly, to be an instrument of doing something that he would have to be done? For my part, I freely own my Suspicion, lest something of Enchantment, have reached more persons and Spirits among us, than we are well aware of."****

Those of us who retain our intellectual equilibrium are not impressed by tales of witches. We know that Karl Marx was a social philosopher, not a sorcerer. We are aware that Communists believe in the socialist organization of society, and that they have the inalienable right to express their views, which can be debated without danger that evil spirits will speak from our lips and convulse our limbs.

But we also know that the powerful interests which spread this propaganda are our enemies as a nation. The only true national interest is that of the people. The demands of the people, and

*New York, 1925, p. 20.
**Ibid., p. 30.
***Boston, 1921, p. 308.
****Wonders of the Invisible World, p. 30.

25

especially of the classes that are underprivileged, are inevitably related to the welfare of the whole nation, because the welfare of the people depends on the general level of employment and income. On the other hand, vested interests pursue aims which do not serve, and which are frequently antithetical to, the national welfare. These aims are expressed in the use of anti-social and divisive propaganda.

Alexander Hamilton and the Federalists were prepared to abandon the gains of the Revolution, to sacrifice the national independence we had achieved—because they could make a better profit by subservience to the bankers and merchants of London. The Southern plantation-owners did not hesitate to destroy the Union to protect their property in human chattels. Recent events in Europe show that men who seek to exploit their own people are utterly impervious to patriotism. Petain was no less a traitor than Benedict Arnold. To call Franco a Spaniard is an insult to the brave people of Spain.

American scholars, artists and writers have played an historic role in fighting for a democratic culture, in championing truth and opposing "every form of tyranny over the mind of man".

In September, 1800, shortly before the national election that would decide the nation's future course, Abraham Bishop was scheduled to give an address before the Phi Beta Kappa Society at Yale. When it was discovered that Bishop intended to make an attack on the *Illuminati* fantasy, the speech was cancelled, on the ground that it would involve Phi Beta Kappa in what the society described as the "political turmoil that disgraces our country."* But Bishop secured a hall in New Haven, and spoke before a crowded audience on the night of the Phi Beta Kappa meeting. The address on *The Extent and Power of Political Delusion* helped to organize the growing public opposition to the witch-hunt. Bishop was scurrilously attacked, but he continued to speak and write, not only exposing the *Illuminati* delusion, but exposing its motive and purpose, as an attempt to subvert democracy and "to prostrate the public mind".**

This is only one of thousands of similar incidents. I should like to quote from a speech that George William Curtis delivered at Wesleyan University in August, 1856, on *The Duty of the American Scholar to Politics and the Times*:

"As the American scholar is a man and has a voice in his own government, so his interest in political affairs must precede all others.

*Stauffer, *opus cit.*, p. 356.
**Ibid, p. 359.

He must build his house before he can live in it . . .

"Young scholars, young Americans, young men, we are all called upon to do a great duty. Nobody is released from it. It is a work to be done with hard strokes, and everywhere. I see a rising enthusiasm, but enthusiasm is not an election; and I hear cheers from the heart, but cheers are not votes . . .

"Gentlemen, while we read history, we make history. Because our fathers fought in this great cause, we must not hope to escape fighting".*

American writers and scholars responded to that call. There was a flood of pamphlets, speeches, broadsides, which supported the new Republican Party, brought Lincoln to the White House in 1861, and preserved the Union.

Almost exactly twenty years ago, on August 22, 1927, I was one of a number of American writers, artists and educators who were arrested in front of the State House in Boston for protesting the execution of Sacco and Vanzetti, which was to take place that night. Among those arrested was Edna St. Vincent Millay. She wrote a poem about it, *Justice Denied in Massachusetts;* this is·one stanza:

"What from the splendid dead
We have inherited—
Furrows sweet to the grain, and the weed subdued—
See now the slug and mildew plunder,
Evil does overwhelm
The larkspur and the corn;
We have seen them go under."

We were released on bail. A group of us walked through the streets of Boston that night. I recall that we stopped and listened as a bell tolled midnight, and we knew that two innocent men, a fish-peddler and a shoemaker, were dead. It seemed impossible that this thing could happen, in Boston, on a summer night in the third decade of the Twentieth Century. We did not realize that their death was part of a pattern that began with the Palmer raids. Their arrest was an incident of the raids. They were taken from a streetcar in Brockton, Massachusetts, in 1920, and accused of a hold-up and murder. Their only crime, as Vanzetti wrote to his friend's son, was that they "fought modestly to abolish crimes from among mankind and for the liberty of all".** As this became increasingly apparent, it became increasingly necessary that they should die—so that the frame-up would not be admitted, so that the policies that were driving toward depression and

*New York, 1856, pp. 42-46.
**Cited, *The Democratic Spirit,* edited by Bernard Smith, New York, 1941, p. 707.

27

another world war would not be exposed.

In the same year, 1927, American marines participated with English and Japanese troops in the attack on Shanghai, which prevented the democratic unification of China and opened the way for further Japanese aggression in Asia. In the same year, a group of Japanese leaders prepared the *Tanaka Memorial;* with the defeat of democracy in China, which was unavoidably bound up with its defeat in Boston, Japan was ready to plan the campaign of war and aggression that culminated at Pearl Harbor.

As we stood in the street and listened to the bell toll, we did not know that it tolled for us, and for millions all over the world; that we were caught in a web of evil; that the failure of our protest was the failure of a world.

Today another intricate and deathly web is being woven around us. But we have learned a lesson. We know that the sword of truth can cut the web. This time, we dare not fail.

At this point, Mr. Bernard Smith read a passage from his book, The Democratic Spirit, *quoting from the writings of John Adams.*

Norman Corwin

Network radio writer and producer since 1938; author, four
books; first winner, Wendell
Willkie One World Flight Award

THE KEYNOTE

THIS conference is met to act upon a concern more vital than any which has agitated this country since the end of the war. I speak of thought control, and when I give it billing above such recent history as the killing of other controls, the passage of anti-labor bills and the short-circuiting of the United Nations, I do so simply because thought control has been seen in the company of them all, and is the chief agency by which, in the past, freedom has been abridged and peace destroyed.

Let me define, at the outset, what I mean by thought control. I mean the control of public thought, hence, public opinion, by distortion, overemphasis or suppression of facts; by concentrated and systematic propaganda tending to create suspicion, hatred and fear; by the manufacture of synthetic hysteria; by the smearing of opposition; by the denial of basic civil liberties and due process of law; by the avoidance of anything resembling a direct plebiscite of the people; and by restrictive action against education in particular and culture in general. There may well be other meanings. If so, I am sure the conference will fill them in.

For the moment, however, let's forget these individual meanings and go to a broad and overall definition. The shape of the main pattern is indicated nowhere better than in Archibald MacLeish's stirring preamble to the constitution of UNESCO. In it he expressed a profound truth, which I believe is the key to the foremost problem in the world today.

"Since war begins in the minds of men," wrote MacLeish, "it is in the minds of men that the defenses of peace must be constructed." In other and lesser words, the mind of man is disputed ground; it is the arena in which the issues of our time must be fought. It follows, then, that what enters the mind of man—what is permitted to enter— influences, if not actually determines, what is to come of the peace and the future.

29

Unfortunately, the first to acknowledge the importance of controlling men's thoughts and the quickest to respond with a program of action, have not been the MacLeishes, the delegates to UNESCO, the people of good will, but quite the opposite of them—men who for personal or partisan profit or power, for selfish interest, have always sought and are still seeking to control opinion. This fight has been going on for a long time now, in dozens of countries, and the annals are wet with blood; the struggle is universal, and covers the globe itself. What we're concerned about here and now is the area of the United States. The fact that thought control obtains in other lands, does not make it any more admirable or acceptable here, and it is only by freeing America from this danger that we can in clear conscience call upon other nations to follow suit.

One could spend hours merely listing the atrocities against freedom of expression which, in the attempt to control thought, have been committed in this country in the past year. Every propaganda weapon in the arsenal of reaction has been used against labor, liberals, minorities and against the populace at large, in the drive to achieve new repressive measures, to enact unpopular legislation, and to keep old pre-war institutions, like lynching and the poll tax, alive and well.

The techniques of biased reporting, barrage propaganda, the red herring and the smear have been around for a long time, and have passed in and out of political storage in cycles. But what makes this crop more dangerous than any of its predecessors is that for the first time the techniques of war have advanced to the point where the catastrophe common to all war must occur this time on an astronomical scale.

What makes it necessary to formulate an immediate program on the broadest possible scale, is that the methods and boldness of current thought control, including the artful creation of a war psychosis, are now so far out of bounds that they can no longer be checked in the forum, or by debate, or by the persuasion of logic. There is no hope for a brief, however brilliant and penetrating, if it must go unheard, or if its advocate is slandered by a self-appointed judge and jury before he comes into court.

The present hysteria and the phony climate of crisis may well force the embattled liberal to last-ditch democratic safeguards of constitutional and civil law. This, and the rallying of the electorate to the awareness of danger in time for remedial action at the polls, may well become the only recourse left to Rooseveltian democracy—a democracy that only a few years ago was good enough to have twice saved the nation from disaster—first, economic, then, military.

I speak continually of danger and menace. It is easy to think, in the casualness of day-to-day life, that these words exaggerate the situation as it applies to Mr. MacLeish's "defenses of peace."

I ask you, then, to take the word of General Eisenhower, who said a few days ago that war could happen within a year.

I ask you to take the word of Fiorello LaGuardia, who said a few days ago that if we continue our present foreign policy we shall certainly get war.

On the specific menace of thought control, I ask you to take the word of the recent Commission on Freedom of the Press, a commission operating on monies granted by Henry Luce and the Encyclopedia Britannica and disbursed by the University of Chicago. The report of the Commission, which I commend to the study of all persons concerned with thought control, says some startling things in its section on the press. It recognizes that the press of America

> "can endanger the peace of the world . . . can play up or down the news and its significance, foster and feed emotions, create complacent fictions and blind spots, misuse the great words, and uphold empty slogans . . . These instruments can spread lies faster and farther than our forefathers dreamed when they enshrined the freedom of the press in the First Amendment to our constitution . . . The press can be inflammatory, sensational and irresponsible. If it is, it and its freedom will go down in the universal catastrophe . . . It becomes an imperative question whether the performance of the press can any longer be left to the unregulated initiative of those who manage it."

I quote these passages not just to underscore the element of danger, but to indicate that the menace of thought control is worrying other than political minorities, progressives, artists, scientists and trade unions. The menace is so well established and documented as to be at the core of this nonpartisan report. The weight of evidence, as I believe you shall find in the course of this conference, is crushing.

It is worth noting the desperate and sometimes lunatic character of reaction in America today. I don't mean only the hooded gangs, the Columbian types, the Christian Fronters. I am speaking now of the widely-circulated and powerful voices which are influencing, or attempting to influence, all American thought. These voices, and their backers, have carried the device of the wild alarm, the smear and the blackout, to degenerate lengths without precedent in our history. It has not been usual for former vice-presidents of the United States to be denied the right to speak in publice places.

According to the self-appointed vigilantes, this country is overrun with Communists ready at any moment to overthrow the Army, the Navy and the government itself. We gather that there are so many Reds in government jobs right this minute that an appropriation of $25,000,000 is needed to clean them out. We gather that the best minds and the finest talents in the United States belong to Communists—that Albert Einstein and Thomas Mann, Orson Welles, Ingrid Bergman, Van Wyck Brooks, Robert E. Sherwood, Dore Schary, Lillian Hellman, Archibald MacLeish, William L. Shirer, Raymond Gram Swing, Leonard Bernstein, Samuel Grafton, Max Lerner, Olivia de Havilland, Katharine Hepburn, Bartley Crum and Henry Wallace are Communists. There was a time when a Communist meant Earl Browder or William Z. Foster, but in recent years and months it has come to mean, from time to time, Shirley Temple, Frank Sinatra, Franklin D. Roosevelt, Mrs. Roosevelt, James Roosevelt, Elliott Roosevelt, Wendell Willkie, Harry Hopkins, Glen Taylor, Claude Pepper, Marshall Field, John Garfield, Myrna Loy, Melvyn Douglas, Edward G. Robinson, Danny Kaye, Christopher Marlowe, Ralph Ingersoll, Fredric March, Gene Kelly, Carlson Evans, Clyde Miller, James Cagney, Franchot Tone, Chet Huntley, Euripides, Clifford Odets, Garson Kanin, Walter Winchell, John Roy Carlson, Bette Davis, Cecil Brown, Robert Kenny, John Steinbeck, Eddie Cantor, the World Security Workshop, Phil Baker's *Take It or Leave It* program, Metro-Goldwyn-Mayer, Sam Goldwyn and the Warner Brothers.

How Marlowe and Euripides got in there I don't know. But the witch-hunters never stop at a little thing like anachronism. They flay corpses just as hard as the living. If the deceased happened to have been the author of a democratic idea, or the *ancestor* of the author of a democratic idea, then his shade must expect to be attacked—if not as a Communist, then as a wife-beater, a warmonger or a dope trader. There was a discovery in Westbrook Pegler's column last month, stating:

> "We have learned that old Warren Delano, the late president's grandfather, was an opium smuggler in Canton, China, and founded his fortune on this criminal trade."

On the previous day, Dr. Charles Tansill, professor of history at Georgetown University, announced that Abraham Lincoln had maneuvered the South into starting the Civil War. He said Lincoln "played fast and loose" with the Southerners and tricked them into bombarding Fort Sumter, thus making them appear the aggressors.

The psycopathic nature of thought control is such that after a while hallucination sets in, and those who are prey to suggestion begin seeing sea monsters and flying saucers. In New York City recently the opponents of a boost in subway fare were branded "leftist". Any catastrophe which is not clearly an act of God is likely to be considered an act of the Kremlin. Thus it was publicly suggested by a congressman from Texas that Communists were responsible for the Texas City holocaust. Samuel Grafton, in the *New York Post,* writes that

"in Washington the theory is advanced that anybody who charges any American with being a Fascist must be a Communist. In business circles anybody who mentions the danger of recession is a Communist, trying to destroy our economy . . . A portion of our population is slowly reaching the stage where it blames Communists when it can't find its socks in the morning."

Thomas L. Stokes, in the *Los Angeles Daily News,* notes that

"it has become almost a crime to speak of cheaper medical care. Urging federal health insurance has caused even some members of Congress to be called Communists."

According to the standards of those who would control American thought, any opposition to the policies, ethics and practices of the right wing of the Republican Party, the Southern Democrats, or the advocates of Anglo-Saxon white Christian supremacy, is either a Communist, a fellow-traveller, or unconsciously under Moscow's hypnotic influence. Hence the avidity with which Jews are linked with Communists, by all true reactionaries.

Nothing of what I am saying is a defense of Communism, American or foreign; nothing of what I am saying is a defense or even a discussion of Russian policy or intentions. The issue of freedom of expression versus thought control would remain the same if focussed, as it has been in the past, upon witchcraft, the theories of Galileo, Catholicism, abolitionism, syndicalism, the labor movement, inoculation, socialism, Mormonism, Judaism, child labor, vivisection, birth control, or the cult of Jehovah's Witnesses. It is merely that Communism at home happens to be a convenient and workable pretext, right now, to abrogate freedom of expression, mostly in the interest of altogether unrelated and nefarious ends. The device is not new. Don't forget that Franklin Roosevelt was obliged three times to go on the air and declare he was not a Bolshevik.

Overnight, at the drop of an issue, you can become a Red, though you may not know Karl Marx from Groucho Marx. Opposition to the Truman Doctrine became *prima facie* evidence of Communist leanings if not connections. Objection to the disloyalty bill on any ground, legal, moral or political, became *prima facie* evidence of disloyalty itself.

If you fight for lower rents, higher wages, better working conditions; if you are against silicosis in the mines or fraudulent advertising; if you are for health insurance and protection of the rights of the foreign-born; if you favor consumer cooperatives and fair employment practices; if you are·for equality of opportunity in education; if you are against Jim Crowism and the poll tax; if you are for foreign cultural exchange; if you stand for One World or any of the doctrines tributary to it; if you believe literally what is said in the great documents of freedom upon which the United States and the United Nations are established, then you are suspect of participation in a colossal international Communist Front.

Even the term "democracy," which up to now has been admissible to the lexicon of American reaction—if only as a cloak—has come to make the reactionaries uncomfortable and self-conscious. Last year Ernie Adamson, Counsel of the House Un-American Committee, wrote to a veterans' organization saying,

"I wonder if you are sufficiently familiar with the history of the United States to be aware that this country was not organized as a democracy."

Only last month the *Saturday Evening Post* felt compelled to carry an editorial on our form of government which practically paraphrased Mr. Adamson's statement:

"It is a 'republican form of government' and not a 'democratic' one that the states of the union are required by the constitution to maintain."

Apparently what we fought for in World War I was to save the world for republicanism, not democracy, and so the great slogan was in error. It is significant that these delicate distinctions in the use of terms apply only when you are calling a country a democracy, but not when you are calling an individual a Communist. It is also significant that the campaign to reduce the power and scope of the word "democracy" materializes at the height of the thought control season.

Of techniques there is no end. One of the corniest and most effective anti-democratic devices is to label an organization Communist-infiltrated, and thus to imply that all its officers and members are tainted red. This is intended to serve the triple purpose of embarrassing the organization, discouraging prospective members from joining it, and frightening old members out of it. The term "fellow-traveller" was coined to describe those who remain in these organizations, and it has become indispensable to the jargon of thought control. I should like to point out, as a matter of definition, that if belonging to an organization which possibly has a few Communists in its membership constitutes fellow-travelling, then the United States itself, as a member of the United Nations, is a fellow-traveller.

The smear is the favorite tool of the thought controllers, because when successful it intimidates. The sunshine-patriot type of uneasy liberals—especially those with wives and children—hurry in out of the rain. They hastily resign from committees, usually denouncing their former associates in the process. Or else, to prove they are impeccably pure and suspicionless, they declare more loudly than the reactionary how much they loathe witches, and they point out a few. The intimidated among the hunted join with the hunters, thus swelling their numbers and adding to the general hysterical effect.

The one consuming fear of the huntsmen is that the American people, who have always had a fine sense of proportion, will become bored with the antic chase, will realize that there are ample laws, detection machinery and agencies of justice to cope with the enemies of our security. It is incidentally somewhat insulting to the prestige of the F.B.I., whose work in the war was nothing short of brilliant, to declare that in peace subversion has gotten out of hand and that the government is in danger of a putsch from within.

There is dread in the hearts of the irresponsibles that the picnic may end. *Newsweek,* which not long ago listed Albert Einstein, along with all of his naughty affiliations, in the rogues' gallery of those who a Soviet newspaper said were friendly to Russia, closed one of its long treatises on Communism in America on a plaintive and almost whimpering note. It was worried about

> "the possibility that the public—as it did after the last war—may weary of the anti-Communist fight, leaving the door open once more to the masters of political and economic infiltration."

Can they mean the masters of political and economic infiltration who between wars took this country out of a Hoover depression, and in war led it to victory? What dire and tragic things happened to this country through that open door, when the public wearied? While the reds were sabotaging the republic through that open door, *Newsweek* became an established and successful capitalist enterprise.

So that the public may not weary of the fight, it is being forced upon them. This may explain the morbid preoccupation, the flailing in all directions, the hysterical fear, the cowardly attacks, the arrogance, the quoting out of context, the invidious associations, the clamping down of censorship.

There are many aspects of thought control even more sinister than those upon which I have touched so superficially. I do not propose to cover them all. But there is one general aspect which we, as members of the arts, sciences and professions, have reason to study in special detail. I am speaking of the general onslaught against culture—against not only so-called progressive culture, but all culture. This attack invariably accompanies thought control, and was among the first accomplishments or Fascism. You will recall the infamous Nazi boast, "When I hear the word 'culture', I reach for my gun." It is remarkable that Germany and Italy, each so highly distinguished for cultural achievements in the past, went completely sterile under Hitler and Mussolini.

Lately the thought control korps has sought to move into the fields of film, stage, radio and even the theater; to intimidate by "investigation" and to inhibit free expression by all of the usual devices. The first step here, whether consciously or otherwise, is to reduce the very dignity of the artist and scientist. Mr. Pegler set the gauge for us in a column last November, when he informed his readers that

> "Singing and acting are so absurdly overrated as arts, now that performers are allowed familiarities with their betters, that few of us bear in mind the origins of these poor trades, above which the current celebrities never rise, however we fawn upon them."

He explained that there was nothing at all, really, to the art of singing:

> "A singer emits certain sounds from the neck, causing sound effects by the expansion and contraction of certain muscles and by regulating the flow of air."

He then disposed of the craft of acting, to which there is also nothing at all, really:

> "The actor utters recitations written for him by a writer; he bawls, whimpers or whispers, and stands here or there according to minute directions after long and patient instruction."

In the same column he gave us an insight into the mind and character of an eminent scientist:

> "Albert Einstein, whatever it is that he has added to the sum of human knowledge, did what he has done not because of any sense of duty to mankind but because he couldn't help it, and has received beautiful rewards in the coin that he values most—a posturing old fellow, delighting in a show of homely and spectacular modesty . . . He lives well, he keeps in print, and he is allowed to express political opinions that antagonize the sentiments of many young men who lost their lives preserving his cozy asylum."

Book-banning, script-baiting, commentator-hounding, and the reviewing of new works according to the political bias of the reviewer—these are merely new variations of old forms of attempted control; but what gives them added impetus is the recent appearance, in higher reaches of government, of discriminatory values respecting art. The State Department's cancellation of an international exhibition of American art was a step backward in the direction of the Dark Ages. And President Truman's letter to William Benton on the subject of modern art is likely to be remembered as long as Lincoln's letter to Mrs. Bixby—although for different reasons.

"I am of the opinion," Mr. Truman wrote, "that so-called modern art is merely the vaporing of half-baked lazy people . . . There is no art at all in connection with the modernists."

This is of a piece with the statement that there is no art at all in connection with singing or acting. A surprising sentiment to issue from the father of the Missouri Nightingale.

The citizen, the man on the street, the innocent reader of editorials, columns, and presidential correspondence, is thus to believe that the Museum of Modern Art is a temple of lazy slops; that Marian Anderson and Bing Crosby merely emit certain sounds from the neck; that Ingrid Bergman utters recitations. After which the citizen is expected to trust the values of these same minds on the political arts and sciences.

Traditionally the United States of America is celebrated in the world mainly for two admirable and enviable qualities—our wealth and our tolerance. No other nation—certainly not among the powers—has contributed so much, over so long a period, to the development of political democracy. Historically, we head by a wide margin the list of asylums for the persecuted, the underdog, the unwanted minority. It is, therefore, all the more tragic and ironic that today, at the height of our power, wealth and productivity, toleration of minority political ideas, toleration of minority races and religions, should be so far forgotten as to be a subject of growing concern in the more freely regulated media of expression—particularly books. It is heartening to find that the No. 1 and 2 best-sellers in this country today are books on anti-Semitism and discrimination against the Negro—but the necessity to make frequent "pleas" for tolerance in books, films, on the radio, or in reports such as that of the Commission on Freedom of the Press, is in itself an indication of the extent to which American thought has been controlled and poisoned. You make a plea for something you haven't got.

The Commission's report, which I quoted earlier, says at one point:

"With the means of self-destruction now at their disposal, men must live, if they are to live at all, by self-restraint, moderation and mutual understanding. Civilized society must make sure that as many as possible of the ideas which its members have are available for examination."

This compass would place outside the pale of civilized society those interests—and we all know who they are—which do just the opposite, which make sure that no ideas contrary to their own are available for examination.

"The press is not free," says the report financed by Mr. Luce, "if those who operate it behave as though their position conferred upon them the privilege of being deaf to ideas which the processes of free speech have brought to public attention . . . Freedom of the press can only continue as an accountable freedom. Its moral right will be conditioned on its acceptance of this accountability. Its legal right will stand unaltered as its moral duty is performed."

For "press", of course, read all other media of mass communication as well. As to the point of legal right, I return to the suggestion made earlier: corrective political action and recourse to law for those who are slandered and assassinated by rumor, innuendo and accusation, who are penalized and damaged for the expression of ideas contrary to those of particular publishers, producers or monopolies.

It is time to explore the extent and validity of legal as well as moral rights; to reinforce freedom of expression with buttresses provided by the original architects of the Constitution, men who were farsighted enough to anticipate that the tyrannies and reaction of their own past might well recur to future generations.

Whether the textbooks of California are to conform to the will of reactionary senators; whether the films and broadcasts of the country are to be circumscribed by Rankin's Un-American Committee; whether every last liberal utterance is to be distorted, misrepresented or silenced; whether every dissident to monopoly prejudice or majority opinion is to be hanged as a witch, is a choice that is up to the American courts and the American people.

We shall watch with interest such actions as Fiorello LaGuardia's* suit for $100,000 against the National Home and Property Owners' Foundation, which called him a Communist because he opposed the

*News of Mr. LaGuardia's death was announced just as this copy was going to press. A tragic loss at a time when he could least be spared.

elimination of rent controls. Mr. LaGuardia's bill of complaint is that such statements made against him were "intended to destroy his good name and reputation as a law-abiding and patriotic citizen, and bring him into public hatred."

We shall watch with interest actions now being planned against publications, organizations and individuals by victims of recent irresponsible attacks.* Meanwhile, this and similar conferences will do more than watch with interest. They will study in detail the nature, habits and dimensions of thought control, and will ultimately recommend, initiate and support counter-measures.

Since the arena is that of the minds of men, and the defenses those of peace, freedom, democracy and tranquility, one could ask for no higher stakes.

---

*Such as the $2,000,000 suit filed by Emmet Lavery, writer, and Martin Gosch, producer, against Mrs. Lela E. Rogers, for stating in a radio broadcast that their *as-yet unproduced* (!) play, *The Gentleman from Athens*, was "un-American propaganda".

the legal aspects

Saturday, July 12, 1947, 10:00 A. M.-12:30 P. M.

Robert W. Kenny, Chairman

Speakers: Morris E. Cohn, Fred Okrand, Sanford I. Carter, Charles J. Katz

Papers in this panel prepared in cooperation with the Southern California Chapter, National Lawyers' Guild.

Morris E. Cohn
Member, firm of Kenny & Cohn; specially interested in law relating to literature, copyright, freedom of expression

THOSE INVESTIGATING COMMITTEES

DURING the Twenties American students and scholars gave serious attention to the problems arising from legislative investigations. Our Supreme Court had passed on questions of powers: the power to punish for contempt, and the power to conduct legislative inquiry. But many questions were left undecided. Distinguished writers urged on the one hand that legislative inquiries merely stirred up the drains of public malady, violated the privacy of the citizen, were wasteful of time and money, and in any event served no public good. Others, surveying the history of legislative investigations, came to different conclusions.

Landis, of Harvard, examined Parliamentary investigations and American colonial precedents and showed that inquest by the legislature was essential in order to supervise the executive department, to con-

40

trol disbursements, and in short to hold all public servants to account. Doctor Dimock, of UCLA, in a long study for the Johns Hopkins University Studies in Historical and Political Science, confirmed Professor Landis' conclusions, and added another cogent reason. The legislative inquiry is the practical means by which is overcome the theoretical separation of the three branches of government; it is the conduit for the flow of intelligence and of political responsibility from the judiciary and the executive, through the legislature, and ultimately to the people. Other writers (Gallway, Ehrman), comparing American practices with those permitted under the French and German constitutions during the past 200 years, concluded that the legislative inquiry makes for responsible government and is a valuable, if not absolutely essential, instrument to prevent corruption.

This preliminary statement is worth making because it is time for further examination of the question, particularly in relation to the Thomas Committee to Investigate Un-American Activities, and also because in considering the Thomas Committee it is necessary to distinguish characteristics which have marked this committee from the attributes of legislative inquiry in general. It will be seen that, of those things which justify legislative inquiry, few if any have proved true of the Un-American Activities Committees, while the dangers of legislative inquiries have been multiplied and intensified by such committees.

The present standing committee is the successor of a line of similar committees extending back to 1919. Shortly after the revolution in Russia, a public meeting was held in Washington, D. C., to discuss the merits and dangers of the new form of government. Newspaper reports of the meeting vary, some treating it as inflammatory and threatening an immediate overthrow of American institutions, others reporting a critical but temperate and intelligent examination of the event. The subject came to the Senate floor in a matter of days, and almost immediately a committee was set up to investigate Bolshevism in America. From that time until the present standing committee was set up, temporary committees have made sporadic forays into the undefined field of un-Americanism. Now with the standing committee in Congress, the California committee, and the possibility of other state committees, there is real danger such committees may become a permanent institution.

The immediate source of danger is the word "un-American." It is dangerous because of its lack of precise definition and because it points in the general direction of the area of thinking, opinion, belief, and conviction. These two factors have had grave consequences on the conduct of some members of the committee. They have defined their powers by personal bent and have oppressed citizens, admittedly innocent of anything the law can punish, solely for difference of opinion. It is this conduct which makes these committees a special subject of the present study, this invasion of the mind of the citizen.

The last citadel of individualism, the domain of the mind, the one place in which the individual has found sanctuary, is now invaded with the trappings of officialdom, the trumpets of press releases, flashbulbs, cameras, and the shadow of prison. Ever since the ascendancy of temporal power over spiritual, when the church relinquished political government to the state, what a man thinks has been his concern alone. Defeated, angered, embittered with the world, he could seek the comfort of criticism and condemnation all within his own mind. He could express the criticism if he chose, but he need not. If he was one of a slender minority, he might well defer expression or, at least, select the time and occasion for saying what he thought.

But now if he is summoned and asked what he thinks, for example, of the Truman Doctrine, he must speak or he must litigate with the Attorney General of the United States. What he says will be heard by members of the Un-American Committee, and if they choose, and only if they choose, by newspaper reporters, radio commentators, his employer and his associates. The history of this committee shows that, chosen to investigate an unmarked field, they have defended a narrow strip of political ground and have attacked the occupants of all other areas of thought. The witness, not blind to the history of this committee, is in effect prosecuted without indictment, convicted without the right of defense, and punished for what the law says is no crime. Above all, criticism, the right to differ, is killed before expression. Democratic principles, civil rights, have been aliens without passport in the hearing-room.

Any objective study of the conduct of these committees shows that, whatever the avowed reason for their existence, whatever the legal justification for their creation, their purpose has been to injure, defame, and intimidate those who differed with the committee on political questions. The committee has attacked not only individuals but also organizations; and it has selected for attack those persons who have been distinguished by the character of their opinions; it has selected for attack those organizations which, either in fact or in unproved allegation, have been formed about some particular branch of political thinking. It would be sheer blindness to urge that the reason for the so-called investigations of these persons and committees was anything other than the notions avowedly held by them.

Nor can there be any reasonable challenge to the conclusion that the committee, or at least some members, have used their positions and the results of their hearings for the purpose of making it difficult and dangerous to entertain currently unpopular notions concerning government. The timing of the committee's releases bears a relationship to political events which cannot be explained by any theories of chance or sunspots. The investigation of the sitdown strike had as its direct consequence, and no doubt as its specific purpose, the defeat of Frank Murphy in his campaign for re-election as governor of Michigan. The announcement that the committee would send investigators to survey the audience attending Wallace meetings is no surprise to those who have watched previous investigations by this committee in pre-election years. The announcement by the committee, a few years ago, that it had an index consisting of over a million cards was the sound of a bell that tolled for anyone who hoped for the right to express disagreement. The right to hold a job or the opportunity to get a new one, for all the dissident knows, lies locked in that monumental, constantly-growing, index file.

Although our Supreme Court has stated that the individual's right of privacy is protected by the Fourth Amendment (*Gouled* v. *U. S.*, 255 U. S. 298; *Harris* v. *U. S.*, 91 Adv. Op. L. Ed. p. 1013), these committees have not yet been challenged on this ground.

Consideration of the conduct of these committees raises two general categories of question: first, whether the conduct of these committees is lawful; and second, what remedial legislation is desirable. Under the first heading, the following questions will be discussed: Does Congress have the power to conduct such inquiries? If it has the power, is the enabling resolution valid, i.e., does it effectively delegate the power?

As was pointed out in the case of *Kilbourn* v. *Thompson* (103 U. S. 168, 26 L. Ed. 377), Congress could not look to the practices of the English Parliament as an analogy for the source of the power to investigate. The British Parliament was originally a court, and was in fact known as the High Court of Parliament. As such, it exercised judicial power. With the rise of Commons, the judicial functions were retained by the House of Lords, which to this day exercises judicial power. The Constitution of the United States, however, vested judicial power in another branch of government. Accordingly, the power of Congress to conduct investigations must be found in the powers delegated to it by the Constitution. While it is true no judicial power as such was granted to Congress, the exercise of certain specified powers required the exercise of the judicial function. These included the power of impeachment and the power to determine the qualifications of its members. However, few, if any, of the investigations undertaken by Congress are related to the exercise of these powers. There remains the legislative function. Most investigations authorized by Congress would undoubtedly seek support from that function of Congress; and the case of *McGrain* v. *Daugherty* (273 U. S. 135, 71 L. ed. 580) expressly held that Congress had the implied power to conduct investigations in support of its legislative function.

What is the legislative function? It includes the power to make laws, but is it limited to that power? Since the power to investigate cannot exceed the legislative function (except in cases of impeachment and the like), it is necessary to determine whether the power of Congress to investigate is limited by its power to make laws.

Students of government and political science, such as Woodrow Wilson, Marshall Dimock, and others, have included in the legislative function other powers such as the right to supervise the executive; the right to call for accountings for the expenditure of appropriations; the duty to educate the public, and finally the so-called informing power by which is meant the power of the legislature to turn the spotlight of public attention to selected areas of current events.

Our Supreme Court has by implication passed upon the power of Congress to supervise executive departments; and no one would care to challenge the existence of that power. Congress is the most nearly direct representative of the people and, as such, should have the power to investigate and to supervise the official actions of all other agencies of government. It may even be conceded that this power exists with reference to all persons who, though not agencies or employees of the government, have contracts with the government, as, for example, contracts for public works and the like; and, if it were necessary, this power could be derived from the duty of Congress to supervise the expenditure of public funds.

But a halt must be called at the exercise of the informing power. As is well-known, Martin Dies, as chairman of the Un-American

Activities Committee, publicly recognized the fact that his range of investigation extended beyond the power of Congress to legislate; but he contended that by reason of the informing power of the legislature, Congressional investigation could properly extend beyond the power of Congress to enact laws.

In the *McGrain* case referred to above, one of the questions presented for decision was whether the investigation had for its purpose a legislative end, specifically, whether Congress had in mind the enactment of laws. The resolution authorizing the investigation was attacked upon the ground that no such purpose was manifested. The Supreme Court, however, indulged in the presumption that the Senate intended to conduct the investigation for the purpose of enacting laws; and it was only by the indulgence of this presumption that the resolution was sustained. From that decision, therefore, it may be inferred that an investigation solely for the purpose of informing the public and without any intention of enacting laws is beyond the powers of Congress, even if the scope of the investigation were within the power of Congress to enact laws. In other words, an investigation must be for the purpose of informing the legislature, not the public. It follows, therefore, that if the subject of investigation were wholly beyond the powers of Congress to enact laws, Congress would have no power to conduct the inquiry.

So far as the Thomas Committee is concerned, the concept of an informing function outside the power of Congress to enact laws is totally foreign to the federal government. Certainly, Congress as an organ of the federal government exercises only limited powers. Conceding that within the granted powers Congress is not limited, still Congress has no powers outside those granted. The informing function beyond the range of the grant of powers is no part of the machinery of a government of limited powers.

States, however, are not governments of limited powers, and their legislatures are usually regarded as the residuary beneficiaries of all governmental power. The objection on the ground of lack of power may, therefore, not be applicable to the legislatures of the states. But, as will be seen, no governmental agency, state or national, can conduct such an inquiry because of the inhibitions of the Bill of Rights.

To summarize the question of power, then, if the scope of an inquiry is either not within the limits of the lawmaking power of the legislature or of Congress, or if being within those limits it is prohibited by the Constitution, then the committee does not have the power to investigate.

The immediate object of the Thomas Committee is the investigation of propaganda. The resolution asks for a study of un-American propaganda in the United States, and of the diffusion within the United States of subversive and un-American propaganda instigated from foreign countries.

There has yet to be submitted a bill suppressing propaganda which, except in time of war or imminent danger, is capable of becoming a law under the Constitution of the United States. Stripping the word propaganda of its emotional charge and looking at it as a court must do, the word propaganda means news, persuasion, literature, the articulate expression of ideas. It is perfectly plain that the subject matter of investigation is precisely the ground occupied by the First Amendment, and while the First Amendment may not in all instances be invoked in order to prevent an inquiry, for example, an investigation to aid in the dissemination of news as by an investigation into the control of press and radio, the Amendment is a shield against any attempt by the state or national government, in the absence of a clear and present danger, to stifle or to discourage the clash of opinion. No valid law can be passed suppressing propaganda.

It seems superfluous, in the face of the great guardians of freedom of speech announced by our Supreme Court, such as *Thornhill* v. *Alabama* (310 U. S. 88, 84 L. Ed. 1093), *DeJonge* v. *Oregon* (299 U. S. 353, 81 L. ed. 278), and others equally well-known, to debate those questions any longer. Between the resolution creating the standing committee and the First Amendment there exists a direct conflict and the most inexorable war. Either the resolution or the First Amendment must bow.

But even if it were to be assumed that, notwithstanding the First Amendment, some power remains in Congress to frame valid legislation and for that purpose to conduct an investigation, the question arises whether the resolution creating the standing committee effectively delegates a part of that power. It is respectfully submitted that the resolution fails to do so; it is void because it lacks reasonable certainty. As a practical matter, the lack of certainty in the resolution is related to the discussion under the First Amendment because both arise from the attempt on the part of the framers of the resolution to designate a particular philosophy. On the one hand, it is plain that the word un-American is not sufficiently precise to be the critical word in a law; and on the other it appears that the general subject under investigation is a philosophy opposed to "Americanism", that is, a philosophy embodying criticism and disagreement.

In *Connolly* v. *General Construction Co.* (269 U. S. 385), the Supreme Court laid down the canons for the determination of certainty, saying in substance that these were sufficient: technical or special phrases having a meaning sufficiently well-known to enable those within their reach correctly to apply them; words defined by the common law; and lastly words defined or otherwise given meaning by the text of the statute.

The resolution holds absolutely no lamp to the search for meaning. The reports of the Committee have at different times offered different and even contradictory clues. For example, the following definitions have been given by the Committee: un-Americanism is the destruction of the American system of checks and balances (76-1, H. Rept. 2, p. 12); Americanism recognizes the existence of a God from whom all fundamental rights are derived (76-1, H. Rept. 2, 1/3/39); un-Americanism is absolute racial and social equality; it includes the abolition of inheritance, a system of planned economy, the promise of economic security. Another report (77-1, H. Rept. 1/1/41) distinguishes between attachment to foreign dictators and those who sincerely desire beneficial changes. The 1946 report includes, as un-American propaganda, endeavoring to secure support for Russia's foreign policy, criticism of Chiang Kai-Shek or of General MacArthur, calling for the dissolution of the British Empire and suggesting that anyone who is 100% American is a Fascist.

When it is remembered that the resolution delegates Congressional power, it should be clear that it fails to meet the requirements for delegation fixed in *Panama Pacific* v. *Ryan* (293 U. S. 388). Furthermore, the resolution is enforced by criminal statutes, making disobedience of the committee a misdemeanor punishable by a fine of not less than $100 and imprisonment in a common jail for not less than a month (2 USC Sec. 192 and 194). It, therefore, requires the certainty necessary for the validity of penal laws. The resolution in question cannot meet these standards (*U. S.* v. *Cohen Grocery Co.,* 255 U. S. 81).

No one, said our Supreme Court in *Lanzetta* v. *New Jersey* (306 U. S. 451), may be required at the peril of liberty to speculate as to the meaning of penal statutes. And the cases are legion which hold that the standards of guilt must be sufficiently clear to be understood by laymen (*Smith* v. *Cahoon,* 283 U. S. 533), the average member of society (*Klein* v. *Frink Dairy*, 274 U. S. 445), and to men of common intelligence (*Connolly* v. *General Construction Co.*, 269 U. S. 385).

No court has attempted to define Americanism or un-Americanism. It would be strange if any court should attempt to do so. As has been shown, the committee has made many attempts at definition, too many in fact. It is therefore submitted that the resolution is wholly void. As has been shown, the vice is not one of phrasing; it is inherent in the purpose of the resolution, beyond remedy by language.

The first step to be taken in combatting these evils is to present these legal questions in pending cases. To this end, the most active support should be extended to those who are today being prosecuted for disobeying the committee. Every effort should be made to see that the far-reaching Constitutional issues involved in that prosecution are clearly presented, so that there will be no mistake that what is at issue is not the liberty of the immediate defendants but the vigor, of the First Amendment.

We should next turn to remedial legislation. This should include, first of all, a repeal of the resolution creating the committee. On the basis of what has been here said concerning the conduct of the committee and concerning the invalidity of the resolution, no further argument should be required.

However, further legislation is desirable. Recognition must be given to the tremendous power for good which resides in] the carefully-restrained exercise of the investigative function. The Rochette and Stavisky scandals in France commemorate the weakness of unenforceable requests for information in dealing with corruption in government. On the other hand, the Truman Committee to Investigate War Frauds, the LaFollette Committee on Civil Liberties, and others, have embodied the most determined expression of a philosophy which exacts ultimate responsibility of officials to the people. Great care must be taken, however, to discourage those who hope, by abuse of power and by unlawful procedures, to accomplish what the Constitution and a decent respect for common justice combine to forbid. This can be done by reconciling the justified exercise of legislative power with the Bill of Rights and immunities generally accorded witnesses and litigants.

In this connection, it is worth observing that while, as the textwriters say, most of the rules of exclusion of evidence have as their purpose either the efficiency of the tribunal or the discovery of truth, there exists a category of exclusions which sacrifices the search for truth in order to preserve rights of the witness. For example, the privilege of retaining inviolate confidential communications certainly sacrifices an opportunity to discover the truth in a contested situation because, if any assumption is permitted, it is just that in such communications the truth is uttered. Nevertheless, the rights of the witness are deemed to be superior to the purpose to be served by the trial.

No such rights are required to be respected by Congressional investigating committees. The witness is not even excused from answering on the ground that he might incriminate himself. He must answer.

It is true that a Congressional act forbids prosecution of a witness for anything said by him in a Congressional investigation (except for perjury); but it is doubtful whether this is the equivalent of the Constitutional privilege against self-incrimination. England's Witnesses Protection Act of 1892 goes farther than the Congressional act, making it a misdemeanor to threaten, punish, damnify or injure anyone for having given evidence before a Royal Commission of Inquiry. It is questionable whether even this law goes far enough.

Without attempting here to formulate a code for the protection of persons summoned to testify, it is suggested that Congress should enact a general law applicable to all investigations except those in which extraordinary reasons require departures. Such a law would regularize procedure and would guarantee to the witness the immunities to which he is entitled in other proceedings for compulsory disclosure. In view of the history of the Committee on Un-American Activities, the protection of the citizen depends not only upon freedom from investigation in prescribed areas, but also upon the fairness of the committee in procedure and the immunity of the witness.

The following proposed provisions, though far from being all-inclusive, relate particularly to Congressional investigations as distinguished from judicial proceedings:

a witness shall have the right to be represented by counsel;

a witness, or any person whose life, liberty, property, or good name is affected by the evidence of other witnesses, shall have the right of cross-examination and the right to present evidence;

prior to the examination of each witness, the officer presiding at the hearing shall read to the witness a statement of his rights;

no person shall be tried or punished for refusal to disclose his opinion concerning political, religious, or economic subjects, nor for refusal to divulge his religious or political affiliation; but this immunity shall not extend to refusal to answer questions concerning his acts or conduct;

no hearings shall be secret, except in cases where the hearing is conducted under a joint resolution of both houses, and then only upon specific application of the committee for a resolution authorizing the secret hearing, which resolution must specify the persons who may be so examined and the subject matter; none of the rights accorded to the witness by other provisions of the code shall be suspended during any secret hearing; no evidence taken in secret session shall be made public by the committee or any of its members until it has been presented to the originating legislature and the publication thereof has been authorized; and if thereafter any is made public, any person injured by such publication shall have the right to make public any other portion of the evidence given before the committee in such secret session;

the defense of qualified privilege shall not be available to anyone who publishes testimony given by a witness in any of the hearings; but this defense shall be available for the publication of the committee's findings;

a publication made by anyone, whether a member of the committee or otherwise, concerning a witness or a person named in the investigation shall render the publisher liable, if the statement is defamatory and untrue, and if it was made otherwise than as a part of the hearing (this is probably a restatement of present law, but it is worth emphasis);

anyone who publishes defamatory material given in a Congressional investigation, regardless of whether it is true, shall be required to give the person defamed equal space for the opportunity to make a defense, and on failure to do so shall be liable in a specified sum as well as for actual damage.

Since case law and the work of textwriters is comparatively scant in this field, little more has been attempted here than to suggest special provisions of the proposed law.

Before concluding, it is worth pointing out that appraisal by namecalling is not new in our history. Joseph Choate in his argument before the Supreme Court called the income tax laws unconstitutional on the ground that they were populistic and communistic. We can go back to Jefferson's time. Foner, in his *History of the Labor Movement,* says:

"The Federalists fought the Democratic Societies and the many Jeffersonian newspapers by an elaborate Red scare. The Societies, the Federalists thundered, were part of a vast, secret and subversive international body known as the Bavarian Illuminati, organized by the 'bloody French Jacobins,' subsidized by Paris gold. Timothy Dwight, president of Yale College, warned that if the people's movement succeeded holy worship would become a 'dance of Jacobin phrenze,' their psalms would be 'Marseilles hymns,' the Bible would be 'cast into a bonfire,' and the wives and daughters of Americans would become 'the victims of legal prostitution; soberly dishonoured; speciously polluted; the outcasts of delicacy and virtue, and the loathing of God and man.'

" 'Every attempt to restore the liberties of mankind, or to check the progress of arbitrary power,' wrote a Jeffersonian in 1797, 'is now styled Jacobinism.' "

Wise policy has come to recognize that freedom of thought and of expression are not luxuries to be indulged only in happy times of general agreement. On the contrary, they are most useful when they are most needed, in times of tension and disagreement. The security of a nation lies not in enforced uniformity but in the opportunity to air disagreement. Freedom of thought and of expression are not only goals for a democracy, something to look forward to after victory over opponents, but they are the methods, the means by which democracy lives.

It is a strange adventure for Congress to hunt an ideal Americanism with the great torch of freedom of thought put out. History will view this fantastic venture into policing opinion as the result not only of unrestrained officialdom but also of an apathetic citizenry. The present report points to remedies in the courts and in the legislature. The time is now, because delay can only operate to make it more difficult to effect a cure.

Fred Okrand

Specialist in Constitutional
and labor law; former student editor, *Southern California Law Review*

LOYALTY TESTS FOR GOVERNMENT EMPLOYEES

WITHIN the last month, a government employee received a letter from his superior in which he was charged with, among other things: being an atheist, always defending strikers, and living in a neighborhood known to be Communist-infiltrated (this at the time of our current housing shortage).

This is an actual occurrence. It represents but one incident that has come to my attention. And, of course, it represents but an infinitesimal part of the huge program that is going on all over the country. This incident should cause us to pause and consider whether we are willing to go back to the days of Salem where men feared witches and burned women. It should make us wonder whether we are willing to go back to the days of the Alien and Sedition Laws. It should make us wonder whether we have forgotten the sane advice given us by President Jefferson in his inaugural address, where he said: "If there be any among us who wish to dissolve this union, or to change its republican form, let them stand undisturbed as monuments of the safety with which error of opinion may be tolerated where reason is left to combat it".[1]

Bear in mind that the purpose of this report is to indicate the legal aspects of the loyalty test program introduced by the President's Executive Order and by the various bills before Congress. We will not discuss directly, therefore, although of course we cannot ignore, the fact that the entire program is but one facet of what has turned into a "witch hunt" against those with whose views the majority at the moment disagree.

The fact that the aspect of loyalty, undefined, is included in legislation unrelated to federal employment, *e.g.*, union officials in private industry under the Taft-Harley Law, teachers in state schools under

---

1. Jefferson, Writings, Vol. 8, Pg. 1.

the Rankin Bill, etc., is ample proof that what is desired is first ortho-doxy and oneness in political and economic thinking, and only sec-ondarily a genuine concern for the security of the nation.

The American Tradition is One That Abhors the
Concept of Loyalty Purges or Test Oaths

"The test oath has always been abhorred in the United States," said Justices Black and Douglas in their concurring opinions in *West Virginia Board of Education* v. *Barnette*.[2] Such an oath, or a proce-dure compelling action which would be accomplished by the exacting of an oath, runs contrary to the concept of a people one of whose rights is Freedom from Fear.

In at least three cases, the Supreme Court has struck down statutes requiring the taking of oaths strikingly similar in effect to the pro-gram now under consideration. In *Cummings* v. *Missouri*,[3] the statute prohibited any person from holding a position of honor, trust, or profit in the State of Missouri or in any municipality thereof or to be a priest or counselor at law unless he took the oath known as the "oath of loyalty." In *Ex Parte Garland*,[4] Congress had enacted that no person could hold any office in the government or practice before its courts unless he too took such an oath. And in *Pierce* v. *Carskodon*,[5] such an oath was required of all litigants before the West Virginia Courts.

Manifestly those statues were all aimed against those who had participated in the Civil War on the side of the South.

The Supreme Court in holding the statutes invalid did so on the theory that they were bills of attainder (though some of the Justices thought they were *ex post facto* laws). Under our present day legal jargon the court might say that the laws were abitrary or unreason-able and had no relationship to the conduct being regulated. Those cases are still good law today. Their rationale is that the loyalty test is an unconstitutional proscription on freedom of opinion—at least in the absence of actual acts which the state has the right to prevent or the exercise of freedom of speech beyond the extent of the "clear and present danger" rule.

Governor Alfred E. Smith of New York in signing the bill that

2. 319 U.S. 624, 642.
3. 4 Wall (U.S.) 277.
4. 4 Wall (U.S.) 337.
5. 16 Wall (U.S.) 234.

repealed the infamous Lusk Laws (laws essentially similar in import to the present proposals) said in 1923:

"I am satisfied that they should not remain upon the statute books of this State because they are repugnant to the fundamentals of American democracy. Under the laws repealed, teachers, in order to exercise their honorable calling, were in effect compelled to hold opinions as to gov-. ernmental matters deemed by a State office consistent with loyalty; freedom of opinion and freedom of speech were by those laws unduly shackled . . . In signing these bills, I firmly believe that I am vindicating the principle that, within the limit of the penal law, every citizen may speak and teach what he believes."[6]

And not too many years later Governor Herbert E. Lehman vetoed a New York act which barred from civil service employment persons who advocated overthrow of the government by force and violence. Said he:

"I am profoundly convinced that any statute which directly or indirectly limits opportunity for free public discussion undermines the very foundation of constitutional government . . . The threat to democracy lies, in my opinion, not so much in revolutionary change achieved by force or violence. Its greatest danger comes through gradual invasion of constitutional rights with the acquiescence of an inert people: through failure to discern that constitutional government cannot survive where rights guaranteed by the constitution are not safeguarded even to those citizens with whose political and social views the majority may not agree . . . Were we of this great liberal state to approve this bill today, we might readily find tomorrow that we had opened the flood gates of oppressive legislation in the Nation against religious, social, labor and other minority groups."[7]

The American way is to meet the problems that face us and not to camouflage them or use a scapegoat to conceal them. The tradition is a noble one and should not be permitted to lose ground to the totalitarian methods we all abhor.

It is precisely because it is so easy for those in positions of power to describe and taint one as "disloyal" that our tradition prohibits it. Presumably because the Congress and the President have determined that for the protection of the United States military aid to Greece is necessary, one who speaks out against such a program is speaking out against the interest of the United States and so is disloyal. But our way of life does not rest on so flimsy a base. Our tradition is noble just because we value so highly the right of the heterodox to make known his views and not to encircle him directly or indirectly by economic threat or force. We battle him, rather, with the superior

6. Public Papers, 1923, Pg. 292.
7. Public Papers, 1938, Pg. 120.

weapon of better ideas.

Though several bills have been introduced in Congress bearing on the loyalty program, only the President's Executive Order is thus far in effect. Hence it will here be discussed as illustrative.

This discussion of the President's Executive Order is taken almost verbatim from a report of the Committee on Constitutional Liberties of the National Lawyers' Guild and published in the March-April, 1947, issue of the *Lawyers' Guild Review*. A few blue-pencil liberties have been taken, but very few. It was felt by the committee that the work done in that paper was of such calibre as to bear repeating here.

The President's Executive Order on Loyalty
of Government Employees

The President's Executive Order 9835, issued on March 12, 1947, prescribes procedures for the administration of an employees' loyalty program in the executive branch of the government. Briefly, the executive order provides that there shall be a loyalty investigation of every applicant for employment in the executive department of the government, and that the head of each department or agency shall be responsible for the removal of disloyal employees from employment in his agency. The order further provides that each employee charged with being disloyal shall receive a hearing before a loyalty board of the agency in which he is employed, and shall have the right of appeal first to the head of his agency and then to a Loyalty Review Board in the Civil Service Commission.

The standard prescribed by the executive order for removal of employees is that "reasonable grounds exist for belief that the person involved is disloyal to the Government of the United States," and the following are listed as "activities or associations which may be considered in connection with the determination of disloyalty."

a. Sabotage, espionage, or attempts or preparations therefor, or knowingly associating with spies or saboteurs;

b. Treason or sedition or advocacy thereof;

c. Advocacy of revolution or force or violence to alter the constitutional form of government of the United States;

d. Intentional, unauthorized disclosure to any person, under circumstances which may indicate disloyalty to the United States, of documents or information of a confidential or non-public character obtained by a person making the disclosure as a result of his employment by the Government of the United States;

e. Performing or attempting to perform his duties, or otherwise acting, so as to serve the interests of another government in preference to the interests of the United States;

f. Membership in, affilation with, or sympathetic association with any foreign or domestic organization, association, movement, group or combination of persons, designated by the Attorney General as totalitarian, fascist, communist, or subversive, or as having adopted a policy of advocating or approving the commission of acts of force or violence to deny other persons their rights under the Constitution of the United States, or as seeking to alter the form of government of the United States by unconstitutional measures.

Before examining this executive order in detail, it would be well to comment briefly on its overall implications. It should first be made clear that this order applies to all employees in the executive branch of the government, whether they be employed in the post office, the mint, the Government Printing Office, or the Bureau of Engraving. It applies as well to clerks, charwomen, mechanics, messengers, typists, chauffeurs, etc. There are roughly 2,500,000 employees in the executive branch of the federal government. Of these, only a very small fraction can reasonably be said to hold policy positions, or positions which can in any way influence the course of government policy. This in no way implies that these minor employees should hold government jobs if in fact disloyal to the Government of the United States. But it should lay at rest the notion or the argument that all government employees need necessarily be in agreement with or endorse the policies of the administration in power. Thus, no one will quarrel with the right of President Truman to remove Henry Wallace from his cabinet because Mr. Wallace differs with President Truman on the proper foreign policy of the United States. But it is another question whether the President can require that all government employees, regardless of what position they hold, share the President's or the Attorney General's views on foreign or domestic policy. It is this danger in the order that requires its critical examination and appraisal.

It is also important that a full realization be had of the scope of the order. The order envisages a loyalty investigation of approximately 2,500,000 federal employees, plus all applicants for federal employment. The investigation would include inquiries of the employee's or applicant's former employers, schools, neighbors, friends, family, etc. It has been estimated that an appropriation of between 20 and 30 million dollars will be necessary to carry out these investigations. There is thus within the consequences of this executive order the rather serious probability of the establishment for the first time in the United States on an official large-scale basis of a political police reaching throughout the country.

This danger is heightened by an examination of the standards themselves. The first four of these standards encompass such acts as sabotage, treason, advocacy of force or violence to overthrow the government of the United States, and unauthorized disclosure of confidential documents. These standards constitute either crimes, or grounds for dismissal from government service, under existing laws. Present law enforcement agencies have full power to enforce these standards without the Executive Order.

The fifth and sixth standards are of an entirely different character.

To the extent that the fifth standard encompasses violation of existing laws such as treason, espionage, sabotage, or disclosure of confidential information, it is unnecessary. To the extent that it may seek to encompass other activities, its vagueness and indefiniteness are such as to render impossible the determination of the area or limits of its application.

The sixth standard, even more than the fifth, gives rise to the clear danger that the order invites an inquisition into political opinions. Certainly, as similarly phrased standards have been applied by the House Committee on Un-American Activities, which the Executive Order recognizes as one of the reference sources for purposes of determining disloyalty, these standards have meant nothing more than the holding of views in disagreement with the members of that committee. This point becomes sufficiently clear, when it is remembered that the President's own nominee to the position of Chairman of the Commission on Atomic Energy has been attacked as "communist," "totalitarian" and "subversive."

The Executive Order Constitutes an Invasion
of the Legislative Province

The Executive Order in thus prescribing standards over and above those set forth by statute invades the function of the legislature. There is no basis in either statute or constitution for the promulgation of such standards by the President. The Congress of the United States has spoken on the subject of sabotage, espionage, treason, advocacy of overthrow of the Government. But never has it proscribed generally membership in or sympathetic association with organizations, or entrusted to the executive the power to dictate the political views of government employees. On the contrary, it has affirmatively asserted that government employees shall be free to express their political

57

opinions.[8]

The President, concededly, may have power to set forth the procedure to determine whether or not standards set out by Congress have been met, but our system of government gives the executive no authority to prescribe standards either greater or less than those prescribed by Congress. The supremacy of the legislative branch is negated if the President by executive order can legislate on so important a subject as to what class of persons shall be eligible to work for the government. So fundamental a matter of policy is clearly under our form of government entrusted to Congress, not to the Executive.

In some quarters this action of the President in enacting new substantive legislation is justified as forestalling Congressional action. These apologists argue that the President, being more liberal than Congress, is thus preventing more drastic Congressional action. But even if we conceded this certainly not obvious conclusion, since it is difficult to see how any action can be more drastic than that taken by the President, nevertheless such conjectures as to the comparative liberality of the President as against Congress should not be permitted to subvert established constitutional principles, or to shift to the executive powers given by the Constitution to the legislative branch. Nor is it to be presumed that the legislature, after full public hearings, and opportunity to get the viewpoint of public organizations and the legal profession, would enact such patently unconstitutional legislation in complete disregard of constitutional principles as laid down by the Supreme Court.

The Procedure in the Executive Order
Denies Constitutional Safeguards

It has been established above that the sole province of the executive on this subject matter is to establish not substantive standards but procedure. But the procedure must conform with constitutional standards. The necessary safeguards are the obvious ones—that the crime or charge to be proved be clearly stated, that the burden of proof rest upon the charging party, that there be a full written record of the proceedings, that the judicial or deciding body make findings of fact and render a written opinion on the basis of the record made before it, that appeal lie from this opinion on the basis of the written record and accepted judicial standards.

In considering these aspects of the order it is well to remember that involuntary separation from federal employment on charges of

8. Section 9 (a) of the Hatch Act, 18 U.S.C. 61 (h).

disloyalty entails severe penalties. The serious curtailment of one's ability to earn a livelihood and the stigma of disloyalty were recognized by the Supreme Court in *United States* v. *Lovett*[9] as being penal in character, so that the imposition of these punishments by legislative act was held to be an unconstitutional bill of attainder. The severity of the penalty is no less when the same result is accomplished by the executive or the administrative, rather than the legislative, process. And even if it be conceded that the relationship of the executive departments or agencies to their employees is such that the standards of criminal proceedings do not apply, the seriousness of the punishment would seem to be sufficiently great to call for the exercise of self-imposed restraints to stafeguard rights that have traditionally been regarded as fundamental in other areas of the law.

Loyalty investigations and removal for disloyalty are not new phenomena in federal personnel administration. The abuses of the personal rights of individuals and the host of baseless charges that have been paraded under the mask of disloyalty are well-known.[10] Violations of traditional standards of fairness have been shocking. The present executive order on its face purports to provide such elementary safeguards as hearings, representation by counsel, information of charges, and the right to appeal, safeguards which have been frequently denied in the past. Despite these provisions, however, the order falls far short of securing to federal employees their exercise of political and other rights free from fear of recrimination. Even if it were necessary to prove disloyalty as a reason for disqualification, the standards and procedures prescribed in the order are sufficiently loose to create serious dangers of abuse. Since it is only necessary to establish reasonable grounds for belief as to disloyalty, the dangers are magnified many times and the need of stricter procedures is more compelling.

Of basic importance is the nature of the hearing afforded an employee. It must be surrounded by fundamental procedural safeguards to afford the individual his full constitutional protection as well as to assure adequate standards for adducing proof and determing the probative value of the evidence.

It may be argued that administrative hearings, dealing only with the internal administration of government, need not proceed with the same caution as has characterized hearing in other fields of public

9. 328 U.S. 303.
10. 328 U.S. 303, *U.S.* v. *Lovett.*

law. But it would seem that the "rudimentary requirements of fair play"[11] should govern loyalty hearings for the reasons stated above, *i.e.,* (1) for the individual's protection, (2) to assure the "maintenance of public confidence in the value and soundness of this important governmental process," and (3) to assure adequate proof.

The procedural safeguards are particularly significant in the light of the sanctions imposed. In *United States* v. *Lovett*,[12] a statute was challenged which prohibited certain individuals whom Congress deemed guilty of "subversive activities" from ever engaging in any government work. The type of punishment was likened to that invoked for "special types of odious and dangerous crimes."[13] The Court, in reviewing the dangers of legislative punishments in terms which would seem equally applicable here, stated (p. 317) that it was the intention of the authors of the Constitution "to safeguard the people of this country from punishment without trial by duly constituted courts." The conditions deemed necessary before punishment could be imposed, which it would seem furnish an appropriate guide for measuring the adequacy of the procedural safeguards of the executive order, were described by the Court as follows:

> "And even the courts to which this important function was entrusted were commanded to stay their hands until and unless certain tested safeguards were observed. An accused in court must be tried by an impartial jury, has a right to be represented by counsel, he must be clearly informed of the charge against him, the law which he is charged with violating must have passed before he committed the act charged, he must be confronted by the witnesses against him, he must not be compelled to incriminate himself, he cannot twice be put in jeopardy for the same offense, and even after conviction no cruel and unusual punishment can be inflicted upon him."

The criminal nature of the penalty of being dismissed because "reasonable grounds exist for belief 'that one is disloyal,'" and the inevitable stigma attaching to one's reputation making it difficult to obtain employment, underline the necessity for procedural safeguards not found in the present executive order.

Neither the provisions relating to the setting up of loyalty boards nor those dealing with the conduct of the hearing assure a fair hearing. The head of each agency is responsible for setting up hearing boards. He is also responsible for setting up the machinery to investigate the loyalty of employees and for presenting charges of disloyalty. Since

11. *Morgan* v. *U.S.,* 304 U.S. 1, 15.
12. 328 U.S. 303.
13. *Ibid.,* Pg. 316.

all these powers reside in a single agency, it is clear that the various functions should be separated so that there is no possibility that those persons serving on loyalty boards are in any way connected with investigating powers or have power to initiate proceedings.[14] The order contains no provisions, however, requiring such separation and thus provides no assurance that the hearing board will be an impartial one.

No greater assurance is provided that the hearings themselves will be conducted in accordance with traditional requirements of due process. Although the order provides that an affected employee "shall be informed . . . of the nature of the charges against him in sufficient detail, so that he will be enabled to prepare his defense" and requires that "the charges shall be stated specifically and completely," it is significant that such charges need be stated only as "specifically and completely as, in the discretion of the employing department or agency, security considerations permit . . ."[15] But despite this apparent regard for the accused individual, even the employee's agency charged with making a loyalty determination has not the means fully to evaluate the facts, for the investigative agency may refuse to disclose the names of confidential informants if it advises the agency "that it is essential to the protection of the informants or to the investigation of other cases that the identity of the informants not be revealed."[16] The very fact that the sources of damaging information may be protected against being discredited by cross-examination or direct rebuttal makes all the more urgent the necessity of fully apprising the employee of the nature of the evidence against him.[17] Equally important rights which are not guaranteed by the order are the right to be confronted by witnesses against the accused and the right of examination.[18]

The order does not even prescribe safeguards which the Attorney General's Commission on Administrative Procedure indicated were essential to the fair conduct of ordinary administrative proceedings, such as complete disclosure of evidence, stenographic minutes of the proceedings, written opinions and findings, and publication of guiding principles of administrative behavior. Of these, the secret collection

14. See Final Report of Attorneys' General Commission on Administrative Procedure (1941)—pg. 55.
15. Part II, Sec. 2B.
16. Part IV, Sec. 2.
17. Cf. *U.S.* v. *Cruikshank,* 92 U.S. 542, 558, 559.
18. Cf. *Motes* v. *United States,* 178 U.S. 458, 467, 471.

of evidence not revealed to the employees is most odious.[19] If file information is not required to be disclosed, it can never be determined whether in fact findings made by the loyalty boards are supported by substantial evidence, the general rule in administrative proceedings.[20] In these circumstances the right of appeal to the agency head and the Civil Service Commission must remain a doubtful one.

Guilt by Association is Not Sanctioned by Our Law

If federal employees may be removed solely because of "membership in, affiliation with, or sympathetic association with" lawful organizations, then, whatever may be true of other citizens, federal employees do not "enjoy a political status as citizens in a free world in which men are privileged to think and act and speak according to their convictions, without fear of punishment . . . so long as they keep the peace and obey the law." This, from *Schneiderman* v. *United States*.[21] It is hardly conceivable that acceptance of federal employment can or should require the waiver of such fundamental political liberties. Nevertheless, the test of guilt by association promulgated by the executive order is the equivalent of such a deprivation.

As a further matter, the Supreme Court has specifically rejected proof of disloyalty by association stating in the *Schneiderman* case "that under our traditions beliefs are personal and not a matter of mere association, and that men adhering to a political party or other organization notoriously do not subscribe unqualifiedly to all of its platforms or asserted principles." [22] And in *Bridges* v. *Wixon*,[23] Mr. Justice Murphy, concurring, said:

> "The doctrine of personal guilt is one of the most fundamental principles of our jurisprudence. It partakes of the very essence of the concept of freedom and due process of law. . . . It prevents the persecution of the innocent for the beliefs and actions of others."

The offense of this mode of proof to our fundamental traditions was stated by Chief Justice Hughes in opposition to the expulsion of Socialist members from the New York State Assembly as follows:

> ". . . it is the essence of the institutions of liberty that it be recognized that guilt is personal and cannot be attributed to the holding of opinion or to mere intent *in the absence of overt acts*." (Italics added.)[24]

19. Cf. *I.C.C.* v. *L & N Ry.*, 227 U.S. 88, 93.
20. *Ibid.*
21. 320 U.S. 118.
22. *Schneiderman* v. *U.S.*, 320, U.S. 118, 136-14.
23. 326 U.S. 135.
24. N.Y. Legislative Documents, Vol. 5, 143rd Session (1920), No. 30, pg. 4.

The dangers of permitting proof of membership or association with organizations to be sufficient evidence to warrant disqualification from office are magnified many times in the instant situation. In the ordinary situation this type of evidence "is subject to the admitted infirmities of proof by imputation."[25] These "infirmities" were thought to exist with respect to organizations whose purposes were frankly stated without any intent to conceal their objectives. But in the past we have seen federal employees' attachment to American principles attacked by virtue of their membership in organizations whose stated purposes were beyond reproach on the theory that they were in fact "front" organizations. The executive order apparently sanctions this practice, requiring only that the organization be designated by the Attorney General. But if membership in an organization whose purposes are set forth without concealment is doubtful proof that all of the purposes are attributable to its members, how much more doubtful if the evidence of the true objectives is not revealed to the members and there is no requirement of proof that the member ever knew of its hidden purposes!

Excessive Authority is Vested in the Attorney General

The section of the order authorizing disqualification from employment because of membership in certain organizations constitutes a threat to basic principles not only because it permits proof of guilt by association but also because it reposes excessive powers in the Attorney General. The Attorney General is given the authority to designate organizations, proof of membership in which may be the basis for disqualification. This designation may be made without the requirement of a hearing for the designated organization. Nor is there any requirement that the organizations designated be made public. The designation may have retroactive effect so that membership in organizations before they have been designated by the Attorney General may nevertheless be the basis for removal. And, finally, the tests of organizations which may be designated (totalitarian, fascist, communist or subversive) are not sufficiently definite to permit individuals to know in advance which organizations will be designated and which will not.

The authority thus conferred and the absence of adequate restraints upon its exercise permit the Attorney General to become in effect a political censor and violate rights heretofore considered sacred. The

25. *Schneiderman* v. *U.S.*, 320 U.S. 118, 154.

abhorrence of political censorship to fundamental American tradition was recently stated by the Supreme Court in *West Va. Board of Education* v. *Barnette*,[26] as follows:

> "If there is any fixed star in our constitutional constellation, it is that no offical, high or petty, can prescribe what shall be orthodox in politics, nationalism, religion or other matters of opinion or force citizens to confess by word or act their faith therein."

The power to place organizations beyond the pale, so to speak, is so foreign to traditional concepts, that we might expect at the very least unusual safeguards to condition its exercise. But, as we have seen, the Attorney General is free to act without even affording an organization an opportunity for a hearing to state its case. On the basis of secret information, obtained from unknown sources not subject to impeachment or cross-examination, an organization may be designated as disloyal. By this designation sufficient evidence is created to justify, under the terms of the executive order, disqualification from federal employment of all the members of that organization. An official act which may have such far-reaching consequences should at least have the basis of action subject to the scrutiny of a hearing. Furthermore, since a designation by the Attorney General would appear to make past membership evidence of disloyalty, the penalty of removal would be the equivalent of punishing past conduct which was not criminal in violation of the constitutional prohibition against *ex post facto* laws.[27] The fact that the order does not purport to pose criminal penalties would not seem determinative,[28] inasmuch as the *"ex post facto"* effect of a law cannot be evaded by giving a civil form to that which is essentially criminal." [29]

The fact that the basis of disqualification may be membership in an organization which the Attorney General has designated but has not publicly disclosed in itself offends due process. Persons threatened with penalties as severe as deprivation of employment should be informed as to what is forbidden.[30] The terms used to characterize the types of organizations which the Attorney General may designate, namely, totalitarian, fascist, communist or subversive, are not "sufficiently explicit" to supply the necessary information. As the Supreme Court stated in *Connolly* v. *General Construction Co.:* [31]

26. 319 U.S. 624, 642.
27. *Calder* v. *Bull*, 3 *Dall.* 386, 390.
28. See *U.S.* v. *Lovett*, 328 U.S. 303.
29. *Burgess* v. *Salmon*, 97 *U.S.* 381, 385.
30. Cf. *Lanzetta v. New Jersey*, 306 U.S. 381, 385.
31. 269 U.S. 385, 391.

"That the terms of a penal statute creating a new offense must be suficiently explicit to inform those who are subject to it what conduct on their part will render them liable to its penalties, is a well recognized requirement, consonant alike with ordinary notions of fair play and the settled rules of law. *And a statute which either forbids or requires the doing of an act in terms so vague that men of common intelligence must necessarily guess at its meaning and differ as to its application, violates the first essential of due process of law."* (Italics added.)

The conclusion reached by the Supreme Court in *Lanzetta* v. *New Jersey* [32] with respect to an attempt of the State of New Jersey to punish "gangsters", is peculiarly pertinent to the provisions of the executive order which permits punishment by removal for membership in organizations to be designated by the Attorney General. The court said (pg. 458):

"The challenged provision condemns no act or omission; the terms it employs to indicate what it purports to denounce are so vague, indefinite and uncertain that it must be condemned as repugnant to the due process clause of the Fourteenth Amendment."

Conclusion

It is apparent from the foregoing discussion that the executive order of the President is offensive to our constitution in many respects. It

(1) Constitutes an unwarranted intrusion of the executive into the sphere reserved for the legislative branch;

(2) Denies the constitutional safeguards of a fair hearing;

(3) Sanctions the unconstitutional doctrine of guilt by association;

(4) Sets up the Attorney General as a high priest of political orthodoxy;

(5) Violates the constitutional doctrine that standards for punishment be precise and definite.

Although these points in themselves constitute clear and convincing reasons for the rescission of the executive order, our discussion of this executive order would not be complete if we did not set it in its background.

We are living today in a period of rising opposition to the civil rights of minority groups. Not since the post-war days of the First World War have we seen so strong a movement to deny constitutional rights to those who hold unorthodox views. Although many proposals have been made, and many bills have been introduced into Congress, this Executive Order is the first of these measures to take a concrete legal form. It would be foolhardy to sup-

32. 306 U.S. 451.

pose that so serious a deprivation of constitutional rights and the freedom of opinion can be stopped at the point of federal employees. The analogy is too clear, its logic, if once permitted, too irrefutable, to prevent its extension to other fields. If these indeed be standards of loyalty to our government, why should they not be extended to state and municipal employees, to officials of our quasi-public institutions such as schools, universities or labor unions? They may well be extended to employees in public utilities or essential industries, who by presidential edict may be declared to be government employees.[33]

The intimidatory effects of the Executive Order have already been apparent to those who observe the Washington scene. Government employees no longer feel free to express themselves. They now weigh the consequence of their words with one eye cocked warily on the House Committee on Un-American Activities. College students interested in future government employment must weigh carefully what courses they take, what opinions they express, what organizations they join. The public service will no longer know the employee with ideals and principles; he must be made over into a sterile creature of political orthodoxy mouthing the shibboleths of the House Committee on Un-American Activities. Then only will he know that he is safe and has passed the test. The executive order thus does serious injury to the integrity and quality of the public service.

Finally, it would be fitting to inquire what crisis compels this wholesale deprivation of civil liberties, this conversion of government employees into politically sterile idea-less automatons. It would be only trite to mention the obvious fact that our government has operated satisfactorily through two wars without such extreme measures. The laws against espionage and sabotage were considered sufficient in wartime; they should be adequate now. We found no inadequacy in the size and competence of our police force during wartime. There should be no need for their multiplication at this stage. It is significant that during the past war, the FBI investigated 1,121 allegedly subversive employees. Of those investigated, two were discharged, and disciplinary action was taken in one other case. The Attorney General, in his report on the results of these investigations,[34] stated,

33. *United States* v. *United Mine Workers et al.* (67 Sup. Ct. 677).
34. 7702 H. Doc. 83.

"The wisdom of assigning experienced Bureau agents to such work in wartime and with such meager results must be seriously questioned . . . As regards a large proportion of the complaints, it is now evident that they were clearly unfounded and that they should never have been submitted for investigation in the first instance. It will be observed from the figures that this is conspicuously true of the list submitted by Congressman Dies. Hundreds of employees, for example, have been alleged to be 'subversive' for no better reason than the appearance of their names on the mailing lists of certain organizations" (pp. 3-4).

No events have transpired that warrant such extreme action. The executive order is silent on this question of experience because the record is barren. All that appears in the record are the complaints of certain Congressional Committees that all the New Dealers have not yet been driven from government posts. In their minds, the danger is that there remain in government positions not disciples of Marx, but disciples of Roosevelt.

Sanford I. Carter

Member New York, California
Bars; member Phi Beta Kappa;
now practicing, Beverly Hills

DISCRIMINATION IN
EMPLOYMENT

IF the freedoms guaranteed by the founders of our country are to have meaning, the thoughts of the people must be free from control. Freedom of speech, of enterprise and of contract become empty theories if masses of people are intimidated and coerced into thinking along lines set down by a few. Thought is father to the deed and freedom of action cannot truly exist where thinking is controlled.

Perhaps the most serious threat to freedom and to our democracy today lies in the attempt to control mental processes by the use of economic discrimination. Too little attention has been given to this problem and it is our purpose here to bring the problem to light, touch upon its legal aspects and offer a few suggestions for constructive action.

This phase of the problem of thought control can best be illustrated by recounting a simple incident that occurred in our own community, an incident that is typical of many others threatening the nation.

During a Presidential election year a large public utility, employing many thousands of persons, sent a letter to all of its employees stating that the Republican candidate was most familiar with the problems of public utilities and *that the welfare of the company and therefore the jobs of the employees* depended upon the election of the Republican candidate. Let us reflect upon this for a moment. Is it likely that an employee may think and act as a free man when he is told that his job is at stake, his livelihood and the physical well-being of his family are in jeopardy unless he votes in the manner prescribed by his employer? The man who is faced with economic insecurity is easy prey for the employer who wields this economic power to control the beliefs of his employees. It is difficult to think freely on an empty stomach and the danger of this form of exploitation, the exploitation of the human mind, constitutes an increasingly serious threat to our democratic ideals.

Those who won our independence believed that the final end of the state was to make men free to develop their faculties and that in its government the deliberative forces must prevail over the arbitrary. They believed that freedom to think as you will and to speak as you think are indispensable to the discovery of political truth; that free discussion affords protection against the dissemination of noxious doctrines; that public discussion is a political duty and that this should be a fundamental principle of American government; that it is hazardous to discourage thought and imagination; that fear breeds hate and that hate menaces stable government; that the path of safety lies in the opportunity to discuss freely supposed grievances and proposed remedies (see Brandeis, J., in *Whitney* v. *California,* 274 U. S. 357).

In the highly industrialized society of today, the power of proprietors to control the thinking of employees is increasingly great. Large portions of our population are employed by relatively few corporations who, because of the dependence of the employees upon their jobs for existence, are obviously in a position to direct the thinking of their employees. Employees, however courageous, are virtually helpless to combat this attack upon their freedom. The ability to change jobs freely or to "go West" no longer exists. The worker today is forced by economic pressure and fear of insecurity to remain at his job. Nazism and Fascism grew and flourished in Europe where the minds of people were controlled by threats of violence. If, in place of violence, we substitute fear of economic insecurity, can we expect a different result? If the power of the few over the many is permitted to go unrestrained, the inevitable result is the domination of our government by the economically privileged minority. To salvage some degree of freedom the public must be awakened to the seriousness of the problem; existing legislation on this subject must be enforced vigorously and additional legislative safeguards imposed.

There has been some legislation enacted designed to curb this power of the employer over the thinking of the employees. As might be expected, the privileged minority, in attacking such legislation, raised the cry of "freedom" and sought shelter behind charges that such legislation violated the due process clause, interfered with freedom of speech and freedom of contract. But the freedom they cried out about is a concept of "abstract absolute freedom", a concept that has not existed since the first law governing society was enacted. Absolute freedom is synonymous with anarchy, since the very existence of government is an abridgement of individual freedom. The liberty guaranteed by our Constitution is not abstract or absolute, but rather actual and real—liberty in an organization of social beings which requires the protection of law against those evils which demoralize and menace the welfare of the people.

California has led the way in recognizing the dangers to the public welfare and to our democratic way of life if employers are permitted to control the thoughts and activities of their workers. In 1937, Chapter 5 of the California Labor Code was enacted, the relevant portions of which read as follows:

> "Section 1101. No employer shall make, adopt or enforce any rule, regulation or policy:
>
> "(a) Forbidding or preventing employees from engaging or participating in politics or becoming candidates for public office;
>
> "(b) Controlling or directing or attempting to control or direct the political activities or affiliations of employees.
>
> "Section 1102. No employer shall coerce or influence or attempt to influence his employees through or by means of threat of discharge or loss of employment, to adopt or follow, or refrain from adopting or following any particular course or line of political action or political activity."

Needless to say, these laws were attacked as unconstitutional and it was claimed that they constituted an un-warranted interference with the right of the employer to hire and fire. However, these challenges were met in the case entitled *Charles* v. *Lockheed Aircraft,* and its companion case entitled *Lockheed Aircraft* v. *Superior Court.* Judge White, in the latter case, analyzed the problems involved in such legislation and disposed of the constitutional questions raised by the employers in an enlightening opinion, portions of which may well be repeated here.

In this case, the plaintiffs, employees of Lockheed Aircraft Corp., alleged that they were discharged from employment by reason of rules, regulations and policies of the defendant which prevented them from participating in politics, all in violation of Section 1101 of the Labor Code. To the objection that the statute interfered with the normal right of the employer to hire and fire, the court pointed out that this argument proceeded on the erroneous assumption that the right to hire and fire is an absolute one—a view that had already been completely answered by the Supreme Court of the United States in *National Labor Relations Board* v. *Jones & Laughlin,* 301 U. S. 145, wherein that court, upholding the validity of the National Labor Relations Act, said:

> "The Act does not interfere with the normal exercise of the right of the employer to select its employees or to discharge them. The employer may not, under cover of that right, intimidate or coerce its employees with respect to their self-organization and representation."

The next challenge to the constitutionality of the statute was on the ground that it is an arbitrary restriction upon the liberty and freedom of contract and therefore violates the Fourteenth Amendment to the Constitution of the United States. However, the court, fortified by many well-considered opinions of the Supreme Court of the United States, laid bare the fallacies of such contention. Freedom of contract is a qualified and not an absolute right. No one is vested with the absolute freedom to do as he pleases or wills or to contract as he chooses. It is the absence of *arbitrary* restraint and *not* immunity from reasonable regulations that liberty implies.

The highest court in our land, more than forty years ago, recognized the dangers existing because of the inequality in the positions of the employer and employee and upheld the right of the legislature to act in the public interest. In *Holden* v. *Hardy,* 169 U. S. 366, 397, the court, in directing attention to this inequality, said:

> "The legislature has always recognized the fact which the experience of legislators in many states has corroborated, that the proprietors of these establishments and their operatives do not stand upon an equality and their interests are, to a certain extent, conflicting, the former naturally desiring to obtain as much labor as possible from employees while the latter are often induced by the fear of discharge to conform to regulations which their judgment, fairly exercised, would pronounce to be detrimental to their health or strength. In other words, proprietors laid down the rules and the employees are practically constrained to obey them. In such cases, self-interest is often an unsafe guide and the legislature may promptly interpose its authority."

To the claim that such legislation interfered with the freedom of speech of the employer, the court made it clear that such a law did not in any way infringe upon the employers' freedom of speech. Nowhere is the employer prohibited from freely expressing his views. *It is only discrimination against the employee because* he *exercised his right to freedom of expression, that is prohibited.*

It thus appears that not only is there a valid constitutional basis for remedial legislation but further that unless adequate legislation is enacted and enforced, economic inequalities threaten the continuance of our democratic ideals.

Thought control is not limited to political beliefs, but may extend to every branch of thought. Discrimination in employment because of race, creed or religion can sow the seed of widespread racial and religious intolerance. Recognizing this danger, the State of New York, in 1945, enacted its Law Against Discrimination, which is frequently referred to as its Fair Employment Practices Act and which forbids discrimination by employers or labor unions because of race, creed, color or national origin. Similarly, during the last war, President Roosevelt, by executive order, decreed the policy of the United States to be that there shall be no discrimination in the employment of workers in defense industries or in government because of race, color, creed or national origin.

Some progress has also been made by labor unions who, by reason of the equality created by collective bargaining, have it within their power to curtail attempts on the part of employers to control the thinking of employees.

These are all steps in the right direction, but much more is needed if our democratic ideals are to be maintained. The public must be awakened to the problem and its dangers. The rights of an employer must be clearly defined and understood. It must be established that except for a determination of the worker's qualification for the job assigned to him, the employer has no right and no control over the lives or thinking of his workers.

The validity of legislation designed to protect freedom of thought having been established, the scope of existing legislation must be broadened and enlarged. For example, the above quoted provisions of the California Labor Code by their terms only apply *after* the relationship of employer and employee has been created. Employers may now circumvent the statute by refusing to hire or discriminating against persons holding adverse views and thus continue to exercise thought control. Also, "political activities" is subject to as many interpretations as there might be interpreters, and whether the statute, as now drawn, prevents an employer from discriminating against an employee with respect to compensation conditions and other rights of employment may well be the subject of legal conjecture.

Our law must be further supplemented by a Fair Employment Practices Act. Religious thought as well as political thought must be free from control and employers and labor unions alike must not be permitted to discriminate because of race, creed, color or national origin.

Pending these legislative advances, the public must be alerted to the dangers that beset our democratic ideals and bring them to light. It is the job—and the duty—of progressives and the progressive movement to lead the way in this enlightment; to acquaint the workers with their existing guarantees of freedom of thought and to lead the fight for necessary legislation in the future. Future legislation must not only guarantee complete cultural freedom, but must give birth to a positive philosophy that guarantees the right to accept or reject any thought or action without fear of economic discrimination. If our American philosophy of government is to be preserved, founded as it is on the recognition of the dignity of the individual as a natural right, every person must be free to pursue his beliefs unhampered by fear, for it is only through the free interchange of thought and expression that we can hope to solve the problems of civilization.

Charles J. Katz

Past President, L. A. Chapter,
Natl. Lawyers' Guild; noted for
handling many important labor
and civil liberties cases

TOWARDS A FREE PRESS

BISMARCK once said that most wars could have been prevented
by hanging a dozen editors, and Napoleon pointed out that he feared
four hostile newspapers more than four hundred thousand armed
men. An anonymous wag in Fleet Street during the reign of Queen
Anne wisecracked that the power of the press is the "suppress". The
brilliance of the statement is not lessened by the anonymity of its
author.

Our American Revolutionaries in the thirteen original Colonies
fully understood what was meant by the phrase "freedom of the
press". They had suffered deeply enough at the hands of the British
to know what Government censorship was and they feared the sterilization that always followed in the censor's path. Before them was the
example of John Milton inveighing as early as 1644 against an Act
which the Long Parliament had passed establishing the Crown's absolute
censorship over the press before publication. In his appeal *For the
Liberty of Unlicensed Printing,* Milton had vigorously defended the
right of every man to make public his views "without previous censor";
and he declared the impossibility of finding any man base enough to
accept the office of censor, and at the same time good enough to
be allowed to perform its duties.

In 1712, Parliament imposed a rigorous control over all newspapers.
Its avowed object was to suppress and prevent the publication of
comments and criticisms objectionable to the Crown. There followed
almost a century of resistance to the measure, and great agitation for
its repeal.

And so, when in 1781 the Constitutional Convention adopted our
Supreme Law for the new nation, containing no explicit guarantee of
freedom of the press, Jefferson, Madison, Richard Henry Lee, Eleazer
Oswald, Patrick Henry, and other patriots, during the debates over
ratification, bitterly assailed the proposed Constitution for failing to

include a provision prohibiting all governmental interference with the press. Historians now assert that the Constitution itself would never have been ratified had the first Congress not immediately adopted the Bill of Rights, with its very opening paragraph guaranteeing in the clearest language possible that Congress "shall pass no law abridging the freedom of speech or of the press".

The admitted aim of those who sponsored the first amendment was to prevent the Government from interfering with expression. The authors of our political system knew that the free society they were seeking to establish could not exist without free communication. As Jefferson put it: "The basis of our government being the opinion of the people, the very first object should be to keep that right; and were it left to me to decide whether we should have a government without newspapers, or newspapers without a government, I should not hesitate a moment to prefer the latter". (We may forgive him this trespass, for in his enthusiasm he could not have foreseen the spectre of our contemporary press.)

The phrase "freedom of the press" had a definitive connotation in Colonial times. It meant the right to publish opinions without fear of governmental suppression. The censor was then the villian. And so Jefferson and his followers were justified in assuming that if by Constitutional command the government could be prevented from interfering with publication, then every condition of a free press would be effectively achieved. In the general report entitled, *A Free and Responsible Press,* just issued by the Robert Hutchins Commission (April, 1947), the following observations are made about conditions in Colonial times, in the face of which our great Constitutional guarantee should be read. Mr. Hutchins says of that earlier period:

> "The only serious obstacle to free expression then was government censorship. If that could be stopped, the right of every man to do his duty by his thought was secure. The press of those days consisted of hand printed sheets, issued from little printing shops, regularly as newspapers, or irregularly as broadsides, pamphlets or books. Presses were cheap; the journeyman printer could become a publisher and editor by borrowing the few dollars he needed to set up his shop and by hiring an assistant or two. There was no great discrepancy between the number of those who could read and were active citizens and those who could command the financial resources to engage in publication."

But with the passage of years this background has changed completely; and with this change, a revolution has occurred in newspaper publishing. A newspaper is no longer the hand press. It is Big Business; pitted against it, the Eighteenth Century concept of freedom of the press, while still retaining much of its basic vitality, has lost a great deal of its primary meaning. In the same Hutchins report, this metamorphosis and its effect are pointed out clearly:

"Literacy, the electorate, and the population have increased to such a point that the political community to be served by the press includes all but a tiny fraction of the millions of American people.

"The press has been transformed into an enormous and complicated piece of machinery. As a necessary accompaniment, it has become big business. There is a marked reduction in the number of units of the press relative to the total population. Although in small communities we can still see a newspaper plant and product that resemble their Colonial prototypes, these are no longer the most characteristic or the most influential agencies of communication. The right of free public expression has therefore lost its earlier reality. Protection against government is now not enough to guarantee that a man who has something to say shall have a chance to say it. The owners and managers of the press alone determine which persons, which facts, which versions of the facts and which ideas shall reach the public. For a considerable period the number of daily English-language newspapers has fallen at a fairly constant rate. At the same time there has been a growth in literacy, in total population, and in total circulation. In only 117 (approximately one out of twelve) of the cities in which daily newspapers are published are there now competing dailies; in 22 states, no cities have competing Sunday newspapers. Altogether 40% of the estimated total daily newspaper circulation of 48,000,000 is non-competitive. Rival newspapers exist only in the larger cities."

Today the business of news gathering is concentrated in the great press associations, the largest of them being the Associated Press. There are 1803 daily English-language newspapers now published in the United States, with a total circulation of some 42,000,000. Approximately 1200 of these, with more than 75% of the total circulation, are blanketed in under the Associated Press, each member of which is under joint contractual obligation not to supply any news to any non-member of the AP.

And the United States Supreme Court (*Associated Press* v. *U. S.,* 326 U. S. 1), in declaring the by-laws of this Association limiting membership in it to be a monopolistic practice, found that a new applicant newspaper could not have entered the morning newspaper field in New York City in 1943 without paying one and a half million dollars to the Associated Press for the privilege. For entering the evening field, it would have to pay a little more than a million dollars to obtain a franchise.

Any new newspaper starting in a metropolitan city today requires an expenditure, it is conservatively estimated, of at least ten million dollars. Access to the news of the world can only come through membership in one of the three great news gathering agencies—AP, UP, and INS—and this can only be obtained at an inordinately high price. Therefore, the rapid decline in the number of newspapers and therefore the increased monopolization of the entire newspaper publishing field.

But this is only one side of the story. Control over the freedom of the press in Colonial times, as has been pointed out, was exercised by governmental censors. Today the control is as effectively exercised by a combination of large newspaper pubishers: a combination found by our Supreme Court to be a veritable extra-governmental Goliath, prescribing its own rules for the regulation and restraint of interstate commerce and providing extra-judicial tribunals for determination and punishment of violators of its own enactments (*Associated Press v. U. S.,* 326 U. S., page 1).

These associations and these publishers determine what shall be published, what emphasis shall be placed on the material published, and who shall be permitted to express their opinions and ideas through the press. And so today a far smaller proportion of our people have any opportunity to enjoy the meaningful blessings of freedom of the press. Once a newspaper was primarily an editorial product, consisting of news and editorial comment, with some miscellaneous features. Today it is essentially a business product.

> "Owners of newspapers and publishers under these circumstances begin to be business men, rather than editorial men. They regard publishing a newspaper primarily as a business to which business rules are to be applied, rather than as a service and a profession. Great sums of money must be invested to house a newspaper properly, to buy the necessary mechanical equipment, to pay the numerous employees required in the various departments and to meet fixed charges and general overhead. Large advertising patronage becomes necessary and large circulations become prerequisite to large advertising patronge. Mass appeal in the news is required to attract large circulation. Mass appeal means excitement, struggle, suspense, humor, pathos, horrors, thrills—elementary things reaching readers' emotions rather than their minds.

> "Owners of newspapers, with their managers, publishers, and chief editors, concerned with these matters, find themselves associating with other business men, also concerned with similar management problems; in clubs, at play, in trade conferences they meet them and come to hold common views. The result: newspaper making is transformed into a manufacturing industry producing newspapers from its factory. This has been the trend in the United States" (Desmond, *Press and World Affairs,* Chapter 8).

The late William Allen White, in 1938, while still editing his

Emporia Gazette, expressed himself thusly:

> "Any newspaper in any American town represents a considerable lot of capital for the size of the town. The owners of newspaper investments, whether they be bankers, stockholders, or individuals, feel a rather keen sense of financial responsibility and they pass their anxiety along to newspaper operatives, whether these operatives be superintendents, known as managing editors, foremen known as city editors, or mere wage-earners known as editorial writers. The sense of property goes thrilling down the line. It produces a slant and a bias that in time become a prejudice against any man or any thing or any cause that seriously affects the right or the title or the interest of any other capital, however invested."

Even William Randolph Hearst, in 1924, had to admit grudgingly:

> "I rather think that the influence of the American press is on the whole declining. This, I believe, is because of the fact that many newspapers are owned or influenced by reactionary and predatory corporations and are used selfishly to promote the welfare of these reactionary interests, rather than the welfare of the public." (See quotation—*America's House of Lords*, Harold L. Ickes, page 160.)

Such is the condition of our free press today. And it is at this pass that we must examine into the question of whether our democracy is strong enough to restore freedom of the press to its envisioned place as the star in the constellation of Constitutional liberties. On all hands the principle is conceded that freedom of the press is an essential condition to political liberty and that where people cannot freely convey their thoughts to one another no democratic freedom is secure.

But so few men today have access to the vehicles of communication, and so one-classed have the owners of the instruments of publication become, that for the great mass of our citizenry the phrase "freedom of the press" has tragically retained little of its original meaning. It is right and proper, therefore, that members of the bar should consider carefully the problem raised by this admitted revolution in news publishing. For here a great privilege falls to lawyers: the privilege of analyzing decisive issues and then reporting upon them to the American people. In the words of Professor Cushman:

> " . . . a heavy responsibility rests upon the members of the American bar not only to aid in individual cases in the legal protection of civil liberties, but to lead public opinion toward a sound and just appraisal of their vast importance. The record of the service rendered to the cause of civil liberties by American lawyers is a very long and honorable one. It stretches all the way from James Otis, defending two Boston merchants against the tyrannical Writ of Assistance in 1761, down to Wendell Wilkie, defending the Communist William Schneiderman, in the Supreme Court in 1943." (R. E. Cushman, *Civil Liberty and Public Opinion*, Cornell University Press, 1945.)

Today the issue no longer lies solely in the arena of the struggle to achieve freedom of content. Rather, the heart-question now is: by what means, consonant with a capitalist-democratic system, can the people be assured freedom of access to the press so that they may enjoy in living practice the Constitution's lyric promise of freedom of expression?

Unfortunately, in the search for the answer to this question, the First and Fourteenth Amendments, standing alone, are not adequate. Indeed, their injunctions against governmental interference have blessedly served to preserve for the press a broad and uninfringed area where newspapers could, if they would, practice freely the high art of publication. And the United States Supreme Court has until now been careful to leave that permissible area of free discussion wide, so that the people's interest in an unfettered press could be served. Thus the Court unanimously struck down an effort of the State of Minnesota to impose a gag law upon publishers who were guilty of continuing and ever-threatened libels (*Near* v. *Minnesota,* 283 U. S. 697), and it rejected Huey Long's effort to bring all Louisiana publishers to his knee via a tax on the circulation of newspapers selling more than 20,000 copies; the small papers then were supporting Long; those with larger circulations were against him. So the Kingfish sought to tax the papers with the larger circulations. The Supreme Court saw through the ruse, and this law of Louisiana was stricken. (See *Crosjean* v. *American Press Co.,* 297 U. S. 233.) The effort of a trial court to punish a newspaper for contempt by reason of its criticism of a pending case was also held violative of the freedom of the press. (See *L. A. Times* v. *Sup. Court,* 326 U. S. 56.)

But these great constitutional amendments, so carefully guarded by our Courts, are nevertheless not self-executing. Their shield, moreover, is set against governmental interference with, and not against private obstructions to, the streams of communication. Valiantly as the Supreme Court has labored to defend the high principle of a free press, it has scarcely been able, as yet, to touch even the outermost reaches of private transgression. The judicial process is ever the brake upon, and never the beginning of, action—however urgent.

The public has now become much concerned with the problem of access to the press, as against the private control over it.

Many proposals have been advanced, all aimed at assuring a free access by the people to the means of communication. We shall examine some of them.

One such proposal is popular with certain old-fashioned liberals, notably Morris Ernst. They express continued faith in the Nineteenth Century postulate that the stimulation of competition between newspaper publishers will insure a satisfactory solution. And so they advocate a vigorous enforcement of the anti-trust laws. Thus far, despite the successful use of the Sherman Act against the Associated Press, the trend toward ever greater monopoly control has not only not been slowed down, but every passing year shows an increasing centralization of control. And one may be pardoned a repetition of the observation, so often made by critics of this liberal view, that as long as it costs at least $10,000,000 to establish a newspaper in any large population center, few potential competitors will ever be found. Men with that much money tend somehow all to think alike. To have more $10,000,000 channels through which to funnel Big Business propaganda into the mass mind seems at best a questionable blessing.

Another proposal advanced—always by the newspaper publishers themselves—is for a system of self-regulation of the press. The fundamental conflict within the press as to whether it should be a profit-making business or a public agency would be resolved by letting the owners of the press decide it for themselves. The motion picture industry with its Hays (now Johnston) Office technique is cited as an example to be emulated. To this end the American Newspaper Publishers' Association, aware of the need for some moral standard, adopted a code of ethics containing seven rules to serve as canons of conduct for the self-regulation of the news publishing business. The code sounds beautiful. Among other rules, it declares straight face:

"1. RESPONSIBILITY. The right of a newspaper to attract and hold readers is restricted by nothing but considerations of public welfare. . . . A journalist who uses his power for any selfish or otherwise unworthy purpose is faithless to a high trust.

"2. INDEPENDENCE. Freedom from all obligations except that of fidelity to the public interest is vital. Promotion of any private interest contrary to the general welfare, for whatever reason, is not compatible with honest journalism. . . .

"4. Good faith with the reader is the foundation of all journalism worthy of the name. By every consideration of good faith, a newspaper is constrained to be truthful.

"5. IMPARTIALITY. News reports should be free from opinion or bias of any kind."

Sic. But not even the publishers themselves believe what their society so solemnly formulated. Shortly after the adoption of these rules for self-regulation, the *Wall Street Journal* wrote editorially on

January 20, 1925:

> "A newspaper is a private enterprise owing nothing to the public which grants it no franchise. It is therefore 'affected' with no public interest. It is emphatically the property of its owner who is selling a manufactured product at his own risk."

But it was not only the frankness of the *Wall Street Journal* which gave the game away. Many editors, aware that their neatly embroidered rules for self-regulation had failed in practice, and that their canons of ethics were being honored only in the breach, have spoken out against the profession's failure to meet its high trust. Thus even one President of the American Society of Newspaper Editors, Grove Patterson, was constrained to say in 1935:

> "I am less disturbed about the 'freedom of the press' than I am about the disposition of so many editors not to do anything with the freedom that is theirs. . . . The press in the United States does not suffer from lack of freedom. . . . But with some notable exceptions we suffer from editorial inactivity and mental indolence. The press does not lack courage but in too many quarters it has grown rusty with disuse."

And twelve years after the adoption of these same moral standards which were to act as rules of self-conduct, many other editors wrote publicly in sharp criticism of their performance:

(1) J. Charles Poe, managing editor, *Chattanooga News*, 1935:

> "Business office pressure and political bias are reasons why we editors do not print the news. . . . We need, not experts with their technical language, but intelligent young men who can understand the social significance of what is happening and interpret it in words the people can grasp. The trouble in America is not so much encroachment on the right of free press, but our failure to make use of this blessed privilege."

(2) Maurice S. Sherman, editor, *Hartford Courant:*

> "A glance at the first page of some of our journals that are supposed to speed enlightenment creates the impression that they are edited by morons for morons. The reader gains almost no information that contributes to his understanding of the real progress the world is making. The purpose of most newspaper publishers is solely to make money; they sell their rather scaly product much as fish is sold at the wharf."

One may surely be allowed a laugh while rejecting this thesis of self-regulation as the way to a more responsible press acting in the public interest.

Then there is the proposal advanced by Harold J. Laski and other progressives. It proceeds from an appraisal of the dialectics of our underlying economy.

> "Our new system," says Mr. Laski, "is, in a word, but a reflection of our social system; there will be no vital change in the one unless there is

a vital change in the other. The press is a fundamental weapon in the social conflict, national and international, in which we are all, despite ourselves, combatants. We shall have truthful news when untruthful news does not pay, but it will not pay only when the major causes of social conflict, national or international, have been removed."

Sometimes this position is phrased thusly:

The drastic means required to effect a meaningful change in the condition of the press is a shift in its economic ownership. But until masses of people find the way to ownership and control of newspapers, the essential evil will continue to exist.

Another corrective is suggested by Harold L. Ickes in his book *America's House of Lords:*

"One possibility is to have a press that would be supported by readers and subscribers, instead of by advertisers. Such a press would consist of nickel or dime newspapers and would, of course, express the point of view, the wishes and interests of the readers instead of those of Big Business. I am not sure, however, that the American people are psychologically prepared as yet for such an alternative."

We think there is a proposal which the American people are psychologically prepared to accept. It is one which finds considerable support in judicial decisions. It is the one we advocate.

It would require newspapers (in much the same way as radio stations have been required) to open their columns to a fairly-rounded presentation of controversial views on all major social, political, religious and economic questions of the day. This could be done by requiring one or two pages of the press to be set apart as the particular pages where the opposing (or the majority and minority) positions on controversial subjects were presented, all without expurgation or censorship by the publishers; these pages would be openly and publicly described as the particular pages where the views of the proponents and opponents of controversial measures were being printed, much as specific pages are now devoted exclusively to news of finance, of sports and, as we who have young children have learned sadly, of comics. Readers would know, and the law would require newspapers to make known the fact, that these were the open-forum pages of their press; here no private censor could operate; here no publisher's slant would be sacrosanct. And here ideas would be allowed to reach the market-place of the readers' minds, there to be accepted or rejected as the reader decided. This proposal is not a substitute for the "Letters to the Editor" column. For here the editor could not unilaterally and discriminatorily select particular communications which he desired to permit to be published. Instead, the firm legal duty would be created to assure a rounded presentation in the open-forum pages of the un-edited writings of the critics and the advocates of the critical issues of our times.

The mechanics of administering such a proposal are, of course, difficult. But certainly no more difficult than the mechanics of administering a Taft-Hartley Bill, as just passed by a Republican Congress. The problems of policing and regulation are soluble by the administrative processes now the subject of much (and such successful) expert attention.

A number of possible modes of enforcement suggest themselves. The cease-and-desist-order techniques employed for years by the Fair Trade Commission appear appropriate; sanctions, after full administrative hearing with fair judicial review, and consisting either of public reprimand or, as a last resort, denial of second-class mail privileges, may be considered as remedies.

And, incidentally, under our existing Postal Laws, the great second-class mailing privileges (without which a *Chicago Tribune,* for example, could not survive) are given by our government to newspapers because of the public service which they are supposed to render. Certainly a vigorous Postmaster General could even without legislation require some showing of fair and comprehensive coverage before allowing the continuance at public expense of this second-class mailing privilege.

If legislation is required, then specific penalties designed to cure the violations complained of can readily be fashioned by the agency charged by Congress with the administration of the contemplated statute.

Our proposal would extend, not diminish, the principle of a free press. If it is true, as many assert, that democracy may perish without an educated citizenry to uphold it, and if it is true that an educated citizenry cannot long remain such if it is without vehicles for the distribution of public information, then assuredly this proposal contributes to such enlightenment.

Legal support for this corrective lies all about us. The right reasonably to regulate private business clothed with a public interest is firmly established. And that the private business of newspaper publication has a direct relation to the public interest permitting reasonable regulation seems clear. Mr. Justice Frankfurter, in his separate concurring opinion in the Associated Press case, said:

"To be sure, the newspaper publisher is engaged in a commercial business for profit. But in addition to being a commercial enterprise, it has a relation to the public interest unlike that of any other enterprise pursued for profit. A free press is indispensable to the workings of our democratic society. The business of the press is the promotion of truth regarding public matters by furnishing the basis for an understanding of them. Truth and understanding are not wares like peanuts or potatoes. And so the evidence of restraints upon promotion of truth through denial of access to the basis for understanding calls into play considerations very different from comparable restraints upon enterprises. Neither exclusively nor even primarily are the interests of the newspaper industry conclusive; for that industry serves one of the most vital of all general interests; the dissemination of news from as many different sources, and with as many different facets and colors as is possible. That interest is clearly akin to, if indeed it is not the same as, the freedom of the press protected by the First Amendment. It pre-supposes that right conclusions are more likely to be gathered out of a multitude of tongues, than through any kind of authoritative selection."

When the Associated Press case was tried in 1943 before a special court consisting of Justices Learned Hand, Augustus Hand and Circuit Court Judge Swan, the newspapers complained that, by applying the Sherman Anti-Trust Act to publishers, the Court was declaring that their business was "clothed with a public interest" and that this was beyond the powers of a Court. Instead, said the publishers, it was up to the legislature to declare whether the business was subject to such regulation. Judge Learned Hand was not misled by this sophistry. He said:

"But there is no warrant for holding that the failure of Congress specifically to say that all activities are to be deemed so 'clothed' whenever the courts find them to be, shall deny power to the courts to effect the legislative will. Indeed, the whole matter is a red herring which should no longer be allowed to break the scent. Since *Nebbia* v. *New York*, 291 U. E. 502, there cannot be any excuse for misunderstanding the matter—there has really been none since *Munn* v. *Illinois*, 94 U. S. 113—'If one embarks in a business which public interest demands shall be regulated, he must know regulation will ensue.' . . . The phrase can, in the nature of things, mean no more than that an industry, for adequate reason, is subject to control for the public good."

"Private property," said Chief Justice Waite of the United States Supreme Court, in *Munn* v. *Illinois,* 94 U. S. 113, "does become clothed with a public interest, when used in a manner to make it of public consequence and affect the community at large."

It is, of course, difficult generally to say in each particular case whether a private business has become clothed with a public interest so that its patrons should not be discriminated against. But it is not difficult to say that newspapers do so directly affect a great public interest.

The principle of the grain elevator case (*Munn* v. *Illinois*) introduced no novel departure. What it did was to call attention to the fundamental relations that existed between the use of private property and the creation of a public interest in such use, and its chief value as a contribution to jurisprudence was that it pointed out clearly that the underlying question is not what the State has done to impress a public interest upon a private business, but rather what the owners and operators had done to draw to, and thus clothe themselves with, a public interest (see *McCarter* v. *Fireman's Insurance Co.* (a New Jersey case), 73 Atl. 80).

In 1920 a case arose in a *nisi pruis* court in Ohio which is of extreme significance here. In the small town of Defiance, Ohio, one weekly newspaper was published. A man named Uhlman conducted a general mercantile business in that city. Three competing merchants of that town disliked Uhlman. They were charged by him with prevailing upon the newspaper publisher to refuse Uhlman's proffered ad. The newspaper declined to publish the ad and Uhlman sued out an injunction. The publisher claimed that his newspaper was his own private enterprise; that he had no contract with Uhlman and therefore could not be compelled to accept his ad. The trial court (*Uhlman* v. *Sherman,* 22 Ohio Nisi Pruis Reports, New Series 225) rejected this contention by declaring that the business of newspaper publishing was one of public consequence which affected the community at large and was thus a business clothed with a public interest so that its patrons who offered to comply with all its reasonable rules *could not be discriminated against.* In reaching this conclusion, Judge Hay of the Common Pleas Court of Defiance County, Ohio, said:

> "Newspapers in this country have become universal. They are now practically in every home. They give to the people daily the news from all quarters of the globe. They gather and publish the many items of local news so much desired by the people of the particular locality in which they are printed. They publish the weather reports, the market reports, and the hundred and one other things which the people desire to read and know. They are favored by the law with the publishing at a liberal price of notices of Sheriff's sales, financial reports of city and county offices, sales of county and municipal bonds, notices of the reception of bids for public contracts, rates of taxation, appointment of executors and administrative and many other public notices of various kinds.

> "These all add to the interests of the public in the business and serve to make it a success, and cause the public to depend upon the newspapers, not only for knowledge of current events, both local and foreign, but also for a knowledge of these matters of public concern which vitally affect every citizen and taxpayer.

"We believe that the growth and extent of the newspaper business, the public favors and general patronage received by the publishers from the public, and the general dependence, interest and concern of the public in their home papers, has clothed this particular business with a public interest and rendered them amenable to reasonable regulations and demands of the public.

"Is is reasonable to say that warehouses, public wharves, taxicab lines, ferries and many kindred lines of business are of more concern and importance to the public than the newspaper business?

"We are of the opinion that it will be difficult to find any one line of business in the present age of the world which is of more vital interest and concern to the general public than the newspaper business. It is a molder of public opinion; the general medium by which local and foreign news is conveyed to its patrons, the vehicle which carries to the people of the locality in which it is circulated the most vital facts concerning its governmental matters.

"We therefore believe that a newspaper company when it has advertising space to sell has no right to discriminate against a local merchant who in his application for advertising complies with the law and the reasonable rules of said newspaper company."

By this same logic, cannot its pages then be required by reasonable regulation to be open to the opponents of the publisher's social and political views, as well as to his supporters? We think this can be done, and may perhaps be done by the proposals here outlined. At least a step in the direction of freedom *to* the press will have been taken.

RESOLUTION

Unanimously adopted by the
Law Panel

The law may be utilized either as an instrument of thought control or as the guardian of freedom of speech, press and assembly, religion and other basic rights which guarantee *freedom* of thought.

Today, the law is developing toward more and more suppression of free thought. The law has failed to meet the challenge of the growth of Big Business and monopoly, with its inherent tendency to utilize as a means of thought control its enormous economic power, including control of jobs and means of communication.

The so-called Un-American Activities Committees—the Thomas-Rankin Committee, the Tenney Committee—in collaboration with the press and radio of the land, attack the Constitutional guarantees of freedom of thought on every front. Their objectives—and thus far they have succeeded all too often—are to subject those with whom they disagree to the loss of jobs and the penalty of the blacklist, the deprivation of access to the means of communication, including the use of meeting places, the radio and the press. For those who will not yield to the unconstitutional demands of the Committee, prosecution, fines and imprisonment are threatened and imposed.

These committees—these unconstitutional instrumentalities of thought control—must be abolished. Those who are being prosecuted for contempt of the committee must be assisted in their defense by every progressive citizen and organization. If the prosecutions of any of those who have taken the lead in challenging the authority of this Committee succeed—and it is immaterial whether we agree with the views or politics of those being prosecuted—no progressive citizen is safe. Their defense is our own first line of defense.

Procedural safeguards affording protection against the flagrant disregard of the right to a fair hearing which the existing committees have indulged in, must be enacted into law. Hearings designed to effect thought control must be replaced by an aroused citizenry utilizing all means of communication to develop fully their political, cultural, scientific, artistic, religious, and all other forms of thought and expression.

There must be a guarantee of access to means of communication—for freedom of thought is meaningless unless the channels of convey-

87

ing that thought are available to those who desire to use them. The press and the radio must be treated—as, in fact, they are—as monopolized industries basically clothed as a public interest. The law must provide access to both of these means of communication, to those who can pay and to those who are unable to do so. This means that, for the privilege of publishing a newspaper or operating a radio station, the publisher and operator must be required to throw open to all points of view without charge a specified portion of the press and of the air, as well as to sell advertising-space in newspapers and time on the air to all without discrimination.

Of late, the growing tendency of those who control meeting places to refuse to rent them to persons or organizations with whose ideas they disagree makes a mockery of the Constitutional guarantees of free speech and free assembly. The public must be aroused to the dangers inherent in this trend and must by their organized pressure compel the renting of halls to those now being denied the opportunity to present their views. Consideration must be given to the enactment into law of civil-rights statutes guaranteeing access to meeting places— without discrimination.

Thought control in government and private employment constitutes a threat to our freedom which in its pernicious effects is second to no other method of accomplishing this objective. The abominable loyalty tests—the Truman domestic counterpart of the Truman Doctrine—must be abolished. The vast number of government employees must not be converted into second-class citizens with the constant threat of economic reprisal and public abuse if they dare to advocate views or belong to organizations which advocate views considered subversive by the administration. Private employers must not be allowed to exercise their economic power over their employees as a means of thought control. Existing laws prohibiting discrimination in employment because of political views or activities must be vigorously enforced. New legislation further protecting employees against thought control must be adopted.

The implementation of this program cannot be achieved by lawyers alone—nor even with them as its principal advocates. Only when progressive organizations mobilize their forces in this criitcal struggle is success possible. When, however, such organizations do move—as they can and must—thought control will be defeated and the law will become the means of truly protecting the rights guaranteed by the first 10 Amendments to the Constitution of the United States.

THOUGHT CONTROL IN U.S.A.

● ● ● ● ● ● ● ●

No. **2**

the
PRESS

the
RADIO

THOUGHT CONTROL IN THE U. S. A.
The collected proceedings of the
Conference on the Subject of Thought Control in the U. S.,
called by the Hollywood Arts, Sciences & Professions Council, PCA,
July 9-13, 1947

Edited by Harold J. Salemson
Designed by Herbert D. Klynn
Published by Hollywood A. S. P. Council, P. C. A.,
1515 Crossroads of the World, Hollywood 28, Calif.

Printed in the U. S. A. by union labor
Aldine Printing Co., Los Angeles, Calif.

(111)

the press

Thursday, July 10, 1947, 8:00-10:30 P. M.

Hugh De Lacy, Chairman

Speakers: Charlotta Bass, Robert Joseph, Darr Smith, Joe Weston, Leo Lania

Charlotta Bass
Editor-publisher, *The California Eagle;* one of first women publishers in U. S.

THE NEGRO AND MINORITY PRESS

TODAY we stand on the brink of a new era and with increasing anxiety, watch a world drama rush through the daily headlines of our newspapers. We have seen Fascism sprout, blossom and bloom in Europe. We have witnessed its conquest, supposedly, in Europe. With the shouts of V-J Day ringing in our ears, we believed that Fascism was really destroyed everywhere.

But today we have a different story to tell. Today, we see the government of the United States of America appropriating billions of dollars to breathe new life into those very decadent governments which lent their support to our enemies during the war. We see the danger of Fascism rising again.

This is true not only of Europe. With deadly certainty, it seems even more true of our own great land. Our Negro boys who fought

89

side by side with their white buddies on the battlefields of Europe and Asia, to destroy a dictatorship that threatened to envelop the earth and annihilate democracy everywhere, came home to find themselves homeless. In the housing shortage, Negro veterans have found themselves at the end of the long list awaiting a place in which to live.

Negro boys came home to find their families in jail. Why? Because they dared to live in their own homes against a court-order which declared they would have to live in some other section of the city—simply because they are Negroes. This happened, in this city, to a family which gave two of its members to fight in World War II.

Hundreds of Negro families have been ordered to leave their homes, which they had bought and paid for, just as their white neighbors built and paid for theirs. The only reason: the high crime of being Negroes.

Have you ever seen any notice of this injustice in any metropolitan American newspaper?

Up to 1938, when a young Negro by the name of Sam Solomon appeared on the scene, every effort of the Negroes of Miami, Florida, to win the franchise had resulted in failure. In that year, however, this active young Negro, defying all the threats of the Ku Klux Klan, successfully staged an election campaign and on election day led 3000 Negroes to the polls.

Did you read any account of the amazing campaign by this young Negro in any white American paper?

The policy of the white American press has to a large extent coincided with that of most native American historians—to suppress everything good about the Negro and magnify everything that is bad.

What, then, should be the role of the Negro press in the affairs of America and of the world today? To answer this question correctly, it is necessary to go back into the history of that press and judge from the role it has played in the history of our country. It has been a notable and a glorious role, although few of our historians seemingly know anything about it.

Negro journalism started in the year 1830. Between 1830 and 1865, about 30 anti-slavery Negro newspapers were published.

The Negro slave, illiterate, bitter in bondage, whom it was illegal to teach to read or write, nevertheless felt glowing within him a spark of that freedom which is universal in all the oppressed. And, despite all handicaps, a few learned to read and a few embarked in the newspaper world in order to help their suffering brothers.

The greatest of these early journalists, beyond doubt, was Fredercik Douglass, who was born a slave in February, 1817, in Maryland. His mistress taught him to read, but his master soon interfered, with the remark, "Knowledge unfits a child to be a slave."

"From that moment," said Douglass later, "I understood the direct pathway from slavery to freedom." Building upon the foundation he had already gained, Douglass learned to read, and later escaped to the North, where he devoted his entire manhood to the eradication of slavery and the upbuilding of the Negro race.

He became active in the Abolition societies, first as a lecturer, then as a writer. He reached his highest peak as the publisher of a newspaper, *The North Star,* in Rochester, N.Y.

Perhaps the most significant single happening of Douglass' journalistic career was his first rift with the standard abolition argument. William Lloyd Garrison, Wendell Phillips, and many other prominent anti-slavery figures, felt that the United States Constitution was an implement of slavery. They believed that it sanctioned the bondage of the black people, and they advocated secession of all free states from the Union which included slave states.

Dramatically, Douglass disagreed. After lengthy consideration of the great document, he published an editorial in *The North Star,* holding that the Constitution was not a friend but an enemy of slavery. He pointed out that the criminal institution of slavery was never mentioned in the "Articles"; that the general spirit of the Constitution was reflected in the statement, "All men are created equal." Certainly, he continued, this sentiment could not be interpreted as an agrument in support of enforced servitude. In conclusion, he stated, "America must remain united under the Constitution."

Such a daring stand, in opposition to the great wall of abolitionist thought, marked the Rochester publisher as a true leader, fearless in the support of his convictions. In no uncertain terms, too, it aided in the preservation of the Union when Secession finally came. President Lincoln in the White House leaned heavily for the support of this cause upon Frederick Douglass, once a slave, but now the outstanding spokesman among his people for freedom-plus-unity.

In 1863, with the signing of the Emancipation Proclamation, the Abolitionists thought the victory was won. There was no longer any need to fight, they said, and *The North Star* closed its doors.

But the discontinuation of an active black press at that time turned out to be one of the greatest tragedies that ever befell colored Americans. The Negro leaders learned only later that, instead of being blessed with peace and victory, they in reality needed to fight more than ever. *The North Star,* however, was not reinaugurated. The fight by Douglass was continued primarily through pamphlets, leaflets and lectures.

There followed a period of dearth in Negro journalism. Only one of the Negro periodicals now being published, *The Christian Recorder,* was established before 1865. Yet, today there are some 250 newspapers and magazines published by and for Negroes.

These publications have come up gradually from the Slough of Despond, lifting themselves by their own bootstraps, encountering all the difficulties small newspapers always face, plus many more because they represent the journalism of an oppressed people.

All newspapers today either fight or submit to the dictatorship of Big Business. It is the advertising of the stores, the shops, the factories, which supply the wherewithal to keep presses running. If the newspaper offends, it can expect to have some of its largest ads cancelled.

An incident from my own experience will illustrate: a Negro employed by the Fifth Street Store was about to be fired because of affiliation with a labor union. He protested to his union, and they threw a picketline around the store. The store sent a cleverly-worded ad to all newspapers, especially the Negro papers, stating what was purportedly its side of the case. The *California Eagle,* knowing the truth of the case, could not print the ad. As a consequence, the advertising of that particular store, although it had appeared in the pages of the *Eagle* for 35 years, is seen there no more.

All this is meant only to show that in the pressure brought upon the press by the National Association of Manufacturers and the Big Business interests of the country, the Negro newspaper has an added burden to bear. Besides this, the Negro newspaper must combat what one editor has called "a conspiracy of silence"—the general deadly tendency to say nothing at all about a Negro unless it be something disgraceful, something bad.

Nor is the Negro, although in the least-favored position, the only minority group which suffers such treatment at the hands of the general press.

There have been, for instance, many examples of anti-Semitism by innuendo in the Los Angeles press. Just recently, the *Herald-Express* ran a front-page four-column photostat of a 500% rent raise by a landlord named Schwartz. The implication in the caption was definitely that here was a greedy landlord taking advantage of a blameless tenant.

The *Los Angeles Times,* some time ago, had an embarrassing incident with its self-imposed editorial policy. It is customary to write an identifying phrase on the body of a story to tie it up to the headline. This is only for the printer's information. In a story about a B'nai B'rith award, between the headline and the body of the story, ran a line of bold type. It read: "JEW STORY."

The *Herald-Express* did a malignant job of distortion on the zoot-suit riots of several years ago. By uniting the words "Mexican" and "hoodlum" through a long series of incidents, they made the two words synonymous. This is deliberate control of thought.

The *Los Angeles Times* has a rigid rule prohibiting the publication of pictures of Negroes. Paul Robeson has never been in the paper, other than negatively. A motion-picture studio, with its expert publicity-department, was unable to have Canada Lee's picture printed.

Strong evidence, indeed, for the crying need of an untrammeled Negro press!

There are some laudable Negro newspapers, such as the labor publications, which follow the progressive line of thought: *The People's Voice,* New York City; *The Black Dispatch,* Oklahoma City, Okla.; *The Journal-Guide,* Norfolk, Va.; and *The Advocate,* Jackson, Miss., whose editor, Percy Green, has been very active in the Oust-Bilbo proceedings.

On the other side, newspapers like *The Boston Guardian,* Boston, Mass.; *The Amsterdam News,* New York City; *The Afro-American,* Baltimore, Md.; *The Pittsburgh Courier,* Pittsburgh, Pa.; *The Philadelphia Tribune,* Philadelphia, Pa.; *The Kansas City Call,* Kansas City, Kans.; *The Topeka Plain Dealer,* Topeka, Kans.; *The Wash-*

ington Eagle, Washington, D.C., and *The Chicago Defender,* Chicago, too often follow the reactionary metropolitan press.

George Schuyler, who writes a column for *The Pittsburgh Courier,* like Westbrook Pegler of the *Examiner,* indicts labor, the Communists, all liberals, and the progressive movement generally.

Despite the fact that 90% of the 250 Negro newspapers in the United States are subsidized by politicians and contribute largely to the building of the organization of slavocrats rather than to freedom of thinking, nevertheless signs point toward a gradual trend to more liberal thought and a liberalized Negro press.

The most radical changes in Negro journalism came about during World War II. The Roosevelt administration brought forth many improvements in the labor movement. Negroes who previously were consigned the menial jobs only, were now white-collar workers and for the first time in history a Negro woman was editor of an Army newspaper—*The Apache Sentinel,* Fort Huachuca, Arizona.

That editor was Mrs. Thelma Thurston Gorham, working in Special Services at the fort, where her husband was stationed. She had already won her university degree in journalism, and had had experience in writing. At first, she was assistant to the editor, but after a short apprenticeship took over the work of the editor entirely.

Instances of the kind I have mentioned briefly could be multiplied by the hundred. They have been given only to show that the role of the Negro citizen and of his spokesman, the Negro press, can be, should be, and in fact is important in the affairs which make for the betterment of mankind in the United States of America and in the world.

In answer to the challenge for a free press and an equal voice and vote in the affairs of the world, I think the time has indeed come for us to meet, as of now, to sit down and together map out a strategy to beat back those forces of reaction and intolerance that are threatening to silence the voice of the fighting press.

We cannot truthfully say that the Negro press, and perhaps the press of some of the other minority groups, are altogether free from such practices as slanting and coloring the news, and sometimes even selling out to the McCormicks, to the N.A.M., the du Ponts, or the poisonous columns of the Westbrook Peglers.

But we do maintain that, in spite of all this, the Negro and minority press, by and large, is fighting constructively for the betterment of all minority groups, and that by so doing the Negro press is also fighting for the advancement of all mankind everywhere—for the creation of that new world which our friend Franklin Delano Roosevelt so strenuously fought for and for which he died, that world in which there shall be real freedom of speech and of the press, freedom of worship, and freedom from want and from fear.

I think it is absolutely essential that every member of this audience should be familiar with the Buckley Bill, H.R. 2848, now pending before the House. This Bill is designed to ". . . suppress the evil of anti-Semitism and the hatred of members of any race because of race, creed or color."

The Act is implemented by making it illegal for the mails to carry material spreading race-discrimination, and making this offense punishable by imprisonment and fines.

When this meeting reaches the action program, I think it essential that we urge endorsement of the Buckley Bill.

To participate in this struggle more intelligently, we suggest that our white friends subscribe to and read the newspapers that constitute the best of the Negro press, as well as those that voice the democratic sentiments of the white American majority.

Robert Joseph

Film officer, ICD, Berlin,
1945-46; co-author, *Hero's
Oak; Berlin at Midnight*, to
appear, Spring, 1948

CREATION OF SENTIMENT
AGAINST OUR ALLIES

ALL of us at school were told the story of Leonidas' heroic stand at
the Pass of Thermopylae against the Persians. We all remember how
5,000 Greeks withstood the onslaughts of many times their number of
Xerxes' men, and how Leonidas' heroism inspired all of Attica to a
renewed fight against the invaders from the East.

1421 years later we heard of Themopylae again. This time the
invaders were the Germans, and the heroic Greeks, aided by a handful
of British troops, were facing Nazi panzers at that famed and historic pass in April of 1941. Our newspaper headlines and stories, our
columnists and editorial writers, worked us up to a fever-pitch of
enthusiasm for those splendid Greek warriors. Democracy, we were told,
had had its origin in Ancient Greece, in the very shadow of the Pass.
Our institutions, our art, our law, our culture—all these elements of
our daily lives were offshoots of a glorious Hellenic civilization. Ours
was a debt which we could never repay. And the newspapers told us
that the modern-day Greek was the spiritual descendent of that Hellenic
glory. We saw in him in 1941 a counterpart of the defenseless Belgian
of 1914, the victim of an unprovoked aggression. This 1941 Hellene
was proud, a fierce bearer of the light of Twentieth Century civilization.
That's what the newspapers said—in 1941.

Six years have passed since our newspapers made such generous
appraisals of our spiritual forefathers, the stout-hearted Greek people.
And now it appears that what had been Hellenic civilization is today
nothing but the ingratitude of shabby guerrillas and anarchists and
pawns of a foreign power. The Greek, the resolute Greek of 1941
who had stood up to Xerxes and his Persians; who had held off the
Roman centurion for centuries; who had fought against the inhuman
Seljuik Turk for more centuries; who had outfought the Italian
Alpinieri in Epirus; who had died in the Pass of Thermopylae, on the

Plains of Attica and before the gates of Athens rather than let the Germans overrun Greece unhindered—this Greek in 1947 is suddenly the willing puppet of a Slavic power of the North, geographically and ideologically as far from him as the Punjab Hindu. The Greeks, those proud bearers of liberty's light, are now allegedly the dupes of a power which has yet to put a foot across their border.

And now today the same newspapers which found our spiritual birth in the Acropolis and the Parthenon have a few headpats for a non-Hellenic king upon a Hellenic throne, and words of praise for his followers and court janissaries. The rest of Greece beyond the palace gardens and the Parliament building seems beyond the pale of our newspaper decency. The Greek people—the Greek people, I repeat—in our press have received nothing but vilification at our hands.

When Paris fell in July, 1940, I think every American must have cried a little. The spiritual father of our own Revolution and much of our history, the France of Rousseau, Voltaire and Diderot, the France which many Americans of the Argonne and the Meuse remembered, this France had fallen. We even wrote one song about it and revived another, *The Last Time I Saw Paris* and *Paris in the Spring*. I think we felt sadder about the fall of Paris than we had about anything in our own history since the time of the death of Lincoln.

Then for four years most of our newspapers told of the spiritual kinship between France and the United States. The Statue of Liberty was a symbol of our common heritage. I think when we went into war, after our own self-protection and ultimate victory, the liberation of France was next in importance. It was symbolic that the invasion of the French coast was the first step toward final victory in Europe: D-Day, Normandy, the road back to Paris and the days of glory. Movie audiences wept as they saw GIs and Tommies and *poilus* stream through the streets of a liberated Paris, past well-known landmarks. The patient resolution of the French people, our newspapers told us, had won France its freedom. Never had a people endured more. And those Maquis and FFI fighters. *Voila!* Their bravery on the South coast of France during the invasion in that sector. Their bravery during long years of occupation. Let the French have the fruits of their victory. Let them set up a Fourth Republic to erase the infamy of the Third. And our newspapers could hardly wait to report the trials of the Vichy cabinet, of Vichy supporters, of collaborationists.

But when the French began to rebuild their government and their country with true Gallic confusion, a confusion to which they have every right in the world, our newspapers began to have misgivings. The Maquis and the FFIs, the underground and the partisans, men and women who had fought with our own men, suddenly became radicals, revolutionists, anarchists. Their program became "red-inspired," "a joiner in the alignment against the Western Bloc," "a wedge against American interests on the Continent," to quote a few headlines and phrases. Frenchmen became "irresponsible Gallic politicians," "dupes and farceurs," "stooges of a distant and hostile power." French cabinets showed "Gallic irresponsibility" and were reflections of the "divisionist tactics of a foreign-inspired claque." The heroes of four years of Nazi suppression and occupation, were "out to gyp the Americans" and were "financial connivers" when the franc was devaluated. France, the Country of Light, *circa* 1940-45, became the nation of bordellos, procurers and dirty-picture postcards, and the nation which reneged its World War I debt.

It was after Berchtesgaden, Godesberg and Munich that an ever-increasing number of American newspapers called occupied Czechoslovakia a "little United States of America in Europe." We felt a strong kinship with that country, the victim of Nazi aggression and penetration. Our newspaper columnists reminded us that Thomas Masaryk had founded his Central European Republic right here in the United States—on June 30th, 1918, in Pittsburgh, Pennsylvania, to be exact. The industry, resourcefulness and fierce spirit of independence of the Czechs and the Slovenes was, we were told, akin to ours. Eduard Benes, Jan Masaryk and General Syrovy became American heroes when Czechoslovakia was overrun by the Wehrmacht, and heroes they remained until the end of the war.

But now we find that Czechoslovakia is within the orbit of foreign domination; the Republic, which is no Republic, in fact, is behind the Iron Curtain; its industrious, resourceful and fiercely independent people have succumbed to the wiles and influences of another power. And headlines underscore the duplicity and chicanery of a people and its leaders who once, for about eight headline years, were very much like us. The tradition of an independent Bohemia, which goes as far back as European history, is suddenly dead—for the headline and editorial writers.

In England's darkest hour, Winston Churchill quoted that most American of American poets, Longfellow, to show the strong affinity between the two English-speaking nations. The concept of Mother Country and Daughter Country was emphasized in many newspaper dispatches and editorials which appeared in American newspapers. After all, one could read in almost every American newspaper up to the time of our entry into the war, and certainly thereafter, blood was thicker than water. The water, in this instance, was the Atlantic Ocean.

Aside from a few disparaging remarks by the responsible American press after Kasserine Pass in North Africa, and during Montgomery's peculiar S.H.A.E.F. behavior before, during and after the Normandy invasion, there were no anti-British clouds on our headline and editorial-page horizons.

Then suddenly came the four-billion-dollar loan to Great Britain. The American press, almost to a column, did an aboutface. The British, it seemed, had many faults. Our newspapers reminded us that the English were cursed with a radical Labor government. We were spending four billion dollars to protect the British lifeline. What right had Britain in India? What about British Colonial policy? Our State Department was the tail to Britain's kite. A nation which could nationalize its coal, among other industries, deserved no help from Free Enterprise America. Some of our papers suggested the House of Windsor was obsolete. We found in our press a hundred different reasons for disliking and distrusting Great Britain.

Then the Bill was passed.

And other emergencies in Turkey and Greece arose, and we rushed to Britain's aid, all the charges cited above notwithstanding. Interestingly enough, we hardly hear a word about the British lifeline, the Colonial Office and the other black patterns of British national behavior.

What is it, then, that makes the peoples of Greece heroic in 1941, and dupes in 1947? What is it that makes the French patient and long-suffering in 1940 and misguided and anarchistic seven years later? Why is Eduard Benes a hero in 1938 and a puppet in 1947? How is it that Father Tiso, the Slovak quisling, is a traitor in 1939 and a martyr in 1946? What makes the British a bad financial risk in American newspapers one month, and the object of some fancy financial underwriting in the Middle East a month or so later?

Nations and States have a national oneness, which as H. J. Laski states, "implies the sense of special unity which marks off those who share in it from the rest of mankind. That unit is the outcome of a common history, of victories won, and of traditions created by corporate effort."*

It is unlikely that the Greeks and the French, the Czechs and the British changed very much within the last ten years. We have our own newspapers which tell us that the fierce and independent Greek of the City State is the same Greek of today. And we refer to these same sources to assure us that there is historical and spiritual continuity in other countries as well.

Nations and their peoples have not changed. And the masters of our press have not changed, for their special and individual interests are still the same. Nothing has changed but the headlines and the news which sometimes supports them.

Why, we must therefore ask, if everything else has remained the same, have our headlines and editorials changed? And what is it that moves our newspaper-chain owners, and our syndicate-wire owners to change the sentiment of headlines and editorials, to slant the news, to color the news, to give expression to personal or special-interest bias? Why is the Greek, a hero yesterday, a heel today? Why is the land of the Acropolis and the Parthenon, the cradle of liberty in 1941, the hotbed of anarchism in 1947?

The answer is to be found in the opening papagraphs of the Report by the Commission on Freedom of the Press, *A Free and Responsible Press:*

"The Commission set out to answer the question: Is the freedom of the press in danger? Its answer to that question is: Yes. It concludes that the freedom of the press is in danger for three reasons:

"First, the importance of the press to the people has greatly increased with the development of the press as an instrument of mass communication. At the same time the development of the press as an instrument of mass communication has greatly decreased the proportion of the people who can express their opinions and ideas through the press.

"Second, the few who are able to use the machinery as an instrument of mass communication have not provided a service adequate to the needs of society.

"Third, those who direct the machinery of the press have engaged from time to time in practices which society condemns and which, if continued, it will inevitably undertake to regulate or control."

There seems to be, in the third reason, the implication that both the Ignorant Press and the Venal Press are guilty of news-slanting and

*H. J. Laski, *A Grammar of Politics.*

100

news-distortion. This seems to refer to well above 90% of the American press and its news-agency counterparts.

A shrewd observer of the American press thus characterizes the Ignorant Press:

"It is small wonder," he writes, "that newspapers are in the main instruments of irritation between people . . . It is the ordinary middle-class newspapers which I have in mind, the papers run as commercial enterprises. With all their faults admitted, no one can possibly assert that their owners are criminal enough to provoke war. Yet in almost every crisis the tension is increased by the newspapers.

"The reason is in part that war is more sensational than peace—the possibility of conflict is a cheaper and more obvious form of news . . . The press cannot shout about the aggression that will not take place, or announce with joy the markets that are not coveted . . . No one has discovered a way of making good will, harmony, reasonableness, easily dramatic. In overwhelming measure the news of the day is the news of trouble and conflict. Those journals which devote themselves to telling of the real advances of mankind—technological progress, administrative triumphs, the conquests of prejudice—are not popular. They lack the 'punch.'

"To this condition of news-reporting international affairs have to conform. As the negotiations of governments are conducted with loaded weapons at hand, and with the pretension to sovereignty by both sides, almost any international situation contains news of trouble. At the same time the editor is publishing his paper for a community in which the opposition is probably not represented. It is easy and natural for him to take a 'strong' stand.

"Sympathy for foreigners is the most disinterested and civilized form of sympathy. It is not difficult to understand why editors display so little of it. There is almost no incentive to understand foreign people . . . They do not often reward their friends in another land. At home the editor faces the fact that ignorance and distrust of the alien is the most natural and the cheapest channel into which high passion and united feeling can flow. It is the greatest object of uncorrected enthusiasm, the greatest drama in which the villian is neither an advertiser nor a reader of the newspaper. It is one field of interest where people are at once unanimous and excited, and not many editors have the strength to resist cultivating that field . . ."

Walter Lippmann, by whom the above words were penned in *Stakes of Diplomacy*, tears into the Ignorant Press, the Ignorant Small-town Press, but characteristically has little to say for the Venal Press. The Venal Press does not slant or distort or stir up suspicion of the foreigner for reasons of excessive jingoism, or taking the path of least intellectual resistance, or for any of the simple-minded drug-store-lobby reasons which Lippmann gives. The Venal Press distorts the news about

101

our Allies as another step in thwarting the people's will, just as the people's will was thwarted in the newspaper headlines and editorial pages on purely domestic issues like the OPA or Federal housing or Federal health protection.

The headlines and the editorials we read about Greece or France are an extension of the headlines and editorials we may have read— if the reports weren't too badly buried—about the FEPC or veterans' housing. We are told that the French are a dissolute race of men not through any malice or personal bias; we are stirred up against our Allies because it serves the interests of those who control the news and news sources to have us thus stirred up. The Czechs are an unworthy people; and the Public Health Bill is Un-American; the patterns are different, but the cloth is the same.

The testimony and evidence that news is biased and slanted is overwhelming. There are sources as divergent as the documentation of various Congressional Committees—TNEC, the LaFollette Civil Liberties Committee, the editorial pages of the *New York Times,* Walter Lippmann, George Seldes and *Editor & Publisher* among the many which have from time to time said in one way or another that a little, some, much or most news is slanted. One or two local instances will suffice.

Ten days ago the *Los Angeles Times* offered the following banner headline: *RUSSIA GIVEN ULTIMATUM.* The *Los Angeles Examiner* said: *SOVIET GIVEN FRENCH-BRITISH DEFI.* The *Daily News* bannered the story in this way: *FRENCH, BRITISH APPEAL TO RUSSIA.* All three stories were based on Associated Press dispatches which said, in effect, that Great Britain and France had approached the Soviet Union and asked Russian cooperation and participation in a European welfare conference.

An eyewitness account of such deliberate news perversion is also supplied by a member of this Panel in the following personal account about his encounter with *Time-Life*-Luce Publications:

"When I was hired in Paris, in May of 1945, after my discharge from the Army, I was assured by my employer in Paris that there would be no objection to my personal beliefs or attitudes toward Luce, as long as I kept them out of my copy. This seemed fair enough, so I went to work.

"My first experience with the policy-makers in New York was a query which I received to cover the World Federation of Trade Unions Congress in Paris late in 1945. The query read something like this: 'We want a story about the extent of Communist domination of the WFTU.'

"From all the information I had gathered from delegates to the convention, from other correspondents and from French observers, the Russian delegation was only one of some 57 attending the convention and had no more influence than any of the other nations. However, I spent the next two weeks covering the convention as thoroughly as I could. I hired interpreters to work with me who could speak to the various delegates. I myself covered the American delegation. I did as complete and as honest a story as I thought it possible to do. Before I sent my story to New York I checked it with other correspondents from the wire-services, individual newspapers, French and British newspapermen and other non-competing press observers. They all agreed with my premise that the WFTU was not Communist-dominated, that it was a representative gathering of trade unions (excluding the American A. F. of L.), from every country of the world, and that it ranged from a Catholic trade union on the right through the middle-of-the-road British trade unions to the extreme-left Russian trade union delegation.

"The American delegation, headed by the late Sidney Hillman, attempted to act as the compromising force between the two divergent views and it controlled the balance of power. The compromise was worked out in committee and a coalition slate of officers was proposed and elected under the sponsorship of the American delegation. The WFTU was thus organized—and it was happy, and the Communists dominated nothing. This was the story as I saw it, and as I sent it out.

"The story ran a full column, but through the clever use of semantics, the interchanging of words, the use of adjectives such as 'flint-eyed' and 'Marxist-sharp', used in referring to the Soviet delegation, the whole sense of the story was changed, so that it appeared as if the convention had been dominated and maneuvered by the Soviet delegation.

"When I protested—not too violently, I am ashamed to admit,—I was informed that my story did not quite check with other sources of information. However, the fact is that the original query itself was 'loaded.' It read, to repeat: 'Do a story on the WFTU being Communist-dominated'."

And similar instances of the deliberate and designed perversion of news could be indicated for additional emphasis from the chief amanuensis of Rameses II's court down to and including the Hearst writer Karl von Wiegand.

The dissemination of false news about our Allies is a direct attack upon our own personal liberty. It is part of that greater pattern of suppression now going on in the United States and which we call Reaction. That pattern is so clear, as one studies it, that the greater design for the gradual usurpation of our political liberties becomes increasingly clear.

"There are," wrote Harold Laski, "two conditions for political liberty. The first of these means the power to be active in the affairs of state. The second condition of political liberty is the provision of an honest and straight-forward supply of news. Those who are to decide must have truthful material upon which to decide. Their judgment must not be thwarted by the presentation of a biased case. A policy may be represented as entirely good or bad by the skillful omission of relevant facts. Our civilization has stimulated the creation of agencies which live deliberately on the falsification of news. We must, very largely, take our facts on trust. But if the facts are deliberately perverted, our judgment will be unrelated to the truth. A people without reliable news is, sooner or later, a people without the basis of freedom."*

There is more at stake in this phase of the Panel than a lurid misrepresentation of our Allies. There is more amiss here than deliberate news-distortion. Yes, there is even more at stake than what some newspapers are characterizing as an inevitable drift toward war. That more which is here at stake is our basic liberty, a liberty which can be secured only through an honest press. This news-distortion and perversion is symptomatic of a cancerous growth in our own vitals.

Yes, we the people, have not changed. Nor have the aspirations of our Allies changed. Nor have the masters of the American press changed. Only the headlines have changed, and the editorials.

In 1941 our newspapers told us that we were spiritually one with the Greek people, that their fight was our fight, and that their hopes were our hopes. There were words spoken then which bear repeating now:

"And then came October 28, 1940.

"In Athens the people and the government were given three hours in which to decide whether to accept Axis slavery or to resist an Axis onslaught from the skies. I repeat, the people and the Government of Greece were given three hours, not three days or three weeks. If they had been given three years, their choice would have been the same.

"Today Greece is a land of desolation, stripped bare of all the essentials of living. Thousands have died of hunger. Thousands are dying still. Today Greece is a gaunt, haggard sample of what the Axis is so willing, so eager to hand to all the world.

"But within their own land, and upon other shores, the Greeks are fighting on. They will never be defeated. And the day will come when liberated Greeks will again maintain their own government within the shadow of the Acropolis and the Parthenon.

"President Franklin D. Roosevelt."

That shadow, which goes back into history, crosses us.

*H. J. Laski, *A Grammar of Politics*, 1925, pp. 147-148.

Darr Smith

Former city editor, *Los Angeles Daily News;* public relations head, Conference of Studio Unions

THE PRESS CAMPAIGN AGAINST LABOR

WE are here to examine the treatment of labor by the daily, commercial press. We are to examine it to see whether the publishers are exerting either positive or negative influence, whether the publisher changes the tone of labor news by acts either of commission or of omission.

In doing so, I ask you to keep two things in mind. The first is that to be a newspaper publisher takes a lot of money—even to be the publisher of a small-town weekly. Having money, the publisher's natural interests are with others who have money.

Secondly, I would like you to bear in mind that while the cases we examine are local in character, they have a logical and natural extension into a national picture.

The first step in analyzing labor news as it appears in the commercial press must be an examination of the qualifications of the people who report it. Other factors certainly affect the final product, but it is the reporter who starts it on its way.

Reporting labor news is a complicated exercise. To develop an intelligent story, the reporter must know his field every bit as well as the science reporter knows his.

The labor reporter must know the union leaders in his community; he must know a great deal about the histories of the local unions he writes about.

He must know—even if he disagrees with them personally—the economic and philosophic reasons for the existence of unions.

He must be highly conversant with the history of labor in America. He must know his labor legislation—both pending and passed.

Most newspapermen I have known are reasonably intelligent

105

fellows, who could master all these necessities of the craft of labor reporter if they were allowed the chance. But in most cases they aren't. The labor story is kicked around the city-room to whatever rewrite man isn't busy at the moment, because the publisher has not provided trained men for that purpose.

Of six commercial dailies in the Los Angeles area, only one has a full-time labor reporter. In contrast, each of the four downtown dailies kepes a crew of full-time men in Santa Ana so that every morsel of Beulah Overell's diaries and letters may be reported faithfully.

The point here is that the dailies are not equipped to report labor news in the most basic phase of reporting—specifically trained manpower. This is not to say that the well-trained, full-time labor reporter necessarily does an intelligent or honest job. But he certainly must be well-trained to give his honesty an even break.

And this is a measure of thought control, no matter how inadvertent or thoughtless it may be.

There have been several notable examples of fine labor reporters being assigned other duty by the publisher when it became clear that accurate labor reportage was contrary to the best interests of the publisher.

Most outstanding of these was the case of Art Eggleston of the *San Francisco Chronicle*. He was a fine reporter, a man who understood his subject. In fact, he had done such a standout job that he was awarded a Nieman fellowship at Harvard University. This is a scholarship awarded only to newspapermen to enable them to study any subject of their choosing for one year.

After his return to San Francisco from Harvard, Eggleston, then a more educated man, was taken off the labor beat and given routine work. His publisher did not want good labor coverage. He wanted confusing labor coverage. He wanted to control the thoughts of his readers.

Poor labor stories, ignorantly or confusingly told, are not the fault of the reporter. They are the fault of the publisher, who refuses to assign one man to study and learn what labor is about. The publisher, as often as not, is delinquent here through a desire to play down labor. Good labor coverage might give ideas to his own help. And, just as likely, he would prefer to play along with his buddies of the Chamber of Commerce.

Then, there are times when a reporter is intelligent and accurate and has thoroughly checked his story. When it leaves his typewriter it can be an unslanted, forthright account; but it often runs into policy trouble at the city-desk—policy dictated by the publisher.

Policy on a newspaper is something you hear about constantly in its city-room. On some papers policy is a nebulous thing. On others it is rigid, unchanging and terribly clear. On still others it shifts from week to week, but it is always very clear for any particular week.

Policy is dictated by several things. The first is the frank one that a certain paper is designed for a certain mentality or class which dictates a policy it likes. Other papers attempt to be all things to all people and the things which appear in them are designed to appeal to all people and to offend as few as possible.

Policy also branches out to particular people, things or organizations which the publisher or editor may or may not like.

The biggest policy-maker of all, naturally, is the guy who makes a newspaper possible—the advertiser.

For the past several months I have operated a news bureau for the Conference of Studio Unions, headed by Herbert K. Sorrell. These unions have been in a dispute for nearly a year, after many of their members were fired and ordered thrown off the studio lots. This we have called—and we feel with some honesty—a lockout. The studios and the press have called it a strike or a jurisdictional dispute. The derivation of these terms I will discuss in a moment—not to convince you of the worthiness of the CSU cause, but to determine whether there is any thought control kicking around in them.

I was trying to propagandize no one, but was merely attempting to report news which affected 7,000 workers, their families and the storekeepers who sold them beans and shoes. Anything affecting this many people is news.

The first startling thing I ran into was the frank admission from three prominent and respected newspapermen that they'd like to make a fair representation of the CSU case, but that they couldn't.

It was pointed out to me that the drama sections carried much advertising from the studios—and at a rate of pay higher than, for example, a department-store. I was further told that the studios would prefer to have everybody forget about the lockout-strike-jurisdictional dispute so that it would die quietly. The studios had passed the word around that the strike was dead, that production was back up and that really there was no sense in giving space to a lost cause.

This I call a conspiracy of silence and I also call it thought control.

One example in many—and I give it because the man involved *should* be better informed—shows the success of this campaign. The man is an editor of a leading daily. I met him recently and he asked me what I was doing. I replied I was working for the CSU. He answered in some surprise:

"Oh, I didn't know there *was* a CSU anymore!"

Here is a case of policy-bites-editor in his thought control.

There are two papers in town which consistently print nothing, or one paragraph accounts, or, if there is an opportunity, extremely nasty, half-truthful stories, about the CSU.

This again is policy—personalities division. One publisher has had a deep hatred of Herb Sorrell for many years because Sorrell and some other painters appeared on a Newspaper Guild picketline in front of the publisher's plant.

The other paper strongly dislikes Sorrell because he recently filed a $1,225,000 libel suit against it for attempting to discredit him by printing a hatefully hysterical (and grossly inaccurate) story about him.

The reception of CSU news by these two papers is traceable to these actions, and in it is revealed the apparent right of a newspaper to control what its readers read and think.

In the commercial, daily press, acts of violence and destruction head the list of newsworthy items. The more startling or horrible a story is, the more newsworthy it is considered.

This is explainable on the basis that newspapers are in business; they have a commodity to sell. The more they dress up their commodity, the better it sells. From this thought evolves the hysterical-headline-writer, a harried, harassed man, working under terrific pressure, who digs deeply for the best "selling" headline. That's his job and that's what he was hired for. I have worked with expert copy-desk men who have said: "I can't sell newspapers on this story; rewrite it so I can get a headline out of it."

Then, too, there have been copy-desk men who have not been so conscientious. They have gone ahead to write a selling head without regard for the contents of the story.

These things lead up to a distortion of the news itself or to misleading the casual reader into believing an inaccurate head is the truth. This is thought control.

There is the gleeful headline and story written to discredit a person or idea opposed to a newspaper's policy. I cite you a recent one having to do with the mass picket trials: *Atty. Leo Gallagher Given Third Contempt Sentence in Week.*

It *is* news when a prominent attorney takes three contempt convictions in one week, but I think you will agree that when the Appellate Division of the Superior Court dismisses two of the proceedings on the basis that the judges involved showed prejudice, it is even greater news. The dignity and the integrity of the court is shown to be footed in clay. But what did this story get?

It got coverage, all right, by all the papers; but in two or three paragraphs, under the heading: *Gallagher Splits Decision.*

And is it or is it not significant that when Gallagher spent a few hours in Lincoln Heights jail on one of the convictions three papers carried pictures of him behind bars, but when he walked out of one of the highest courts of the state, having proved his theories were right, there were no photographers present?

It was not news. Or, might I say, the newspapers didn't want it to be news. That's thought control.

The gleeful story came up again recently when four film pickets were sentenced to one year in jail. This was played big.

But the next day the Appellate Division of the Superior Court ruled that the City parade ordinance under which many film pickets had been arrested was unconstitutional.

The court ruled that to give the Police Department power to say who would and who would not parade was an abridgment of free speech. The ruling merely went along with the basic philosophy of our democracy.

One paper, the *Daily News,* thought this was important and displayed the story in its most prominent position. The others kissed it off. Incidentally, the *News* was the only paper to observe that the same ordinance had been declared unconstitutional by the same court some years before. The ordinance is still on the books, and the next time somebody gets arrested for parading without a permit, he will have to spend $20,000 to go to the Appellate Division to prove he was within his constitutional rights.

I would like to talk for a moment about misleading phrases, phrases which are distorted from the truth, perhaps through ignorance, as we have discussed, or perhaps through design.

In writing stories of the Hollywood labor situation the commercial daily press has often used the phrase, "The confused Hollywood labor situation was further confused today."

The Hollywood labor situation, I submit, is confused only because the producers want it that way. And there is most certainly no intra-union strife, because it takes two unions to make such a thing, and again, I submit, the CSU fight is not with any other union, but with the producers.

The Producers' Association would prefer that newspaper readers throw up their hands in disgust and say, "I can't understand this; let these people fight it out amongst themselves." The issues of the Hollywood lockout are very clear, and it has taken an extremely high-priced producers' public relations department to confuse the issues of the Hollywood lockout.

As I said before, I don't bring these points in to convince you of the worthiness of the CSU cause. I bring them in because I am familiar with them and I think they comprise a suitable segment for examination which can be expanded to the national scene.

The use of the phrase "confusion compounded" has root in the Producers' Association. There is an effect sought here, and to a large degree the effect has been obtained.

There is another discrediting tactic I have found. This Spring, three local unions left the CSU, but two of them under entirely different circumstances from the other.

This sum total of comment on the defection of Electricians' Local 40 and Building Service Employees' Local 278 was that they had "deserted" the CSU.

The actual truth was that both locals had been taken over by their international unions and had been "ordered" out of the CSU and back to work. The word "desertion" can hardly be applied here and its use by the papers was a further attempt to lead people to believe that the CSU cause was a lost one.

The Screen Story Analysts, the third union to leave the CSU, did so democratically, and its leadership declared it was not a desertion, but an effort to save the remnants of a weak and staggering local.

Archbishop John J. Cantwell's report on the Hollywood labor situation, which said among other things that the producers were at fault for the lockout and for their failure to negotiate a settlement of it, was given a once-over-very-lightly treatment in the commercial press. Only

110

the labor press gave space to the statement of the leading Catholic of the West.

When CSU attorneys obtained an affidavit from a former Culver City policeman that he and all other members of the department were placed on the MGM payroll last September, the papers virtually ignored it. The power and might of Loew's Incorporated is not something to tamper with.

I said I would discuss the words "strike" and "jurisdictional dispute" used in the commercial press to describe the CSU fight. I believe their use is bedded in thought control. The simple history of the dispute is that workmen were fired and ordered or thrown out of the studios. This fact is inescapable. These men then set up picketlines and other men respected the picketlines. There is no strike here and there is no jurisdictional dispute, nor is there any intra-union strife or confusion of issues. By the use of the employer-sponsored phraseology, the press has permitted itself to become a partner in compounding the confusion. That is how thought control works.

The instances I have cited here are purely local, but they are of a pattern with the national scene.

John L. Lewis has been enjoying an extremely bad press for several years. He has been charged with endangering national safety. But there has been no mention in the wire-service stories of the mine operators who forced Lewis' miners to go on strike. They, naturally, had no responsibility. It was that willful man.

Before the war, the United Automobile Workers (CIO) struck the Inglewood plant of North American Aviation Corp. It was discredited in the press as a "wildcat" strike and as an "outlaw" strike. As a matter of fact, it was an honest, legitimate strike for recognition, wages and hours.

Then, there was the Sewell Avery incident. This stalwart was lauded in the press because he wouldn't give up his office. The big play here was a picture and endless discussion of Avery being carried out of his office in his own chair by two soldiers. Nothing was said of the $27.50 a week his employees were being paid.

The excellent wartime record of labor was ignored during that period and instead we saw daily box-scores of man-hours lost through strikes. We read nothing of the many unions which voluntarily refused to strike, of the many unions which would not strike for higher wages— wages which were legitimately theirs because of the enormous profits they were making for the employers.

111

All of this is thought control, and it built up into one of the greatest campaigns to condition the public mind we have seen in this country. Strikes are crippling the nation, we are told. Labor must be made to accept the same responsibilities as management. This campaign has been carried on long and vigorously, with the full cooperation of the commercial publishers. I submit to you it was successful. It prepared the minds of enough people to make possible the passage of the Taft-Hartley Bill.

Joe   Weston

Publicity director, Wurtzel
Prods.; formerly, Time-Life,
Paris, Stars & Stripes, ETO

THOUGHT CONTROL
IN AMERICAN ADVERTISING

PROBABLY very few of you are familiar with a democratic document printed in the Congressional Record of 1946, Report 1996, House of Representatives, 79th Congress, 7th Session. It is titled, "Sources of Financial Aid for Subversive and Un-American Propaganda," and it is a recommendation by Mr. Wood of the Committee on Un-American Activities to the House. The Committee on Un-American Activities asks the House to revise the income-tax structure in order to eliminate tax-deduction for advertisements publicizing subversive propaganda and ideological theories which bear no relation whatever to the sale and distribution of a product made or sold by the advertiser.

This looks fair on its face, but it is as full of vicious jokers as the Taft-Hartley Bill. The main joker is the definition of "subversive propaganda. For, as used in the past by both the Wood-Rankin and Thomas Un-American Activities Committees, this phrase "subversive" is as elastic as Tommy Manville's protestations of undying love.

Stripped to its essentials, this report calls upon Congress to deny to the American people the fundamental, Constitutional liberty of freedom of expression, and to establish Congressional censorship of public opinion, thereby threatening the entire structure of civil liberties in this country. Under the guise of revising tax exemption regulations, the Un-American Activities Committee seeks to establish itself as a "Thought Police," with power to determine what constitutes Un-American or subversive propaganda, and with the concomitant power to determine who shall be allowed to publish opinion advertising.

To illustrate what the Committee considers subversive, I should like to quote from the report an advertisement which was published March 14, 1946 by the International Latex Corporation of Dover, Delaware. The ad is, in substance, a quotation from an interview with an un-named American Army officer in Germany, criticizing a speech made by Winston Churchill in the United States. This advertisement

113

was listed in the Report as typical of subversive advertising which would not be tax-exempt.

"It has been brought to my attention," the American officer said, "that the morale of the civilian population of Wuerzburg and vicinity has been greatly raised as the result of a speech made in the United States by a British politician relative to our Allies, the Russian people.

"The Soviet Government is an ally of the United States of America, and you are individually and collectively representatives of our government. I will not tolerate any disparaging remarks against our Allies to the German people.

"Millions of Russian soldiers and civilians died to save our skins. Just remember that. If propaganda causes you to hate the Russians, stop and think. They died for you, too.

"If you want to fight again, encouraging these Frauleins that we hate Russia is a good way to get things going.

"An ancestor of my name was killed in the War of the American Revolution. But the Russians are our Allies. They have guts. They kept hordes of Jerries off of us and, by God, I never want to fight again. Think it over."

This, my friends, according to the Congressional Record, is now considered subversive.

At just about the same time that this was being entered into the Congressional Record, the following letter was written by William Holden, assistant managing editor of the *Los Angeles Times,* to Mr. W. J. Bassett, Secretary of the Los Angeles Central Labor Council:

"Dear Mr. Bassett: Following receipt of your letter pointing out that Will Rogers Jr. is a candidate endorsed by the American Federation of Labor, I have called attention of that fact to our political department and others of our editors, and I believe a story has been published emphasizing that fact. However, it may be necsesary, in our campaign to defeat Mr. Rogers, to refer to him occasionally as endorsed by CIO-PAC, feeling that this is one of the effective means of bringing about his defeat. We do not feel that it is required of us, as a matter of newspaper practice, to mention at the same time, that he is also backed by the A. F. of L."

I am certain that both Mr. Holden and his boss, Norman Chandler, would swear a holy oath that this constitutes a free and responsible press, giving equal representation to all shades of political opinion and complete information to the voters of this community.

I am also certain that the publishers of the *Los Angeles Times,* whose editorial policy in this instance was also anti-Rogers, felt that it was only logical to sell the majority of its political advertising quota to those with whom they agreed editorially and news-wise. This they did, claiming a shortage of newsprint, and frankly admitting the

114

impossibility of giving equal advertising representation to both Mr. Rogers and Mr. Knowland.

It is indeed extremely difficult to make a case against the *Los Angeles Times* in this matter on either its editorial or its advertising bias. It is only natural, they claim with some justice, to apportion a limited amount of advertising space to those with whom they agree.

But, in the face of this attitude, which seems to be common among members of the American Newspaper Publishers' Association, it would seem that Wood, Rankin, *et al.* are tilting at windmills. There would seem to be no necessity of legislation to prevent newspapers from running what they do not care to run anyway.

You might be interested, at this point, in a blow-by-blow description—and most of the blows were below the belt—of how PCA tried to reach the American people with reprints of Wallace's Madison Square Garden speech, via the simple "American" process of paying cash on the barrelhead for advertising space.

The day after Wallace spoke, Los Angeles citizens got this much out of the news columns. In the *Times* and *News,* five paragraphs on the back page, containing only one four-line direct quote, from a United Press dispatch. This, the net result of twenty-three-and-a-half minutes of speech-making. The *Herald* and *Examiner* did not even bother. So it became necessary for PCA to take on the responsibility of trying to inform the citizens of this area.

On April 1, the George Stiller Advertising Agency—in accordance with democratic procedure—requested a full page in the *Daily News, Times, Examiner* and *Herald* for the purpose of printing in full the Wallace speech. Stiller asked no favors. The money was on the line at full political advertising rates, in accordance with what I am sure is the same established advertising procedure when the National Association of Manufacturers tries to buy space. Stiller was asked by the advertising managers of the respective papers why he wanted to buy the space. This is the reason he gave: that the metropolitan papers in Southern California had given practically no space, as mentioned above, to the Wallace speech, and the PCA wanted to let people know of the speech and what had been said in it.

All four of the papers, with a unanimity of opinion which has rarely been shown before on any question, refused to let him purchase a full page. They refused to let him have a half-page. They refused to let us have one-quarter of a page. They refused.

That took care of Los Angeles. The Agency then checked papers in San Diego, Santa Barbara, Bakersfield, Sacramento and San Bernardino. We thought, perhaps, that the unanimity of the publishers would not extend outside of the city limits. But we discovered that bargaining with newspaper publishers in this area, at least, was collective and industry-wide. We couldn't buy a line of space in any of these papers.

The excuses given Stiller ranged from a frank, "We don't like it," from the Hearst press and the *Times*, to a "lack of space" from the pseudo-liberal *Daily News*. But the fact remains that while the Pacific Telephone and Telegraph Company was able to buy all the advertising space they needed in order to break the recent telephone strike, we were not able to buy a line. I submit, in my humble opinion, that this is absolute thought control, and flagrant violation of the most elementary principles of the buy-and-sell democracy under which we are currently operating.

On or about May 20 of this year, PCA attempted to buy a civil liberties ad in the local press. This was indeed a subversive document. As a matter of fact, it was just loaded with "Un-American" propaganda. The ad stated that we were opposed to the banning of Henry Wallace from the Hollywood Bowl; Number Two, that the State Legislature vote no more funds for the Tenney Committee; Three, we called for the discontinuance of the Rankin-Thomas Committee; and Four, we were opposed to the outlawing of the Communist Party. These four statements of policy had a rough time. This is what happened to the ad. Amazingly enough, its title was . . . "This Gag Isn't Funny".

In the face of our request for at least a half-page, the *Daily News* came through with an offer of a fat 10-inch ad which was of no value whatsoever, and which we did not accept.

The *Times* arranged for the necessary space, and the copy and lay-out were sent to them. When they got the copy, they backed out, giving the following as their reasons: they agreed with Point One, that the banning of Wallace from the Hollywood Bowl was ill-advised; they also agreed in opposing the outlawing of the Communist Party. They contended that they had covered these two issues thoroughly on their editorial page and that therefore they felt it redundant to repeat this stand in paid advertising. They disagreed with the statement calling for the discontinuance of the Thomas-Rankin Committee, and they also disagreed with our policy that the State Legislature vote no more funds for the Tenney Committee. These last two points, they said, they considered unimportant and not worth selling advertising space for.

What the *Times* said in effect was that they refused to accept advertising copy with which they disagreed editorially.

The *Examiner* did not like the tone of the ad, and turned it down cold. The *Herald-Express* did not like the tone of the ad, and turned it down. And even after we agreed to write a new ad for the Hearst men, they still said no. The ad finally did run in *Variety*, the *People's World*, the *California Eagle*, *Los Angeles Sentinel* and *Labor Herald*.

To protest the high cost of living, the Valley Chapter of PCA sponsored a mass meeting in Burbank on July 2. Advertising space was sought in the *San Fernando Valley Times*. Despite the fact that the advertisement was non-political and was subject to the community service advertising rate of $1.75 per inch, the *Times* decided that it was political advertising and subject to the political rate of $2.80 per column inch . . . if they decided to handle it at all.

The advertising manager, Mr. Smolte, said it was too important for him to pass on it himself. This kind of advertising was something for more responsible shoulders than his, something for wiser heads, more practiced in making weighty decisions. So he passed it on to the management for decision. The management declared that it was political advertising because it was a controversial subject, and that as such it could not qualify under the newsprint quota for political advertising for this year. The ads were refused. A letter of explanation was requested from the management and thus far has not been received.

As for management's political space quota explanation . . . let's check the record. Two or three weeks before, the *Valley Times* ran a large ad for the Pacific Telephone and Telegraph Company presenting their side of the strike. About the same time they ran NAM ads sponsoring the Taft-Hartley Bill. Only a week before this present episode happened, an advertising agency with no contractual agreement placed a thirty-inch ad in the *Valley Times* with less than twenty-four hours notice. And, the *Valley Times,* on its rate card currently says that the only requirement to buy advertising space is to get ads in by noon of the day before publication.

It is probable that you are all thinking, at this point, that the Los Angeles press is not a fair example on which to indict the nation's newspapers. So perhaps we had best detail a few experiences anent that giant in a land of giants, the *New York Times*.

In February, 1946, the *New York Times* refused advertisements from *In Fact*, describing that weekly. They said it was too controversial. This decision was made after the *Times* had kept the ad for some fifty hours without telling George Seldes they would not run it. But on the same day on which the *In Fact* ad might have run, had it been accepted, the *New York Times* ran a half-page ad for the NAM extolling the virtues of a free economy and demanding the end of OPA controls.

Now, I am sure that the *New York Times* considers its right to refuse an ad with which they disagree editorially, and to run one from the NAM, with which they agree editorially, as freedom of the press. I guess it just depends on whose freedom you're talking about.

Case Number Two against the *New York Times*: in February, 1946, ex-Mayor La Guardia of New York City wrote a paid column which was offered to the *New York Times* as an advertisement from a New York furniture company, with a yearly advertising contractual agreement. The column described a New York *Daily News* editorial about the United Nations as "moronic." The *Times* said that this was libel. La Guardia said that he would stand the full cost and responsibility if the advertisement started a libel suit, in order to keep the *Times* immune from damage claims. The *Times* refused to run the column. A few weeks later, another advertising column written by La Guardia was refused by the *Times*. This column was so subversive as to say:

> "A paper that imposes censorship on views it does not happen to like is not a free press in the American sense. It is a proprietary press, abusing its privileges. I have as much right to express my views on any political subject as the owners and publishers of the newspaper. I do not expect a newspaper to give away its space free of charge, but I do demand that, in paying for space, a citizen should have the right to express his views although contrary to the views of that particular paper."

As noted, the *Times* did not think so. The advertisement did not run. But again, a few weeks later, another advertisement by a large industrial corporation, beating the drums for private enterprise—the NAM way—appeared in the *New York Times*.

Why newspapers are so amenable to the ideas of the large corporations may be seen in the fact that these corporations will spend more than three billion dollars this year—the highest sum in history—for advertising space. Since newsprint is scarce, publishers are assured of all the advertising they need—therefore, they need no longer keep up the pretense of being open to ads from all groups. In addition to this, the NAM recently began a million-dollar advertising campaign to propagandize itself and free enterprise. It bought space in every newspaper in America with fifty-thousand circulation or over. Naturally, a newspaper cannot gild the NAM lily in its advertising pages, and blacken its fair name in the editorial and news pages.

However, despite all the pressure put upon newspapers by the advertising revenues derived from conservative or reactionary business elements, it is only a damned fool who will claim that advertisers completely dictate a newspaper's editorial or news policies. *They don't have to.* Among the tightest groups in the country today are the American Newspaper Publishers' Association, and local groups, such as the California Newspaper Publishers' Association. These people toe the reactionary line because they know on which side their bread is buttered. They don't need any prompting from the sidelines.

It is when a newspaper publisher tries to buck this solid wall that he finds out just what freedom of the press means, and to whom. A case in point is that of Dan Matchen, the editor and publisher of the *Times-Record* in Valley City, North Dakota. Matchen, a liberal, came out editorially against the Truman Doctrine and for Wallace. He took a liberal line on domestic policies, as well. Before he could say "boo," almost every merchant in the small town of Valley City had threatened him with an advertising boycott if he didn't mend his ways. You would think, at this point, that newspaper publishers from coast to coast would have raised a cry of "foul," and rushed to Matchen's defense, purely on the ground of a free press, if nothing else. But damned few did. And despite all the publicity from such "liberal" magazines as *Time* and others, the net result of Matchen's fight was an ad in *Editor and Publisher* offering to sell his newspaper.

We might mention here that Matchen really took on a tough customer. He plumped for the Missouri Valley Authority, which, like all public-power projects, is anathema to the large private utility companies.

And speaking of the utility companies, I would like to digress for a moment to tell of a personal experience that happened to me in Provo, Utah, some ten years ago.

At that time, another chap and I were working as reporters of a Salt Lake City newspaper. We were called to Provo by the owner of a small printing plant, who had a few thousand dollars to spare to start and run a small weekly newspaper. The objective of the newspaper was that it be a voice for the 50% of the 12,000 townspeople who were fighting for the erection of a municipal power and light plant, to operate in competition with the established Utah Power and Light Company. The only paper in town, when we came there, was a daily owned by the Scripps interests. Before our arrival, this paper, which had taken an editorial stand for the Utah Power and Light Company, had been receiving one full-page monthly from the utility company.

We started our little sheet on a shoe string. Our editorial policy was strictly "Jack-the-giant-killer." We were fighting, with nothing but guts, one of the biggest power and light companies in the West. With half of the people of the town behind us, we began to be effective. We began to get advertising. We became a voice. But then the sky fell down. Money came into operation. Our advertising rates were much lower than those of the opposing paper, and we were doing quite well financially. But suddenly the opposition began to run full-page ads every day, bought and paid for by the Utah Power and Light Company. This added revenue enabled the opposition papers to cut their advertising rates below their cost level. It amounted to a subsidy. Naturally, we lost much of our advertising revenue which we needed for our existence. But even then, a few of the larger stores stuck with us. Suddenly, they too dropped, and we were told that they had been threatened with impairment of their electrical and telephone service if they didn't come into line. Other advertisers told us that they had been promised rebates on their electric bills, and on their power bills, if they would quit advertising with us. Suddenly, in the high schools, and in Brigham Young University, teachers and professors were espousing the cause of private ownership of utilities against public ownership.

The net result of all this was that after six months we went broke, and had to stop publishing. The 50% of the people who were with us were again left without a voice in a one-paper town. The advertising rates of the opposition paper went back to normal. I went to Cheyenne, Wyoming, to try to get another job, and the Utah Power and Light Company, according to the best of my knowledge, still supplies light and power to Provo, Utah. And, as far as I know, the *Provo Journal* still gets its full page a month.

By this time, I hope I've made my point clear. It is my contention that the United States, via the thought control practiced by the American press, which, through its Newspaper Publishers' Association, is as tightly controlled a union as there is in the nation, is driving toward Fascism with energy and determination.

This is being done through the single process of denying impartial, factual information to the American public. It is being denied them by deliberate suppression and misrepresentation in the news columns. It is being denied them by deliberately inaccurate editorials. And now it's being denied them through the last and only means left in a "them-as-has-gits" economy—paid-for advertising space.

L e o   L a n i a

Playwright; author, *Land
of Promise, Darkest Hour,*
etc.; former European
journalist, now in U. S.

THOUGHT CONTROL IN NAZI GERMANY

IN surveying the present political scene in America and the problems that concern us at this conference, we must be careful not to overestimate political analogies. Stupid as the slogan "It can't happen here" may be, it is just as dangerous on the other hand to draw political conclusions merely on the basis of what seems a historical parallel. These superficial analogies, these parallels, are very tempting; they can be made convincing by illustrating them with facts and figures. But, in my opinion, we will be able to learn a lesson from history only if and when we come to understand that the knowledge of historical facts and figures alone is not enough. What we need most here in America today is a broad perspective, the ability to integrate facts and figures into a comprehensive whole, into an overall picture.

Aldous Huxley said once, "Facts are ventriloquist's dummies. Sitting on a wise man's knee they may be made to utter words of wisdom; elsewhere they say nothing or talk nonsense or indulge in sheer diabolism."

Factual reporting, which the American press is supposed to have chosen as its guiding principle, is of course a very honorable goal. We are told that it is this basic difference between the factual information which the American press provides and the opinion-loaded and editorialized information of the European newspapers, which best guarantees against the evils of state-controlled propaganda and assures freedom of thought here in America.

The strict separation of news and editorials has for a long time been the greatest asset of the American press. The average newspaper in pre-Hitler Germany did not have so good a record. Over

122

there, practically every paper was the mouthpiece for one or another Party, and published only the news that fitted into its editorial policy—or arranged and edited it accordingly. Aside from the official news-agency, W.T.B., subsidized by the government, the only world-wide news-service upon which all the German newspapers depended was the *Telunion*, owned by Stinnes, openly servicing the interests of the nationalistic right, the financial backers of the Nazis. Those few papers with large circulation, which could afford their own news-service, dictated and controlled the news-reporting of their correspondents. Here in America, correspondents doubtless enjoy far greater freedom and independence.

Unfortunately, the last few months have shown a growing tendency on the part of the American press to abandon its former news policy. It is being replaced by a way of reporting which reminds me of a very similar technique that was practiced by the few truly-democratic papers in pre-Hitler Germany, when they gradually started to censor themselves of all news that might be objectionable to the growing forces of militarism and reaction.

I think there is a lesson to be learned from the developments in the German newspaper field before Hitler. It is simply not true that the Nazis had to come to power and turn their terror against the democratic press in order to make it conform to their wishes and orders. Long before, most of the liberal papers—those with the largest circulation, like the papers of the Ullstein group,—gradually, and step by step, retreated and stopped printing the truth. They did not wait until they were confronted with strict censorship—they started to appease their future masters long before, so as not to be drowned in the mounting "wave of the future". Of course, they were drowned anyhow, in spite of their "careful" and "objective" treatment of controversial facts and events.

The first lesson we can draw from our German experiences is that it was not the overwhelming power, the dynamic drive, or the intelligence of the Nazis, which destroyed the progressive forces and democracy, but the inner weakness, the defeatism and the complacency of the liberals. *Gleichschaltung* (which means conformity and which can truly not be improved upon as far as the American press of today is concerned) had already been accepted by the democratic German press, coerced into such a position by its financial backers, before it was ordered by Goebbels.

Here is an example of how that method worked. In 1924, I published the first exposé of secret rearmament in Germany and of the alliance between the Nazis and the armed forces of the German Republic. I had gathered the material during a ten-day stay in Hitler's headquarters in Munich. I had gone there in the guise of an Italian Fascist, pretending to be an envoy of Mussolini. I got away loaded with documentary proof of Hitler's conspiracy and his rearmament program. I published the material in a book titled *Gewehre auf Reisen* (Traffic in Arms). On the day after publication, the Minister of Justice for the State of Prussia declared that I would have to stand trial for high treason. Mind you, high treason! For having dared to expose the high treason of the Nazis and their allies in the Reichswehr Ministry. This was 1924; Germany was still a democratic republic and, what was more important, still very much afraid of the power of France. The Prussian Government realized immediately that it would run into a lot of trouble if by prosecuting me it gave the French a cause for accusing Germany of officially backing the illegal rearmament of the militarists. Therefore, the accusation of high treason was dropped. Instead, I was asked to name the source and the persons who had supplied me with the documents and information in my book. Of course, I refused. I was willing to stand trial for high treason or to face punishment if my documents should be proven false, but I could not see any reason for giving away my informants. They were dissenting Nazis whom I had to protect because I needed their further cooperation in the fight against Hitler.

Whereupon, the Prussian Minister of Justice declared that I would go to jail for violating my duties as a witness—here it would be called being guilty of contempt of court or committee,—and that I would stay indefinitely in prison, i.e., until I should change my mind and name my informants. It was only through the tremendous pressure of all democratic forces in Germany and the skill and energy of my attorney, the famous Deputy of the Reichstag, Paul Levy, that the Reichstag was forced to pass a law *(Lex Lania)* stating specifically that journalists in fulfilling their duties should be exempt from divulging their professional secrets, in the same way as physicians or priests are exempt. I won my case.

It did not help us too much. Nine years later, Hitler was in power. It did not help the Prussian Minister of Justice, a Social-Democrat, to have shown so much concern with and understanding of the wishes and interests of military reaction. He and his Party had to pay the same terrible price in blood and tears as those who had fought from the beginning in the forefront of the struggle against the Nazis.

Here, another question arises. Why did, and do, the Nazis everywhere single out journalists, writers as their first targets? Do they not firmly believe that the sword is mightier than the spirit, that physical terror is more decisive than all ideas and ideals? The answer is: Nazism cannot win if it does not first destroy the ability and the will of the people to think. To make people think, to support them with the tools that they need in order to think freely and correctly, is the most urgent and holiest mission of intellectuals, writers, journalists and artists. Nazism cannot succeed as long as these men fulfill their mission, because in contrast to old-fashioned dictatorship, Nazism is dependent upon the ideolgcial support of a large part of the intelligentsia, the middle-class, the workers.

This being Lesson Two, we can now go to Lesson Three. I would like to call it the strategy of the smokescreen. Nothing more quickly destroys the ability to think freely and independently, to analyze issues, to gain a clear perspective, than to arouse primitive emotionalism and, by subjecting the people to slogans and standardized formulas, make their thinking mechanical and stereotyped.

I am not a Communist. As a journalist and writer whose books, plays and articles are on public record, I could not hide my beliefs and political credo. I believe in democracy primarily because, as Al Smith said: "There is nothing bad in democracy that cannot be cured by more democracy". I believe so much in that principle that I have never let my opposition to Communism push me into an alliance with Nazism, Fascism and their equally evil handmaidens. For 20 years, in every European country, we have seen the Nazis conjure up a so-called Communist danger and, by presenting themselves as the saviors from that danger, destroy the forces of democracy and progress.

There was no Communist danger in Italy when Mussolini marched on Rome, no Communist danger in Germany when Hindenburg delivered the Reich into the bloody fangs of Hitler. Goering, and not the Communists, burned the Reichstag. The workers who were slaughtered in Vienna by the stormtroopers of Dollfus had for 20 years—and they were years of famine and misery—refused to become

Communists and had been praised as members of the most democratic Workers' Party in Europe.

The day when I read in our papers that 26 Communists—or 20—or 10—or even 2—have entered, by force, the house of a banker or an industrialist, kidnapped him, murdered him, been arrested, admitted their guilt in court and been set free—as it actually happened recently with 26 lynchers in our South,—that day, but not before, shall I cease to consider the Fascist danger as real and the Communist danger as a smokescreen. The more so when the same Committee that works overtime chasing so-called Communists, declares officially that there is no Fascist danger in America. It is true that, as my good friend, Frank Kingdon, stated: "Judging by the people the Thomas Committee is attacking, its spies are not investigators, but talent scouts". Yes, one *could* laugh about the grotesque performance of these self-appointed defenders of American democracy among whom we find so notable a Democrat as Representative John Rankin, who has, according to Drew Pearson, attested to the fine Americanism of the Ku Klux Klan.

"Just recently 16 members of an organization were convicted of contempt of Congress. Yet, troublemaker Joe Kamp, cited for contempt of Congress more than a year ago, has not been brought to justice". Is Walter Winchell, from whose column I quote this statement, a Communist too? It seems so, because I have seen not *one* of the big newspapers allocate to exposures of the Fascist danger in America 20 or even 10% of the space they devote to the Communist "menace".

We who witnessed the same methods in the different European countries are surprised only by the lack of ingenuity the forces of reaction show. Same words, same melody. One would think that people, having seen the same show, staged with the same actors, dozens of times,—and what a stupid and obscene show it was!—would at least refuse to attend such a performance again and again, that they would finally say, "This is where we came in".

Maybe the French author was right who said: "The only important lesson one can learn from history is that nobody has ever learned from history".

Ladies and gentlemen, let us not delude ourselves. This battle which we are now witnessing—and it has only begun—is not directed primarily against the Communists, but against all liberal and progressive forces. They shout Communism, but they mean the social re-forms that the American masses have gained during the last 15 years. They shout Communism, but they mean the abolishment of rent-control. They shouted against the Communistic and subversive writ-ers and journalists in Germany, but when the bookburning started they burnt the books of Freud and Lessing, of Zola and Romain Rolland, of Heinrich Mann and Upton Sinclair. And the flames which consumed these books became the fire which consumed human flesh in Belsen and Oswieczim.

But this time, and this is the real difference between Germany in 1932 and America in 1947, the reactionary forces will not win; I am sure of it. America is not Fascistic; there are threats, dangerous threats, there are symptons, but the chances for defeating them are far, far greater.

In closing, I want to state briefly two more lessons we must learn and apply if we want to win.

First: Let us rid ourselves of the fact-and-figure myths. Let us learn the facts. Let us not underestimate the importance of factual information. All journalists must defend it to the utmost against distortion and coloring. But people do not live by facts alone. The more hopeless and hungry they are, the more they hope for a light to show them a path out of the spiritual jungle in which they find themselves. Until we extend and deepen our political education—until our intellectuals, journalists and writers are no longer satisfied with merely reporting events but make a sincere attempt to trans-late the basic concepts of our Democratic beliefs into a concrete program of action in community, state and country,—until that time, we will not have unity, and not even a struggle between clearly-defined conflicting interests, but general confusion.

Second: Let us beware of negativism, beware of the sectarians and perfectionists. In that respect, we sinned very gravely in Ger-many. We cannot win merely by debunking the policies and short-comings of democracy. The debunkers have had their say. They have exposed many false gods, they have destroyed many lies and half-truths, but since we were not able, not strong enough, not quite united enough, to replace the false values by truer ones, we did not replace a weak democracy in Germany by a more honest and better one, but gave Hitler a chance to cash in on the growing despair and disillusionment of the German masses.

127

Nothing is so cheap as the indignation of the perfectionist who, very proud of his spiritual superiority, looks at the world in disgust, gives humanity a bad mark, and decides he does not want to have any part of it. He paves the way for frustration and Nihilism. Right now in America we have a lot of these brilliant and gifted intellectuals, columnists, novelists, all of whom aspire to play the part of a Savonarola or a Cassandra. Their irresponsibility is as great as their lack of humility. They all end, sooner or later, in the camp of the Fascists.

If we apply these last two lessons intelligently, if we do not tire in our efforts, and if we accept as our battlecry the one phrase of F.D.R.'s which in times of crisis and doubt always proves its magic power, we will win sooner than we may expect. That battlecry should be, "We have nothing to fear but fear itself".

DISCUSSION

The discussion opened with a suggestion that the papers presented be made available to the public through publication in *In Fact* or elsewhere. It was also suggested that a Continuations Committee be created for carrying on the work done at the Conference.

In response to a suggestion that things were moving too slowly, the Chairman of the Panel stated that PCA was making every effort to reach the people, and that the organization was growing constantly and gaining momentum.

At this point, a member of the audience rose to move that "Congressmen in the various districts be urged to support the pending Buckley Bill, HR 2848, to outlaw racial and religious discrimination, and be informed that those of us gathered here have endorsed it." This resolution was seconded and unanimously carried.

Returning to the previous point, the Chairman of the Panel pursued further elucidation of the policies and program of PCA. Stating that the organization is making history, and recalling its meeting for Henry A. Wallace in Hollywood, he said: "More than anything that has happened in the last six months, the Los Angeles meeting inspired hundreds of thousands as it encouraged Mr. Wallace and the rest of us in PCA."

The PCA, Mr. De Lacy added, has a program of real action: jobs, labor conditions, lower cost of living, better housing, health action. It stands for these, and for the policies inaugurated by Franklin Roosevelt.

Calling on personal experience, Mr. De Lacy showed how the work done here strengthens the cause in Seattle, how the work in Seattle is felt in Chicago, and so on.

"This great work takes hope, faith, work and guts . . . The only miracle we have to count on is the daily program to meet people's needs for jobs, housing, medical care, personal security, and national security in a world of peace and universal brotherhood.

"Our faith rests on the great democratic accomplishments which the American people from the beginning of our country's history have always made in the face of adversity and discouragement, in good times and bad, to preserve to themselves and their posterity the economic and spiritual blessings of liberty."

the radio

Saturday, July 12, 10:00 A. M.-12:30 P. M.

John Brown, Chairman

Speakers: Reuben Ship, Milton S. Tyre, Marvin Miller, Sam Moore

Participating in discussion: Harry W. Flannery, Victor Shapiro, Emil Corwin, Sam Balter, and members of the audience

Papers in this panel prepared in cooperation with the California Committee for Freedom of the Radio.

Reuben Ship
Radio writer, on *The Life of Riley* for the past four years

RADIO IN A FREE CULTURE

THERE is a tendency to sneer at radio as a cultural medium. To raise the question for discussion is to risk, in some circles, either guffaws of contempt or pitying smiles of tolerance. This attitude is easily understandable in the face of the inept vulgarity of radio's jokes, the lugubrious unreality of its soap operas and the crude melodrama of its mystery programs. Frequently, such an attitude leads one to the position that it is pointless to discuss thought control as it relates to the cultural output of radio, since, being for the most part barren of ideas, there is no thought to be controlled.

This argument is, of course, fallacious. It is the same argument, used in a slightly different form, by the defenders of the status quo in radio. This is the argument that maintains there is such a thing as "pure" entertainment and that it is possible to portray allegedly real and typical characters against a background of alleged social reality without commenting even unconsciously on the nature of society. Proponents of this view deny that radio entertainment exerts any influence on the public, or that it makes any attempt to enforce acceptance of certain values and rejection of others, thus predisposing the listener to some form of action. The supporters of this theory conveniently overlook the fact that they are also among the staunchest supporters of censorship which, if it is anything, is certainly indoctrination.

Viewed from the perspective of a single program acting upon the mind of the listener for a brief half-hour, it is true that the degree of influence seems negligible, indeed; but this is a false perspective. We must remember that the listener listens not spasmodically but regularly, not to one program but to many, and thus over a period of years absorbs a complete philosophy of life the keynote of which seems to be that there is nothing drastically wrong with our society.

Economic control. This is the starting point for any discussion of cultural trends in radio. Through its economic control—and the whole trend has been towards an ever-increasing degree of concentration of power—Big Business is in a position to control the content of the majority of programs at their inception. We are confronted with something of a paradox in radio. Here is a potentially great art medium, delivered into the hands of groups whose primary aim in utilizing this medium is to sell mechandise. They are not concerned with the dissemination of culture *per se*. These men have nothing but contempt for a vital democratic culture; they also fear it. True, when they hear the word culture, they do not reach for a gun—at any rate, not yet. They reach instead for the nearest sales chart.

Mr. Harold J. Ryan, a former president of the National Association of Broadcasters, offers us confirmation:

> "One must consider balance sheets to measure the progress of radio . . . American radio is the product of American business. It is just as much that kind of product as the vacuum cleaner, the washing machine, the automobile, and the aeroplane . . . If the legend still persists that a radio station is some kind of art center, a technical museum or a little piece of Hollywood transplanted strangely to your home town, then the first official act of the second quarter of the century should be to list it along with the local dairies, laundries, banks, restaurants and filling stations."

The head of a large advertising agency (the Duane Jones Company) made his contribution to the philosophy of radio art by stating, just a few years ago, "The best radio program is the one that sells the most goods, not necessarily the one that holds the highest Hooper . . . No program can long endure that does not sell goods."

Culture, then, is the medium through which soap, toothpastes, cigarettes, deodorants, coffee, etc., are sold. Thus, the corporations are confronted with a dilemma. Will not the dissemination of a truthful and vital culture, portraying honestly and accurately the reality of American life, giving expression to the aspirations and struggles of the people for a better world . . . will not such a culture, exposing as it inevitably must the real nature of society and the evils therein, tend ultimately to influence people to exercise their democratic right to correct those evils? And will not such social action prove to be detrimental to the interests of monopoly?

The contradiction is obvious, and so is the manner of its resolution . . . thought control, in the sense that the content of radio programs is a falsification and distortion of American life. The rejection of reality and the projection in its stead of a vast complex of false ideas and distorted images is one of the ways in which the thought patterns of the people are controlled by the forces of reaction. This conspiracy against the minds of the people is further revealed by the scrupulous policy of omission and suppression carried out by those who control the content of radio programs. There are wide areas of American consciousness which no writer may explore. A rigid system of taboos for the creative writers in radio has been erected. Daily, hour after hour, the loudspeaker blares out a seemingly endless recital of the trials and tribulations of typical fathers, typical mothers, typical sisters and brothers, typical doctors, lawyers, merchants and thieves. But where are the typical factory workers, the typical Negroes, the typical native Fascists? Radio does, indeed, hold the mirror up to nature, but the reflection is a gross caricature. For large segments of the glass are missing entirely, and those that remain are cracked and blurred.

The conspiracy against a free culture does not end with the dominant role of the advertisers. The networks, comprising 600 of the 900 radio stations, are accessories by virtue of their subservience to the interests of their clients. The custodians of the people's air have betrayed their trust. Consider the large percentage of their business handled by a very small number of advertising agencies and advertisers. Consider the large proportion of time devoted to sponsored programs, and the relegation of sustaining programs to the least favorable hours of the day.

Consider, too, the frequency with which a majority of the affiliated stations reject a program of vital public interest, carried by the network, in favor of a locally-sponsored program.

Who will doubt the words of Mr. Niles Trammell, testifying before a Senate Committee on Interstate Commerce? The President of the National Broadcasting Company left no doubt as to where his organization stood. He said:

> "The argument is now advanced that the business control of broadcasting operations has nothing to do with program control. This is to forget that he who controls the pocketbook controls the man. Business control means complete control and there is no use arguing to the contrary."

The pattern of economic control, through which thought control is effected, is now complete. What Big Business could not accomplish by direct control, is achieved indirectly through intimidation of the networks.

The more overt forms of thought control, by suppression, seem to be taken for granted in radio. It is possible to find an item like the following, printed in *Variety* under the heading *The Skin is Tender*:

> "Maybe you think the sponsor ain't sensitive. Helen Hayes recently expressed a preference to play the lead in *The Corn is Green*. The play, which concerns the hardships of the workers in a Welsh mining town, was kayoed by the brass at U. S. Steel for the simple reason that negotiations are going on between John L. Lewis' United Mine Workers and the owners of the soft coal mines. And the U. S. Steel has coal mines of its own. Miss Hayes may do the part but not until a coal contract is signed."

The item is significant, not so much because of the evidence of thought control which it presents, but because the casual tone of the reporter implies complete acceptance by radio people and the public of such practices. Such apathy is dangerous. We may wake up some morning to find that Congress had a late session the night before, and that we are no longer even the legal owners of the air which we never controlled.

But suppression is merely one aspect of widespread thought control. Is the contention that the thought patterns of the people are being controlled by falsification, distortion and omission, borne out by the facts? There's one sure way of finding out: by a twist of the dial. Suppose we start on a local level by examining the radio fare offered to the public by station KIEV in Glendale. KIEV may very well be a typical example of how local stations are serving the community. The following is the log of KIEV for June 4, 1947, as recorded in *Radio Life*:

8:00 A.M.—News

8:15—Musical Bandwagon
8:30—Public Interest
9:00—Bing Crosby Time
9:15—Kate Smith Sings
9:30—Nothing listed—evidently Kate still sings
9:45—Rhythm Road
10:00—News
10:15—Stars of Song
10:30—Western Tune Time
11:00—Show Tunes
11:15—This Rhythmic Age
11:30—Latin Musicana
12:00 Noon—News
12:15 P.M.—Lunchtime Melodies
12:30—Glendale High
12:45—Gals on Record
1:00—Meet the Maestro
1:30—Organ Moods
1:45—Swing Stylings
2:00—Midday Melodies
2:30—Musical Potpourri
3:00—A Matter of Records
4:15—Modern Concert Hall
4:30—Bing Crosby Sings
5:00—Record Ride
5:30—Melodies Mardi Gras
6:05—Twilight Tempos
6:30—Dinner Music (This offering is apparently presented on the assumption that the regular listeners to KIEV are still able to swallow food.)

Thus, with the aid of a thesaurus and several thousand records, KIEV fulfilled its cultural responsibility to a community of several hundred thousand suffering, struggling, groping human souls.

We twist the dial to a network station and we encounter the soap opera. We encounter dozens of soap operas. We twist the dial desperately, but there is no escape. So, we listen and are treated to a veritable orgy of suffering in an unreal world compared to which Alice's Wonderland has the clarity and authenticity of a documentary. It is a world peopled predominantly with middle-class professionals and housewives, living mostly in middle-size or small towns, rather than metropolitan centers. There is no working-class in this world. Presumably, it can get along without the labors of miners, factory-workers and laborers, skilled or unskilled.

The problems in this world of the soap opera are largely personal ones, relating to courtship, marriage, family, friends, jobs or professions. But these problems do not arise from the nature of society. They

134

are caused primarily by the weaknesses or corruption of individuals, who make trouble for the good people. Perfect justice reigns in this world. The good suffer, but only temporarily. No harm comes to the pure in heart in the long run. The wicked are always punished, and the weak are reformed.

Yet, an explanation of this ideal justice is never forthcoming. It is the work neither of God nor of man. By inference, all social problems can be solved in the same mysterious way. The characters and the problems of the soap opera are presented to us as typical cases. Generalizations on the basis of such cases must inevitably lead to a distorted view of the real world.

There are other worlds in radio. Perhaps they offer a more valid picture of reality. So we twist the dial. We hear a shot, the splash of a body striking water, the low throaty laugh of a nymphomaniac, the gurgle of a bottle of rye being rapidly emptied. This is the world of the mystery program. What does the increasing trend toward this form of drama signify? Conflict is the essence of drama, for it is the essence of all reality. Yet, the creators of these dramas, pressured into an avoidance of reality, must seek out forms of conflict which, in their emphasis on adultery, blackmail, phychopathology and murder, are removed from the main currents of the life of the people. Crime exists in society, its origins are in fact rooted in society, and as such it is a subject worthy of the serious dramatist. But the crime portrayed by radio is for the most part a thread ripped from the fabric of life, conflict without meaning, crime without reason.

We twist the dial again, in search of the world of fifteen million Negro citizens—a world of share-croppers and factory-workers, of seamen and stevedores, of great scientists and artists, of oppression and exploitation, a world in which forty Negro veterans were lynched since V-J Day. And we find the stereotype of the indolent, childish, amusingly-moronic, crap-shooting, gin-guzzling menials—the Uncle Toms, the Topsys and the Mammys.

No amount of protestation by the networks can conceal the fact that they are fostering and perpetuating vicious prejudices against the largest minority group in this country. Nowhere do we find a sustained attempt to portray the real life of the Negro people. The rare biography of a George Washington Carver, an emasculated version at best, or the even rarer broadcast of an *Open Letter On Race Hatred*, gratifying as they are, cannot compensate for the daily libels against the Negro people, for the injury to the cause of American democracy.

We twist the dial in search of laughter. We find it—too much of it. We find some of the best comedy in the world, and some of the worst. Too frequently it is anti-Semitic, and anti-labor. It is one of the greatest offenders with respect to the portrayal of national and racial stereotypes. Governed by a sense of profit rather than sense of proportion, much of it has been rendered uninventive, repetitious and trite. Too much of it is based on highly individualized personal character, too little of it on social character. Its potentialities for satire directed against social evil are tremendous. Yet, most radio satire, gratifying as it is, is ingrown, directed against the abuses of radio itself. A plea for a more vital culture is often misinterpreted as a snobbish attack on comedy. It should be stressed, in making such a plea, that we are for comics, all kinds of comics, but especially for those who, as George Jean Nathan put it, "think and argue with laughter".

We can turn our dial endlessly, only to encounter everywhere the fog of thought control. The fog is thickening, threatening to blot out all truth. We must know and publicly brand thought control for what it is. Its results are the general debasement of culture, the corruption of creative talent, the pollution of the public taste, and the progressive deterioration of the public intelligence. It seeks to perpetuate social myths, acceptance of which immobilizes social action for true democracy. It is the lever with which the crushing weight of Fascism can be lifted onto the already-burdened backs of the people.

One more question remains to be raised, one more argument must be demolished. Is the present-day culture of radio what the public wants? The sponsors and the networks disavow responsibility, by claiming they are giving the public what it wants. There is considerable quoting of the Hooper ratings to prove the point. But the Hoopers, assuming for a moment that they are accurate, merely establish a preference for one existing program over another existing program. By no stretch of the imagination can they be interpreted to mean a preferential choice of an existing program over a non-existent one. This whole argument is shot through and through with fallacy. The term "public" is an abstraction. Actually, the "public" is made up of many publics, and in terms of specific well-defined tastes there is no majority. We are a nation of minorities, each having a stake in the air, and it is the proper function of radio to provide outlets of cultural expression for all.

The role of radio in wartime is significant in this respect. During the war years radio gave expression to, and intensified the anti-Fascist feelings of the people in such programs as Corwin's *This Is Your War*, *Pacific Story*, *The Man Behind the Gun*, and *Free World Theatre*. It came to grips with social reality in presenting *Assignment Home* and *Reunion, U. S. A.*

Today, on the question of the people's concern for world unity and peace, there are only faint murmurs. On the subject of Fascism, there is only silence or irrational nonsense of the kind expressed by a recent prize-winning show on *Dr. Christian*, which explained the rise of German Fascism by this novel theory: Hitler, when still an as-'sistant paper-hanger, found a ring upon which there was an ancient evil curse.

The same networks that eagerly accepted the Hollywood Writers' Mobilization *Free World* series during the war, now reject its series on the atom bomb, based on a number of seminars conducted by eminent scientists. The scripts submitted to the networks presented the thesis that the danger is not the bomb itself, but the people who may use it, and that unless the manufacture of the bomb is outlawed it may become available to Fascists. Further, the series pointed out that there is no defense against the bomb, that its secret cannot be kept, and that trying to keep it involves restrictions on scientific research and education, and that secrecy and fear can be used to whip up hysteria useful to native Fascists.

The series was rejected by the networks on the grounds that it was controversial.

Whom did they fear to offend—the Fascists? Admittedly, the series *was* controversial. Was not Fascism a controversial question? Are we to assume from today's trend in radio that the people are no longer anti-Fascist? Or will it be argued, in spite of the Taft-Hartley Bill, the Truman loyalty purge, the witch-hunts of the Thomas-Rankin Committee, the lynching terror in the South, the war hysteria being whipped up against the Soviet Union, that the American people are no longer menaced by the possibility of Fascism?

We must reject as utterly fallacious, as well as suicidal, the notion that culture must be noncontroversial. If culture is to survive at all, it must take sides against the forces that would destroy it. The writers, actors, directors—all the creative people in radio, must proclaim their bias against Fascism and for peace and democracy.

We must call for a renaissance of culture in radio: a truthful, dynamic, socially-purposeful culture, probing every aspect of life.

We must restore to radio that diversity of cultural expression which is the only guarantee of freedom of thought, and which must allow the voice of labor and the Negro people to be heard.

We must fight for a free culture, both as creative workers and as citizens. The fight cannot be won by limiting the area of our struggle to the community of radio, for it is linked with the fight against the drive of reaction nationally.

As creative workers, we must be deaf to the blandishments of bribery. We must resist the tyranny of intimidation which daily grows more widespread. As writers, we must strive day by day for the injection of positive content in our writing. Compromise may be inevitable at times; but compromise without struggle must eventually blunt the sharp edge of talent. That edge must be maintained at razor keenness. For, with it, we shall cut through the jungle of lies and prejudice that is a barrier confronting the people on their march toward a free and peaceful world.

Milton S. Tyre

Member, Gallagher, Margolis,
McTernan & Tyre; presented
Hollywood Community Group
case for AM, FM before FCC

FCC AND FREEDOM
OF THE AIR

This paper would more appropriately be entitled "Freedom to the Air" rather than "Freedom of the Air". At the outset, we should understand that it is not the radio station's unfettered use of the airwaves which we seek to protect. The station procured its license in the first place from the people. It is the people's freedom to have access to those airwaves, which the First Amendment to our Constitution, the Free Speech Amendment, is intended to protect.

That freedom is now threatened, not by the Federal Communications Commission, but by those forces who, under the veil of "free speech", would deny it to those who have no power, or cannot use that power, to make their voices heard. When 140,000,000 people depend in whole or in part upon the radio as their source of day-to-day information, education and entertainment, radio has taken its place as the most influential single medium of mass communication.

Where in the Constitution does it say that 4 radio networks, or 20 advertising agencies, shall have the unrestricted right to broadcast to 140,000,000 people only that which those networks or agencies want the people to hear? Who seriously or honestly can contend that our Constitution was intended to protect the right to speak of 4 powerful radio networks and 20 advertising agencies, denying that same right at the same time to the other 140,000,000 citizens?

Our Constitution was not framed with a view to give to a few the power to prevent the masses from being heard. A radio license by its very nature can be given only to a few. Those few cannot have the privilege without certain obligations to the many who can have no license.

In the early stages of radio broadcasting on a commercial basis, no one denied that a Federal agency had the Constitutional power to regulate the radio—to regulate both technically and program-wise. But

139

as the radio has become a powerful medium for the transmission to the people of "free enterprise" propaganda, carrying in its wake suppression of any other ideas, the *laissez-faire* exponents begin to fear for their "freedom". Now it is censorship if the FCC should concern itself in any way with program service. It is for the radio station to determine the program; it is for the FCC to act merely as traffic cop of the airwaves.

The position of the FCC in the field of preventing thought control in radio is necessarily a changing one. When the first statute regulating radio was passed, in 1910, no thought was given to the use of the air to disseminate information to the general public. Certain controls were required then in order to insure uninterrupted communication with ships. Even then, however, it was recognized that the government had the right to regulate the radio for the public use. Only, then, the public use was confined to ship-to-land communication.

But, as the public use became more extensive, it became evident that more regulation was necessary. Thus, in 1927, the Radio Act was passed, setting up the first Federal Radio Commission appointed by the President. That Commission did not recognize any immediate or pressing need for specific regulation of the radio, other than to insure that no licensee interfered with the broadcast-frequency of any other licensee, and only generally that the licensee was using his license in the public interest. At this stage, the radio was still experimental. It was not yet the tremendous source for profits and for the dissemination of thoughts and ideas that it was to become in two short decades.

But, even in 1927, the Commission had to adopt some standards to determine "public interest". Applicants for license renewals were asked to state the average amount of time which had been devoted weekly to the following services: (1) entertainment; (2) religious; (3) commercial; (4) educational; (5) agricultural; and (6) fraternal.[1] Thus, the Commission was already inquiring into the nature of the program service. And no one then seriously contended that this was not the necessary prerogative of the Commission, if it were to determine whether the licensee was operating in the "public interest, convenience and necessity" as required by the Act.[2] In 1928, the Commission in

1. Federal Communications Commission, *Public Service Responsibility of Broadcast Licensees,* p. 10 (March 7, 1946; reprinted by the National Association of Broadcasters).
2. The Act of 1934, which is similar in this provision to the Act of 1927, provides as follows:
    "(a) If upon examination of any application for a station license

its Annual Report stated (p. 161):

> "The Commission believes it is entitled to consider the program service rendered by the various applicants, to compare them, and to favor those which render the best service."

In 1929, the Commission publicly set forth what it considered as a standard of program service. It said it should consist of entertainment, including music of both classical and lighter grades, religion, education, and instruction, important public events, discussion of public questions, weather, market reports, and news and matters of interest to all members of the family.[3]

By the time the Federal Communications Act of 1934 was before Congress, the Constitutional right of the Commission to consider program service was virtually conceded by all. But, of course, the power of radio had not yet been recognized. At the House Committee hearings on the Bill, the National Association of Broadcasters submitted a statement which contained the following:

> "*It is the manifest duty of the licensing authority,* in passing upon applications for licenses or the renewal thereof, to determine whether or not the applicant is rendering or can render an adequate public service. *Such service necessarily includes* broadcasting of a considerable proportion of programs devoted to education, religion, labor, agricultural and similar activities concerned with human betterment. In actual practice over a period of 7 years, as the records of the Federal Radio Commission amply prove, that has been *the principal* test which the Commission has applied in dealing with broadcasting applications." [4]

With this background before it, the Congress proceeded to pass the Communications Act of 1934, containing language identical to that of the Act of 1927 concerning the necessity of the licensee's showing of operation in the "public interest, convenience and necessity."

The Congressional mandate to the Federal Communications Commission to consider program service in determining whether or not a licensee is operating in the public interest, convenience and necessity, has on a number of occasions been upheld by the courts. The claim of the broadcast company that it was being censored when the Commission refused to renew its license in part because of its program

or for the renewal or modification of a station license the Commission shall determine that public interest, convenience, or necessity would be served by the granting theerof, it shall authorize the issuance, renewal, or modification thereof in accordance with said finding . . ." (June 19, 1934, c. 652, Sec. 309, 48 Stat. 1085, 47 U.S.C.A. Sec. 309).

3. *Matter of Great Lakes Broadcasting Company,* Federal Radio Commission, Third Annual Report, pp. 33-35.
4. Footnote 1, *supra*, p. 10.

service was rejected by the Court of Appeals for the District of Columbia. The Court said:

> "It is apparent, we think, that the business is impressed with a public interest and that, because the number of available broadcasting frequencies is limited, *the Commission is necessarily called upon to consider the character and quality of the service to be rendered.*" [5]

This position was affirmed in a later decision in which the Court said that it was the "duty" of the Commission "to take notice of the" applicant's "conduct in his previous use of the permit." [6]

In the most recent case, the National Broadcasting Company contended that the Commission had no power to consider program service, but was limited to technological matters only. The Supreme Court of the United States differed with National Broadcasting Company, saying:

> ". . . the Act does not restrict the Commission merely to supervision of the traffic. It puts upon the Commission the burden of *determining the composition of that traffic.*" [7]

The obligations imposed upon the FCC to insure that the limited facilities of the radio are devoted to the public interest cannot be overemphasized.

Radio is today probably the most influential medium of mass communication. The statisticians tell us that an American installs a radio even before he has a telephone. More than 9 out of every 10 families own radios.[8] This means that some 130,000,000 people are listening to the radio, are influenced by what comes over it or deprived of that which has been suppressed.

Radio has probably surpassed the press, possibly even the pulpit, in its influence. Despite the fact that every newspaper, with but a few exceptions, editorially opposed the re-election of President Roosevelt in 1940, he was re-elected. Certainly, one of the factors was the relative freedom from editorial control of the radio. Only through the radio were Roosevelt and his proponents able to find any real avenue of communication to the people. A 1940 public opinion poll showed that 38% of the people felt their votes were influenced by the radio;

5. *KFKB Broadcasting Association v. Federal Radio Commission,* 47 F. (2d) 670, 672 (1931).
6. *Trinity Methodist Church v. Federal Radio Commission,* 62 F. (2d) 850, 852 (1932).
7. *National Broadcasting Company v. United States,* 319 U. S. 190, 215-16 (1942).
8. Broadcast Measurement Bureau, Inc., *Radio Families v. U. S. A.* 1946, p. 11 (1946).

only 23% felt they were influenced by the press.[9]

As radio has become a more influential factor in the American scene, it has taken on a comparable obligation. As K. B. Bartlett has so ably stated it:

> "The price of scientific advancement has always been the acceptance of greater responsibility, and greater responsibility means less time for foolery. Let us, then, get down to the business of improving the material from which people make up their minds on which they base their actions."[10]

From whence comes this material which determines people's thoughts and influences their actions? Is it a cross-section of ideas of all the people? Unquestionably, it is not. A comparative handful of advertisers or the advertising agencies determine this material. More than 65% of the 1005 standard broadcast stations are affiliated with national networks, and about 60% of their total time is devoted to national broadcasts. These affiliated stations utilize 95% of the night-time broadcasting power of the country. Almost half of their revenue comes from national networks. It is economically sound to affiliate, as evidenced by the figures for 1942, which are the latest available. The net income before taxes of the average network-affiliated station was more than 15 times that of the average unaffiliated station.[11]

The voluble voice of the NAB has been so effective that too many of us have come to think only of political limitations on the freedom to speak. And the NAB would prefer to have it that way. Actually the economic restraints are far more dangerous and in fact are the only ones we need presently fear. With such a high percentage of programs being heard over national networks, with only 144 advertisers sponsoring 97.2% of that time, and with 20 advertising agencies devising 90% of the network programs, we can readily see how the economic viewpoint of Big Business monopolizes what we hear on the radio. Commissioner Clifford Durr says that we are "warranted in asking whether or not the freedom *from* control over broadcasting which is being so vigorously urged carries with it freedom *to* control." [12] Mr. Niles Trammell, President of NBC, frankly stated before a Senate Investigating Committee in 1943:

9. Lazarsfeld, *The People's Choice*, Duell, Sloan & Pearce, pp. 127, 131 (N. Y., 1944).
10. Bartlett, "Social Impact of the Radio", *The Annals of the American Academy of Political and Social Science*, p. 96 (March, 1947).
11. Durr, "Freedom of Speech for Whom?", *The Public Opinion Quarterly*, p. 395-96 (Fall, 1944).
12. Footnote 11, *supra*, p. 393.

"The argument is now advanced that business control of broadcasting operations has nothing to do with program control. This is to forget that 'he who controls the pocketbook controls the man.' Business control means complete control, and there is no use arguing to the contrary." [13]

Thus the lines are clearly drawn. "The air belongs to the public, not to the radio industry," says the Hutchins Commission on Freedom of the Press.[14] We have delegated the F.C.C. to distribute licenses to use those airwaves but only in the "public interest, convenience and necessity". Is it in the public's interest to permit the broadcast only of those programs which 144 advertisers, or 20 advertising agencies, all of whose political and economic ideas happily coincide, may determine? Or is it more in the public interest for licenses of our airwaves to be obligated to devote a certain amount of unsponsored time at a popular listening hour every day for the discussion of important social, political and economic issues by the people and for the people? At a time when the Senate Subcommittee Investigating Small Business tells us that a dozen banks control 75% of the invested capital in the United States, we can no longer hesitate in demanding that the power of economic concentration on the radio be stemmed.

How far the people can go in stemming that power depends, as it does in every political issue, upon the use which the people make of their own power. This paper is not intended to suggest all or even a few of the ways in which the radio can be made an instrument for the real education as well as entertainment of the people. We suggest at least one realistic objective that can be attained right now. The Federal Communications Commission through its legislative power to issue and revoke licenses dependent upon the "public interest, convenience and necessity" served by the applicant *must require that radio stations serving certain localities, especially metropolitan areas, devote a certain period of time every day during popular listening-hours to stimulating social, political, economic and educational programs.*

These programs, must be written with the same pains and by the same talent employed in broadcasting the most expensive commercial program. Various groups and individuals must be given access to appear on these programs and express their views. This time

13. *Op. cit.*
14. "Report of Commission on Freedom of the Press", Robert M. Hutchins, Chairman, *Fortune* (Supplement), p. 6 (April, 1947).

shall be unsponsored and uncensored. Legislation should be passed to protect the station from libel and similar liabilities on such programs. The network affiliate should not be permitted to use a national program every day for this purpose. *It should be required to have at least some programs each week originate locally.* In this way, at least to some extent, the radio industry will begin to fulfill the obligation which it owes to the public. This recommendation is in line with the recommendation of the Hutchins Commission, which suggests that agencies of mass communication accept responsibility of common carriers of information and discussion.[15]

At the same time, the American people must demand that their Congress through legislation make mandatory upon the F.C.C. the regulation suggested above. The F.C.C., on March 7, 1946, published a carefully-prepared report entitled "Public Service Responsibility of Broadcast Licensees." By this publication, the Commission served notice that it is aware of the shortcomings of the radio industry. It knows in what respect the industry has failed to serve the public interest. Further, the Commission is aware that it has the legislative authority now to act along the lines suggested by us. However, the Commission has shown every sign of refusing to carry out its power. This reluctance, at least until a few months ago, was probably due to a fear of reprisal rather than to a failure to see the need.

The Commission's rule that no newspaper would be given a license to a radio station had to be withdrawn because of pressure mostly from the press and its legislative lackeys. Because Commissioner Ray Wakefield saw his duty in terms of protecting the public interest in radio and proceeded to carry it out diligently over a period of 7 years, he was rewarded in June, 1947, by President Truman in being refused renomination to the Commission. In his stead, the President nominated Congressman Jones of Ohio, who has the approval of Senator Taft of the same state. Jones is alleged to have been a member of the Ku Klux Klan and Black Legion.

The fear of fighting back against the economic giants will affect the Commission just as it affects so many others who fear that their very existence is dependent upon the good will of the industrial or financial magnates. Therefore, not only is it necessary to show the Commission that it has the backing of the real power in America, namely, the people, but at the same time it is necessary to give the

15. Footnote 14, *supra,* p. 19.

Commission further legislative mandate to protect the "public inter-est, convenience and necessity."

But we must act fast. Already the forces of reaction are busy in warding off the growing demand to give the air to the people. Big Business has now become fully aware of its potentialities through radio. Senate Majority Leader Wallace White, Republican of Maine, and Republican Charles Wolverton, Chairman of the House Inter-state and Foreign Commerce Committee, on May 23, 1947, intro-duced identical bills in the Senate and House known as the *White-Wolverton Bill*.[16] Since some parts of the proposed bill have been criticized by the NAB, some people have thought that it must be beneficial to the public and harmful to Big Business. But the source of criticism is misleading. Senator White apparently did include a few good provisions for the purpose of drawing fire to them, so that he could later have them deleted. In introducing the bill, White said: "There may be much to be added and some to be subtratced. We shall have hearings and all who have suggestions to offer will be heard."[17]

This paper cannot begin to analyze the many hidden motives of the bill. A careful reading of it clearly shows that it will result in a restriction of the F.C.C. powers, in limiting the ability of min-ority views to be heard, and in general in threatening civil liber-ties and the public's right to access to the air. Only a sampling can here be given. Section 15 of the bill prohibits any broadcast during a political campaign except (1) by a legally-qualified candidate for the office, or (2) by a person designated in writing by such candi-date, or (3) by a regularly-organized political party whose candidates' names appear on the ballot and "whose duly chosen responsible of-ficers designate a person to use such facilities." This would effectively prevent most minority political parties and individuals and organ-ized groups, such as Progressive Citizens of America, League of Women Voters, Bar Association, labor organizations and others, from expressing freely their views through the most effective com-munication medium: the radio. This section would be a violation of the most elementary principle in a democratic government since, as the Supreme Court of the United States recently pointed out:

> "The maintenance of the opportunity for free political discussion to the end that Government may be responsive to the will of the people . . . is

16. 80th Congress, 1st Session, S. 1333; H. R. 3595.
17. *Broadcasting*, p. 14 (May 26, 1947).

a fundamental principle of our constitutional system."[18]

Chairman Denny of the F.C.C. has recently also pointed out that this section would probably prevent news analysts or commentators from discussing political campaigns during the campaigns.[19]

The bill also foolishly prohibits any political broadcasts for 24 hours before the election and extending through Election Day. This is an open invitation to be guided by the misguiding newspapers.

Section 17 would require time to be given to prevent views in opposition to those expressed on another program on political or public questions, but at the same time the station is given dangerous censorship powers.

Section 18 would require that all news items or discussion of current events be identified generally as to source, and that all editorial or interpretive comment concerning such items or events be identified as such and as to source and responsibility. This is another effective restraint on free discussion and exposing of public evils. Many reporters and commentators are not in a position to divulge their source. This means that much information will have to be suppressed. Commentators will be forced to rely only on monopoly press agencies. It will probably be difficult to separate editorial or interpretation from news, and in order to avoid the difficulty the station could easily ban the broadcast entirely.

Section 19 prohibits the Commission from adopting a policy which would deny newspapers the right to own radio stations. Any flexibility in a Commission rule on this subject is removed.

These sections indicate some of the reasons why Senator White, Representative Wolverton and the other members of the Interstate and Foreign Commerce Committee of both Houses must be told that the people seek more freedom to the air, not limitations, and that, therefore, the Bill must be defeated.

This bill represents the very thing which we have tried in this paper to warn against. It would let only the powerful broadcasters determine program. The people's rights are further proscribed.

The danger of this approach was ably expressed by Commissioner Durr when he said:

> "In thinking of radio, we are too much inclined to think in terms of what radio can bring to the people—a one-way pipeline of news, ideas

18. *Stromberg v. California*, 283 U. S. 359 (1931).
19. *PM*, p. 4 (June 18, 1947).

and entertainment—and too little in terms of its value as an outlet through which the people may express themselves. Democracy thrives more on participation at its base than upon instruction from the top . . . In this country, we are dedicated to the principles of democracy. If the pattern of the future is to be a democratic pattern . . . it must be based upon the desires, beliefs and feelings of the people themselves. Democracy can function only in an atmosphere of full information and frank discussion. In determining the course of the future, radio can play its part for good or evil, depending upon whether it is the voice of the few or an outlet for full information and free expression, as uncurbed by commercial as by political restraints." [20]

20. Footnote 11, *supra*, p. 406.

M a r v i n   M i l l e r

Radio announcer, actor, writer,
narrator; featured in 11 films;
recorded 5 albums for children

CONTEMPT OF
THE AMERICAN PEOPLE

"**T**HE ether is a public medium, and its use must be for public benefit. The use of radio channels is justified only if there is public benefit. The dominant element for consideration in the radio field is, and always will be, the great body of the listening public, millions in number, country wide in distribution."

That is the radio doctrine as laid down in 1925 by the then Secretary of Commerce, Herbert Clarke Hoover. Mr. Hoover is not usually considered a dangerously progressive citizen and hence I feel safe in assuming that there is nothing subversive in the idea expressed by him.

I feel even safer in assuming that this doctrine is not subversive, because the Communications Act passed by the Congress of the United States expressly reserves to the people the title to all radio channels and directs that licenses—*temporary* licenses, at that, —may be granted only to applicants who demonstrate their qualifications and their intention of using the publicly-owned channels in the "public interest, convenience and necessity."

Further, if the air belongs to the people, I feel safe in assuming that freedom of the air, if it means nothing else, must at least mean freedom for the people to hear all sides. I am strengthened in this assumption by the decision of the Federal Communications Commission in the case of station WAAB, now generally referred to as the Mayflower decision. Said the FCC: "A truly free radio cannot be used to advocate the causes of the licensee. It cannot be used to support the candidacy of his friends. It cannot be devoted to the support of principles he happens to regard most favorably. In brief, the broadcaster cannot be an advocate. Freedom of speech on the radio must be broad enough to provide full and equal opportunities for the presentation to the public of all sides of public issues."

149

It is on this basis, then, that I ask the question, "Is there thought control in radio?" It is on this basis that I present the following bill of particulars:

Organized labor, together with its members' families, comprises about 40% of the people. That is a sizable portion of the American public. If we consider the fact that organized labor speaks for *all* labor, whether organized or not; if we consider further the fact that the interests of labor are not narrow, individualistic interests, but coincide with the interests of the farmer, the professional, the small merchant—then it becomes even more manifest that the treatment accorded labor may well serve as an index of how well radio is serving the public interest, convenience and necessity.

But, when we turn to labor and the radio, we find a most sordid array of distortion, slander and discrimination. How is this possible if the air belongs to the people?

We have to answer this question in two parts. For, up until 1945, the answer was written down in black-and-white for all to see. It was written in the Code of the National Association of Broadcasters, the NAB. This code, a set of regulations with no official status but solely the private affair of the NAB, precluded the possibility of labor having any voice at all on the air. For this is what the code said: "Time for the presentation of controversial issues shall not be sold except for political broadcasts." The code then went on to explain that if time *were* sold for the presentation of controversial issues, then the rich people could buy up all the time. And this is bad. Therefore, said the Code, "It is a public duty of broadcasters to bring such discussion to the radio audience regardless of the willingness of others to pay for it."

So no one could buy time to present a controversial issue unless it was a political broadcast. That's fine. But how did this affect labor? Well, what is a controversial issue? Did the code say anything about that? Oh, yes. It defined controversy very carefully: "Discussion (or dramatization) of labor programs on the air is almost always of a controversial nature. Even the so-called 'facts' about labor are usually challenged." Please note that according to the NAB there are no facts about labor, only 'so-called' facts. Please note, too, that these so-called facts are usually challenged. In case there was any doubt as to who might do the challenging, the code continued: "Employers as a whole won't discuss their labor problems on the air and

150

are inclined to frown on those stations . . . which open their facilities to labor leaders."

And there you have it. You are hereby warned, said the NAB to radio station managers, that you risk a boycott on advertising revenue if you dare perform your public duty to the overwhelming majority of the American people.

The extent to which this closed-door policy for labor operated is evident from the testimony of Mr. Mark Woods, former president of the Blue Network, when he appeared before the FCC in 1943. Asked if he would sell General Motors time to put a symphony orchestra on a national hookup, he replied that he certainly would. Then he was asked if he would sell time to the A. F. of L. to put the same program on the same hookup. He replied he would not.

This philosophy, that a program sponsored by labor is *ipso facto* controversial, was finally challenged by the United Automobile Workers, CIO, four years ago by bringing the case of Station WHKC of Columbus, Ohio, before the FCC. On time bought by the union, the station had refused to allow the union to appeal to its listeners to write to Congressmen urging them to support the price stabilization program; the station had refused to allow the union to attack the Smith-Connally Act when that bill was up in Congress; the station had refused to allow the union even to mention "America First" or "Coughlinites;" and the station's program director had made the most amazing changes in dramatic scripts, even going so far as to take words out of the mouth of the union leader and put them into the mouth of the company superintendent!

John Moutoux, of the newspaper *P.M.,* commenting on this, said:
"The station did a neat job in doctoring the scripts so that they would offend no one—at least, not the Curtiss-Wright Co., for whom the local employees worked—but the result was such that the company, rather than the union, might well have paid for the time."

This case dramatized the grievances of the entire labor movement against radio, and the immediate outcome was a clearcut triumph for labor. The station agreed to eliminate censorship, to maintain a fair balance among various points of view, and to make time available to labor for the discussion of issues of public importance, including controversial issues.

The FCC, in handing down its decision, declared that any ban on the sale of time for the discussion of controversial issues was not in the public interest. Two months later, the NAB revised its code.

But there is more than one way to skin a cat. During the war, the National Broadcasting Company granted time to the CIO and the A. F. of L. alternately to sponsor a *Labor for Victory* program; but, as the 1944 election campaign got underway along about June, N.B.C. dropped the program. One of the reasons given was that during an election campaign the subject-matter of *Labor for Victory* would be controversial and therefore embarrassing to the network. As an example, it cited a CIO broadcast in which all citizens were urged to exercise their right to vote. You can readily see how such a controversial issue would be embarrassing.

If you remember the *Labor for Victory* program, you no doubt recall that it was exclusively devoted to furthering the war effort and at no time did it present a narrow, partisan, so-called "labor point of view" on any controversial issue. The dropping of the program at the time can only be construed as a political move to silence the voice of labor as a crucial election approached.

But where are we? Labor cannot buy time for controversial issues. It cannot have free time for controversial issues. Very well, labor still has another angle. Remember the NAB Code said, "Time for the presentation of controversial issues shall not be sold *except for political broadcasts.*" How about it, then? Why not *buy* time for a *political* broadcast?

Consider, then, the case of the Ship Scalers and Dry Dock Workers, A. F. of L. This union bought time on station KOMO, Seattle, for a political broadcast during the election campaign. It bought time, paid its money on the line, and—the program was cancelled. Not only couldn't the union get on the air; it had to sue the station for the refund of its money. Why? What was the matter now?

Nothing, except that the program exposed the activities of the PEACE NOW agitators in the Northwest. It called upon the government to jail those who were sabotaging the war effort by advocating a negotiated peace with the Axis countries. It called for the election of Senator Wallgren as a pro-Roosevelt, Win-the-War candidate.

But what's wrong with that? Why cancel the program? Because, the station declared, "PEACE NOW is not a political issue and therefore cannot be discussed on a paid political broadcast"!

The picture is complete. Nobody may buy time for controversial issues unless they are political broadcasts. Everything that labor says is controversial. Labor may not have free time for controversial issues. Labor may not buy time for political issues because nothing labor says is political.—You're damned if you do, you're damned if you don't, and I'm damned if there's any apparent consistency.

I say *apparent* consistency, for it is only on the surface that there is any *in*consistency. It is only in the words that there is any *in*consistency. In the philosophy behind the whole mess, there is *devastating consistency.*

And it keeps coming through. If labor cannot get on the air any other way, why not buy its own station? Well, the United Auto Workers, CIO, applied for a permit for a radio station in the Detroit area. Opposed to them was the Grosse Point Broadcasting Corporation, a commercial outfit seeking the same wave-length. The motion made by this corporation, on file with the FCC, petitioned that the auto workers not be allowed a permit to operate a radio station. On what grounds? Get this: on the grounds that a labor union has no *right* to get into the radio business!

Shall I repeat the question with which I started? "Is there thought control in radio?"

The treatment accorded labor itself is, after all, only half the picture. To round it out we must examine the treatment which is afforded labor's opposition. Now, who would be opposed to labor?

Well, first of all, there is a little outfit called the National Association of Manufacturers—the N.A.M. Sponsored by this organization is the National Industrial Information Committee—the N.I.I.C.

May I read you a few paragraphs from a letter sent out by this committee on June 14, 1944, to some 900 radio stations? "To give your listeners a preview of the businessman's side of the question, the National Industrial Information Committee has completed a 13 week fifteen minute transcribed series called 'Businessmen Look to the Future,' available to you without cost." And let me remind you that "without cost" means "for free". And, in view of the current housing situation, you might be particularly interested in this paragraph from the letter: "The broadcast dealing with Housing was made by Miss Elizabeth Gordon, Editor of *House Beautiful* Magazine, Mr. Joseph Close of Owens-Illinois Glass Company and Mr. E. W. "Pat" Smith of Johns-Manville. They will provide accurate answers to such questions on housing as: What are the homes of tomorrow going to be like? How much will they cost? Will building actually provide jobs to help cover the change in employment after the war? and countless other bits of first hand current information in the housing field." No comment.

But the privilege of carrying these charming broadcasts at no cost to themselves might not be sufficient inducement to the station. The letter goes on to say:

> "We will proceed immediately to back your broadcasting of 'Businessmen Look to the Future' with the kind of audience building material that will bring to the attention of every worker and business man in your merchandisable area the fact that you are carrying this very important series. Letters will be mailed to all of our member organizations in your territory (there are 12,000 members of the National Association of Manufacturers and over 6000 members of the National Industrial Information Committee) calling attention to this series over your station.
>
> "They will be provided with office and bulletin board posters bearing an imprint of your call letters. Included with these posters is a special printed announcement to be signed by an executive of the organization calling attention to the program series to be broadcast over your station. In like manner, there will be special releases prepared for use by these organizations in their house organs.
>
> "Special press releases descriptive of the program will be submitted to the editors of your local papers along with your broadcast schedule. This will include feature stories and mats that can be used effectively to tie in with the broadcasting of the series in your listening area."

That isn't all, but that's enough to give you a rough idea.

Well, did any station fall for this magnanimous offer, which could be had absolutely free, without even sending in a box-top? Did any station go for this?

Turn now to the official report of the National Association of Manufacturers for November, 1945, wherein we read: "Over 300 stations in 48 states with an estimated audience of five million listeners accepted the series of 13 recorded weekly programs entitled 'Businessmen Look to the Future.' Another series is now in preparation."

While we're at it, here's some more from that same report: "Announcers and commentators of over 500 radio stations receive NIIC's weekly service, 'Briefs for Broadcasters,' and in 1944 two of every three stations in the country used material from it in whole or in part."

Footnote to the above: on another occasion, the Association boasted, through its president, that in a single year it received free radio time which, had it been obliged to pay for same, would have cost one million dollars.

154

Note: please place the foregoing in relation to what was said previously about labor and radio, while I ask once again the question, "Is there thought control in radio?"

But the N.A.M. itself is not the only outfit that is, shall we say, not pro-labor. Shouldn't we consider some of the NAM-front organizations, some of the NAM-inspired outfits, some of its satellites, or should we say, NAM fellow-travellers? These organizations also get on the air, you know.

The American Economic Foundation, in its brochure, *Wake Up, America,* enumerates six reasons why this program should prove profitable for local radio advertisers to produce. One reason is that the subjects chosen for this program keep abreast of national problems presented without prejudice or partisanship, yet with fairness and courage. Now, among the red-white-and-blue speakers pictorialized in the brochure are Hon. Clare Booth Luce, Hon. Herbert Hoover, Hon. Robert A. Taft and Louis Fisher. Without the Honorable.

Consider another N.A.M. fellow-traveller: the American Legion. Am I wrong in calling the American Legion a fellow-traveller of the N.A.M., when Major General Smedley Butler of the U. S. Marines is on record as saying that the Legion has been used to break more strikes than the National Guard and the police forces? Am I wrong in calling the American Legion an N.A.M. satellite, when last year it gave its high award, its Americanism medal, to that sterling purveyor of the NAMerican way of life, William Randolph Hearst?

Well, anyway, the *National Legionnaire* proudly announced: "The Legion Radio Voice is Never Silenced. There's a 15 minute program for every quarter hour in 1946." According to George Seldes' *In Fact,* the radio branch of the American Legion National Public Relations Division obtained 35,200 quarter-hours free. This is in addition to the Legion's nationwide hookups on special occasions.

I've forgotten now. How many hours did labor get free?

Thought control in radio?

How does radio treat minority peoples? Does the sum-total of radio programs give the American public an enlightened view, a well-rounded knowledge of minority groups? Do Amos and Andy and Rochester and Beulah give a true picture of the American Negro? Are dramatic programs presented which give the real problems, the hopes, the aspirations of the Negro people? The Jewish people? Mexicans? Japanese?

Several years ago, *The March of Time* decided to dramatize Margaret Halsey's best seller, *Some of My Best Friends Are Soldiers.* You no doubt recall that Miss Halsey's book is bright and amusing, the pith of it being an attack on anti-Semitism and Jim-Crowism. Malcolm Meacham, hired to do the radio version, was instructed by the agency to confine himself to the romance and keep the script "non-controversial," meaning eliminate the very aspects of anti-Semitism and Jim-Crowism out of which the lovestory develops and evolves. The script was what you might expect it to be under the circumstances, and after several hours of rehearsal, *The March of Time* killed the whole thing.

Miss Halsey wrote to Frank Norris, director of the program, for clarification on the philosophy that anti-Semitism was controversial. Mr. Norris replied that, indeed, anti-Semitism or any other form of race prejudice is not controversial, but that a good speech about it is far better than a dramatization, because the latter is "likely to create a great deal of misunderstanding" among listeners.

The March of Time is, of course, thoroughly convinced that a good speech is far better than a dramatization. That is why *The March of Time* is 99% dramatization.

When Helen Hayes was starring in the Broadway play, *Harriet,* she tried to pursuade radio executives to let her do the play on the air. Now, ordinarily, Miss Hayes' offer to do a radio show would be snapped up. But not so in this instance. *Harriet,* you see, is the story of Harriet Beecher Stowe. And she wrote *Uncle Tom's Cabin,* remember?

Here is a more recent incident affecting the thoughts of the American people about certain minorities. Sergeant Ben Kuroki, of Hershey, Nebraska, came back from the war. He had been on combat flights in Europe, including the suicide raid on the Ploesti oilfields. He wore the Air Medal with four Oak Leaf Clusters. When he was in Los Angeles, a local radio station cancelled a broadcast in which he was scheduled to take part, on the ground that the appearance of a Japanese-American on a radio program in California would raise a "controversial issue."

"Thus once again," says Charles Siepman commenting on this disgraceful incident in his book *Radio's Second Chance,* "a controversial issue became a radio station manager's convenient alibi for avoiding his responsibility and a plausible excuse for unjust discrimination." To which we add, and thus once again is the American people denied knowledge—the very knowledge that can help banish prejudice. Denying the American people that knowledge, is thought control.

There are other means, too, of inflicting thought control. Said FCC Commissioner Durr: "Censorship by overloading the air with programs which sell goods to the exclusion of programs which do not, may be as effective as a complete denial of access to the air, or censorship by blue pencil."

The mere fact that a network makes available a sustaining program to its affiliates, is no assurance that the affiliates make that program available to their listeners. The FCC found a deplorable situation in this regard, local stations not carrying public service programs in order to carry in their stead local commercials. A few items culled from the survey of a sample week (in 1944) are revealing.

Invitation to Learning was a program on C.B.S. in which good books were discussed by a panel of distinguished critics. 136 stations were free to carry it. It was carried by 39.

"The American University of the Air" offered *Land of the Free,* a program on NBC dealing with democracy. Of 114 stations, 24 saw fit to carry this program.

A while ago, we spoke about the *Labor for Victory* program and about labor's struggles to get on the air. At the time under review, *Labor for Victory* was the only nationally-organized labor program offered on any network. Of 104 stations which might have carried it free, only 35 did.

On the other hand, 228 radio stations in the United States are currently carrying a six-week series on the Soviet Union, prepared by the Knights of Columbus. Now, if there is any time in world history when the people of America need to have straight-from-the-shoulder information about Russia, it is now.

Listen, then, to this dialogue from the platter called *Labor in the Soviet Union,* as reported by *P.M.* It is the story of Akim and his wife, Titania:

"I forbid you to buy meat," Titania says. "How will we save enough for your shoes?"

"We're lower than hogs in our great classless Utopia," says Akim, bitterly. He tells Titania that that morning he went to "Boronoff, the pig who heads the union," and asked Boronoff "for work to make enough to buy food."

"Boronoff," says Akim, "pig that he is—he folded his greasy hands on his fat belly. He told me I was a wrecker. He picked meat from his teeth."

There is a knock at the door. It is the Russian police. "I believe you are the counter-revolutionary swine, Akim Voroshev," says the officer. Akim winds up in a prison camp beyond the Urals.

This sort of thing is being fed the American people over 228 stations. Two hundred and twenty-eight stations are carrying this as a public service, giving the Knights of Columbus the time free of charge.

The production manager of the New York station which broadcasts this series is quoted by *P.M.* as saying, "If someone had something equally good on the other side of the question, and if we felt that the point of view was justifiable, we'd broadcast it, no doubt."

"If we felt that the point of view was justifiable."

Thought control?

No one in Hollywood will forget that fateful day in February, 1945, when out of an apparently-clear sky, Earle C. Anthony, "California distributor of Packard motor cars" and former president of the National Association of Broadcasters, summarily fired six sponsored news-commentators, among them, Alvin Wilder, Sam Balter and Peter de Lima. No charges were preferred against them, nor were they permitted to give any explanation for their departure on their final broadcasts. Henceforth, under the new station policy only newscasters on the station's payroll, under its control, could broadcast news over its facilities.

The die was cast, and in the months that followed, things happened on other stations. John B. Hughes, Bill Pennell, John Dehner and Averill Berman, among others, were dropped by their sponsors or were switched to other departments or were broadcasting on sharply-curtailed schedules.

In New York and Chicago, the axe fell on liberal commentators with similar precision. Commentators like Frank Kingdon, Quincy Howe, Johannes Steele, William Gailmor and Dr. Raymond Walsh disappeared from the air completely or found themselves working in a political straitjacket. The latest to feel the purge is William Shirer.

But there are lots of other commentators on the air who are still broadcasting, still going strong, and still untouched, so that the American people are not really being denied an analysis of the news. They may still listen to Fulton Lewis, Jr., Hans V. Kaltenborn, Sam Pettingill, Lowell Thomas, Gabriel Heater . . . oh! we've got a million of 'em!

An advertising executive representing commentators wrote last June:

> "During the past few months reactionary pressure has been brought to bear in unprecedented volume to force liberal voices off the air. Sponsors of liberal commentators have experienced everything from veiled threats to outright boycotts from certain groups and individuals."

The crime of these commentators? Fearlessly and consistently they spoke in behalf of the American people; they spoke for racial and religious equality and for world unity; they spoke in behalf of price control and in behalf of FEPC; they spoke against Gerald L. K. Smith and against the KKK, and against anti-labor legislation. Well, they're gone now. And so is price control. And there's no FEPC. And Gerald L. K. Smith marches on. And the Taft-Hartley Bill is here.

There is one station owner in this town whose antics were described by Dixon Wecter in *The Atlantic Monthly* for June, 1945—antics which seemed at the time too fantastic to believe, but which subsequently have been entirely corroborated. Wecter wrote:

> "We hear reliably of one station owner who frequently sends snippets from the Hearst editorials up to his newsroom ordering that they be read on every newscast that day; who commanded that Henry Wallace's name never be mentioned over the air; who sent his music department an order 'not to play anything by that damned Communist choir' referring to the Cossack Male Chorus, and banned songs by Paul Robeson who offended both on the score of politics and of race. When one of his commentators interviewed on the air an officer sent by the Navy, Commander Goldberg, the owner administered a tongue-lashing. 'Next time,' he growled, 'tell the Navy to send us somebody named Casey.' It is worth remark that in the past three years he has fired seven successive news editors."

It is worth remark in passing, too, that this station last summer conducted a contest in which prizes of a new car and cash awards were offered for the best letters on the theme—guess what? On the theme, "I believe in free speech because . . ."!

It is interesting to note, too, in passing that Mr. Earle C. Anthony, "California distributor of Packard motor cars" and onetime president of the National Association of Broadcasters, who fired his commentators because in his opinion they monkeyed with politics, this Mr. Anthony just happens to be the only station owner in the entire NBC network who refused to carry one of the fireside chats of the late President Roosevelt.

Thought control in radio? There is no end to the means and the devices and the tricks by which this thought control is exercised. Did you ever consider the effect of the discriminatory use of the disclaimer? I'd like to read you the opinion of a former commentator who, for reasons of security, shall remain nameless. To help quiet any speculation as to his identity, let me assure you he is not one of our local commentators. This is from a personal letter he wrote concerning the tacking of disclaimers onto controversial programs:

"My understanding of the disclaimer is that it is no defense against libel. It gives the station no legal protection. But it operates to the disadvantage of the liberal commentator in an obvious fashion. The Fulton Junior Lewises can spread any fantastic fabric of alleged facts and nobody croons a disclaimer—they're only 'reporters' giving you the lowdown. But if the liberal commentator digs up evidence that Junior is fibbing and presents it and says that Junior is working for the wrong people and ought to be ashamed of himself—then that commentator is 'attacking' Junior and he's controversial; and the local station proceeds to tell the audience hurriedly (on the commentator's time, not on the station's), 'The preceding punk is entirely on his own. This station does not hold with a word he has just said and indignantly refuses to accept the slightest moral or legal responsibility for the trash you have just been listening to. The jerk will, however, return to the air tomorrow evening at the same time.' The political disclaimer has much the same effect. The reactionary can rant for 15 minutes about free private enterprise and it 'ain't' political—he's talking about the great American institution of free private enterprise. But if a Democrat gets up and tells them that half the hooey they hear about free enterprise is Republican hooey and the other half of the hooey is bought and paid for by the NAM, then the station will carefully warn the audience that what they've just been hearing is 'a paid political broadcast' and please forgive us for peddling the time for it."

Now, we come to the radio forums. Now, we're on high ground. There's no problem of controversy here. The very essence of the forums is the controversial issues. And the forums meet the situation head-on by proudly proclaiming that they give both sides of the question. Both sides, that is. Ultra-conservative and reactionary.

Referring back to the NAM report from which I quoted a while ago, we read also the following:

"Spokesmen for management have been provided on such influential radio programs as *March of Time, America's Town Hall Meeting, American Forum of the Air, People's Platform,* and *Wake Up, America.* Special network time is also secured for industrial leaders to answer radio attacks on American Business."

The fakery of George V. Denny's *Town Meeting of the Air* is so voluminous that *In Fact* claims it could fill ten issues—some 50,000 words—with evidence. Mr. Denny admits he plants questions in the audience. He admits questions are censored. During the war, he excused this on the grounds that it prevented a Fascist spy from getting in a question over the radio which might be a tip to the enemy. Nevertheless, during the war, in the program originating in San Francisco, the first of four audience participants was Homer Maerz, liaison man between the German-American Bund and the Silver Shirts. Maerz got across this question: "Isn't it a fact that the proposals before the San Francisco Conference are precisely what the Jewish World Zionist Organization has advocated for decades?"

Denny also explains the planting of questions by saying it is done so that there are no delays, no dead air. But everyone who has ever attended a *Town Meeting* says there are always more persons with questions than there is time for. Mr. Denny emphatically denies that the *Town Meeting* program is loaded. "I did state," he says, "and will continue to affirm that we reserve the right to plant questions in the audience when it seems advisable and appropriate for us to do so." He also expressed regret that on a particular broadcast, George Romney, representative of the National Association of Manufacturers, had his question asked for him by a stranger who exposed the routine.

Other speakers on *Town Meeting* have been Lawrence Dennis, one of the Sedition Trial defendants and the so-called brains of American Fascism. He spoke four times. Merwin K. Hart, spokesman for Spanish Fascism and Franco, head of the National Economic Council and sponsor of Upton Close, was afforded the *Town Hall* platform on two occasions.

One of the most recent examples of the *Town Hall* tactics occurred last April, when one of the speakers was Edward A. Hayes, National Chairman of American Action, Incorporated. Hayes and American Action have been exposed as the Big-Business-backed successor to the old Liberty League and the discredited America First organizations. But Mr. Hayes was introduced merely as "a prominent attorney and former National Commander of the American Legion."

Thought control?

I have tried to point out the many forms it takes—direct and indirect. But now we come to what decent Americans consider to be the most insidious form of all—the direct pressure of the government, as exemplified in the nefarious tactics of the Committee on Un-American Activities.

This committee first thrust its fingers into radio by requesting the scripts of some eight or nine commentators. The scripts were to be scrutinized to see if they were subversive. Now, which commentators were included in this dragnet?

Did it include Upton Close, that expert on the Far East who explained the Pearl Harbor attack as being a possible coup by a small portion of the Japanese Navy or some other Japanese group? No, Upton Close was not suspect.

Did it include Fulton Lewis, Jr., one of the most violent Roosevelt-hating, labor-baiting commentators on the air? No. Junior is one of the darlings of the Un-Americans.

Did it include Henry J. Taylor, who Jew-baited Sidney Hillman on the air, and who wrote articles for *Reader's Digest,* one of which was rehashed and reprinted in Hitler's propaganda magazine, *The Signal?* No, Hank is O.K. with the Un-American Committee.

Did it include Sam Pettingill, leader of Frank E. Gannett's pro-Fascist front, the Committee for Constitutional Government? Of course not. What's subversive about that?

Well, then, could it include Earl Godwin? Uh-uh. Earl Godwin uses up a good deal of his air time defending the Un-American Committee. *Variety* reports him as saying on one of his broadcasts that the Committee is engaged "in the age-old fight of God and the devil; light vs. dark; Christian vs. heathenism." Those who oppose its work and tactics are trying to keep the Committee from finding "the strands of a world plot against American freedom to own property." They go so far as to accuse the Commitee of being "Fascist—whatever that means." So says Earl Godwin.

Variety goes on to ask, "Is there a gold star father in the house? He might tell Godwin what 'Fascist' means."

Well, was Godwin one of those whose scripts were requested by the Un-American Committee. Perish forbid!

No. You know the dangerous commentators: Quincy Howe, Johannes Steel, Sidney Walton, Raymond Swing, William Gailmor, Hans Jacob, J. Raymond Walsh. The liberals again. Just in case the economic pressure of the NAM boys themselves wasn't enough, the political pressure from the Un-American Commitee was thrown in. It did the trick. As Hugh de Lacy put it on the floor of Congress:

> "The Rankin Committee is setting itself up as a congressional radio thought police. Here is how the smear-fear technique works. Simply asking the radio stations for radio scripts spreads fear. Advising the press of the request spreads fear. The commentators whose scripts are sent for are plainly warned that they are under government surveillance, that their thoughts are under house arrest. Radio stations are put on warning that if

they want to stay out of the center of a smear controversy they had better get other commentators."

The extent to which this Committee protects the American people from subversive influence can best be seen from the letter which the Committee's counsel, Ernie Adamson, sent to Drew Pearson:

"Several people," wrote Adamson, "have called my attention to the closing line of your Sunday night broadcast, 'make democracy work.' I should like very much to have your definition of the word 'democracy' as you are using it over the radio. If you will be good enough to supply this information, I will give the matter further consideration to determine whether it should be called to the attention of the members of the committee for such action as they deem proper."

There you have it. It is the right of Americans to project and support the concept of democracy that is challenged by the Un-American Committee. But getting liberal comentators off the air just whetted the appetite of this Committee.

It isn't funny, ladies and gentlemen. American citizens are right now facing fines of $1000 and jail sentences of one year for refusing to comply with the unconstitutional demands of this Committee. Such refusal is contempt of Congress.

But, ladies and gentlemen, I say that the complete disregard by the Un-American Activities Committee of this country's hardwon democratic rights is contempt of the American people; I say that the utter scorn with which certain sacred-cow organizations ride rough-shod over every principle of equality and justice is contempt of the American people; I say that the cynical arrogance with which lies, distortions and propaganda are pumped into our homes over the radio with a complete lack of concern for the general welfare, is contempt of the American people; I say that the insolent denial of freedom of the air to the voice of democracy is contempt of the American people.

I say it is time for the American people to prefer charges. It is time for the American people to act.

(The above paper, presented by Mr. Miller, was written by him in collaboration with Harmon Alexander.)

S a m   M o o r e

National president, Radio
Writers' Guild; formerly
wrote *The Great Gilder-
sleeve*, with John Whedon

THE THREAT TO FREEDOM

THE preceding speakers have shown—and in my opinion they have shown all too clearly—that radio, the voice of the people, has a muzzle on it—or at least a muffler.

The air is full of programs which have only one object—to corral the greatest possible number of listeners for a given expenditure of program money. Stations in general do not give a hoot about whether they educate their listeners or not; and in this respect the networks appear to give just enough of a hoot to be able to defend themselves somewhat before the bar of public opinion and the FCC.

Education? Radio is far below that. Radio is chained fast in the swamp of entertainment subject-matter which is considered acceptable in pictures, slick magazines, and newspapers. Stories about cool-headed detectives who are attractive to women murderers; stories about charming young people whose only problem is to marry each other, and God help them after that; stories about people who travel, people with cars, airplanes, college degrees, and housekeepers.

7,000,000 farmers in the United States, but mighty few stories about farmers; 15,000,000 members of organized labor, but mighty few stories about unions, and few enough with ordinary working-people as heroes; 13,000,000 Negroes in the country, and mighty little about them on the radio.

On the radio, everybody is happy except a few mixed-up characters who are obliged to commit the crimes solved by the horde of private eyes now patrolling the airwaves. The only other discomforts are those caused either by temporary difficulties in love, or by psychological disturbances which have become increasingly popular. If money trouble is ever mentioned on the air, it is as something young people should face bravely if they expect to be happy.

In addition, radio's forums are stacked; the news comes from the AP and the UP, controlled by the press which went 90% against

Roosevelt; the commentators soon will represent only one point of view.

Yes, indeed, we have certainly got thought control on the air. And pretty soon we will have worse. Here's a quote from a speech by a man named Arthur C. Nielsen, head of the A. C. Nielsen Company, market researchers. He was talking to the Grocery Manufacturers of America, Inc., at the Waldorf-Astoria, New York, on November 19, 1946, on the subject "Postwar Trends in Food Marketing."

Here is his point No. 6, the closing point of his "postwar plan for the food industry":

> "While selling your products, make sure that you *also* sell the American public on your company and on the American system of free enterprise which has given the American public the world's highest standard of living.
>
> "There is ample proof that while American people esteem the products of industry, they are generally hostile to the companies which have contributed so greatly to better living and the creation of the common wealth."

He goes on to recommend an advertising program which will sell not only the product but the economic system which produced it, and says:

> "One of the world's greatest corporations has developed 100 different ideas for such advertisements. While their executives originally feared that such copy might prove subnormal in ability to sell the product, they are now firmly convinced that this advertising will sell more goods than the usual type of copy. And they have allotted a substantial percentage of their total advertising appropriation to this purpose."

Mr. Nielsen concluded:

> "I hope that your industry, representing the greatest aggregate national expenditure in America, will recognize the *unbeatable educational* power at your command, and put it to work, without delay." (The emphasis is Mr. Nielsen's.)

Presumably, when the grocery manufacturers start putting forth this kind of propaganda, the networks, under their present policies, will accept it without question. Free enterprise is presumed to be a non-controversial topic.

There have already been a few efforts at this type of propaganda by radio sponsors. But this threat is as nothing compared with the threat to the freedom of the air represented by the Thomas Committee on Un-American Activities. When the Thomas Committee subpoenas scripts of various liberal commentators, and the mere fact of their being called in question is enough to throw them off the air, we have indeed government censorship of radio by a means which was never envisaged in the Federal Communications Act.

This Act specifically provides there is to be no censorship of radio programs by government—yet the Thomas Committee is able to censor them.

Mr. Justin Miller, president of the National Association of Broadcasters, asserts that the FCC's proposal that stations should live up to their pledges to operate in the public interest or be denied license renewal, is censorship. He would like every station to be allowed to operate like a newspaper, frankly espousing the views of its owners on all social, economic and political questions. So far, Mr. Miller has won little support for this view in Congress, which is just as well, as radio is in bad enough shape already.

Bad shape? The entertainment offered is at extremely low cultural level, reflects no kind of reality whatsoever, stimulates no thought but daydreams. The news and commentary offered, to a degree rapidly approaching totality, supports actively the reactionary anti-democratic and imperialist designs of Big Business.

Why does radio support these policies of Big Business?

Because, in the first place, radio IS Big Business. Time sales totalled $310,000,000 in 1945.

In the second place, who are the radio industry's biggest customers? 38% of the networks' revenue in 1944 came from four advertising agencies. The networks were paid $82,000,000 in revenue in 1944 by 46 advertisers who are also among the biggest contributors to the hope-chest of the NAM.

We recognize that the NAM is behind the Taft-Hartley Act to crush the labor unions, and the Truman Doctrine of American imperialism in Europe.

The press is behind these policies, too.

If the NAM is able to tighten a little further its grip on the radio, to take it away from the people and let it operate on a free enterprise basis, as Justin Miller demands, the people will never hear any arguments at all against NAM policies.

If none of us had access to any newspapers but Hearst's, how would we know what was going on in the world?

If the NAM gets hold of radio, 140 million Americans will be totally in the dark.

And they want to get hold of it—because thought control is really not thought control at all, but *action control.*

Why do big corporations find it desirable to advertise free enterprise? Is it because they see a depression coming, and they don't want people to blame the system? Is it because they don't want people to think depressions might be unnecessary if distribution were better planned? One thing is sure: they hate to hear Henry Wallace talk about public ownership of railways, mines and power.

The NAM doesn't want us to hear even the single voice of Henry Wallace raised against the Truman plan, if it can be silenced. They don't want us to hear the facts about the sabotaged housing-program, the threat of inflation and unemployment while profits continue at peak levels, the injustices of restrictive covenants and the barbarity of lynchings. All they want us to hear is the danger of Communism, and that "Russia says no, Russia walks out, Russia blocks agreement," and that we should drive carefully over the Fourth of July weekend. The last warning is brought to us as a public service.

Big Business wants to control the world. To do this, they may try to drag America into war. But, in spite of their hurry, the sand in the atom bomb is running out—in spite of their hurry, they can't go to war as long as the pressure of organized labor is against them. Hence, the Taft-Hartley Act, to cripple or destroy the labor movement. What's more, Big Business can't go to war against the pressure of an informed public opinion. Hence, the drive for Thought Control.

The NAM wants us kept in the dark about these matters, because the NAM is afraid of democracy. They are afraid the people will find out, get together and do something about it.

That is why the threat of further business control of radio is a threat to the freedom of every American.

That is why it must be fought. If we lose control of the only means of mass communication which is still theoretically free, we are beaten on every front.

Radio can be free. We have a chance to organize the fight against inflation—people are already beginning to realize they were swindled when the OPA was thrown in the ashcan. With a free radio, we can fight American imperialism, fight the Congressmen who passed the Taft-Hartley Bill and killed FEPC, and who keep the Thomas Committee functioning as a threat to the freedom of every decent, democratic-minded citizen.

How can we keep the radio that is supposed to belong to us?

In the first place, we have to publicize the fact that radio *does* belong to the people. Too many of us, even in the radio industry, have forgotten this prime fact, if we ever knew it. Millions of Americans are unaware that the soap-peddlers and patent-medicine salesmen are getting a free ride on the *public* air—and that when stations change owners for as high as $2,500,000, most of that money is for a license which is actually owned by the public.

We must learn that radio is ours, and that we have a right to demand it be operated in our interest.

We can make this demand in two directions. We can demand it politically, by support of the generally-progressive policies of the Federal Communications Commission; and we can demand it simply as listeners, by writing to station operators and advertisers.

The FCC is a body appointed by the President and confirmed by the Senate. Appointments to it depend on the general political climate to some extent, but an aroused public awareness of the importance of the job could put far more pressure on the President and Senate than they have felt from the public up to now.

We must write to the progressive members of the FCC, expressing support of the policies outlined in the Blue Book issued in March, 1946; we must demand better balance of programs, more public service programs, a fairer representation of all points of view on controversial questions. And we should also write to the President and our Senators about these questions, and tell them we want a progressive FCC that will remember radio belongs to the people.

As listeners, we can take up our case directly with the big advertisers who depend on our good will for their sales, and are also, according to Mr. Nielsen, desirous of our affection for the corporations themselves.

Suppose a sponsor got 10,000 letters from people in organized labor, and their families, asking why there aren't any union members on any of the sponsor's 31 programs? I believe the writers of several of those shows would get a memorandum in a hurry.

I believe that similar pressure could compel other desirable changes in the content of radio drama and comedy. The same kind of pressure could eliminate the onesidedness of radio news and commentary, but such protests should be addressed to the FCC, as well as the sponsor or station manager.

Organized labor must take an even further step. The A. F. of L.

spent hundreds of thousands of dollars for actors, scripts, and air time in the fight to beat the Taft-Hartley Bill. It wasn't too little, but it was certainly too late. Organized labor should be on the air 52 weeks of the year—not with 15-minute discussion programs, but with the kind of shows that will build a mass listening-audience for the voice of labor

In order to get this kind of mass awareness going, the PCA in New York has already adopted a plan which has been discussed out here with much interest. The plan is to set up Listening Posts of interested ciitzens to try to keep radio fair.

Have you ever heard a program deliberately distorting the political scene, howled an imprecation at the speaker, and let it go at that? This does no good.

I would like to suggest a specific course of action.

I suggest that a Radio Division of PCA be set up, within the framework of the Arts. Sciences and Professions, and that for this division we try to mobilize at least 500 people employed in radio in Los Angeles, as actors, directors, musicians, technicians, office workers, writers, or whatever.

That this division set up at least three committees: Production, Research, and Speakers' Bureau.

The Research Committee would dig up facts on the current radio situation, would analyze program content, check up on commentators, try to provide a general line of attack.

The material from the Research Committee would be turned over to the Speakers' Bureau, which would send speakers to groups of any kind, provided they were interested in the project of setting up Listening Posts. The speakers would explain the basic facts, the need for pressure on the FCC and advertisers, and might suggest specific listening-projects for the new post to take up.

The Listening Post could then organize its members' listening, organize its protests, and make regular reports to the Radio Division on projects carried out and results observed or assistance needed.

The Production Committee would fill another kind of function. This committee would be a service group prepared to utilize specialized radio skills in preparing programs to assist PCA's general political program, or to help other groups—labor groups, for example, who are fighting the same battle.

I believe those of us who work in radio can perform a tremendous service to democracy by carrying out this project. PCA has a growing number of neighborhood chapters which are anxious to get speakers from the ASP division—radio members who know their own industry can get Listening Posts started in every chapter. Labor unions in this area must be told about this project—veterans' organizations, civic groups of all kinds will be interested.

And, of course, radio writers, actors, and musicians have a special stake in this proposal to support the FCC. The keystone of the FCC Blue Book is its demand for more local live broadcasting. That's what Petrillo wants—it's also what AFRA wants and the Radio Writers Guild wants. More local live broadcasting will make more acting, more writing, more live music.

If for this reason alone, support of the FCC should be demanded by every member of AFRA, the Radio Writers' Guild, the Musicians' Union.

But, just as all of us in radio began to see clearly, when we were helping labor's drive to defeat the Taft-Hartley Bill, that our interest was identical with the interest of the A. F. of L. carpenter and the CIO longshoreman, so we must realize that this new fight is not the job of radio workers alone. We must undertake the job of organizing the fight, but it is a fight in which all champions of democracy must join, if we are to keep democracy. I think we can keep it.

DISCUSSION

The first speaker from the floor put a question as to how effective liberal and progressive groups could be now.

The Chairman called upon Reuben Ship to answer.

Reuben Ship: "I think they would be tremendously effective, but they haven't been operating as pressure groups. Sponsors particularly worship letters. Every letter that comes in is placed in a safe and then transmitted down the line with dozens of memos. I recall one instance on a certain program, when a teachers' group—just a small group—wrote in objecting to a certain characterization of a teacher. That was last year. They said, 'Here are teachers trying to raise their economic level and they are presented on the air as silly, incompetent people, and thus public opinion turns against them.' Well, that show did not get on the air and it is doubtful that it ever will.

"Mr. Moore pointed out that, if labor did that, the same thing could be accomplished. Negro organizations, in conjunction with other minority groups, could write this same kind of pressure letter, and it would bring results, because sponsors worship the dollar and, rather than risk losing it, they will give in to a certain extent."

Chairman Brown: "This is interesting to note. A few days ago, I listened to a news commentator, and this fellow, who is not a liberal, mentioned this Conference. He said it was being attended by *Life, Newsweek* and *Time,* and that it was considered an important political item in present American history. He made great haste to follow it up by saying that the NAM had just issued a pamphlet which asked, 'Do you wish to be told what to write? What to think? Preachers, do you wish to be told what to preach?' and so on. That's pretty good proof that they are not taking any chances on pressure groups being unanswered on the air."

Marvin Miller: "You will find, I think, that the public's conception of the mass of letters that most programs get is pretty much a press agent's dream . . . Of course, any program that sponsors a contest and gives away a car, refrigerator, etc., gets a terrific amount of mail. But the day when the so-called radio fan sent in bags of mail to his favorite air idol is over. It just doesn't happen. I make exception for such phenomena as Frank Sinatra, and the like. In that case, you have a lot of so-called fan-mail. But actual expression of opinion about what the program does, or does not do, is very rare indeed. In sixteen years in radio, I have only run into a dozen such letters, more or less. People who listen to the radio underestimate their own importance. They just don't write letters."

Harry W. Flannery, news commentator: "May I also comment on what the last speaker said? He is on a program on which they probably don't get letters. I get a lot of them. I have been called a Fascist and I have been called a Communist. I quoted this Conference in my broadcast, and the pamphlet on the NAM came to me the day after the meeting opened, and I considered it significant. I considered it the sort of thing you would mention and I, therefore, mentioned it.

"In regard to letters, they do have their advantage, because I think they are not as numerous as they were in the old days. Most of the writers do not write in on the soap operas but on news-commentary programs, which is the type I have; and every letter is read. I consider it important to figure out what the people are thinking about and whether they are for or against what I say. Everybody has a right to disagree with what I say and I have a right to give my opinion.

"Some of the letters will be effective, but I hope you won't go so far as to carry this to the point of embargo. The late Boake Carter went off the air because of an embargo. I have been threatened many times from both sides. People have written my sponsor saying they don't want me on the air because they don't agree with my opinion. I have a right to my opinion, but I think your method should be fair and not deprive anyone of expressing an opinion."

Victor Shapiro, publicist: "I want to take exception to what Mr. Flannery said. I understand a young man called him up and objected to some remarks he made, and Mr. Flannery answered, 'You have the same right to speak as I have.' The gentleman doesn't happen to have CBS to speak on, and I think that was the most unfair crack he could have made to this man."

A member of the audience: "I would like to suggest that a Listening Post be set up here in Hollywood to transcribe programs that have consistently shown wrong presentation of facts, and thoroughly analyze these programs sentence by sentence. We could then write constructive letters on them, as individuals or as a group. We could also have a discussion of the contents of the programs, even if they originate in New York, by taking what actually went over the air, an air-check record, and analyzing that."

Chairman Brown: "Mr. Emil Corwin may be interested in saying a few words about the FCC Committee hearings he attended."

Emil Corwin, writer: "I wasn't prepared for this, but I would like, indirectly, to answer the first question that was made by the young lady who wanted to know how effective pressure groups can be. I think there are three instances that come to mind immediately which would answer that. Marvin Miller mentioned the NAM program, *Businessmen, Look to the Future.* I happen to remember that the time was given free in New York over the Mutual network and the first program had to do with the housing situation. The point of view of businessmen only was given, and the Political Action Committee, then forming, protested to the Mutual station, WOR. Mutual, without quibbling, said 'You may have a quarter-hour at an equivalent time to answer the NAM.' PAC ·put on a program to answer the NAM, transcribed that program and had it broadcast over several stations which had previously carried the NAM program. Which shows you how simple it can sometimes be to get time to answer the other side.

"Another good example of protest action was cited by Marvin Miller, in the Columbus, Ohio, case. The UAW decided to do something about the censorship on Station WHKC there, and because they decided to do something about it the NAB revised its Code, which I consider one of the most important developments in free radio.

"A last instance of the effectiveness of protest and pressure can be found locally in the case of the Emergency Committee on KFI, which for more than a year protested the arbitrary dismissal of a half-dozen commentators from the station. Many of you may not know it, but FCC decided not to renew the KFI license outright. They gave only a temporary renewal from month to month, or three-month period to three-month period, and that very greatly worried Mr. Anthony who owns and operates one of the most powerful stations in the country.

"In that connection, the California Committee for Radio, which grew out of the Emergency Committee on KFI, did quite a bit of protesting on its own at the FCC hearings here. I hope that when the new committee Sam Moore has spoken about is organized at PCA, it will be very much concerned with the hearings held here supposedly for a handful of applicants for radio-stations. These are public hearings. The people can attend and can ask questions of people who want to run radio-stations, as we have done here and in San Francisco."

A member of the audience: "I would like to suggest another channel of exerting pressure through those sections of the press which are available to the people, the Negro press, the labor press, the community press. As an example of that, here is something that happened on the Red Skelton show. They have a Negro on that show, Wonderful Smith, and they had been pointing bad jokes at him about his color, all in very bad taste. One week, they had a particularly bad joke and when he got to it he hesitated and said, 'You know, there are certain sections of the Negro people who won't like this. I've seen columns in the Negro press criticizing me for doing these lines.' The Skeltons were appalled that anybody would feel that way, so they pulled the joke out of the script. I don't know what they've been doing since then; I haven't been listening in. But certainly that kind of pressure is effective and it corroborates the fact that broadcasters are sensitive to public opinion."

Sam Balter, news commentator: "I don't know what I can add to this discussion.

"I'm thrilled by the speeches that have been made here. I recognize sections from them. I have made similar talks in the past and I'm always worried about the one important question, 'What can we do about them?' I think we're aware of these facts. I'm aware of Mr. Richardson of KMPC and I'm happy to mention his name, the Little Colonel McCormick in town who sends in seven paragraphs of Upton Close which have to be on the next newscast, and if they are not there the newscaster is fired. He forbade the mention of Henry Wallace's name and refuses to have Negro music played on his station.

"There are sponsors who have tried to buck the NAM. They felt a voice should be heard, but they had to stop because they couldn't get their goods. They were threatened that they wouldn't get merchandise or material to sell, and finally had to cease sponsoring liberal commentaries. What do we do about people who are liberally-inclined and progressive, who want to sponsor these things, but are frightened out of it? I think that's an important fact. Most of us know about thought control. It certainly exists, and I think Mr. Flannery can vouch for that, even though he tries to steer a middle course. I think Mr. Flannery tries to express an opinion here and there; otherwise he would be just a newscaster."

A member of the audience: "I think one of the most exciting things in a Conference like this is that the problems of radio people and film people are put on the same floor for discussion and out of it comes a common program. One thing that has been suggested in the

174

other panels is that the Arts, Sciences and Professions Council of PCA, nationally, immediately raise the money for a national broadcast of at least a half-hour once a week, looking toward a half-hour or fifteen-minute every-day broadcast. This should be one of the major things coming out of this Conference. We should set up our own national broadcast with some of the talent, artists, writers, musicians, news-commentators that are available to us. I think we are the only group that could put Einstein on the air, for instance. I would like to suggest that this be adopted as a resolution."

Chairman Brown: "In connection with that, we do hope to set up a meeting of the people who have attended this Panel and those interested in this subject for further discussion."

A member of the audience: "There has also been a proposal that the ASP, nationally, working together with all of us, set up a Mental Consumers' Union. They have told us in the past about impure foods and poisoned drugs, and I think we should have a Mental Consumers' Union to tell us if our kids are getting poisoned in school, if we are seeing anti-Semitic plays, and I think this Union should embrace all the fields of the Arts, Sciences and Professions. It should put out a monthly, or fortnightly, Mental Consumers' Guide News. It should take in books, radio-programs, magazines, films, schools, schoolbooks, etc. I think that this, too, is another good idea that would work with the individual Listening Posts."

Chairman Brown: "You're suggesting on a national scale what can be called a Mental Consumers' Union to issue Mental Consumer Reports to PCA and all others it can reach. At this point it is most important to say that those of us who are so tremendously interested in these problems can't do much about them without organized strength. That is the main purpose and promise held out by these Thought Control Panels. If we get together and fight against the abuses we see, we can accomplish something. If we try to do it alone, in the privacy of our homes, we cannot. Therefore, I urge you to join PCA and ASP. If you're interested in radio matters, then join the Radio Division of ASP. As you leave this hall you will find radio cards on the desk. Sign them and designate the division you wish to join. You will be doing a service to the PCA and, more important, a service to yourselves."

During the course of this discussion, the following five resolutions were moved, seconded and unanimously carried:

RESOLUTIONS

I. ON LISTENING POSTS.

Whereas, freedom of the air is under relentless attack by the forces which control radio today; and

Whereas, the preservation of liberty demands that this attack be met by a concerted counter-attack on the part of the American people;

Now therefore be it resolved, that the Radio Division of ASP set up people's Listening Posts to keep constant vigilance over the manner in which the people's air is being utilized;

Be it further resolved, that the Radio Division correlate the findings of these Listening Posts and recommend appropriate action, both of approval where it has been earned and of censure where it is due;

Be it further resolved, that the findings of these Listening Posts and the recommendations of the Radio Division be publicized in the widest possible manner.

II. ON FREEDOM OF THE AIR.

Whereas, the radio-stations of this country have been following a policy of systematically dropping liberal commentators or of seriously curtailing their right of free expression; and

Whereas, the number of conservative and outright reactionary commentators has, on the other hand, been allowed to increase;

Now therefore be it resolved, that the Radio Division of ASP undertake to rouse the American people to the dangers inherent in this thought control;

Be it further resolved, that the Radio Division co-operate with the California Committee for Radio Freedom and all other organizations in the fight to secure freedom of the air for the American people;

Be it also resolved, that the Radio Division protest to the local Los Angeles stations and the networks demanding a reversal of their discriminatory practices; and

Be it further resolved, that the Radio Division call upon the Federal Communications Commission to carry out its stated policy of guaranteeing the right of the American people to hear all points of view.

III. ON RACIAL DISCRIMINATION.

Whereas, we believe in radio as a potentially great medium of art, reflecting the aspirations and struggles of the people for peace, democracy and security and as a cultural force capable of contributing to social progress,

Be it therefore resolved:

1. That the Radio Division of the Progressive Citizens of America organize forums, seminars, lectures and publications in order to stimulate greater interest in radio as an art medium, to raise the cultural level of radio and to achieve a dynamic social content in radio;

2. That a committee be formed, including representatives of national Negro, Jewish and other minority groups and organizations, whose goal shall be the elimination of stereotypes from radio programs, and the portrayal on the air of the life of the Negro people, the Jewish people, and other minority groups in a positive, truthful and realistic manner;

3. That in addition to fighting for the elimination of stereotypes in radio characterizations, PCA and the specially-formed committee mentioned above bend all efforts toward curbing discrimination against Negroes and other members of minority groups seeking employment in the radio industry.

IV. ON THE WHITE-WOLVERTON BILL.

We find that the Federal Communications Commission under the present law has the power to require certain program service for the public interest, convenience and necessity.

We further find that the White-Wolverton Bill now pending in Congress will not serve to carry out this purpose, but that this Bill will tend to jeopardize civil rights and real freedom of access to the air by the people.

Therefore, we resolve that the Federal Communications Commission be urged to carry out at once such power and its duty to the public by requiring of every licensee or applicant for a license or for a renewal, that it devote each day a percentage of its broadcast-time during popular listening-hours to sustained programs concerning public, social, economic, educational and political problems and issues, and that all segments of the public be afforded an opportunity to be heard on such programs.

We further resolve that Congress be urged to pass legislation making mandatory upon the Commission to enforce such obligations on licensees, applicants for licenses or applicants for renewals of licenses.

We further resolve that this Conference go on record as opposing the passage of the White-Wolverton Bill.

V. ON LABOR-SPONSORED PROGRAMS.

Whereas, radio is becoming increasingly the voice of America's vested interests, and progressive programs are being driven from the air; and

Whereas, the voice of organized labor should be heard regularly through union-sponsored programs from coast to coast;

Be it resolved, that the Radio Division of PCA form a committee, with representation from its own membership and from the ranks of organized labor, to investigate the problem of labor-sponsored programs and make recommendations which will help put such programs on the air.

THOUGHT CONTROL IN U.S.A.

• • • • • • • •

No. **3**

LITERATURE
MUSIC
THE ARTS
ARCHITECTURE

THOUGHT CONTROL IN THE U. S. A.
The collected proceedings of the
Conference on the Subject of Thought Control in the U. S.,
called by the Hollywood Arts, Sciences & Professions Council, PCA,
July 9-13, 1947

Edited by Harold J. Salemson
Designed by Herbert D. Klynn
Published by Hollywood A. S. P. Council, P. C. A.,
1515 Crossroads of the World, Hollywood 28, Calif.

Printed in the U. S. A. by union labor
Aldine Printing Co., Los Angeles, Calif.

(111)

literature

Friday, July 11, 1947, 8:00-10:30 P. M.

Donald Ogden Stewart, Chairman

Speakers: Philip Stevenson, Albert Maltz, George Tabori

Participating in discussion: Arnaud D'Usseau, Millen Brand, Wilma Shore, Berkeley G. Tobey, Leslie Edgley, Arthur Laurents, George Sklar, Milton Merlin, Dorothy B. Hughes, Leo Penn, Waldo Salt

Philip Stevenson
Author, novels, The Edge of the Nest, The Gospel According to St. Luke's; co-author, play, Counterattack, screenplay, G. I. Joe, etc.

BACK WHERE WE CAME FROM

THE political events of 1947 have a strangely familiar ring. We've been here before. In fact, we might define the American way of life as an uninterrupted struggle by the people to establish, preserve and extend basic civil rights—the rights of free expression, assembly and organization—*in their own interest*—against a powerful few who would impair or abolish them.

Those of you who attended the opening session of this Conference were given a scholarly, overall picture of the history of thought control in America. I can assume, therefore, that you understand the function of the smear—of name-calling and denunciation—in paving the way for the destruction of constitutional rights by legislative and juridical means. You have had a look through the tele-

179

scope. Now, perhaps, it may be useful to examine a small segment of that field under the microscope—to analyze one battle of this never-ending war.

Three months ago, when Henry Wallace went overseas to plead the cause of the United Nations and world peace, he was denounced as a traitor to his country—a foreign agent—a tool of the Kremlin. In the American Congress it was seriously proposed that on Wallace's return he be prosecuted under the Logan Law of 1799.

What was the Logan Law?

The question is interesting. To answer it, we must go back where we came from—back to the time of the Founding Fathers,—specifically, back to the fateful year of 1793.

In 1793, the Jacobin Society took over control of the French Revolution. The French King and Queen were tried for treason, convicted and executed. Understandably enough, the castles and courts of Europe trembled — this was *lese-majeste* on the grand scale, and henceforth no crown and no title was safe. To protect their prerogatives, therefore, all the crowned heads of Europe came together in a coalition under the leadership of George III of England to make war on France, to smash the Republic and the Revolution that had established it.

What did this European quarrel have to do with America? A good deal, it seems. "This summer," Thomas Jefferson wrote in May, "is of immense importance to the future condition of mankind all over the earth, and not a little to ours." King George was our traditional enemy. We had fought a revolution to free ourselves from his tyranny. In that revolution France had been our only, our indispensable ally. In 1793, she was the only other republic on earth, and we were bound to her by a treaty of friendship and mutual aid.

So, the American people took these events in Europe with great seriousness. Clearly, the majority were grateful to and sympathetic with the French. Crowds wearing liberty caps surged through the streets of American cities calling for all-out aid to the French Republic.

However, there was a powerful minority that sided with the coalition of Kings—the people Hamilton called "the rich and well-born",—the bankers, speculators, merchants trading on British capital, Tories who had been on the British side during our Revolution. Quite frankly these gentry feared that unless the Jacobin revolution were crushed in France, America might "become infected with democracy."

The Hamiltonians were well entrenched in the government. Through their Federalist Party, they controlled both Houses of Congress and could count on the support of two, sometimes three, out of the four members of the Cabinet. If America became involved in the European war, it must be on the side of England, they decided.

The main obstacle to their plans was, of course, the majority of the people, who were beginning to organize in the Democratic-Republican party. The leader of this party, Thomas Jefferson, had a tremendous popular following. He was the revered author of the Declaration of Independence, which had asserted that whenever any form of government destroyed the inalienable rights of a people and subjected them to despotism, "it is their right, it is their duty, to throw off such government, and to provide new guards for their future security." He passionately believed that "the mass of mankind has not been born with saddles on their backs, nor a favored few booted and spurred, ready to ride them legitimately, by the grace of God." Of the French revolution he had said in January: "The liberty of the whole earth was depending on the issue of the contest . . . Rather than it should have failed, I would have seen half the earth desolated." To Lafayette he had written: "We are not to expect to be translated from despotism to liberty in a feather-bed." In 1793, there could be no question where he stood. As Secretary of State he could fight Hamilton face to face in the Cabinet and perhaps influence the crucial decisions of President Washington.

In Congress he had such able lieutenants as Madison, Monroe and Gallatin. Philip Freneau, the celebrated Poet of the Revolution, edited the *National Gazette,* a Democratic-Republican paper in Philadelphia. Benjamin Franklin Bache, Thomas Adams, Thomas Greenleaf, William Duane, fought the people's cause in other newspapers, and countered the war propaganda in the Federalist press. Through the efforts of such men as these, war with France was barely avoided in 1793. As soon as the crisis was past, Jefferson resigned from the Cabinet.

But the minority did not give up its plans. France continued to be treated as a potential enemy, and sympathy for her struggle against the Kings was denounced as "subversive of every American principle."

To cut the story short, after five years the Federalists managed to bring on another war crisis.

By 1798, George Washington was in retirement. John Adams was President. Jefferson, who had barely missed the presidency by three electoral votes, was Vice-President. The Federalist party was in the saddle and spurring hard toward open war with France. 1798 was a Congressional election year. It was now or never for the Federalists, one of whom, Fisher Ames, candidly declared: "We must make haste to wage war, or we shall be lost."

To point the crisis, President Adams, at Hamilton's suggestion, declared May 9 a day of national fasting and prayer. But it produced little fasting and no prayer. War-like speeches thundered in public squares, in college halls, even from fashionable pulpits. And that night violence broke out. Democratic editor Bache's windows were smashed by a mob, and a statute of Benjamin Franklin in Philadelphia was smeared with mud.

This was the signal for a deluge of war propaganda in the Federalist press. Columns were filled with hysterical reports—from the usual "unimpeachable source," no doubt—that the French had already landed on American soil, were burning and pillaging settlements, murdering babies and raping women.

The Democrats saw no honest reason for war—particularly not war on the side of the European Kings against our sister republic— and they vigorously opposed all measures leading to war. As a result, they were denounced as "French Jacobins," "anarchists," "atheists," "spies," "traitors" and "foreign agents." Jefferson, Vice-President of the United States, was under surveillance. Snoopers in the Post Office interfered with his mail, so that for two years he wrote almost no political letters. Hired musicians played the *Rogue's March* under his windows at dawn.

A Federalist paper replied to the Democratic plea for peace:
"And yet the word 'peace' re-echoes through our land! O Shame! O Lasting Disgrace! Rivers of blood will not wash it away! The only reply is a blow on the head—a smashed mouth—a kick in the guts!"

As we now know, no French soldier ever set foot on American shores. Nevertheless, the propaganda worked. Hysterical fear seized the people. Congress was in panic. There were smashed mouths and kicks in the guts on the floor of the House. In a frenzy of haste, bills were passed creating armies, a brand-new navy, fortifications, heavy taxes, war-loans.

It is interesting to note that although the "rich and well-born" applauded these war measures, their patriotism was not sufficient to induce them to buy war-bonds at the legal rate of six percent. They demanded—and Congress promptly gave them—eight percent.

There were the inevitable scandals over defective war-materials and profiteering in supplies. When it came to commissioning officers for the new army, Democrats were virtually excluded on the ground that their loyalty was in question. And Federalists demanded the firing of all Jeffersonians among the workers in war-plants.

Even these measures failed to give the Federalists the security they needed for an open declaration of war. The people still resisted. All opposition, therefore, must be suppressed.

First, an Alien Bill was passed that made thousands of immigrants liable to deportation.

But the climax came when the Federalists steam-rollered through Congress the infamous Sedition Bill.

Although war had not been declared, the Sedition Bill specifically named the French people as the enemies of the American people and condemned sympathy for France as sedition. Still worse, under this law *any* criticism of *any* act of *any* government official could be construed as "criminal libel," punishable by heavy fines and imprisonment.

That, mind you, was the "moderate" form of the bill, as finally passed by Congress. In its original draft, it had carried the death penalty.

In summing up the Democratic opposition to these bills in the House, Edward Livingston declared:

"Like the arch-traitor we cry 'Hail Columbia' at the moment we are betraying her to destruction; we sing 'Happy Land' when we are plunging it in ruin and disgrace."

James Madison, too, saw clearly what was going on. "Perhaps it is a universal truth," he wrote to Jefferson, "that the loss of liberty at home is to be charged to provisions against danger, real or pretended, from abroad."

As for Jefferson, he characterized the Alien and Sedition Acts as "a libel on legislation . . . an experiment on the American mind to see how far it will bear an avowed violation of the Constitution."

"The friendless alien," Jefferson declared, "has been selected as the safest subject of a first experiment; but the citizen will soon follow—

183

or rather, has already followed, for already has a Sedition Act marked him as its prey." These laws, he warned, "unless arrested at the threshold, necessarily drive these States into revolution and blood, and will furnish . . . new pretexts for those who wish it to be believed that man cannot be governed but by a rod of iron."

In other words, the real war was against the American people—against the republican form of government. The undeclared war on France was an hysterical device to blind the people with patriotic fervor while they were being systematically robbed of their hard-won liberties.

Among those who believed in a peaceful settlement with France was Dr. James Logan, a Philadelphia Quaker. Dr. Logan paid his own way to France to study at first hand the sentiment of the people and their leaders toward America. Presently, his letters home were stressing the fact that the French did not want war—least of all with their brother-republicans in the United States. And naturally the Democrats did not keep this evidence secret.

The Logan letters were a telling blow at the plans of the Federalists. In retaliation, they denounced the gentle Quaker as a traitor, and their partisans in Congress rushed through the Logan Law, making it a felony for a private citizen to meddle in international affairs. Doctor Logan was able to establish that he had in no way meddled—that he had merely asked questions—and he was not prosecuted. Merely smeared.

So far as I know, no one has ever been prosecuted under the Logan Law. Which makes it all the more appalling that after 148 years it was trotted out as a threat against a former Vice-President and member of the Cabinet.

It is significant that only Democrats were prosecuted under tne Sedition Act. Against them, the law was enforced with ferocity. U. S. marshals were instructed to keep Democrats off the juries. In the first three months of the Act, 21 Democratic editors were jailed and fined for opposing war or criticizing the government.

Congressman Matthew Lyon, who edited a paper called *The Scourge of Aristocracy*, was fined and thrown into a dungeon in spite of the fact that he was an elected representative of the people. Another publisher, Dr. Thomas Cooper, was convicted for criticizing President Adams' warlike measures in time of peace—the new army and navy, the eight percent war-loans, etc. The notorious federal judge, Samuel Chase, solemnly decided that the very existence

184

of the army and navy were proof the country was *not* at peace—that Cooper had therefore published a criminal libel! He fined Cooper $1,000 and sent him to prison for six months.

In New York, a State Senator was convicted for the crime of circulating a petition for the repeal of the Sedition Act. In the same state a paper editorialized: "When a man is heard to inveigh against the Sedition Law, set him down as one who . . . deserves to be suspected."

Some printers who escaped arrest had their presses smashed and they themselves were beaten up by soldiers of the new army. Mobs attacked signers of petitions in churchyards. It was the reign of terror.

What did the American people do about it? They did what they have always done when their liberties were destroyed. They fought back. They reelected Matthew Lyon to Congress while he was still locked up in jail. And they organized—openly where they could—secretly where they couldn't. They formed a network of Democratic Clubs in preparation for the presidential year of 1800. And they never relaxed their pressure against the phony war with France—the new "army without an enemy"—the eight percent loans—war taxes—but especially against the Sedition Act.

In 1799 Jefferson could write: "This summer is the season for systematic energies and sacrifices. The engine is the press. Every man must lay his pen and his purse under contribution." New newspapers appeared to take the place of those suppressed. Pamphlets and petitions circulated by the hundreds of thousands.

The Federalists had sown the wind of oppression; now they reaped the whirlwind of depression. There was a sharp financial crisis that sent some of their own leaders to debtor's prison. Even so, they made a half-hearted attempt to turn hard times to good account. A Federalist paper promised that "war with France would within two months revivify every department of society, commerce would be invigorated, and the funds would rise." But it was already too late. War now was impossible—not only because of depression, but because Napoleon was beating the combined military brains of Europe. The Federalists' only chance was to win the election of 1800 by hook or by crook.

They tried both. There has never been a more vicious campaign. Congressman John Allen warned that the election of Jefferson would destroy the Constitution, result in anarchy, wreck the financial system, and bring on civil war. The New England states, he threatened, would secede. The Reverend Cotton Smith accused Jefferson of having acquired his property by robbing a widow and her children of their estate while acting as their executor.

But the full flavor of the Federalist campaign comes out in the solemn jeremiads of the Reverend Doctor Timothy Dwight, President of Yale College, better known as the Pope of Federalism. Why, asked the reverend doctor, should good Americans vote for Jeffersonians?

> "Is it that we may change our holy worship into a dance of Jacobin frenzy? and that we may behold a strumpet personating a goddess on the altars of Jehovah? . . . Is it that we may see the Bible cast into a bonfire? . . . Is it that we may see our wives and daughters the victims of legal prostitution? soberly dishonored? speciously polluted? the outcasts of delicacy and virtue? the loathing of God and man?" And so on for pages.

To cut the story short, the people answered the rhetorical questions of Pope Dwight by voting in a landslide for the Democrats. Jefferson—the "Jacobin," the "anarchist," the "atheist," the "foreign agent"—became President.

What did the Federalists get out of their seven years of effort? They didn't get their war with France. They didn't get a return to monarchical forms. They didn't even secure their own aristocratic rule. At most, they postponed democracy a few years. But, in the end, like every clique of the favored few that has tried to suppress the people's rights, they got—oblivion. They never won another election. Within a few years, their once-powerful party was extinct.

That is the lesson of the 1790's—a lesson it is well to remember in 1947. Now, as then, under threat of war with a radical foreign government, hysteria is being created. Now, as then, all who resist panic—including a former Cabinet member and Vice-President— are branded as radicals, tools and agents of a foreign power. Now, as then, the people are being subjected to thought control—by dubiously constituted Un-American committees—by thought-police operating under arbitrary executive decree—by legislation like the Taft-Hartley Act. Now, as then, the friendless alien is persecuted for asserting his right to speak, and citizens are prosecuted for such newfangled crimes as "conspiracy to commit contempt"—whatever that may mean. And finally, now, as then, under cover of this patriotic frenzy, the people's pockets are being picked by inflation; their rights and their standard of living are being systematically destroyed.

History does *not* repeat itself exactly, in spite of the startling parallels it presents to us. The fact that the American people have always fought successfully against all attempts to reduce them to subjection by the favored few, is no guarantee that they will win again this time. If we .look at history in perspective—as we must,— we will find they are in a worse jam today than they were in the 1790's. Then, they had a young and vigorous party, under inspired leadership, to help them fight their cause. The vote on the Sedition Bill in the House was very close — 44 to 41. Today . . . well, the vote on the Taft-Hartley Bill was 331 to 83.

Nevertheless, our task, like that of Jefferson and the Democrats of his time, is to arrest at the threshold these libels on legislation, and to organize the fight for a progressive democracy.

That's why we're here. And, for this task, our inspiration can be our own proud history.

Albert Maltz

Author, screenwriter; novels, *The Cross and the Arrow, The Way Things Are, The Underground Stream*

THE WRITER AS THE CONSCIENCE OF THE PEOPLE

IN the year 1902, Anatole France stood by the bier of Emile Zola and said this: "Zola was good. He had the candor and simplicity of great souls. He was profoundly moral. In his last books he revealed completely his fervent love for humanity. He sought to divine and to foresee a better society." [1] And a few moments later, in reflecting upon Zola's role in the great political struggle that convulsed France and that established the innocence of the abused Alfred Dreyfus, he said to the other mourners, the thousands upon thousands who had come to the funeral of this writer:

> "Envy him! He has honored his country and the world through an immense work and through a great action. Envy him his destiny and his heart, which made his lot that of the greatest: *he was a moment of the conscience of mankind!*" [2]

Profound phrase, profound tribute! The comment lives and has come down to us. Yet, perhaps we speak it too easily these days. We forget at what cost, by what effort, by what determination in the face of slander and hatred, Zola won the right to be called "a moment of the conscience of mankind." No man was more loathed and more calumniated in his time than Zola. It is too easy for us today to accept Zola as a great writer, to accept Dreyfus as innocent, to approve Zola's role in defending him. But what would we have said then? Would we have come forward to support Zola if we were his contemporaries and government officials called him a liar, generals in our army called him treasonous, newspapers and magazines distorted his words, lied about his purpose, maintained that he was an agent of foreign interests? Would we have been Zola's friends when, for his physical safety, he could no longer sleep in his own home—would we have been part of his body-

1. Matthew Josephson, *Zola and His Time*, p. 509.
2. *Ibid.*, p. 510.

guard on those several occasions when only force saved him from lynching? And would we have raised our voice or been silent when he was found guilty of libel in a court of law and sentenced to a year's imprisonment? The question has its relevance today.

Zola was not alone. He had allies in France and internationally. It was a young student, Marcel Proust, who went from door to door to gather signatures on a petition in favor of Zola. Men of science and men of letters came forward to support him. France, and then the world, were divided by the Dreyfus question. Anton Tchekhov wrote in a letter: "Our only topic is Zola and Dreyfus . . . Zola has grown three yards higher . . . and every Frenchman realizes that there is still justice on earth . . ."[1]

And so it is clear that Zola's right to be called "a moment of the conscience of mankind" was won very dearly. For the sake of truth and justice, Zola risked fortune, fame, security, personal freedom. He won and we honor him.

But there is a question to be asked: "What was Dreyfus to Zola?" Zola was an author, not a lawyer or a politician—what had he to do in the first place with the defense of a man on Devil's Island? Zola could write books whether Dreyfus was innocent or Dreyfus was guilty—or so it would appear. Was Zola a busybody—or a seeker after publicity—or a misguided author who was allowing his Socialist ideas to pervert his great literary talent? All of these things were said of him in explanation of his behavior.

What is the truth? It is this, of course: Zola *could not* write his books in peace while remaining indifferent to the fate of Alfred Dreyfus. The kind of writer Zola was followed from the kind of man he was. This is an obvious comment about all writers. The author who wrote *Borinage,* a compassionate portrait of French coal-miners, was the same man who was moved to defend Dreyfus.

The life and work of Zola are no accident. Nor is Zola an unusual type of man in the history of literature. Only by the degree of his success and prominence, perhaps, is he to be separated from the hundreds and thousands of other writers who, to the best of their ability, during all their lives or a part of it, also sought to be a moment in the conscience of mankind.

And none of this is accidental. It derives from the nature of the

1. *The Life and Letters of Anton Tchekhov,* translated and edited by S. S. Koteliansky and Philip Tomlinson, p. 253.

writing process, from the nature of writers and from the nature of Man.

I am not one to maintain that art is the product of only one type of mentality or temperament—or that it should have only one method or concern. There have been some writers, although not many, who have written out of a consuming hatred of life and people, and whose pages burn with cynicism, venom and despair. One reads them or not as one chooses. They are not without their insights and, if the belly can stand it, their protest has a meaning.

There are other writers whose preoccupation, both as citizens and authors, has been narrowly with themselves. It would be a great error to deny them their achievements in letters or an honored place in society. Our world is complex and we have seen that from the lyrical outcry of an individual, who may be neurotically maladjusted to his fellows, or pitiably narcissistic, there may come a work of literature that endows us all with a unique treasure.

And there are still other writers who are marked in their work, as in their lives, by a cool impartiality toward events, people, their times. Somerset Maugham once wrote of himself that the reason he could never be a truly great writer was that he didn't like people enough. Perhaps the future will judge that Maugham was wrong in so estimating his own work, I don't know. It is interesting, however, that Maugham here is regretfully commenting upon his temperament— he is not advancing an aesthetic. In this, he disagrees with not a few important, intelligent, well-meaning and respected arbiters of literature today, who would have us believe that the touchstone of a true artist always has been, and is, a cool impartiality toward social events. The mark of some writers has, indeed, been their indifference to the events of their times. This is what they were temperamentally as men, and we will evaluate their work for what it has to offer.

But the whole history of literature demands that we reject those who would build for us an aesthetic of impartiality, of dispassion, of cool indifference. These thinkers exist only by ignoring the record and the very lives of authors they frequently admire. "To see life steady and to see it whole" has been transmuted by them into the act of viewing life from the outer side of a plateglass window and both regarding it and writing about it as though it were a fascinating puppet show. Fascinating it is, indeed, but the action is real, the laughter or groans issue from human hearts, the blows draw blood—and it is not a show of puppets.

It has never been a puppet show to most writers and they have not been indifferent to the outcome of the action.

The history of literature is largely dominated by writers distinguished in their lives and work by their compassion for people and their love of people—rather than by their cynicism; distinguished further by their *partisan* espousal of those social movements in their time that were forward-looking, often radical. This is not the complete history of all literature, but it is as a matter of record its dominant trend. And how could it be otherwise? Writers, being human, have been moved by the suffering of other men. What is a writer to use as his material, if not the lives of his fellows? And if his heart be compassionate, his mind inquiring, his eyes perceptive, how can he avoid the portrayal of an imperfect world—or close his own heart to the longing for a better one? Since writers began to write, men have been in turmoil, and the world has been either in motion or convulsion. There has been not one day of tranquility, one day without human suffering, one day in which some human hearts have not hoped and dreamed of change.

Out of this fundamental has come much of the world's literature. Out of it also has come the fact, too little known and celebrated in our time, that vast numbers of the literary men and women of the past have been guerrilla fighters for unpopular causes. Not dispassion and impartiality, but the most intense partisanship, the career of citizen-author, author-warrior, in the defense of justice, of truth, of the cause of the poor, the suffering, the afflicted. The list of the great in literature is heavy with names of those who in their time were objects of censorship, who were social radicals, who were the subject-matter of police reports and the object-matter for slander, ridicule, misrepresentation and, always, bad advice. They were not all Zolas, these forebears of ours. Some grew weary, some became smug, some were confused, some were intimidated. Yet, it is to the eternal credit of many that they scorned the police reports with defiant courage, they accepted the slander with stubborn dignity, and they rejected the bad advice. Indeed, if only the literary and political Bourbons of each period had written their own histories of literature, it would reveal to us today that the writers of each generation have suffered to an astonishing degree from a series of related distempers, contaminations and corruptions; among these corruptions would be listed: the possession of ideas that were unusual and unaccepted or, even worse, unpopular with the powers that be—even radical; the corruption of leaving the writing-desk to talk and walk in the marketplace with other citizens, particularly members of political parties in opposition to the status quo; the corruption of being impolite, even noisy and demonstrative, in the face of human injustice; the corruption of having convictions and a measure of courage about them. And all of these contaminations and corruptions are the very reason we honor them today—the reason why they not only lived as they did, but wrote as they did.

There is a record here; it is too little known, too little honored, it has been persistently obscured. It is fitting that at a gathering of American authors in the year 1947 the record be dusted off and tribute paid—because tribute is needed for our own souls' sake. This is our heritage, whether we know it or not; it is one of the reasons that we today can write at all; I like myself to think of it as a shawl of finespun wool with which to warm ourselves in troubled times. We are all of us embattled in the present; a brief glance into the century gone by may lend us clarity.

In the year 1863, George Stearns, a Boston merchant who was an Abolitionist, sent a bust of Captain John Brown, only lately hanged as a criminal, to Victor Hugo. Why to Hugo? Because he was then in the course of 17 years of exile from Royalist France as the result of his participation in the Republican uprising of 1848; because he was a passionate democrat, a spokesman for the people, a supporter of the Abolitionist North in the war against slavery; because he was the author-citizen who, a few years later, was to support the Paris Commune.

Earlier in the century, in the year 1828, the Chief of Police of Milan sent a report to Vienna concerning a Frenchman newly-arrived in his city, by the name of Henri Beyle, whose pen name was Stendhal. The author of *The Red and The Black* was characterized as holding "the most pernicious political ideas," of having the insolence "to hold forth in the most damnable manner against the Austrian government" (then master of Italy), of being "an enemy of religion, an immoral man, and dangerous to royalty." [1] Stendhal was commanded never again to enter the territory of Lombardy.

It was four years before the writing of this police report that the first poet of Europe, Lord Byron, went to Greece as a volunteer to the revolutionary army fighting for Greek independence—and there died. We will recall that in our time other English writers died

1. Matthew Josephson, *Stendhal*, p. 319.

as volunteers in Spain—Ralph Fox, John Cornford, Christopher Caudwell.

And so let us ask of Byron, Zola, Anatole France, Stendhal—was their work great *in spite* of their passion for social justice, as some would have us believe, or because of it?

It was later in the century, in the year 1891, that the wife of Leo Tolstoy sent emissaries to the Tsar in an attempt to forestall the threatened imprisonment of her husband.[1] The occasion? There was famine in sections of Russia, it had been kept a State secret and the Tsar himself had denied that there was any famine. The Tsar was a liar. Tolstoy published the truth and was censored in Russia. He published abroad and the Minister of Interior recommended imprisonment if he would not keep silent. The newspapers attacked him, the Minister of Education prevented discussion of his work at Moscow University, spies watched him, poison-pen scribblers denounced him.

This was not the first time or the last that Tolstoy offended the powers that controlled his people. It was no different with other writers of his time. The great works of 19th Century Russian literature were not written by impartial observers to whom life was a puppet show. The police files of the period show otherwise: Sentenced to penal servitude in Siberia for revolutionary activity—the student, Fyodor Dostoevsky! Sentenced to prison for revolutionary activity—the author and playwright, Maxim Gorky! Arrested for entertaining dangerous political figures in his home—Leonid Andreyev! Resigned from the Academy of Arts and Letters—Anton Tchekhov, in protest at the Tsar's order to the Academy to expel Maxim Gorky. It is not recorded whether the professional literary blackguards of the time received Pulitzer Prizes.

This is part of the record of European writers in the 19th Century. Was it otherwise in our own land? Emerson, Thoreau, William Cullen Bryant, Longfellow, Whittier—selections from their work are to be found in the textbooks of literature used in every public school. No stench attaches to their name; they have been washed clean.

Their names stank in good society once! Do we recall what it meant, even in the Northern states, to be an Abolitionist in the bitter years between 1825 and 1860? Do we know that Abolitionist meetings were broken up by mobs, that Abolitionists were beaten, murdered and lynched, that William Lloyd Garrison, the editor, was dragged

1. Ernest J. Simmons, *Leo Tolstoy*.

through the streets of Boston with a rope around his neck, that the Reverend Lovejoy was shot and killed—that to be an Abolitionist was to accept slander, ridicule, misrepresentation, ostracism from certain circles, violence?

If we know all this, then we are ready for a rollcall of the writers who were not silent, who were not indifferent, who were not always in good taste, let alone good repute.

John Greenleaf Whittier! His first poem was published in a newspaper edited by Garrison. Prophet and poet of the Abolitionists, defender of so-called lawbreakers, he dedicated one of his poems "to friends under arrest for treason against the slave power." [1]

Richard Henry Dana! Author of *Two Years Before the Mast,* a lawyer as well as an author, legal defender of runaway slaves and those arrested for helping them.

Henry Thoreau! Member of the Abolitionist Vigilante Committee of Boston. He traveled the illegal Underground Railroad to guide a fugitive Negro to Canada. In protest against slavery, he refused to pay taxes. Thoreau, gentle, retiring author of *Walden,* who opened the doors of a Concord Church with his own hands and, despite warnings of violence, delivered from the pulpit "A Plea for Captain John Brown."

William Cullen Bryant! Newspaper editor as well as poet, fiery Abolitionist, defender of the rights of union labor when participation in a strike for higher wages was conspiracy against the law.

Walt Whitman! Fired from the editorship of the *Brooklyn Daily Eagle* for radical political sentiments, writing his first poem, *Bloodmoney,* in a burst of rage at the passage of the Fugitive Slave Law.

James Russell Lowell—Abolitionist; Henry Wadsworth Longfellow—Abolitionist; William Dean Howells, son of an anti-slavery journalist, partisan of labor unions, outspoken enemy of imperialism, defender of Tolstoy and Zola.

And let us pause for a moment over a man who gave funds and support to Captain John Brown. On the day that Brown was executed, he spoke of a gallows made glorious as a cross.[2] A leading member of the Abolitionist Vigilante Committee of Boston, he entertained in his home Harriet Tubman, notorious runner in the Underground, a lawbreaker with a price on her noble, black head. Platform speaker, agita-

1. *The Democratic Spirit,* edited by Bernard Smith, p. 236.
2. Henrietta Buckmaster, *Let My People Go,* p. 269.

tor, dangerous member of society—this is the record of Ralph Waldo Emerson.

These are some of the men who gave us our literary heritage. And the American national conscience as we know it today is, to no small degree, an inheritance also from them—from their works, their lives, their passion. But we have something to remember: it was Henry Thoreau, upon the passage of the Fugitive Slave Law, who said: "We have used up all our *inherited* freedom; if we would save our lives, we must fight for them." Let every American writer tack those words upon his desk and ponder them.

When we read our history and note that Emerson was denied the right to speak in Philadelphia in 1856, and prevented by a mob from speaking in Boston in 1861—do we observe with agitation that in the current year 1947, Paul Robeson was denied the right to speak in Peoria, Illinois, and in Albany, New York?

When we read Walt Whitman's poem, *Blood-Money*, do we ask if he would have been outraged by the Taft-Hartley Bill? Are we agitated? Do we protest? Do we muster our forces to repeal it?

When, in the year 1947, we read that *Citizen Tom Paine*, a magnificent and glowing novel by Howard Fast, has been banned from the public-school libraries of New York and Detroit, are we nauseated and alarmed? Do we raise our voices?

One of Emerson's associates in the Abolitionist Committee in Boston was a physician, Samuel Howe. Earlier he had been Chief Surgeon for the Greek revolutionary army, a volunteer like Byron. We honor him. Is it hard for us today to recognize that Dr. Edward Barsky, of New York, is owed equal honor? He served as a volunteer physician in the Republican forces in Spain, ten years ago. And are we aware that Dr. Barsky has just been declared guilty of contempt of Congress, and that he is now liable to a year's imprisonment?

We are writers; we honor Zola, we cherish the arts, we cherish our freedom. What shall we say, then, of this: that Professor Lyman Bradley of New York University—and nine others—physicians, lawyers, housewives, trade-union organizers—have equally been declared guilty of contempt of Congress and that they are now under sentence to jail?

And what shall we say of the fact that the novelist Howard Fast stands in their number, liable to a year's imprisonment? Howard Fast, more than any other writer in the history of our nation, has sung a hymn to democracy in his novels. What shall we say when the

195

prison gates close on him—we, who honor Zola and know that Dreyfus was innocent?

Of what are these eleven men and women guilty? They comprise the Executive Board of the Joint Anti-Fascist Refugee Committee, a charitable organization that has been sending aid to Spanish refugees from Franco. This is their crime, their real crime. The ostensible charge is that they refused to turn over their membership records to the Rankin-Thomas Un-American Activities Committee.

What a loathsome spectacle in our national life, when individuals who are the political scum of our nation are seated in Congress, and when they are given the power to intimidate decent citizens!

These eleven have refused to be intimidated. These eleven refuse to turn the names of anti-fascists over to the mercies of those who would reduce America to one vast concentration camp, who poison the atmosphere with slander and racial hatred, who are a living embodiment of all that is corrupt and evil in America. And, if ten thousand courts and ten thousand juries were to declare Howard Fast and his ten colleagues guilty, they would still be innocent of anything save human decency.

In our time, as in every other, citizens are forced to choose the way they will travel. This is a cruel problem and we might wish that life made things easier for us. It never seems to and we, who are writers, must also choose. When Howard Fast is declared guilty of a crime and is liable to a year in a penitentiary—then the shadow of Rankin has fallen across the desk of every other American writer. It will not leave of its own accord. The time has come for honest men and women of letters in America to spring to awareness. If free thought is a heritage we cherish, it begins to need defending. We will not continue in possession of it if too many of us are complacent or confused or too easily intimidated by the ancient cry of "radical." The men of letters we honor in the past were not complacent, they were not confused, they would not be intimidated.

At his trial for libel, Zola said:

> "All seem to be against me, the two Chambers, the civil powers, the military powers, the great newspapers, the public opinion which they have poisoned. And I have nothing for me but the Idea, the Ideal of truth and justice. And I am calm, I shall conquer." [1]

1. Matthew Josephson, *Zola and His Time*, p. 462.

And Garrison, in publishing the first issue of *The Liberator,* wrote this:

> "I will be as harsh as truth and as uncompromising as justice . . . I am in earnest—I will not equivocate, I will not excuse, I will not retreat a single inch—and I WILL BE HEARD!"

This is our heritage. What we inherit, we have an obligation to defend and to enrich and to pass on. And if we do that, then we will be worthy of the name of writers.

George Tabori

Author, *Beneath the Stone,*
Companions of the Left Hand,
Original Sin; Hungarian-born,
now settled in England, visit-
ing U. S.

WHAT EUROPEAN WRITERS EXPECT FROM AMERICAN WRITERS

THE writers of Europe are facing fundamentally the same problem as you are over here.

Briefly, this is the problem of survival. Not in the mere bio-
logical, but in a higher, sense of the word; for a writer lives as long
as his works are read. This may perhaps sound too heroic. But
physical death has become a bore in Europe; it is too familiar to
terrify.

For the past thousand years, there have been persistent threats
to literary survival; sometimes by authority, sometimes by the writer who cut himself off from the sources of his inspiration—that is,
society; at times by society itself, when it felt that the writer was
either ahead of his time or lagging behind.

In our generation, the threat has been threefold, but from time
to time the emphasis has changed. Before and during the war,
authority was the main source of menace. Today, strangely enough,
it is the writer. He has more objective freedom than ever before;
both in the absence of restrictions and in the presence of opportunities. For a variety of reasons, a great number of European writers
are hesitating to make use of this new freedom. But, whenever you
hear the thin voice of despair from across the ocean, remember this:
the last decade may not have produced great and startling talents;
but it has created an immense and articulate audience. This audience
is waiting for guidance and inspiration; and, at the present moment,
it has to look for them beyond the boundaries of Europe; mainly,
to America. Hence I should like to speak tonight not as a writer, but
as a reader.

198

Interest in America is one of the few common factors which unite the two camps in Europe. More American books are being published and plays produced in Europe than ever before. Some of the greatest Europeans, as you know, have come to live in the United States. More will come, on a visit, to learn from you.

This new interest is both quantitative and qualitative. You may find it among the leaders and the people; those who work for peace and those who hope for war. A few months ago, for instance, I listened to a discussion about the fundamental similarity between the world of *Tobacco Road* and that of Eastern Europe. Last winter, there was a heated debate in London about the relationship between the Marquis de Sade, imperialism and Mr. Raymond Chandler. Three months ago, in Paris, we attended a crowded meeting which analyzed the social implications of a movie called *Mildred Pierce*. Dreiser, Hemingway, Steinbeck, Faulkner, O'Neill and others are now an integral part of European inspiration; similar to what Proust or Joyce used to be for the American writer. You may be flattered to know that the Existentialist novelists are vapid epigons of your own "tough school"; that Graham Greene, perhaps the most brilliant talent writing in England today, employs the method of the American thriller for his own brand of Catholic pessimism; that the monosyllabic sentimentality of Hemingway has invaded large parts of Western Europe.

On the other hand, people on the extreme Left often feel that it is the American novelist who has rescued realism from becoming dull and arid reportage. American prestige, in the best sense of the word, is higher than ever. Books like *For Whom the Bell Tolls* or *Grapes of Wrath* have given us hope and inspiration and the sense of being part of the same world; movies like *Winterset, Boomerang, Citizen Kane,* to mention a very few only, have convinced us that the film may after all develop into the most appropriate art-form of our age, the one which will truly express this rapidly-changing and always-inter-connected reality.

This literary interest is, naturally, connected with a political orientation, from which to some extent it emerges. Most Europeans today are convinced that the dynamism of our times lies in America; that the issue of war and peace will be decided not at the Dardanelles or on the Danube but mainly along the shores, in the mines and mills of the United States. Whatever happens in Europe today is largely a reflex conditioned by America. Every item of news from the States, a speech, a trial, a strike, is studied with the greatest interest, and often results in a corresponding speech or trial or strike. America is the battlefield, we believe; and let me add that those whom I should like to call the true friends of America have little doubt as to the outcome of your conflict. This may sound to you unduly optimistic. But we should never have survived without optimism; and, after all, there are some objective reasons for being hopeful.

Take, for instance, the various persecutory activities that seem to be so popular again. The other night, Mr. Lawson gave us an impressive survey from the American angle. Well, Europe has known these inquisitions for several thousand years; like death, in general, they terrify no more. The best and biggest of them all started in our generation. It managed to kill and burn about 35,000,000 people, but—to put it mildly—was a complete flop, achieving the exact opposite of what it set out to do. Europe today is more liberal than ever before; it is a liberalism won in blood and fury. It won't be lost.

There are, I think, two broad conclusions we have drawn from these inquisitions. First: they start by concentrating on a particular group of people—Chartists or Catholics, Jacobins or Jews,—but they usually go beyond their original task and try to engulf everyone who loves freedom and decency, and grow into one of those hyphenated Goebbelsian monsters such as the Judeo-capitalist-bolshevist-liberal-catholic-marxist menace. Secondly: so long as some people refuse to be intimidated, the inquisition will always defeat itself.

Thought control, part of all inquisitions, is a very familiar thing in Europe. We are past-masters at dodging censorships, which, as you know, may be of all sorts and degrees. 150 years ago, the actors of the Comedie-Francaise were discouraged from using the word "handkerchief" on the stage. Ten years ago, Attila Jozsef, one of the finest revolutionary poets that ever lived, was banned from reading his poem of welcome to Thomas Mann because he called Mann "among us mere whites a true European." A great-grandfather of mine was incarcerated for disseminating the ideas of a comparatively unknown French thinker named Jean-Jacques Rousseau. Four years ago, Budapest cafes had to remove the markings from certain doors because they corresponded to the initials of Winston Churchill. Successive European governments have used murder, imprisonment, threats and bribery to squash and pervert freedom of thought and expression.

But what should be of particular interest to you is the attitude of European writers toward this menace.

A century ago, at the time of an ascending liberalism, the choice was clear. Byron, Shelley, Schiller, Heine, Petofi and Boteff provided the argument that the poet should stand at the head of his society instead of lagging behind in isolation. They fought, they went into exile, they died for freedom. From 1848 on, the threat became more subtle, the choice more difficult. Then, the mission of liberalism was to solve its own contradictions, to renew and extend itself. Romanticism wasn't enough; those who clung to it became nostalgic squires like Flaubert, or apostles of heroic vulgarity like Wagner. By 1879, William Morris was speaking of an art cultivated by a few and for a few who would consider it necessary to despise the common herd. The artist thus withdrew from the world and fumbled with form, until we arrived at the brilliant mutterings of Proust, Joyce and Kafka on the one hand, the comic strip and the Nazi mass-meeting on the other. The generous and open realism of Tolstoy or Balzac had been forgotten, and the area of literature gradually reduced to a padded room, a spiral staircase and, finally, the tiny world of the nightmare. Politics—that is, the affairs of the public—were excluded from inspiration. A mythical character was invented and baptized the Individual; someone rather like the Wild Man of Borneo, who lived in a jungle of instincts and was supposed to be completely unaffected by war or peace, poverty or prosperity.

Thus, the "common herd" was left to the totalitarianism of trash. Those who set out to control thought had an easy time. The public, despised and rejected by its poets, was fed on irrationalism, mysticism and other forms of escape; literacy seemed to grow into a Frankenstein monster. But, so long as some writers kept their reason and so long as the heritage of freedom remained alive, the thought controllers had to proceed warily, according to a careful pattern. First, the means of mass-communication—press, wireless, cinema— were subjected to censorship; then, the stage, another direct and collective form of art; and, lastly, the novelist and the poet. Some of them, though very few, became outright traitors. Others were tricked into what Thomas Mann called state-protected escapism, a form of gentlemen's agreement between the State and the writer, under which the writer gave up his attack on the central abuses of the system in exchange for so-called poetic freedom. He was permitted to associate freely—not, of course, with his fellow-beings, but with words only; he was graciously allowed to invade and explore his own mind, provided he closed his eyes to his environment.

But it is in the nature of thought control that it can never be satisfied; that the greater the control, the greater the demand for freedom it creates; whence, a greater urge to control. So, in the end, the limited freedom of the poet and the novelist was also taken away; and in Europe books began to burn. The choice became clear again: fight back or keep silent; and silence is a terrible admission of defeat.

Some kept silent; and silence created guilt, and guilt more silence. But there were others, too. Lorca was murdered in Spain, Peri in France, Thomson in Bulgaria. Silone, Aragon and Malraux fought with gun and pen alike. Despite the monstrosity of occupation and mass-murder, the Forties were one of the most hopeful periods in European history. That unity of all good men which was and still is the condition of our survival was established. Perhaps you have heard the story of the French nobleman, an ardent Royalist if ever there was one, who kept an army of serfs on his estate, ready to attack the prefecture of the neighboring village the moment the Bourbons, or whoever the pretenders to the French throne are, came back. Instead of them, the war came, and the Germans. The Vicomte, who, I suppose, would have considered Neville Chamberlain a dangerous radical, became the head of an important Resistance group, his chateau a meeting-place for an assorted group of liberals. When he was asked by one of his former friends how he could possibly consort with such despicable rabble, the Vicomte drew himself up and replied: "I prefer a France going Red to a France growing red with shame."

You may now ask: What has happened to that unity? Was it merely a temporary response to danger? Was it ever sincere or practical? Could it be revived? And applied outside Europe?

At the first glance, the picture is fairly gloomy. Malraux, in his arduous search for a hero, has finally found him in Charles de Gaulle. The brilliant Koestler, on the other hand, brushes heroism away as a mere sublimation of childhood guilt, and has become so fascinated by the false dualism of ends and means that he has ended by not knowing what he means; condemning one kind of violence while eulogizing the other. The cops of Graham Greene have of late been chasing not Spanish Republicans but Mexican priests. Stephen Spender, who once wrote a book entitled *Forward from Liberalism,* is now afraid of being chased "down the communal corridors"—whatever he may mean by that. Others, finding salvation in Indian philosophy, are advising us to build mystic oases; this at a moment when India is at long last exchanging that philosophy for a more practical one.

Apart from the fraternity of pessimists, there is a new wave of irrationalism, a revival of the pre-war days when eminent scientists like Eddington and Jeans explained that the universe made no sense, expecting us to believe that they, being part of that universe, did. Then there are the various esoteric souls who ignore the dictum of the best of literary aristocrats—Thomas Mann—that modern man must state his spiritual problems in political terms; and the various exponents of philosophical idealism who want to persuade us that Dunkirk or Pearl Harbor, the gas-chambers or the atom-bomb, do not really exist except in a few superior minds.

But this is one side of the picture only; for, as the greatest European of the last century, Goethe, said, "There is nothing wholly tragic in existence." There are new voices, too; and they will have to be heard; for there is a new type of audience in Europe and Asia; about a thousand million people in the process of becoming literate. Some writers are frightened by this prospect. It may become very frightening indeed if true art and literature disappear in a kind of black market. This new audience wants to know about its world and itself; for knowledge is freedom. They will look for inspiration and information wherever they can get it. They are still patient; they wait and listen. They do not seek escape; for they have only just arrived; they're at our gates.

European unity, as I said before, is partly broken. But this creates the condition for a new and higher form of co-operation. Our unity has been broken mainly by extra-European pressure. If the writers of Europe are unwilling or unable to repair that unity, we, the readers of Europe, will look beyond our frontiers. The conflicts of the 19th Century created the great European novel. That background is not unlike the American scene today, and we hope that the writers of the new world will carry on the tradition of realism, and develop it, that they will give us perhaps a new Homeric art, for and by the people. The audience is there. What will they be like—people, conscious of their needs and hopes and fears; or an amorphous mass of morons for whom the world is but a "big, buzzing confusion"? It is a tremendous task, and there is only one way for the writer to perform it: by writing. Silence will be suicide for him and possibly for humanity.

And here I'd like to mention a man who has become quite a symbol in Europe. His name is Miklos Radnoti. He was a poet; and he had the unique privilege of being executed twice by the Nazis. First, he was severely wounded; then, lying in a pool of blood, before being propped up again and finally killed, he found time and courage to write a poem; it was discovered in his grave. It wasn't a very good poem; but a writer at his best.

FROM THE FLOOR

The discussion at the end of this Panel was extremely lively, including, outside of questions from members of the audience, some fairly lengthy presentations by well-known writers. Extracts from these statements, based upon notes taken during the debate, are presented below:

Arnaud D'Usseau, playwright: "As far as the theatre is concerned, thought control is not as severe as in the movies, but that is the only difference. A relative difference. People in the theatre cannot feel smug about it. The situation on Broadway is extremely serious. What you have to combat is not so much a thought control like a Hays Office, but a climate; and it can become very dangerous. I have been connected with two plays and they have been rejected by the top producers. In each case, Jim Gow and I had to go out and raise the money to put them on. After the plays opened, we got a visit from the Dies Committee. A road company of *Deep Are the Roots* looked set, and then it turned out the chief backer was a Southerner.

"*The Big Two,* for instance, seems innocuous, innocent. The play was well watered-down, it straddled, got nowhere and died. I don't think you can write anything in the theatre today. I think the critics are wielding a very bad influence in this country. The State Department is playing politics with the Vatican. I think it would be extremely difficult to put an anti-imperialist play on Broadway today. If a producer could get it on, the critics would turn thumbs down on it. I don't think we can be smug. That climate must be resisted. If one is familiar with the theatre, he knows there has always been censorship. Today in America, what censorship there is is political. While things are a little easier on Broadway than in Hollywood, I still think we have a long way to go."

Millen Brand, novelist: "I was teaching literature last summer at the University of New Hampshire. A representative of the Hearst press asked me for a statement on filth in literature and then I began looking at the Hearst press to see what they were doing about obscenity. I began reading a few of their headlines on obscenity. 'It is much better to have houses of prostitution than to talk about them in novels.' I thought about that and then I read on. I came across this handsome statement: 'Never in the history of American writing have books sold on the open market been so saturated with such degeneracy . . . They write their filthy stuff for one purpose—money'.

"There is a device called 'projection'. When you feel guilty about doing something horrible, you think someone else is busy doing it too.

"Then, in the news-columns, I saw Dr. Torrey Johnson, president of *Youth for Christ,* say, 'Nothing would catch the imagination of the people in the United States better than a bonfire of the lewd and filthy books in America'. The Nazis were fond of hollering about degeneracy. At the same time that the *Horst Wessel* was their song, they broadcast to the United States on three levels—high-class, popular and smut. There is a tie-up between this and the Hearst campaign . . ."

Wilma Shore, short story writer: "The magazine makes money not so much from your buying it as from the advertising that is sold. The connection between the source of income and the stories is fairly apparent. The editor of a magazine is in the middle, between the advertiser and the readers, and he has to suit both.

"Many people consider there is really no censorship except for minor taboos, but when a policy becomes pretty nearly universal it leaves the realm of individual taste and becomes *thought control.*

"The tendency to prefer the story with a happy ending, for instance, has a very definite effect on the thoughts of those who read the magazine over and over again. It tends to remove them from the realities of life. There is also the tendency to limit the subjects stories may deal with. For example, editors don't want any more stories about the housing problem, though many people are still living in garages and with their 'in-laws' and in other unpleasant conditions like that. If you had more stories dealing with the housing problem you might have more people working for adequate legislation for more housing.

"Some people feel that the editors try to give the people escapism. However, four or five of the current best sellers, fiction books, deal with race prejudice, and people are spending two or three bucks for these books . . ."

Berkeley G. Tobey, publishers' representative: "Before the war the book publishers in New York went along at a pedestrian pace, on the whole. They published a certain number of prestige books, a number of bread-and-butter books, and a few that might correspond to praying-for-rain. That is, they were always hoping for that phenomenon, *the best-seller.* Incidentally, who can predict what a best-seller will be? All the apocryphal stories in the world couldn't be as fanciful as the true ones on that subject. But let's leave the Cinderella books.

"There has been a decided change in publishing since the war. Before the war the publisher looked on himself as a public servant. He expected his cut on movie rights and admittedly cheap fiction to pay for what he seemed to think was his philanthrophy. But, at least, he did think of himself in the light of the humanitarian, the altruist, sometimes feeling somewhat degraded over the claptrap that kept the altruism in motion. He regretted in the old days that he didn't have the cash to run a purely literary house.

"The war saw the end of that fiction. There was a great change in publishing during the years of the war. In the first place, people began reading more. They bought more books everywhere. They were so hungry for books that they bought out the first editions in record time. In the Twenties, considered rich at the time, 1500 copies of a book was a good first printing, and if it sold out completely the pub- lisher at least broken even. But, if it didn't, the publisher often car- ried the writer through several books. Hemingway was considered a break because he was carried through only one book before he paid off. Sinclair Lewis was carried through three or four before he wrote a *Main Street*.

"But during the war the publisher tasted the big money. All at once, there was more than a profit in books. There was a possible jack- pot in every book. Those prestige first-novels, those socially-mature books that had been looked on as the jewel in the crown, were now selling. The usual 1500 edition jumped to five thousand, then to ten thousand copies at a first printing.

"That was when the publisher stopped fooling himself that he was a public servant. If he had been, he would have printed more books—that is, those books that he had been claiming for years that he would publish if he could afford it. Here was his chance. With everything he published either paying its way or making a small for- tune, he had now his opportunity to make good his boast.

"He didn't do it. Those controversial books that he had always claimed he wanted to publish were still being shunted aside. He was still haunted by fear. But a different fear. Now it was the fear that a book would not go into a reprint, that it had no chance with the book-clubs, that the movies would not buy it. And there was the in- creased cost of production.

"So, there was still the runaround. The publisher published as small a segment as before of the left-wing literature. That was one faction of talent that he was not yet ready to gamble on.

"Why? On the whole, all publishers have published an astonishingly limited number of books of a progressive nature. They are the first to be dropped, are seldom reprinted, and must completely pay their way, as is not true of other books—say, religious books, or art books. The publisher will still carry those, but not the novels, plays, biography and criticism of a socially-progressive nature that don't pay their way.

"Now, the back office—the sales staff—has really joined the front office, the editorial staff, not to mention the Board of Directors, in what may, in a sense, be termed thought control . . ."

Leslie Edgley, novelist: "In any discussion of censorship, I think we have to realize the lynchers' noose of the Wood-Rankin-Thomas Committee is also backed up by the invisible thumb screws of economic pressure. Writers have an understandable obsession about feeding and clothing themselves and their families, and publishers all agree publishers ought to make money. Right now, publishers and booksellers are engaged in a fight over the book-club question. In many cases, book-club subscribers are paying less for their books than are booksellers.

"I appreciate the financial problem involved and I think this fight is germane to a brief look at the book-club as a cultural force in our society—and as an instrument of thought control. Twelve months out of every year, some two million families have their reading material chosen for them and shipped to them like so many boxes of Wheaties or Pepsodent. There are fifty-two American book-clubs. One publishing firm alone controls four of the largest. That's Doubleday, with the Literary Guild, which has a million-and-a-quarter circulation, and three other clubs whose memberships run into the hundred thousands.

"Twenty-one years ago, the Literary Guild's first selection was *Anthony Comstock,* by Heywood Broun and Margaret Leech; it went to less than six thousand members. Its membership has increased twenty thousand per cent since then, and now its selections run almost entirely to novels like *The Black Rose* and the Daphne du Maurier effusions.

"The Book-of-the-Month Club had a modest start, too. Today I believe it has a membership of some 900,000, and its offerings are not always on the side of the angels. Book-of-the-Month and Literary Guild are the largest of these clubs, but many of the remaining fifty stick pretty closely to the traditions they've established. Their influence on the American reader is obviously tremendous. Their influence on the American writer is equally significant—and perhaps equally pernicious. With publishers telling both booksellers and writers that publishers need book-club sales to show a profit, it's just barely possible that the editorial boards that choose the monthly selections will determine what should and what should not be written by American writers.

"A few years ago, this might have seemed a little far-fetched, but not today. Publishers are taking fewer and fewer chances nowadays. The cost of publishing books keeps going up and up. Publishers consequently are going to accept only those manuscripts that look like possible sellers—and possible book-club selections. Writers are aware of that and, consciously or not, they're likely to write with one eye on those book-clubs. When this happens, of course, the novelist in particular finds himself using the novel as a mass medium, and writers for the mass media have a very real social responsibility.

"I know that *Kingsblood Royal* and some other recent book-club selections may appear to invalidate what I have said, but I am not suggesting that we damn the book-clubs out-of-hand. They are undoubtedly here to stay. But it seems to me progressive writers might start thinking about book-club methods of distribution for progressive purposes. Some years ago, I believe the UAW in Detroit formed its own book-club. I don't know what its present status is, but an investigation of the trade-union field might well be worthwhile for writers who want to be able to publish without benefit of censorship, and want to be able to say, 'This is the fight against reaction, here is the enemy, here is the role each of us plays if we wish to survive'."

Arthur Laurents, playwright: In comparing thought control in the theatre with thought control in Hollywood, the speaker felt that there was not very much, although it is true that the social play has a harder time getting on the boards because of producers, backers and actors. He thought that although most producers prefer plays like *John Loves Mary,* Bloomgarden and Clurman are not inclined to play safe . . .

The greatest thought control, he felt, comes from critics. Sometimes this is unconscious, although Atkinson, in reviewing *The Whole World Over,* used the opportunity to review Russia. In the case of *Finian's Rainbow,* the *Journal-American* raved about it, then suddenly turned against it.

He explained that sometimes thought control on the part of the critics is due to their double standard in viewing plays. An author, when trying to write a social play, of necessity is trying to write a good play, since you cannot write an artificial play about real people and real problems. And so the critics' standards go up, and they are apt to review such a play as if they were reviewing Ibsen or Shakespeare. The critics have never given an unqualified review to a social play, but they rave about things like *Life With Father* and *Harvey*. He felt that this accounted for the beating taken by *All My Sons*.

He also thought that in a way this affects playwrights. They are sometimes inclined to give up, rather than knock themselves out. But writers who succumb to this type of thing are more abundant in Hollywood than on Broadway.

George Sklar, playwright and novelist, pointed out that this is no time for complacency. *All My Sons* is the only social play of this year. Mr. Laurents' play was the only one last year, and Mr. D'Usseau's the only one the year before. In looking back over his own experience in the theatre, he realized that, of his six plays produced, four were censored in one form or another. In thinking about the history of the Federal Theatre Project, he felt that it was not something to be complacent about. He referred to the Federal Theatre as the high-water mark in the American theatre, mentioning Hallie Flanagan's *Arena*. The Federal Theatre was a people's theatre: prices at twenty-five to fifty cents; produced a thousand plays for an audience of twenty-five million; plays were brought to the people—on trucks, in schools, churches, town halls; everything from the Greeks to Marlowe; it brought out the talents of hundreds.

But what is most interesting in reading *Arena,* he said, is what happened to the Project—what the Congressmen who created the Theatre did to knife it, and the methods and mentality of hatchet-men who killed it: J. Parnell Thomas, Dies, Rankin. This is pertinent today, because we are dealing with the same mentality and methodology, the direct and indirect danger of the technique of the smear and of the red herring. The trouble started early, when *Ethiopia,* the first living-newspaper, was suppressed. Then *Turpentine,* the first Negro play, was attacked. *It Can't Happen Here,* co-authored by Jack Moffitt, was attacked by Dies as subversive. And, after a long series of bans and attacks, the big guns were turned on, with the Dies Committee investigation in 1938 and the Woodson Committee hearings in 1939. They attacked every play the Federal Theatre put on as either salacious or bearing the trademark of Red Russia.

It is a tragic commentary, he added, that it takes major calamities of war and depression to make things like the Victory Committee and the Federal Theatre Project. It is about time we started to make plans and fight for a national theatre. He hoped that we could someday have these things in peace.

Milton Merlin, book reviewer and radio writer, referred to the lack of thoroughgoing thought control in the book reviews he writes, and attributed this to the fact the *Los Angeles Times,* at the moment, does not consider literature as very important. *Dorothy B. Hughes, mystery writer,* stated that she believed writers in her category were especially favored and experienced no thought control at all. *Leo Penn, actor,* made a plea for writers to prepare material for a topical cabaret, which the Actors' Division of PCA, Cabaret Committee, is organizing.

Chairman Donald Ogden Stewart, who had stated earlier that ". . . one of the great dangers now is that you become your own censor, in terms of thought control. We ourselves are becoming a little bit afraid and we aren't writing what we should write because we know that nobody is going to buy it. That is going on and that, each of us must fight within himself . . . ", said in conclusion:

"I came here to be encouraged and I have been . . . It is terribly important to organize a continuations committee to organize PCA to do what we can about thought control. I think it is up to you to put yourselves in touch with that committee and carry on this fight."

Waldo Salt, screenwriter, rose to cite the growing importance of and attention to *Consumers' Union,* and felt that it was time we had an ASP Mental Consumers' Union, which would cover films, radio, school-books, to warn the parents and the readers of the impurities and poisons which exist in books, etc. It was resolved that there be an ASP-PCA Mental Consumers' Guide, published monthly or semi-monthly.

In addition to the above, the following resolutions were moved, seconded and unanimously carried by the Panel on Literature:

RESOLUTIONS

To the Board of Education, Detroit, Michigan
To the Board of Education, New York City, N. Y.

No author in recent years has done more than Howard Fast to rouse the interest of our people in the living reality of our national past. His novels re-dedicate the reader to a profound love of country, based on old struggles which are brother to struggles present and still to come, to maintain our American democracy and widen it so it may be truly a democracy for all peoples, races, religions, political viewpoints.

The students in our high schools, who are now forming the principles on which good citizenship is built, need to know our history, not only intellectually by text-book, but emotionally in a way the text-book can never teach it.

Therefore, we, 600 citizens of Los Angeles, in the Panel on Literature at the Thought Control Conference of the Progressive Citizens of America, strongly protest the withdrawal of Howard Fast's historical novels from the high-school libraries of Detroit (and New York City). We urge that your decision be immediately re-considered and these moving, honest books be returned to the shelves.

To the Los Angeles City Council, and to the
Office of the Los Angeles District Attorney:

The attempt to censor and control the thinking of the American people takes many forms. In a Los Angeles City court, Harry Wepplo and the Pickwick Bookshop are now being prosecuted for the possession and sale of Edmund Wilson's book *Hecate County*.

Conviction would set a dangerous precedent, because the concept of "obscenity" has always been an extremely tenuous one. It has varied with both time and place, meaning one thing in Boston, and another in Los Angeles. It is a convenient catch-all label for the peculiar prejudices of the censoring person or agency. The fact that this case has received major attention in the Hearst press, not widely known for high moral principles, leads us to believe that more is at stake than the alleged obscenity of Mr. Wilson's book. This case can open the way for attacks on all works which attempt honestly to deal with reality, both political and personal.

Therefore, we, 600 citizens of Los Angeles in attendance at the Literature Panel of the Thought Control Conference of the Progressive Citizens of America, strongly urge that charges against Harry Wepplo and the Pickwick Bookshop, be dropped. And that the whole basis for this type of censorship be seriously re-considered.

To the Hon. J. Parnell Thomas, Chairman, and the Members of the House Committee on Un-American Activities:

We, the novelists, short-story writers, poets and dramatists of the Hollywood Arts, Sciences and Professions Council of the Progressive Citizens of America, believing that the actions of the House Committee on Un-American Activities in their recent visit to Hollywood were those of a body determined to spread fear, not truth—and believing that a further proof of this un-American tactic of intimidation in place of fact-finding is the unjust persecution of the writer Howard Fast, the play-producer Herman Shumlin, and other members of the Executive Board of the Joint Anti-Fascist Refugee Committee,— do therefore, in the tradition of free American writers, protest the use of your Committee as an instrument of those who would, through fear and threats of imprisonment, suppress and control the expression of free thought in this country.

music, the arts and architecture

Thursday, July 10, 1947, 8:00-10:30 P. M.

Dr. E. A. Cykler, Chairman

Speakers: Mildred Norton, Phil Moore, Jarvis Barlow, Reginald D. Johnson, Edward Biberman

Participating in discussion: Sam Albert, Vincent Price, Earl Robinson, and members of the audience

Mildred Norton
Music critic, *Los Angeles Daily News*

THE MUSICIAN AS A CITIZEN

THE musician today lives and works in a world in social convulsion. Neither he nor his music can remain aloof. Both are inexorably caught up in the tide of history, and they can achieve significance, validity—perhaps even survival, only as they affect and reflect the most vital and progressive currents of our time.

It has always been the musician's function to chronicle his time. Homer was one of the first historians. The troubadors of the Middle Ages carried on the saga of the people in ballad and song. The musician of the 18th Century never doubted that he filled a definite place in the organization of the body politic.

Not until the rise of industrialism, with its need of a great, inarticulate laboring class, was the musician encouraged to betake himself to his ivory tower and leave the business of running the world

214

to less "impractical" people. The romantic fetish arose of the musician as a creature half-child, half-genius, who must not concern himself with the struggle his less talented brothers were making toward a more democratic life.

Inevitably,—Robert Burns to the contrary,—we come to see ourselves as others see us. Told that it was somehow "ill-bred" for a creative artist to concern himself with matters more concrete than his own psyche, the musician obligingly withdrew from the world's arena, his art became less actively identified with the social scene, the product of his talent became a luxury, and he himself became economically expendable.

Just whom is such a state of affairs designed to benefit? Surely not the musician, who forfeits his franchise as a human being when he accepts less than the full privileges of citizenship. Surely not the people, who have relied on the artist in every age to discover and codify the multiform needs of the human spirit.

Who does profit, then? Only one segment of society—the reactionary segment. The men of ill-will, who would make the hands of history stand still forever at the hour of their own greatest aggrandizement.

Reaction, which can only destroy, is in mortal terror of the artist's power to create. It must at all costs keep him from realizing his potency as an intellectual and moral force in his community, as an agency of progress throughout the world—as, in short, a citizen of his time.

The need for the artist to exercise these functions has never been so acute as in the present era of vicious anti-labor legislation, of federal "investigations" into the lives of private citizens, of spiritual and economic retrenchment from the ideals of the Four Freedoms, and of that arrogant, 21-gun salute to "dollar imperialism"—the Truman Doctrine.

Whether from the standpoint of artist *or* of citizen—and the two are indissolubly linked,—the musician cannot ignore the threat to his own security, menaced by an age that has split the atom only to split the world. Radioactivity is ruthlessly impartial. It makes no distinction between the possessor of absolute pitch and his tone-deaf neighbor.

Like anyone else, the musician is amenable to physical laws. He must eat. He must have a roof over his head. He must earn his living by the labor of his hand and brain. For, let's not be highbrow about it. The musician, like all productive ,workers, is a laborer.

The composer doesn't just *dream* his ideas onto paper. The concert pianist and the jazz trombonist alike spend millions of man-hours practicing their craft. Inspiration is fine, as far as it goes; but it takes plenty of perspiration as well, as any musician here tonight can tell you. The fact that the American Federation of Musicians has rolled up a national total of 175,000 members is proof that the musician recognizes his need for a strong union body to represent his interests as a workingman.

There is no longer any ivory tower to which he can flee from the reality of daily living. Our society is so complex that, when any sector of it is rocked, the musician feels immediate reverberations. When Congress enacts and the Supreme Court upholds a piece of legislation such as the Lea Bill, aimed, among other things, at cutting down the size of orchestras and thereby limiting job opportunities, the musician's professional and living standards both are placed in jeopardy. When reaction sponsors and our Senate and House of so-called Representatives jam through a Taft-Hartley Bill over the nationwide protests of the American people, the musician's right to bargain collectively as a ciitzen is placed in jeopardy.

When Hollywood Bowl, in the interest of "culture," denies its stage to the humanitarian message of Henry Wallace; when Paul Robeson's great voice is refused audience in Peoria and his program emasculated in Albany; when a respected composer such as Hanns Eisler is subjected to the brand of persecution from which he fled in Nazi Germany; when actors and writers of the motion picture industry are made the target for the latest Congressional witch-hunt,—the musician's right to reflect the truth as an artist is placed in jeopardy.

Today—our California textbooks are being "purged" by self-appointed arbiters of what our children may be taught. Tomorrow—may we expect to witness book-burning ceremonies in Pershing Square?

Today—Chaplin's latest film is faced with boycott by the theaters of Memphis. Tomorrow—shall our movie screens be permitted to reflect only the twisted precepts of Fascist dogma?

Today—our radio commentators are being silenced, one by one, whenever they try to present an undistorted picture of the economic scene. Tomorrow—shall we wake up to find our airwaves given over wholly to the calculated lies of Fascist demagogues?

Today—our Los Angeles County Museum is under attack for ex-

216

hibiting the works of contemporary artists. The President of the United States has embarrassed the American people before the eyes of the cultivated world by applying to our country's art the measuring stick of a Babbitt mentality. Tomorrow—may we expect to find all art except the most banal stigmatized as "decadent" and "subversive"?

The pattern of these instances is too defined to be purely coincidental. It is, moreover, a pattern we have come to recognize. We have seen it take shape in other countries, and we have seen the results.

Deliberate, organized control over words and pigment and tone is not new in the world. The Japanese under Hirohito and his warlords spent many years perfecting their own brand of thought control before they felt they could safely launch their people on a widespread war of aggression.

In Nazi Germany, only a certain kind of "art" was permitted, only a certain kind of writing, only a certain kind of music. Under the cultural tutelage of Hitler—who also didn't approve of "modern" art, you may recall,—an entire generation of German boys and girls grew up to consider prettily-colored picture postcards the epitome of artistic expression.

You may say that, compared with other things Hitler did to the German people and, through them, to humanity, this was a minor crime. But, if you do, you ignore the basic lesson we have learned from Fascism.

That lesson is, that a people's taste, a people's own culture, must first be thoroughly degraded and corrupted before that people is ready for the physical, military annihilation by Fascism of other peoples, and other people's cultures.

The timid, the inept, the imitative, the sterile, are the portion of the arts under Fascism. What great art emerged from Nazi Germany? None. Its legacies were the torture-rack and the gas-chambers of Maidanek and Dachau. Italy forfeited her artistic conscience as the price of Axis membership. Spain's great artists in every field are scattered in exile throughout the world—Manuel de Falla, who died last year; Pablo Casals, who carries on the fight against Franco as a signal example of a man who combines in his own person the most sovereign features of both artist and citizen.

Let us not fool ourselves that reaction in this country will somehow deal more indulgently with culture and with cultural workers than it has done in other countries. As Katharine Hepburn pointed out recently:

> "It is precisely these people—the writers, actors, scientists, educators—who have been chosen as a primary target by the Rankins, Tenneys and others of that ilk . . . Silence the artist, and you silence the most articulate voice the people have."

No matter how subtle, no matter how brazen, any attack against a country's artists has a twofold objective: one, to depress the living standard of the artist; two, to gain control over his product. The two go hand in hand, since any lowering of the artist's economic security makes him increasingly vulnerable to thought control and to artistic corruption.

Economic depression is the gestating period for political oppression. Rob the artist of his security, destroy his self-respect, and you inevitably drive him into the cartel of the thought control merchants, and their commodities of hate and tyranny.

But perhaps you may feel that the case in this country does not justify such alarm. It is true that there has been a little sniping, here and there, you say, but must we give it too much importance?

I cannot answer that. But there are men in this audience tonight—writers, painters, composers—who have seen with their own eyes the shaping forces of tyranny take form in their own lands. They can answer it.

These scattered attacks, which our artists have so far suffered at the hands of reactionaries, are merely the opening skirmishes of an all-out campaign which *will* be launched against art in *all* its phases, if we, as musicians, as artists, as American citizens, fail to challenge them, here and now!

How are we to go about this most effectively?

First. Let us take our place beside other proud, progressive Americans, who are too conscious of their country's heritage of freedom ever to accept any abridgement of their sovereign rights of citizenship.

Second. Let us begin, at once, to work for the election to Congress in 1948 of sincere, democratic men and women who will represent *us*, the people, and not the entrenched interests which forced through a Taft-Hartley Bill.

Third. Let us keep actively informed about the current political and economic situation, so we can pull our weight—and if we all pull together, it's a lot of weight—in promoting fair and equitable legislation for all facets of the nation's economy. The FEPC has been defeated, but *we* have not! Let us see that a comparable bill is brought to the Senate floor in 1948, and that a democratic, enlightened Congress permits it to become a law.

Fourth. Let us be quick to fight discrimination against minorities wherever we encounter it, but, most especially, whenever we come across it in our own field. Make no mistake about it—the interests that promote race-prejudice are the very same interests that would throttle the artist. If we are to combat them successfully, we cannot fight them on one front and join forces with them on another. So long as any of our artists is reduced to the status of second-class citizen—so long as the concept of second-class citizenship remains in the world,—not one of us is secure.

Fifth. Let us, as musicians, lend our support toward an increasingly strong, progressive Musicians' Union, one capable of promoting our economic well-being by virtue of informed and militant leaders, and an active voting membership. Let us take steps to eradicate the Jim Crow union, by demanding that our brother members be hired on the basis of their *tone-color* and not on the basis of their *skin-color!*

Sixth. Let us do all in our power to encourage performance of music being written by composers living and working in our own time. Here we shall have to deal with the virus of thought control in its less obvious manifestations. The symptoms are less pronounced; the patient can sit up and take a little nourishment, but the malady lingers on.

The fact is, that music, which has long been considered the most intimate and inaccessible of the arts, has now become "Big Business." The rattle of the box-office till has become the criterion of a work's musical value, and both performer and music are subject to the interests of management. No performer, however talented, may be booked through any major circuit unless he is under contract to one or the other of the country's two large concert-agencies. This means that an enormous segment of American talent is never going to have a chance to be heard by the American public. It means that only those pieces which have proved their merit at the box-office are going to be encouraged on the programs of concert performers.

Music differs in one respect from other entertainment media. The public demands new plays, new movies, new books. But it is content to accept only that music with which it is already familiar.

Monopoly has not been slow to recognize this. Surefire concert war-horses continue to form the concert lion's stock-in-trade, and if works by contemporary composers are included at all, they are apologetically appended near the program's end, after the critics have gone home, and after the audience has presumably been given its money's worth in "standard" fare.

How is the public going to become familiar with any new work unless it is given a chance to hear it, not once or twice, but many times? Our modern composers are capable of writing, and do write, pieces more substantial than the bagatelles that our concert performers and symphony conductors occasionally sandwich between the familiar concert bromides. But the scarcity of major contemporary works in our concert-halls is merely another instance of the way in which thought control operates against a healthy, dynamic expression of our musical culture.

In the operatic field, the same reluctance to perform new works is encountered. The Metropolitan Opera Company, which is even now about to extend its hegemony to Los Angeles, has not been reluctant to accept contributions from the American public toward its own continuance, but it has been singularly reluctant to spend any money in the performance of new American operas.

In the popular field, Tin Pan Alley's assembly-line technique has efficiently vulgarized, for commercial ends, the healthy, normal urge to rhythm and song. Under its aegis, the jukebox begins to assume the place religion once held as a soporific of the masses. There is a world of difference between a healthy folk expression and its perversion to commercial ends. The essence of truly "popular" music is that it is participated in by the people. The hypertense atmosphere of the jazz-hall and the raucous blare of the jukebox feed the neurosis of under-privilege and pave the way for a people's resentment to express itself in aggressive wars.

Let us protest these subversions of our musical life to the interests of "Big Business." Let us encourage our concert performers to play more new, unhackneyed concert pieces. Let us demand a more ad-venturous spirit on the part of Tin Pan Alley, and suggest that there are other avenues to the human heart besides the heavily-trafficked ones marked "moon" and "June" and "spoon." Let us ask that our recording-companies discover the delights of chamber music, of the madrigal, the folk-song, of the vast, unexplored territory outside the boundaries of 19th Century concert literature.

Seventh. And this is our long-range project. Let us never cease to work for the establishment of a Federal Bureau of Fine Arts, and for Federal and state subsidies of music-schools. Let us make it incumbent upon Congress to encourage and develop a national culture and to promote and foster a native American culture by encouraging the use and development of the work and talents of American composers, playwrights, painters, sculptors, actors, and all other persons working in the Fine Arts.

The artist is one of the most valuable assets a nation has. America is the only major country in the world content to let her artists scrabble for a living. There is enough money in the American treasury to maintain an Un-American Activities Committee. There is enough to carry on experiments in newer and more efficient methods of exterminating mankind. There is even enough so that President Truman can offer millions to the service of reaction abroad. Is it too much to ask that a tiny segment of this amount be put to the use of our country's artists?

With all this—and the list is endless,—let us strive to expand the horizons of our own thinking beyond the borders of nationalism. Let us encourage the use of music in building international understanding by periodic exchanges of students and conductors. In this age of shrinking distances, nationalism is going out of fashion in music, as it must in our thinking. If the musician is ever to realize his fullest potentials as an artist, he must begin to regard himself, not only as a citizen, but as a citizen of the world.

Music is a positive force. And it is up to the musician, as a citizen, to see that the work of his hand and brain shall serve a constructive purpose in the world today, and in the world his children will inherit.

Phil Moore

Ranking jazz composer
and performer; heads
his own band

MINORITIES IN MUSIC

THE title of this paper is "Minorities in Music". It is obvious there is an art form termed "music"; it is obvious there are people termed "minorities"; it is obvious that there exists this national cancer termed most politely "a problem."

We are here gathered for an analysis of this disease, to examine scientifically whether these problems really exist, whether in our national thinking there is antipathy toward certain sections of the American population by other sections. As a Negro, I need no such scientific analysis. I know the American mind has been conditioned to accept these problems as part of our way of life, conditioned by thought control.

We were not born with these ideas. Where have these ideas come from—these deadly germs that pass from mind to mouth? Somebody started them. Who was responsible? Scientifically, I believe that those who are responsible are the powerful mighty few who first conceived the economic truth that there is "profit in prejudice," real profit.

Where does this profit come from? The 14,000,000 Negroes? The 5,000,000 Jews? Or the few millions of other oppressed minorities? NO! Those are petty markets, much too small to be the chief concern of these ambitious monopolists. The real market is YOU, the 100,000,-000-odd other Americans who ultimately are the real sufferers.

Every time a Negro factory-hand is paid a lower wage, the wages of a white factory-man are depressed. Every time a Mexican is tossed back into the pool of labor to be fished out when the crops are ready to be picked, the white agricultural worker buys one less bottle of milk for his children. Every time a Jew is baited or the word Communist or International Banker echoes behind him, some trade union is threatened, and the security of all of us is in danger.

I have mentioned factory-hands, agricultural workers and trade unionists. What do they have to do with music, a most cultural

222

form of expression? They have a great deal to do with it. Or, rather, the other way around. The culture of a nation is the way a nation thinks. Control the culture of a nation and you control the actions of a nation, its work habits, its thinking and its life. Let me cite a few instances:

A Civil War was fought. Negroes in the South were given the franchise. In South Carolina, a Negro who had once been a slave was sworn into the Legislature but, meanwhile, the banking-houses of the North and South joined in marriage, and the wedding-ring was an iron one, clamped on the Negro, and the groomsmen rode horses and wore sheets of white. The Negro was forbidden to tarvel from his own territory.

Then suddenly there appeared upon the scene a most wonderful and amusing new form of theatre and music: the minstrel-show, complete with bandanna and chicken-stealing and rolling eyes, and the woman whose hips melted men if you paid for it. The whites loved it. The first Jim-Crow show—a smashing success. It became typical of what the whites wanted others to think of the Negro. A stereotype was born that even today is not dead, its insidious work goes on in millions of minds.

It is only fair to point out that Jim Crow and his minstrels were whites—whites from New England, but the charcoal on their faces was pure, deep South.

For years after that, only those Negro actors who would mimic the Jim-Crow antics could get work. That's how Jim Crow was born. Let's investigate how it operates in the field of music.

The Negro must be kept in his idiom. In the classical field of music we find few American Negroes and few American Mexicans. A Marian Anderson, having finally made the grade, is practically compelled to include many spirituals in her repertoire; whereas, it is a fact that Reginald Forsythe and Rogulio create and perform any type of music they wish and are both accepted wholeheartedly. Why? Forsythe is an English Negro, Rogulio from Martinique. Prejudice is national, not international; a matter of geography, not "race". In other words, the foreign-born Negro has an advantage over us because he isn't American.

Schools of music are in universities where the quota-system reacts against all minorities. Student orchestras, the training-ground for the fine musician of tomorrow, have alarmingly few Negroes in them.

Only four Negroes are at work as staff musicians in all the major networks and motion picture studios. In every city except New York and Detroit, there are Jim-Crow unions. This is how it works: the white union—in Los Angeles, Local 47—exclusively contracts all motion picture and radio stations. Result: two Negroes in these fields. There are 900 members in the Negro local. Believe me, there are many, many capable Negro musicians in this jurisdiction.

This is a pattern, and it does have reason. Its reason—segregation; division in culture, so division among labor becomes easier.

But in the field of jazz the Negroes' path was made easier, and opened to them in many cases. Great stuff, this jazz, real jungle stuff. But something unforeseen happened. Jazz music became part of the culture of the American people. Jazz music became a major cultural form, bringing Negroes and whites together, playing together, working together. The attack against jazz started in the Deep South.

Let us look at this Operation Prejudice:

Hazel Scott—pianist, wife of a Congressman,—banned in Washington. Reason: color and player of jazz. This ban of the Daughters of the American Revolution was endorsed by Mrs. Harry Truman. Addenda: Jazz music and Negro musicians were banned in Hitler's Germany. Addenda: Last week, Mr. Harry Truman, speaking to the National Association of Colored People, asked for the immediate end of bias and prejudice. Doesn't Mr. Truman speak to Mrs. Truman? They ought to get together.

A trade-magazine, reviewing my little band at Loew's State, New York, said: "Just four colored fellows and one Ofay (meaning white) and that's about all." Pointing up the mixed band, they forgot to mention whether we sang, played, or were acrobats!

A Los Angeles paper, reviewing Julian Work's *New England Sketches,* praised the composition, but suggested that Mr. Work might accomplish much more in his own native Southern idiom. Addenda: Mr. Work does not live in the South, mentally or physically.

"Sweethearts of Rhythm", an all-girl orchestra of all races. In order to play in the South, two Jewish girls had to pass for colored. In New Jersey, the darker Negro girls had to be temporarily replaced and the lighter Negro girls had to pass as Mexicans. In Dallas, the Mexican girls had to pass as Negroes. In Washington, a Negro girl in the orchestra was arrested for speaking to a white Army officer who was waiting for her friend, a white girl in the orchestra. The charge:

soliciting. The punishment: jail or get the whole goddam orchestra out of town!

Phil Carreon and his Orchestra. All veterans. All races. The Police Commission of Los Angeles refused to permit them to play outside the Mexican area on the advice of a police lieutenant. "Mixed orchestra incite to riot." Permit was finally granted after a delegation headed by the Independent Citizens' Committee appeared on behalf of Carreon. Result: there have been no riots.

Billy Berg's—Vine Street, Los Angeles. Permit refused for dancing. Reason: danger of mixed dancing inciting to riot.

Another facet of Operation Prejudice:

Assassinate the character of jazz-musicians. Play up the marijuana and plant the idea that all jazz-musicians, Negro and white, are strictly different.

Pasadena—Eddie Heywood and his band searched by the FBI on the Santa Fe train, the Chief, enroute to an engagement in Los Angeles, looking for weed, for marijuana. Result: They found none, but one more band was supposed to have been put in its place.

A white guitarist beaten in Philadelphia because he played with a mixed band.

Lena Horne, during the war, not permitted to sing before mixed Negro and white soldiers in the South, but requested to sing for mixed white American soldiers and German Nazi prisoners of war. She refused.

Jim-Crow transportation. Jim Crow at hotels. All part of the pattern of thought control.

Now, sex is the new artillery of the bigots. During the Civil War, the plantation-owners left their women in the care of their slaves, confident that no harm would be done. Today, the lie is that every Negro man has eyes only for white skin, and every Negro woman is ready for a dollar. What does this have to do with music?

Here is a list of the hit Negro musical shows of the last few years: *Porgy and Bess, Cabin In The Sky, Beggars' Opera, St. Louis Woman,* and the stageplay *Anna Lucasta.* All have one element in common: a Negro woman prostitute and a Negro male whose sole mission in life is to be a stud. This is real thought control on author and composer. Whose work are they doing?

The dancehall-owner who books a Negro band and, to show he's a

225

good Joe says he likes colored folks, but he can't stand Jews; the dancehall that permits Negroes, but not Mexicans; the owner can't stand Mexicans. That is, on Monday, Wednesday and Friday. The other days, he can't stand Negroes. "Dancing for Mexicans only", those days. Keep them apart. That's their battlecry . . . It means that some day someone might ask a white man to rewrite Ellington, as someone in another country asked Strauss to rewrite Mendelssohn's *Wedding March* so it could be played without taint of the Jewish name on it.

This is thought control. But just one phase of it. Let's term it "Thought Control 'A'". Now, for "Thought Control 'B'".

My people have lived for a long time with "Thought Control 'B'". "Thought Control B'" is a gag, but not a joke. A dirty hand clamped over your mouth, the hand of Hitler, of Rankin. The Negro knows the smell of that hand all too well. The perfume on it is his blood! You've heard the expression "Uncle Tom". It was the result of "Thought Control 'B'". The Negro who had to mouth the phrases his master wanted to hear, or else be flogged. An "Uncle Tom".

The Negro who had to bow and scrape to hold a job which paid off in crusts—an "Uncle Tom". The Negro who had to "yessah" and "yes'm", even though it meant accepting the guilt for something he hadn't done. Which is better? A few lashes of the whip or the lynch-rope? My people know. We have felt them both!

Thought Control 'B'"—the gag, is about to be applied to the mouths of the American Nation. Think of it—a nation of "Uncle Toms". The new stereotype for the children of nations seeking democracy to pity, because they will see the pain behind our ever-obedient eyes.

The President of the United States has issued an edict asking for loyalty, the so-called loyalty pledge. Loyalty to whom? To the Committee on Un-American Activities, whose record of bigotry is infamous. To be loyal under this pledge, one must speak only words that please the Rankins and the Thomases and think only thoughts they have planted in our minds. It means guilty without trial. It means guilty without knowing the charge. It means TERROR.

Will this affect our music, our work? Here is a straw in the wind.

I personally do not like war. I wrote a song, *Get Aboard the Peace Train*. To quote a line, "You've found war an awful pastime. Let's make sure that that was the last time." A prominent Hearst columnist printed the lyric and commented, "a perfect example of Communist propaganda." Peace—Communist propaganda. No comment.

Will the George Sokolskys and the Westbrook Peglers—the Pegler who said that "Lynching is as American as an icecream soda,"—be fortified by the Truman edict? Will fighting for a decent land and being against racial or religious prejudice be subversive? It already is. Rankin has accused every organization in the country which militantly fights race-prejudice as being a Communist-front. This can be the beginning of no JEW music—no NIGGER music—no SPIC music— no nothing, but red hot goosestep jive;—and it won't be the Blues.

But we can stop this. I offer this for your consideration in order to combat "Thought Control 'A' ".

Taxes are paid by millions of Americans now being treated as second-class citizens. I propose that legislation be enacted which should make it unconstitutional for any institution of learning receiving Federal funds either directly or indirectly to discriminate !

The minorities are part of the labor movement and have always solidly supported the trade unions of this country. I propose that Jim-Crow unions be abolished!

It is an axiom that when people work side by side fears and prejudice depart. I propose that a Federal FEPC Bill be enacted.

I propose that those who have prejudice, hate it ACTIVELY, join organizations such as the Progressive Citizens of America. That they consciously consider their own creative work to eliminate all traces of prejudice which may unknowingly have crept in. That they patronize no establishment that is anti-Negro, anti-Jewish, anti-Mexican, all of which means anti-American.

As for "Thought Control 'B' ":

I propose the immediate abolishing of the Committee on Un-American Activities, which prosecutes and persecutes any liberal, but withheld damaging evidence against the K.K.K. for almost six years!

I propose that pressure be brought on the President of the United States to withdraw his so-called Loyalty Pledge.

These notes I have read are not all of the composition, however. There are other notes—good notes. My being here tonight is one of those good notes. Paul Robeson, although attempts will still be made to stop him, will add his good note. And the Marian Andersons and the Lena Hornes, Duke Ellingtons, the William Grant Stills and an

227

increasing number of others, will add theirs. It is not all the Blues. There's Red and White in it.

Organizations such as Progressive Citizens of America are part beginning to hear, and they are frightened.

I say, let us make them hear it!! Make this symphony so powerful that it will be heard in every corner of these United States, and only those who fear the harmony of the voice of the people will run from it, while all the others will join in with us, in a chorus that can well be heard around the world.

(The above paper, presented by Mr. Moore, was written by him in collaboration with Henry Blankfort.)

Jarvis Barlow
Well-known Los Angeles and
Pasadena architect

MUSIC AND FINE ARTS
UNDER FASCISM

OF all the sacrifices that Germany made for the glorification of Hitler's Third Reich, one of the most tragic was the sacrifice of its genius in the arts and letters, and in music.

It should be remembered that Germany, no less than America, had a tradition of humanism that arose out of the libertarian struggles of the 18th Century. Its expression in philosophy, literature and music embraced the same humanitarian concept of man and society enunciated in such political documents as our own Declaration of Independence, the Constitution and the Bill of Rights.

How this tradition was weakened, how the losing of it paved the way for National-Socialism, and how the German people were finally bereft of the moral fibre to resist all the evil that Hitler personified— all this tragic process is worth reviewing, however briefly, as part of our analysis of thought control in Amercia. For, in the United States, 1947, the same type of forces that brought Hitler to power are hammering at *our* finest traditions of liberty and human dignity. How far can these attacks go before *our* liberal traditions crumble as did the humanist tradition in Germany?

In Germany, the process of thought control of the arts was complicated. In order for National-Socialism to brutalize its followers, to degrade them and to achieve its goal of world conquest under the banners of "Aryan supremacy" and "German nationalism," it was necessary to destroy old values, to silence the liberal and to inject into the German mind a new distorted sense of values, of man's relationship to man.

The work of philosophers and artists which had culminated in universal masterpieces like *Faust* and the Ninth Symphony, gave way to an increasing nationalism sponsored by schismatic philosophies under the aegis of the New Order.

Nietzsche's conception of a "re-evaluation of all values," a fan-

229

tastic shakeup of human fundamentals, was used as one of the weapons to destroy the integrity of the German people. Other contributing factors were the use of the Fascist mythology of Wagner's *Ring* operas and the pseudo-Christian mysticism of *Parsifal;* the aggressive pan-Germanism of Wagner's son-in-law, Chamberlain; the pessimism of Spengler, who denied the powers of the human intellect and the whole idea of progress inspired by the theory of evolution.

Thus, Nazism found useful ideological supports for its educational propaganda. Great names to cite as witness for cause and creed, names to help bring about the surrender of the intellectuals. But most important: Nazism attempted to translate into action, into living terms, the decadent philosophies already widely disseminated and accepted.

What were the symptoms of this state of affairs in the arts? One of the most important was what Dr. T. W. Adorne has called the decultivation of the German middle-classes.

This is well-illustrated, for instance, by the work of Richard Strauss. Strauss was the most typical and the most representative exponent of Germany's imperialistic period, the holder and treasurer of Wagner's heritage. His music was rife with intoxication and clamor, with recklessness and expansionism, developing in such a manner that a recent work like the *Metamorphosis,* 1945, marks the near-end of a regression clearly apparent to alert critics as far back as *Rosenkavalier.*

But there was another level of musical activity that existed side by side with this one. For the anti-humanist spirit of Strauss was the very spirit against which everything rebelled that was responsible and productive in German musicianship. This rebellion had set in with Schoenberg at the beginning of the century and had been reverberating ever since in the work of the *avant-garde.*

Such was the intellectual and artistic climate in which Hitler made his bid for power. The political picture was the rising progressiveness of the German people and the awareness of world reactionary forces that this must be defeated. The international cartels of Wall Street, Threadneedle Street and the Bourse selected Hitler as their frontman to head their drive for world Fascism. That part of history which shows how Hitler turned on his original financial backing need not be gone into here. It is too well-known.

It is an integral part of the Fascist plan that music and the fine arts must serve politico-economic ends. How these ends are secured

230

may vary widely, depending on the circumstances. In Italy, for instance, the artistic policies of Fascism were subtle. Mussolini fancied himself a patron of the arts. In order to finance official patronage, a tax was levied upon motion-picture admissions and appropriated for the cultivation of the arts. For composers it was a great day. They could live by their art. Ostensibly, they had to do no more than compose.

But was the Italian composer free? He was free only to cover with the mantle of his art all the rottenness that underlay Italian life. This was the kind of freedom that Toscanini rejected. But it was good enough for most musicians. Many of them, Casella, for instance, dutifully wrote dithyrambs for Fascism. Danger was recognized only when the anti-Semitic laws were imposed in 1938, and when a few fanatic critics began to hurl the charge of "Communism" against some of the progressive men like Dallapiccola.

On the whole, Italian composers were reduced to a kind of second-class citizenship. The results were a music that was effete, inconsequential and, in the sense that it had no vital relationship to life-phenomena, as decultivated as its German counterpart. Music, as meaningful human speech, had been bribed into silence.

In Germany, the policy was not so mild. Immediately after the Reichstag fire, a Ministry for Popular Englightenment and Propaganda was established under Goebbels. Every key position in German intellectual and artistic life was opened to Nazi Comrades, to thousands of untalented careerists. They were made the heads of radio stations, conservatories, orchestras and opera-houses, just as they have been in Peron's Argentina. Musicians (as well as writers, painters, actors) were assembled into Chambers. The primary duty of each Chamber was to control its membership—and thus the traffic in artistic merchandise. The principal weapon was discrimination. It was mainly, but not only, used against Jews. Jewish contributions to music were traced far back into the past and eliminated with elaborate demonstration. Mendelssohn, Meyerbeer, Offenbach, Mahler, and countless others, were forbidden art.

When the weapon of discrimination could not be employed, there was the useful charge of *Kulturbolschewismus,* or degeneracy in the arts. This wide-sweeping weapon eliminated from the musical scene nearly all the composers not already proscribed under other bans: Hindemith and Schoenberg, Kurt Weill, Krenek, Webern, Berg, Franz

Schreker and, among others, Hanns Eisler who, today, is again in our own country finding this pattern repeated, Bruno Walter, Otto Klemperer, Arthur Schnabel, and more and more.

Bolshevism was the charge brought against all progressive music and its composers were labeled "Communist." There was no appeal against the decisions. Hitler's Cultural Minister, Rosenberg, said, "There can be no opposition to the sovereignty of National-Socialism. Its decisions are final."

The results of these policies were quickly apparent. The instrumentalist and the conductor became the targets—pianist Leonid Kreutzer, cellist Emil Feuermann, violinist Karl Flesch, and conductors Oskar Fried, and Stediry and Brecher, and again more and more.

In Vienna, 3,000 musicians, actors, writers were made into slave-labor. On V-E Day, of this 3,000, only 150 were still alive. And thus, in Germany and in the area under Nazi domination, the repertoires of orchestras and opera-houses were reduced to insignificance. Living composers or real talent went underground, wrote music only for the Day of Liberation, as Webern did. Living composers acceptable to the regime were actually "hangovers" from the oldest generation—Paul Graener, Hans Pfitzner, Strauss and Von Resnicek. Music became valued for one purpose, its *dope-character*—whether it was the music of Wagner and Strauss or Beethoven.

The Nazis were not slow to recognize the poverty of available musical material. Therefore, the government, through propaganda, violence and publicity, promoted its own exponents of *Kultur*. Thus, in Dresden, when the conductor Busch, an Aryan, had to be removed by force from the rostrum of the opera-house by 60 uniformed Nazis, he was replaced by another more suitable. A split policy had to be pursued—as illogical as the scientific policy that let the Nazis reject and denounce the scientific contributions of an Einstein, yet required them to continue with the Ehrlich treatment for syphilis. Regenyi and Egk (to mention two of the few) actually followed the road of the international *avant-garde* schools. The former's music is a poor imitation of Kurt Weill's; and the latter's an imitation of Milhaud and Stravinsky. Twelve-tone music was acceptable when written by Klenau—but not Schoenberg. And Paul Hoffer tried to build a career on Hindemith's aesthetics—but without Hindemith's talent.

Strauss composed a Paean of Praise glorifying the Japanese Empire, and the sale of this hymn was forced upon the German people.

232

It became quite clear that those who "accepted" had within them the weaknesses which made the capitulation of their talents in abject surrender to Hitler's race and military policies a matter of small time.

In short, an utter poverty of creative talent plagued the Reich. From time to time, there appeared a number of one-day wonders, built up to importance by advance publicity and then retired to the storerooms by an apathetic public and disgruntled officials. Thus, nothing that could be called Nazi music ever developed.

Insofar as the field of the visual arts was concerned, the young German National-Socialist State lost little time in translating the broad tradition of humanism into a narrow and restricted nationalism. In 1933, the Minister of Education of Wurtemberg, Herr Mergenthaler, wrote a pamphlet titled, *A Cultural Program for the New State.* Let me read some quotes from this document:

> "It is a mistake to think that the national revolution is only political and economic. It is above all cultural. We stand in the first stormy phase of revolution. But already it has uncovered the awarness that all the expressions of life spring from a specific blood, a specific people, a specific race!"

The effect on the German artist was immediate. Two lines of attack were pursued. Most experimental art forms, as in music, were immediately proscribed as being *Kunstbolshewismus*—Bolshevik art. The subject-matter of painting was exposed to just as rigid scrutiny as the technique employed. For example, a drawing by George Grosz of the slums of Berlin was attacked, but the same artist's portrait of his mother was passed by. Added to the attack made on painters for unacceptable technique, and/or acceptable subject-matter, was, of course, the economic proscription of any artist of Jewish blood. Under any one or a combination of bans, came every vital contemporary painter and sculptor in Germany, living or dead. Barlach, Kokoschka, Grosz, Klee, Kandinsky, Feininger, Franz Marc, Hofer, Beckmann, Schlemmer, Lieberman, Lehmbruck . . . the list is almost endless. And the museum-directors who showed or championed these artists were summarily dealt with.

What was the character of the "traditional" German art to which the Nazi artist was asked to revert? Was it the great tradition of such names as Cranach, Durer, the Holbeins, Gruenewald, Schongaver and others whose names are honored in the history of Western European art? Not at all, for these men were leaders, experimenters and searchers in their era. Nazi painting became one which had no "tradition" in the finest sense—copies of copies of copies became the new pattern. Says Lincoln Kirstein:

> "Nazi painting was . . . a further corruption of the Munich Academy's dilution of the lowest common denominator. It was occupied neither with the investigation of nature, personal sentiments of the painter, nor the technical extension of means of painting. In sculpture, the Nazis took refuge in an ideal naive perfection, the arrantly monumental, which was seldom heroic, but simply out of scale."

In the field of architecture, the Nazis also had a complete program. We must remember that some of the greatest names in contemporary architecture are either German or architects who were given an opportunity to develop the new idiom in certain German buildings or housing projects: Mies van der Rohe of Berlin, Lecorbusier-Jeanneret of Paris, J. J. P. Oud of Rotterdam, Gropius, the onetime director of Bauhaus, Daiber of Stuttgart, Eric Mendelsohn, Richard Docker, and others. These men, and others like them in other parts of the world, had been pioneers in the development of what has come to be known as the "international" style. But the very word "international" was anathema to the thinking of the "blood and soil" National-Socialists. Here are some excerpts from a Nazi manifesto, the section of which devoted to architecture was written by Schmitthenner:

> "The architecture of a period is the best cause of its general cultural level. The nature of German architecture reveals itself at its most significant in tradition. The new 'objectivity' in architecture is nothing but the utilitarian become form, that very utilitarian spirit which has dominated the contemporary period to such an extent that grace and dignity have been readily sacrificed to an 'international' phantom."

On this subject, Lincoln Kirstein says elsewhere:

> "Hitler had but one basic architectural notion: absolute symmetry at any cost . . . two of everything in crushing balance. To Hitler, classicism meant first of all uniformity, the arbitrary repetition of a single module of design. Nazi classicism . . . was 'earnest,' serious not luxurious, solemn not rich, 'powerful' not 'playful.' It was functionalism in a straitjacket. As in painting and sculpture, the password was: 'not internationalism but universalism'."

Stillbirth was the inevitable consequence of the premises upon which Fascism had intended to erect its cultural monuments. All was thrown into the sacrificial fire which consumed the German spirit twelve horrifying years. And when the final catastrophe came, there was not even one voice left to intone decently the final service for the dead.

Reginald D. Johnson
Architect; fellow, American Institute of
Architects; member, Board of Trustees,
Good Samaritan Hospital, Los Angeles

ARCHITECTURE
AND THOUGHT CONTROL

T HE purpose of this paper is to present a brief analysis of the forces at work which determine the character of our cities and our homes.

Quite evidently, many of these forces have value and are responsible for much of the technological progress of which we are justly proud. On the other hand, those who are close to the picture are convinced that thought control is often being used, and with success, to obstruct progress.

As to the plan of any city or region, it should always be borne in mind that it is simply the reflection of the economic, social, and political thinking of the period. Throughout the ages, this has been true. The feudal, walled city told its story by the architectural importance of the castle and the church: the walls themselves clearly stated, to the least observant, that this was a small principality, no part of a great united nation.

And so today our American cities, by and large, reflect our society, our economic way-of-life, and the determination of some to maintain the "status quo". In a period of advancing thought, it should be pointed out, "status quo" is tantamount to going backwards. Our towering skyscrapers advertise to the world the importance and power of the giant private corporations in our economy. The many churches demonstrate our financial as well as our spiritual devotion and our attitude toward religion. The large area given to our slums is ample proof that at least one-third of our people exist under substandard conditions. And, in our constantly-expanding segregated sections, the most casual observer can recognize that the restrictive convenant is being used to oppress the minorities.

Hence, if we are to rebuild a worthwhile city of the future, we must be quite sure of the soundness of our economic, social and political

235

philosophy. *Life* magazine, describing the New York City skyline, proudly boasted that it was the result of non-planning, or, in its terms, "the irrefutable law of the jungle where the strong are well rewarded." There was no mention in the article that in New York City, today, there are over 10,000 dwelling-units without toilet facilities. This, too, is a result of non-planning, in the greatest and wealthiest city of the world.

Fortunately, the philosophy of the law of the jungle has not been accepted by the more advanced architectural publications. However, it is doubtful that the truth about architecture and city planning, as it is related to our current economy, can be expressed in any architectural school.

Today, it is not Federal laws which retard progressive advances in architecture. We find that private corporations "thought control" the design of America. These private corporations are the major lending-institutions, which control the mortgages of America, and which, by influencing government agencies, determine the nation's living facilities.

The effect is the same, however, as that of Federal laws. These lending-institutions prohibit flat roofs, concrete floor-slabs, livingrooms on the garden side of a house, or community parks and playgrounds, to select a few of their restrictions. It is quite evident that although the law of the jungle is advanced as a thesis for the majority of Americans, these lending institutions are not adverse to their own planning. Their argument in favor of their controlling-design can be reduced to simple terms:

> Institutions lend most of the money to the builder of the house or project. The builder or owner may default on his obligation, forcing the institutions to sell the house to recover loan and interest: therefore, they must be certain that the property meets the taste of the majority of the American people.

They do not state that they have controlled the taste of the American people, nor do they openly state their fear that the existence of modern dwellings will depreciate present values of older property, reducing the value of their mortgages.

This censorship, now reflected in the attitude of F.H.A., is stifling the free creative expression of the architect. It is making it more and more impossible for the American people to live in houses which should, by all rights, represent the advanced scientific thinking of today.

The architects of America are more deeply concerned with this problem, since the recent attacks on other divisions of the fine arts. For the first time, these attacks are emanating from official sources and recall similar attacks that once occurred in Hitler Germany.

On March 24, 1933, the newspaper *Neus Tablet* commented on a recently-completed church, as follows:

> "German cultural sensibilities will be wounded by this building. Neither the principle of efficiency nor the principle of artistic freedom excuses this public offense. We must resolve to support the State Minister of Education who will direct his attention to architecture."

It was announced in Germany, at that time, that "the contemporary belief that art is international is misleading." And "if one should ask what is left of freedom, he will be answered, there is no freedom for those who would weaken and destroy German art."

According to Alfred H. Barr, Jr., who made personal observations in Germany, the New Order invaded every intellectual and cultural activity with thoroughness and rapidity. Official architectural thought control immediately followed the official control of fine arts.

In view of the direct connection between the control of painting and architecture, it is not surprising to find the following quotation from Mr. Edward Withers in the *Los Angeles Times*, May 22, 1947:

> "One painting", Withers said, "apparently depicts the decay of the church, the state, Renaissance architecture, and classic architecture. We are used to having things of known beauty held up to the people", he added. "Every man likes to look around a known world. When he does not see that, he begins to lose faith—and there is where Communism steps in."

We architects, therefore, find ourselves in the same category as the painters. A threat to freedom of thought in painting is a threat to freedom of thought in architecture. Every threat to this freedom must be challenged, regardless of its source.

The architects understand this threat. *The Architectural Forum*, of May 1947, commenting on the decision of the Fifth Avenue Association of New York to set up a board of experts to pass on architecture, stated:

> "Where censorship rules, the commonplace is never far behind. Distinguished men serve with devotion and without compensation but never to the public's long run gain. When such individuals cease to act as individuals but as an official group to pass upon or reject the works of their neighbors, violence is done. Then anonymity and mediocrity rule."

George Fred Keck, prominent Chicago architect, states:

> "Complete regimentation in Germany produced one type of mediocrity. The regimentation of design and technical control of the FHA produced another type of mediocrity."

Today, mediocrity is not confined to design. It has been extended to the lack of understanding in our Congress of a major problem confronting the American nation, the acute shortage of housing. There has been a distinct attempt to "thought control" the people so that the blame for this shortage should lie entirely on labor, on high wages and on strikes. But those who have most closely examined the history of housing in this country realize this is not true.

The so-called "American way", when it comes to supplying adequate shelter for the average American family, is, and has been, far from satisfactory. This statement can easily be branded as subversive, but not if one is willing to look at the matter realistically rather than emotionally. The facts in the case are that for several generations the great middle economic class of Americans, for whom we make so many claims,—and naturally the many millions below that group,—has been unable, from a sound economic point of view, to purchase a new house in an average urban or suburban area.

It is generally accepted by American sociologists and economists that the average family should not pay more per month for shelter than one-fourth of its *monthly* income, or that the purchase price of a house should not exceed twice that family's *yearly income*. Those of you who have followed the plight of the middle and the lowest income-groups in relation to housing, will know that at the present time there is a continuous barrage of thought control being hurled against any legislation on the state or Federal level, designed to help solve the housing problem for these great segments of our population.

Helen Gahagan Douglas, in speaking of a well thought-out Veteran Housing Bill which she introduced into Congress, recently said:

> "Of course the housing profiteer's lobby will say in a voice made loud by all their organs of publicity, that the whole idea is Socialistic; or Communistic; or crackpot; or professional Do-good-ism; or, at the very best, that it is a plan put forward by sincere sponsors who have been duped by sinister, subversive influences."

Much research by competent, non-profit foundations, such as the Twentieth Century Fund of New York, has been done on this subject of the excessive cost of housing in relation to the average American's income.

The shortage of housing is making a field-day for certain interests who, rather than have the government enter the picture—even as proposed by Senator Taft—are apparently willing to jeopardize our entire social and economic structure, that very structure which, on the other hand, they are so valiantly defending against attack.

The present is often discouraging and baffling, but I feel sure that all really progressive citizens of America will agree with this thought, expressed by Lewis Mumford in the closing lines of *The Culture of Cities*:

> "The cycle of the machine is now coming to an end . . . We can no more continue to live in the world of the machine than we could live on the barren surface of the moon. Man is *at last* in a position to transcend the machine, and to create a new biological and social environment in which the highest possibilities of human existence will be realized, not for the strong and the lucky alone, but for all cooperating and understanding groups, associations and communities.
>
> " 'Men come together in cities', said Aristotle, 'in order to live; they remain together in order to live the good life.'
>
> "Only fragments of this purpose are fulfilled in the modern world; but a new pattern of the good life is emerging."

The important part which the Progressive Citizens of America can, and must, play in this picture is not hard to visualize.

Edward Biberman

Painter; one-man shows, Paris, Berlin, New York, Chicago, Boston, Philadelphia, San Francisco, Los Angeles; 3 murals for U. S. Section of Fine Arts

THE ATTACK ON THE AMERICAN ARTIST

Two years ago, we were still at war. Two years ago, we were mourning the then-recent death of Franklin Delano Roosevelt. Two years ago, President Truman assured the world that he was aiming to carry out the policies of Franklin Roosevelt. In January, 1946, with all hostilities six months over, the Department of State had, among its other activities, an art program and an Office of International Information and Cultural Affairs. By October of 1946, this Department had prepared an exhibition called "Advancing American Art." The exhibition consisted of two sections—one scheduled for showing in Cuba, Haiti and the Dominican Republic, then to go south to Venezuela, Brazil and other countries in this hemisphere. The second section was to open in Paris in November, during UNESCO Month—thereafter to travel to Switzerland and Czechoslovakia, then for an indefinite period of years to go through Europe and the Near East.

The exhibition opened brilliantly at the Metropolitan Museum of Art in New York City. The Assistant Secretary of State for Economic Affairs, William Benton, in the official statement of sponsorship, said that this exhibition

"bore testimony to all those abroad who thought of the United States as a nation of materialists, that the same country which produces brilliant scientists and engineers also produces creative artists."

As to the paintings in the exhibition, Mr. Benton said:

"The pictures have been selected, on the basis of pleas from our missions abroad, to show the newest development of American art. It is an exhibition in which I believe the United States may well take pride."

The exhibition was shown very successfully in Havana, and Santiago-de-Cuba, and in Port-au-Prince, Haiti. The European section was received in Paris and Prague with equal enthusiasm.

240

On April 4th, a strange story broke the front pages of newspapers throughout this country. The *Los Angeles Examiner* carried a front-page headline reading, *Radical Art Tour Halted—Marshall Stops Showing Abroad.* The Hearst story referred to the paintings as "degenerate portraits authored by radical artists which 'reflected Communistic influences' in picturing American life at a deteriorated level" and were "exaggerated portrayals of alleged low standards of American life, all in conformity with the Communist theme." The *Los Angeles Examiner* took great pride in announcing "the true nature of the exhibit was first revealed last fall by the Hearst newspapers." As to the official position of the State Department, Secretary of State Marshall was quoted as follows: "This is being done in the best interests of the State Department in view of the controversial issues involved." State Department officials were quoted as saying that the exhibit was "a fantastic, silly thing, and unrepresentative of American modern art." This, the exhibition which Assistant Secretary of State Benton, six months previously, had praised unreservedly! Said Marquis Childs, *New York Post* (April 24, 1947) commentator:

"It so happened that, at that very moment, the pictures were being exhibited in Prague, where they attracted so much favorable attention that President Edward Benes asked permission to show them in other cities in Czechoslovakia; he even had the Czech government put up $6000 to pay for the cost of sending the exhibit around the country."

Less than two months later, a second art exhibition made Page One in a strange fashion in Los Angeles. This time front-page headlines in the *Los Angeles Times* said, *Art Club Flays Museum Show As "Subversive".* The story quoted the California Art Club as attacking the annual exhibition of works by artists of Los Angeles and vicinity at the Los Angeles County Museum as "'radical art' and containing 'subversive propaganda' . . . inimical to our form of government."

And now a third story. One of the most famous artists associated with mural painting in Mexico is Xavier Guerrero. Ranking in stature with such names as Orozco, Rivera and Siqueiros, Guerrero has also painted murals in Chile, and his paintings are to be found in collections in every part of this hemisphere. In 1941, he was in the United States as a guest of the Museum of Modern Art, in New York City, where he won a prize in the Museum's Inter-American Competition. In May of last year, Guerrero was again in New York and signed a contract with the highly-respected Knoedler Gallery for a one-man exhibition of easel painting, drawings and the development of his fresco technique. But the exhibition contained only a fraction of the intended works. For Guerrero himself never reached New York. The U. S. Embassy in Mexico refused him a visa, on the grounds that he was an enemy of the United States, because of his political opinions.

What accounted for these two violent attacks on American artists in less than 60 days and the barring of one of the foremost contemporary Mexican artists from our shores? What is the meaning of a new evaluation in which political epithets replace aesthetic criteria? Let us examine the pattern.

Back of these three episodes lies an interesting story. There has always been, on the part of reactionary forces in society, resistance to change in the cultural fields, as well as in the economic and political fields. However, it is a simple matter of history that the form of art and its content as well have not been static. To attempt to stop the mutations in the form and content of art is as futile as King Canute's ultimatum to the tides. Society is not static, and art, which is a reflection of society, cannot be static. It has been in constant movement.

In our own country, the social realism of the so-called "Ashcan" School, before the First World War, shook the academic canons of subject-matter. The Armory Show in 1913 had a tremendous influence on the matter of a re-evaluation of contemporary art-forms. The influence of government art programs under Roosevelt was formidable, and the impact of the popular Mexican mural movement of the 20s was a strong one. Similar essays into new form and content have been a constant leaven, provocative of an alert and developing 20th Century art idiom. But reaction was frightened by these vital new developments and the camp of art reaction realized that a new and drastic attack was needed if they were to have any success. Their efforts to fight the battle on an aesthetic plane had been of no avail. What they needed was political censorship of the most drastic and official nature.

With the end of the war, the golden opportunity suggested itself. Congressional Committees which had been set up to investigate "Un-American activities" began to terrorize, intimidate and silence all voices which spoke for liberalism and progress in sociology, politics and economics. Why not use the hysteria created by these inquisitorial bodies against the artist? Why not declare that all change in art form is "Communistic", in that it destroys established, hence sacred, tradition? Why not declare that any art work which in its subject-matter attempts to record, examine or comment upon contemporary life in all its aspects, paves the way for conclusions which might then also be labelled "radical?" From then on, the path would be simple. Paint traditionally! All change in form is dangerous! All comment in subject-matter is dangerous! Cultural censorship becomes the prelude to economic compulsion. Follow the rules or else!

This is the pattern which worked beautifully in Nazi Germany. Let us trace some interesting parallels:

Dr. Otto Zur Nedden, quote from Kulturminister Mergenthaler (Minister of Education), April 9, 1933, Stuttgart, Germany: "It is an important cultural duty of the regime of the new national resurgence to set free from any foreign, external influence our native creative personalities."

Board of Directors, California Art Club, Los Angeles, May, 1947: The California Art Club "is interested only in the promotion of an art containing no 'ism' but Americanism!"

Dr. Otto Zur Nedden, April 9, 1933, Stuttgart, Germany: "The widely held contemporary belief that art is international is absolutely misleading."

American Artists' Professional League, November 15, 1946: "Our association groups question the cultural value of any exhibition which is so strongly marked with radicalism of the new trends of European art. This is not indigenous to our soil."

Alfred Barr, from Germany, 1933: "The newspapers began to publish announcements which suggested beyond doubt that—the German museum director who has concerned himself in any way with modern art must act with extreme circumspection."

American Artists' Professional League, Art Digest, March 15, 1947: "Our museums and art schools are being rapidly filled with the forward-looking boys who have absorbed the alien ideologies and are getting a stranglehold."

Edward Withers, Retiring President of the California Art Club, Los Angeles, May, 1947, calls for the resignation of James Breasted, Director of the Los Angeles County Museum, for permitting the "modern" show in the Museum.

Art critic of the *National Socialist Courier,* Germany, 1933: "Who wants to take these pictures seriously? Who respects them? Who wants to defend them as works of art? They are unfinished in every respect. One may say that in their decadent spiritual attitude they might as well be left on the junk heap."

Pres. Harry S. Truman to William Benton, April 2, 1947: "I don't pretend to be an artist or a judge of art, but I am of the opinion that so-called modern art is merely the vaporings of half-baked lazy people. There is no art at all in connection with the modernists, in my opinion."

Incidents such as these represent the overt acts against which liberal opinion can be most easily aroused. Since they are flagrant examples of direct abuse, protests have poured into Washington from American Federation of Arts, *Art News, Art Digest,* Artists' Equity, and countless critics.

But there is another and extremely subtle aspect of thought control at work, which is harder to identify, which contains a half-truth at its core and which, because of its hidden nature, is more difficult to isolate and to refute. In the field of aesthetics, the search for contemporary forms is a healthy manifestation, being, basically, a desire to relate the visual idiom of a culture to its other social manifestations. That is why it was attacked by the Nazis and why it is attacked in our own country. However, reaction has forged a double-edged weapon.

We have already seen that it attacks experimentation with one edge of the sword. The second and more subtle attack is to establish the primacy of formal values and to negate all else. At this point, experimentation may well lose its progressive nature and become a serious stricture upon the artist. For a sole and unique preoccupation with form and formal values, to the exclusion of any concern with subject, can limit the exploration of man's relationships to his fellow-men and to his struggle with the forces of nature and seriously limit the basic function of art as communication. Making a fetish of form can be made to *seem* the ultimate in progress, yet, in effect, serve anti-social ends.

Let me read some quotes from Barrows Dunham, who explores this thesis magnificently in the chapter, *You Can't Mix Art and Politics,* in his recent book, *Man Against Myth*:

"The belief that art and politics are incompatible has its social uses. The primary purpose is to silence and disarm. Everyone knows that ideas, when transmitted in the excitement of aesthetic experience, have a powerful effect upon the mind. Not only are they then more readily accepted, but they are more readily acted upon.

"Reactionaries therefore take no chances. So far as they can manage it, there will not be any novels or plays or paintings expressive of human suffering and the means of remedy.

"A secondary, though valuable, use is as a weapon of attack against those works which, despite all cajolery and enticement, continue to plead the hopes of mankind.

"There must be some irony in the spectacle of artists striving to avoid politics on behalf of a doctrine whose purpose is political.

"The preoccupation with design, so brilliantly shown in French paintings, has been enormously fruitful. Reactionaries, however, were not slow to see how the corresponding aesthetic theory could be put to other uses—how, as a dogmatic and exclusive principle, it could silence undesirable voices."

Now, one may ask why so much attention is being paid to the artists? Are they so great in numbers? No. But their potential influence is what reaction fears. For art is not only communication. It is also inspiration, and can, in its most intense form, result in direct agitation. For, even though we live in a world of high literacy, we must not underestimate that old and well-worn Chinese proverb, "A picture is worth a thousand words."

But is it only the artist who is being silenced? Not at all. We have seen the pattern. After the "degenerate" artist comes the museum, which must not have collections of, nor directors who favor, "decadent" art. Museums are vulnerable, being for the most part tax-supported. Next, move in on universities. Art departments can be examined, art libraries gone over with a fine-toothed rake. Then, follow through on public schools, supported, like state universities, by public funds. The concentric rings spread out, until not a phase of visual life is left untouched. And the outermost rings of this whirlpool will affect every member of society. The result is the degradation of taste, the stultification of creative energy and finally the complete artistic sterility of the whole people.

What is the answer? There may have been a time when the thesis that politics and culture had no relation had a limited validity (though I doubt even that). But certainly, today, the relationship is clear. The American Artists' Professional League, which prides itself on having taken the lead in the attack on the State Department's exhibition; "Sanity in Art", which beats the drum for cultural paralysis; the directors of the California Art Club—all have a new string to their bow. And who has supplied it? The new political climate made by the old Dies Committee, the present Thomas-Rankin Committee, and the rash of so-called "loyalty" tests which stem from the Washington parent.

Two things are immediately necessary. One, for the artists to close cultural ranks—to fight back unitedly against events such as have occurred, and to forestall similar episodes which may be in the making. Secondly, to realize that art cannot be considered as being separate from the greatest good of all the people—and that only in a political climate of freedom can the conditions obtain which will release the full creative genius of man.

245

DISCUSSION

The discussion opened with a question on whether there is freedom for the artist in commercial and advertising art. It was answered as follows:

Edward Biberman: "The painter who works independently, in terms of actual creation, does not have censorship until possibly after his work is done . . . It is obvious that when a person is not working for himself, and his work is subject to policy of the agency or client or the medium in which it is to appear, it is pretty impossible for any freedom finally to come through . . . In terms of technical limitations, there are probably fewer limitations, however—but aside from this, little freedom in the field . . ."

A member of the audience: "How would you go about establishing a Ministry of Fine Arts in the Government?"

Sam Albert, musician: "There was a bill presented (by Congressmen Coffee and Pepper) in Congress a few years back; it died in Committee . . . PCA must spearhead the fight for such a bill through the election of a progressive 81st Congress . . . The United States is practically the only major government in the world which does not sponsor its artists . . ."

Mildred Norton announced that she had with her the proposed Fine Arts Bill which had been prepared by the New York Independent Citizens' Committee of the Arts, Sciences and Professions, around a year ago. She read several passages from this, then added: "When we consider the amounts our government allocates to other purposes by no means so constructive, the proposals of this Bill seem like a very modest sum ($5,000,000) . . . This proposed Bill has a number of very good points which could be incorporated into a permanent Bill if we devoted our time and energy to seeing it through."

Vincent Price, actor: "It seems to me that artists and musicians should back their local art centers; they should belong to the Museum Association . . . And who wants a fine arts policy in the hands of Truman?"

Sam Albert: "NY-ICCASP drew up the proposed Bill when Roosevelt was alive. It is not a final draft. We must support local organizations to build up sentiment for such a Bill."

246

Edward Biberman: "I agree with Mr. Price, but I believe there is one fallacy in his statement, which lies in the fact that timing is of the essence. The Fine Arts Bill was never submitted to Congress because it was felt the political climate was not favorable . . . If we can get a good 81st Congress we then can press for a Fine Arts Bill."

A member of the audience: "Don't you think it is important to open new markets for the painter in the labor unions?"

Edward Biberman: "A survey was made on this question by Walter Abel, critic and curator of one of the Mid-Western museums. It was called *Art and Labor.* The article dealt with not only a compendium of what had been done with labor organizations, like murals; but Ben Shawn's artwork for political campaigns during the last elections . . . The article was fully documented on the commissioning of art by labor organizations in this country; also cooperation of museums and labor organizations (*i.e.,* the Metropolitan Museum of Art has had a liaison with leading unions in the East, etc.)."

Additional discussion from the floor included the following statements:

Earl Robinson, composer: "One aspect of the discussion that can stand a little more emphasis is that the best defense against thought-control is a counter-attack. Join PCA. Counter-attack with our art. There will be a strong tendency on the part of artists to be afraid, but this is the time to put our feeling into our art in strong terms and attack the Tenneys and Rankins through our art . . . The PCA audience is looking not only for speeches, but for art . . ."

Vincent Price: "All members of PCA, I think, must go out and do missionary work in the broad section of people yet untouched; we must work for the arts, instead of just talking about theories . . ."

After this discussion, a series of resolutions were moved, seconded and unanimously carried by the Panel on the Arts. They were:

RESOLUTIONS

1. That those present unanimously demand that the Committee on Un-American Activities be abolished.

2. That we work for the establishment of a Federal Bureau of Fine Arts and creation of Federal and state subsidies for music schools.

3. That the Musicians' Division of PCA participate actively in the opening of opportunities for Negroes and members of other minority-groups in student-orchestras and comparable projects.

4. That all those who believe that prejudice should and can be eliminated from the American way of life, determine in no way to support or patronize those establishments which discriminate because of race, color or creed.

5. That we work for enactment of legislation which would make it unconstitutional for any institution receiving Federal funds directly or indirectly to discriminate against minorities—this to include colleges and universities.

6. That we work for the abolition of Jim-Crow unions.

7. That every effort be expended to effect the passage of state and Federal FEPC laws.

8. That, universal and equal franchise being inherent in a free culture, the blot of the poll-tax be eliminated from our democracy.

9. That we ask the State Department to reconsider its action in Xavier Guerrero.
allowing the United States Embassy in Mexico to refuse a visa to

10. That we urge the State Department to reinstitute its policy of circulating international exhibits of contemporary American art.

11. That we urge the County Board of Supervisors to change its suggestion that the annual exhibition of the works of Los Angeles artists be removed from the Los Angeles Museum.

12. That all those present enlist in the fight for the abolition of restrictive covenants.

13. That it be made part of the program of this Division of PCA to work for the enactment of the Taft-Ellender-Wagner Housing Bill.

14. That a Continuations Committee for the Music, Arts and Architecture Panel be started tonight to carry out the action resolved upon here.

THOUGHT CONTROL IN U.S.A.

● ● ● ● ● ● ● ●

No. 4

MEDICINE SCIENCE and EDUCATION

THOUGHT CONTROL IN THE U. S. A.
The collected proceedings of the
Conference on the Subject of Thought Control in the U. S.,
called by the Hollywood Arts, Sciences & Professions Council, PCA,
July 9-13, 1947

Edited by Harold J. Salemson
Designed by Herbert D. Klynn
Published by Hollywood A. S. P. Council, P. C. A.,
1515 Crossroads of the World, Hollywood 28, Calif.

Printed in the U. S. A. by union labor
Aldine Printing Co., Los Angeles, Calif.

medicine

Friday, July 11, 1947, 8:00-10:30 P. M.

Dr. Don MacQueen, Chairman

Papers in this panel prepared and presented by members of the Medical Division, Hollywood Arts, Sciences and Professions Council, PCA.

MEDICAL CARE AND THOUGHT CONTROL

IN discussing this subject, it is necessary first to present facts which show the necessity for improving our system of medical care. For in this field the control of our thoughts operates to prevent and slow down changes sorely needed. Does the people's health require improvement?

Mr. A. J. Altmeyer, Chairman of the Social Security Board, answered this question in December, 1945:

"The answer is twofold. In the first place, while we have made notable progress in reducing the deathrate in this country, we are not the healthiest nation in the world. In the second place, while we have achieved high standards in medical and hospital care, this high quality care is not within the actual reach of large numbers of our people."

Mr. Altmeyer pointed out that in our infant mortality-rate we stood seventh, and as we compared mortality rates for older groups we stood lower and lower. Furthermore, since 1930 there has been practically no reduction in our deathrate. Of more importance than foreign comparisons is the fact that in many parts of the country, and among many groups of our people, death and sickness rates are far higher

249

than in others. The result of various surveys of medical costs adds up to this: that the amount of medical care received by persons in the low-income bracket has been about one-third as adequate as the care received by those in the upper-income bracket. Medical care as it exists is in much closer relation to income than to need. Financial barriers are the cause of the inadequate medical care our people receive.

Those of us in practice know that these barriers to the best care exist and operate constantly in our daily work. The American Medical Association in 1941 admitted that families with incomes below $3000.00 per year require assistance in paying for medical expenses— and in 1941 Americans in that category made up 80% of the population!

Organized medicine, despite the obvious problem, has maintained the consistent attitude of opposing change and only gradually giving in when it must to prevent greater changes. It is worth glancing for a moment at the record, since the present attitude of the American Medical Association and its member societies is in direct continuity with its past performance.

In 1932, an American Medical Association committee, the Committee on the Costs of Medical Care, proposed voluntary health insurance as an approach to the problem. The House of Delegates condemned their report as "socialism and communism inciting to revolution." As late as 1934, the American Medical Association opposed Blue Cross Hospital Insurance. The formation of medical groups giving prepaid medical services has been strongly opposed by organized medicine. At one time, Drs. Ross and Loos here in Los Angeles were expelled from the Los Angeles County Medical Association and the California Medical Association because of this. Its opposition to the Group Health Association of Washington, D.C., including expulsion of physicians from medical societies and hospital appointments, resulted in the Supreme Court of the U. S. ruling that the A.M.A. was acting as a trust in restraint of trade. The A.M.A. opposed the prepaid hospital-insurance service in Boston and more recently was against the development of the Kaiser Health Plans in California.

You may wonder at this past attitude, at the lack of a progressive, experimental approach. It is certainly not the approach of scientific men. It is so because organized medicine is led by a hierarchy of officials who control the policies of the American Medical Association and constituent societies, and their publications. There is recorded no opposition to nominees for official A.M.A. posts. The societies do not permit the expression of a minority opinion. The majority opinion is considered unanimous. In 1941, Garceau in his book, *The Political Life of the A.M.A.*, explained the manner of accomplishing this without openly transgressing democratic principles. The university and research men, those who are chiefly responsible for advances in medical knowledge, are not a part of the hierarchy. They do not take an active part in Medical Association politics. Several years ago, some of our leading professors were attacked for forming a committee and independently publishing several proposals which stated that the health of the people is the concern of the government, and implying that there was room for improvement in medical care. This is thought control with a vengeance.

But what about the present picture? The A.M.A. is now in favor of voluntary health-insurance plans, organized and directed by physicians. The record shows that this position was at first opposed. Has there been a change of heart? Are all points of view and proposals fairly presented to the public and the profession? Or do organized medicine and its allies feel that their first concern is the preservation of the status quo?

Since 1939, there has been in existence an organization misnamed The National Physicians' Committee for the Extension of Medical Service. While technically independent of the A.M.A., it has its official endorsement. It is governed by its doctor-members, all prominent in the hierarchy. This committee, in testimony before a Senate committee, called itself "a non-political, non-profit organization needing the systematic, organized support of all county and sectional medical societies, insurance underwriters, and interested units of business and industry." Its financial sources are unpublished, but are very large. It has distributed millions of pieces of literature, flooding doctors and the public alike, but especially doctors, with vicious propaganda depicting proposals for national health-insurance as attempts to communize America. This committee apparently is the political propaganda agency for the A.M.A., through which it has effected an alliance with Big Business and drug-manufacturers. Consider this alliance! The Medical Association, responsible for the people's medical care, Big Business—the single force most responsible for the people's ill-health, and drug-manufactures—who yearly sell billions of dollars' worth of nostrums and bitterly oppose Federal regulation through pure-food and drug laws.

Some of the leaders of organized medicine have other strange friends. Recently, in California, many of the leaders of the Los Angeles

251

County Medical Association formed a group called Medical Friends of Upton Close. They appealed to all physicians for financial support to keep Mr. Close, whom they term medicine's best friend, on the air. I quote from their letter:

> "Obviously, if we are to be successful in arousing and mobilizing public opinion, we must take advantage of every possible medium. There is one radio commentator on the air today whose background, ideals, past performances and energetic fighting qualities seem just tailormade for our cause. He is Upton Close."

We are not aware that this pro-Fascist has ever been noted for his concern with the health and safety of the American people. Quite the contrary. But prominent medical men do not hesitate to ally themselves with him, and why should they? On the subject of medical care, at least, their views coincide.

It is more serious, however, that many facts have been kept from the members of the medical profession. The scientific journals, read by the profession, and freely discussing controversial scientific questions, have never presented the argument in favor of national health-insurance. Despite repeated suggestions, to my knowledge, no forums or debates presenting all viewpoints have been held at Medical Society meetings. When the Medical Council of the P.C.A. recently sent a letter to the *Bulletin* of the Los Angeles County Medical Association, detailing Mr. Close's unsavory record, the letter was not published and the "open page" in that *Bulletin* has since been discontinued.

Let us for a moment look at the scientific objectivity with which foreign experiences with health-insurance are discussed in our medical journals. The system of socialized medicine in the Soviet Union, how it is set up, its functioning, its results—none of this is mentioned at all. England, after three to four decades of experience with health-insurance, has just passed a law instituting health-insurance for the entire population. British physicians have had several points of disagreement with certain features of the new plan. For the past year, almost every issue of the *Journal of the A.M.A.* has elaborated the objections of the English doctors. What has not appeared is the most important fact of all, namely, that based upon its extensive experience the British Medical Association approved the extension of National Health Insurance to the entire population!

Charles Hill, secretary of the British Medical Association, has written protesting the misrepresentations regarding the British experience. Hist most recent letter appears on Page 600, one of the back pages, of the November 9, 1946, issue of the *Journal of the A.M.A.* It concerns the testimony of Dr. Edward H. Ochsner of the Chicago Medical Society before the Senate Committee on Education and Labor. Dr. Ochsner told the following story, supposedly illustrative of how health-insurance operates in England. He said,

> "A Chicago physician visited a panel-physician in England, and went with him to see how he handled his waiting patients. As the doctor stepped into the waitingroom, the English physician said to the more than 40 patients seated there, 'Will those of you who are troubled with headaches please stand,' and 6 stood up. He then reached into his desk and took out 6 identical prescriptions and handed one to each patient and dismissed them."

What was the answer to this?

> "This is not the first time," said Hill's letter of protest, " (that) I have had occasion to protest against the misleading and inaccurate accounts given, evidently at second hand, by certain American doctors who are endeavoring to avert the introduction of any health insurance scheme into their own country by denouncing the British scheme. In the present instance Dr. Ochsner appears to have accepted as fact a story that must surely have passed around as a joke, and it is most deplorable that he should have repeated it in public as responsible evidence to a Senate committee. It is gross libel. I can assure American readers that such methods are never adopted by British insurance practitioners and would indeed never be tolerated by patients or insurance committees. I challenge Dr. Ochsner to bring forward evidence to substantiate his allegations."

But the *Journal* has not editorially corrected its onesided presentation. I have not found it telling American doctors that the Canadian Medical Association has gone on record as favoring the principle of compulsory health-insurance. New Zealand has had national health service since 1940. In April 1946, the editors of the *Journal of the A.M.A.* commented,

> "The system, of course, is shocking and it is not surprising that the standards of medical practice have deteriorated. Altogether New Zealand affords a wonderful example to the rest of the world of how not to do it."

However, a letter from a practicing physician in New Zealand, entered into the record by Senator Murray at a hearing on Senate Bill 545, states that under their compulsory health-insurance program the infant mortality-rate, once higher than in any country in the world, is now lower than that of the U. S., and even lower than the rate for the state with the best record in this country. Of New Zealand's health program, this doctor said, "Its advantages so far outweigh its disadvantages that few people would now suggest its repeal."

This withholding and misrepresentation of facts represents thought control. Many doctors, basically open-minded, have been led to feel that the sole intent of the health-insurance proposals is to obtain political control of medicine with the consequent rewards to the politicians.

Organized medicine goes further than this, however. The Los Angeles County Medical Association now requires that before admission to membership all applicants attend an indoctrination course. One of the subjects presented (onesidedly, of course) is compulsory health-insurance.

For the past two years, all members of the California Medical Association have been assessed yearly, in addition to their regular dues, the sum of $100 for the explicit purpose of building up a fund more effectively and widely to present medicine's official point of view to the public—in other words, to fight national health-insurance.

But most vicious of all have been the pressures exerted on physicians who disagree with the political leaders of the medical profession.

Appointment to the staff of an accredited hospital requires membership in the County Medical Society, and this is where a doctor can really be hurt. As mentioned earlier, medical societies in the past have expelled members who disagreed with the majority. Two current examples of pressure will suffice. The Physicians' Forum is an organization of doctors, members of the American Medical Association, which works for national compulsory health-insurance. In San Francisco, 15 doctors were in arrears in June, 1946, in their Medical Society dues. The bylaws of the Society require reinstatement in good standing if delinquent dues are paid up before the Fall meeting of the Executive Board. Three of the 15 men in arrears are leading members of the Physicians' Forum, and they sent in their dues checks some time during the summer. Of the 15 men, all were readmitted to the Medical Society, except for the three members of the Physicians' Forum. These doctors appealed this decision. They were Robert Evans, Chief of Pathology at Stanford, Leona Bayer, Assistant Professor of Medicine at Stanford, and Ernst Wolf, Chief of Pediatrics at Mt. Zion Hospital and Assistant Professor of Pediatrics at the University of California. Other members of the Society resented this decision, and one wrote specifically asking about the failure to readmit Dr. Evans. The answer received was to the effect that Dr. Evans had once taught a class at the California Labor School and that was why he did not deserve to be reinstated. Dr. Evans threatened legal action and, 1½ months later, after much pressure from other members of the Stanford faculty, the Board of the Medical Society reversed its decision in Dr. Evans' case and rein-

254

stated him, but not Dr. Bayer or Dr. Wolf. They were notified in June, 1947, that they were not to be reinstated. They have been granted no hearing, despite requests therefor, and have been given no explanation for the action of the Medical Society. A physician who today works for compulsory health-insurance, sponsored by many lay organizations, endorsed by President Truman and Gov. Warren, is threatened with loss of his Medical Society membership and hospital appointments.

Many doctors who would join us in the fight for improvements in the system of medical care, do not because of this intimidation. An incident related to this conference illustrates the current atmosphere. A prominent physician, now in this city, who had formerly practiced in Austria and had taken a leading anti-Nazi stand, was invited to deliver a paper on Medicine under Fascism. After several days' consideration, he regretfully declined. He would not speak at the conference on a medical subject, since he is only a naturalized citizen.

Before closing, we must mention some restrictions currently being attempted. In Connecticut, some Catholic physicians have lost their hospital connections for advocating education in birth control. Thus, the general Red-bating drive and witch hunt threatens doctors just as it affects all others.

It is obvious that in the science of medicine, and especially in its sociologic aspects, our thoughts and actions are being restricted. In this field, some political leaders, for various reasons, are in favor of progressive change. The group primarily responsible for the lack of information and the pressure on individuals is the leadership of organized medicine. By their propaganda, they have kept the great majority of physicians in the dark and have turned them against change. This is a real threat, since the cooperation of the doctors is essential to the success of any health plan.

We have not discussed the case for compulsory health-insurance. That has not been our subject. What has been attempted is the demonstration of a very important fact, that the same un-American pattern of thought control that exists in other fields also operates in medicine.

ADDENDUM

In Bureau Memorandum No. 57 of the Social Security Boards, 1944, the many barriers to adequate medical care are listed. These are:

1. The unpredictability of illness and unpredictability of costs which make budgeting difficult or impossible for families of modest means.

255

2. The neglect of preventive measures.

3. The inability of a large proportion of the population to pay for adequate services through the present method of fee for service payment at the time services are needed.

4. The competition between doctors' bills and other costs of medical care, such as hospital bills.

5. The hesitancy of physicians to propose consultations, additional tests, hospitalization, because of the expense to the patient.

6. The inability of many low-income families to obtain hospitalization except for very serious illnesses or emergencies, and that only in certain munities.

7. Inability of smaller and less prosperous communities to provide hospital and health facilities.

8. The consequent reluctance of doctors to practice in these communities.

9. The necessity for specialists, in particular, to locate where hospital and laboratory facilities are available.

10. The expensive training of doctors and complexity of modern medicine, which makes costs high and emphasizes the need for increased efficiency and economy in method of providing service.

11. Overspecialization because of larger incomes of specialists.

12. Inability of doctors to get away for post-graduate work.

It is obvious that medicine is one of the many fields of science in which advances in technology have outstripped social needs.

MEDICAL RESEARCH
FOR WHOM?

WHEN we first contemplated writing a paper on the subject of thought control in medical research, there was considerable doubt as to whether such control actually existed and, if it did, whether it was widespread or effective. Some members of the Medical Council felt that medical research might even be the one shining example of a field of intellectual endeavor that was free of any control. Others among us thought that there might be occasional instances of profit-motivated commercialism in the laboratory, but that these would be the exceptions rather than the rule. That is why we decided to put the title of this paper in the form of a question—Medical Research for Whom? We really did not know.

Deeply impressed upon our minds is the romantic picture of the lonely investigator peering at a test-tube held against the light, or through a microscope, always, of course, in the late hours of the night, fighting the good fight against the enemies of mankind. And in this good fight he is supported by some kindly millionaire or by a generous foundation. True enough, he himself may suffer from a lack of the comforts of life, his suit may be frayed and shiny, or that noble little woman, who spurs him on with her great faith, may have to cook his dinner over Sterno cans—but for his laboratory there is always enough. Nor would his benefactors ever be *crass* enough to influence the course of our hero's scientific investigations, let alone the results!

Well, if such ever was the case, things have changed considerably. In the first place, the easy pickings are gone and medical research has gotten to be a very complicated, difficult and expensive process. Equipment and materials run into high finance, teams of investigators are usually necessary, much technical and secretarial help is essential. Financing such operations and projects requires large sums of money, and with them goes the opportunity for exercising control. Furthermore, large sums of money frequently demand results, and so the investigator is harrassed, not only by the suffering of mankind, but by the necessity to produce results or else lose his support. Then, too, such large sums of money are usually derived from sources that have a vested interest in some established product or process, and the affection of such interests must not be aleinated.

Now it begins to appear that there are not only possibilities but also probabilities of thought control in medical research. When the gathering of the material for this paper was completed, we no longer felt there was much question left in the title.

Then we discovered that we were not alone in these suspicions. Here are a few quotations from Professor Goodpasture, of the Vanderbilt Medical School. (Ernest W. Goodpasture, *Research and Medical Practice*, Science, Vol. 104).

Dr. Goodpasture is one of the leading medical investigators in the United States. His main work has been in the field of cell-parasite relationship in bacterial and virus infection, for which he has received universal recognition. His most recent contribution was the original development of the method for propagation of viruses in pure culture by inoculation of chick embryos.

In an address in May, 1946, Dr. Goodpasture discussed the support of medical research by philanthropic foundations. He said:

"The aid provided has been helpful and often essential to bringing initiated research to a useful conclusion, but the price paid is, to a considerable extent, a release by the investigator, the teacher and the university, of the only thing worth while academically—the responsibility for originality and initiative in the free pursuit of intellectual curiosity."

He goes on to say:

". . . The determination and direction of fields of research by the distant control, often from beyond the grave, is . . . inhibiting and stultifying. . . .

"So, in the rapid development of medical research and teaching in this country, a dual mechanism has evolved: the university, the institution of learning, is largely controlled in its research policies and provisions by extramural influences.

"Industry has not devised means of affording a free financial aid to universities; if anything, its aid, with few exceptions, is the most restrictive."

And he concludes:

"Unfortunately, the universities have become merely the operating agencies for trustees and administrators of funds, who reserve for themselves, in large measure, the privilege of responsibility of determining the trends of research, the training of scientists, and the extent and quality of the result."

We have chosen a few of the many examples of control in medical research. There are included some instances of the suppression of new knowledge resulting from uncontrolled research. We have purposely excluded the everyday practices of drug-industry control and manipulation of price and supply when research is not involved. Though these monopolistic practices have a profound effect on the health of our nation, through the creation of artificial scarcity and increasing the cost of medical care, they are not pertinent to the subject of this paper.

An example of how research and vested interests are closely related is furnished by Stilbestrol, a pharmaceutical which has the same action as the female sex hormones. Stilbestrol was discovered by a group of scientists, headed by E. C. Dodds, at the University of London and Oxford University; the research was financed in this case by the British Government, through the Medical Research Council. This new medication could have been available as early as 1939 at a fraction of the price of hormones controlled by the cartel of four major drug-houses. These companies were distressed by the danger of Stilbestrol upsetting their price structures and control of the market. A conference was held on August 1, 1939, at which were discussed various proposals for keeping Stilbestrol off the American market.

Dr. Stragnell of Schering Corp. advised the conference that "the European 'groups' were working primarily in order to find any fault or shortcomings with Stilbestrol . . ." (Kilgore Subcom. on War Mobil., *Monopoly & Cartel Practices,* Part 10, p. 1118).

A memorandum concerning this conference was found in the Schering Corp. files, which stated: "Ciba and Roche-Organon want it (Stilbestrol) just in order to be able to knock it with physicians. They say the hormone business in England has been destroyed by this new product." (This information came to light when the Alien Property Custodian seized German-owned Schering in 1942.)

The cartel never introduced unpatented Stilbestrol, even to knock it. It was finally introduced to the American market late in 1941 and is now being manufactured by over 30 firms. The effect on the price of the other hormone products was as the cartels feared—prices immediately came down more than 50%.

The large firms have carried out a whispering-campaign against Stilbestrol through their retail-men and trade-publications, emphasizing the side reactions of Stilbestrol. To a large extent they have succeeded—Stilbestrol is regarded by a great number of physicians as a dangerous drug.

After investigating the activities of the cartels in this country, the Department of Justice prosecuted these four companies, and fines totalling $54,000 were assessed and paid in December, 1941. Wendell Berge, Assistant Attorney General, stated that "research has been seriously affected by restrictions imposed by foreign cartel members."

If anybody thinks justice was done in the interests of the public, consider what a piddling sum $54,000 is to four large corporations compared to the fantastic profits they made for years, and still make, from one item alone like female sex hormones.

A classical example of control in medical research is furnished by the story of Vitamin D, a specific remedy for rickets, the poor man's disease. Vitamin D is synthetically prepared by irradiating ergosterol with ultraviolet light, by a process discovered and patented in 1923 by Dr. Steenbock, a professor at the University of Wisconsin. The Wisconsin Alumni Research Foundation was promptly set up for the purpose of marketing this valuable product, protecting the public and preventing unscrupulous commercialism. At any rate, that was their *stated* purpose. The foundation has no formal connection with the University of Wisconsin. A summary of the investigation of this Foundation by the Anti-trust Division of the Department of Justice reveals the following points:

1) The Foundation has been the vehicle for creating a domestic monopoly —and limitation of potency of vitamin products.
2) It has exhibited a lack of interest in research unless a commercial advantage could be obtained.
3) It has suppressed the use of competing processes.
4) It has attempted to suppress the publication of scientific research data which are at variance with its monopoly interests.
5) It has used its licensing scheme to discourage research by its licensees.

For many years, the Foundation maintained a complete monopoly on synthetic Vitamin D, controlling prices so that they remained high at all times. The poor people of our country, who needed it most, benefitted little by this great discovery of medical science. Finally, about 1935, a new process was discovered and patented by General Mills, namely, irradiating ergosterol with cathode rays. Unable to prove patent infringement, the Foundation undertook to establish that its product was superior. Dr. Alonzo Smith, of Howard University, and Dr. Nolan Owens, of Freedmen's Hospital, both Negro institutions in Washington, D. C., were given a grant of money, and commissioned by the Wisconsin Alumni Foundation to make comparative tests on the two products, and to prepare an article for the medical journals on the results.

On June 17, 1936, Drs. Smith and Owens submitted their results to the Foundation. Their conclusion was that *there was no significant difference in the two products.* One of the officers of the Foundation wrote shortly thereafter that the Foundation was opposed to publication of the results in any form, and that Drs. Owens and Smith would be advised that publication of the work was *not* desirable. The Foundation then arranged an agreement with the owners of the new process to keep it off the market and to use only the Steenbock process in order better to maintain the price structure. Thus, the results of the Foundation's program have been to stifle its own research activities. Certainly, these are peculiar results of a program instituted "to protect the public" and "to prevent unscrupulous commercialism."

That is an example of the procedure used when a new discovery threatens an established patent—if you can't prove patent infringement, then try to prove the inferiority of the new product, and if that doesn't succeed, then buy it out and destroy it.

Finally, in 1946, a Federal Court in Illinois forced the Foundation to surrender its patents on Vitamin D to the people of the United States of America forever.

Another example, and a personal one:

Your reporter has been working with a group of physicians for several years in the Arthritis Clinic of a local hospital. We were using the usual measures for the treatment of arthritis. Some two years ago, we were approached by the representatives of a pharmaceutical house that had launched on the market a new cure for arthritis. This was done with much fanfare and high-pressured publicity. This house offered us, free of charge, unlimited quantities of their expensive drug. Finding surprisingly little substantiation in the medical literature for their rather exorbitant claims, we proposed to these representatives that we test the value of their drug by a simple process of administering it to one group of patients and using a dummy capsule prepared to look like their product on another group of patients, and comparing results. After much consultation with their home office, they agreed. They were even willing to supply us with the dummy capsules and pay the salary of a full-time secretary, but they made one stipulation: all control of publication of the results must be in their hands. *They insisted on the power to suppress publication.* Needless to say, this investigation was never undertaken, there being insufficient funds to buy the large quantities of the drug; previously-donated supplies were withdrawn, and what would have been an honest estimation of a questionable product never reached the profession. Most authorities on arthritis now regard the drug as worthless, but without critical comparative tests having been made.

Even the field of research on the costs and availability of medical care has not been without controls. Less than 10 years ago, at the height of the last great depression, at a time when our people were suffering from lack of medical care, amongst other things, several foundations undertook research and investigation in this field with a view to finding a solution. At that time, the American Medical Association had been forced into the position, after many years of opposition, that voluntary health-insurance might help the people provide medical and hospital care for themselves. The Milbank Memorial Fund carried on for several years valuable research work on the cost of medical care. They finally concluded that voluntary insurance, because of its expense and the widespread unemployment of that period, was not the ideal solution to the problem and recommended a universal system of prepaid compulsory health-insurance. Now, the Milbank Fund is largely supported by its capital investment in the Borden Company, a producer of milk and milk products. The President of the Fund was also the head of Borden's. A boycott against Borden's was threatened and partially carried out by the opponents of compulsory health-insurance. The Fund immediately abandoned its program of research in this field and liquidated its plans for publication. The boycott was lifted. Several other foundations, similarly threatened, dropped out of this controversial medical-care field, including the Rosenwald Fund, vulnerable because of its dependence on the Sears, Roebuck interests. (See J. A. Kingsbury, *Health in Handcuffs,* and J. Rorty, *American Medicine Mobilizes.*)

Recently, on May 28, 1947, an interesting item appeared in Drew Pearson's column about the fight against cancer. The facts of this story have been checked in the files of the *New York Times* and they are accurate. This is the story:

The House of Representatives had appropriated $17,300,000 for cancer research. In hearings before the Senate on this item, James Adams, Chairman of the American Cancer Society and also Chairman of Standard Brands Corp., urged the Senate to cut the appropriation by more than 5 million dollars.

This remarkable performance must have astounded the august

Senators, for, from time immemorial, the plea in such instances is always for more money. And here was the head of a society pledged to fight a disease which claims the lives of 175,000 Americans annually, urging that the Senate *cut* the appropriation passed by the notoriously penny-pinching Lower House.

This money was to be spent under the supervision of the U. S. Public Health Service, headed by Surgeon General Tom Parran, who incidentally, has espoused the cause of compulsory health-insurance. Mr. Adams did not want too much money in the hands of Dr. Parran, because then there might be some competition to his privately-supported Society. Tax-deductible contributions from industrial magnates in the now-popular fight against cancer have great publicity value. Mr. Adams finally proposed that what little money was appropriated should be administered privately, by Mr. Kettering of General Motors and Mr. Frank Howard of Standard Oil. Apparently private control of this field in something to fight for.

Quite irrelevantly, Pearson points out that this same Frank Howard, after the Nazis invaded Poland, made a deal with I. G. Farben, delivering into his hands some 200 patents for safekeeping *"through the term of the war, whether the United States came in or not"* (direct quote from letter by Howard to home office). These are the men who would safeguard the interests of the public and who struggle for control of a field of research as if it were a commercial fight for sales supremacy!

Two or three years ago, one of our leading members, a book-dealer, was Secretary of the local Barlow Society for the History of Medicine, a recognized and respected group devoted to study and research in the field of medical history. Our member committed the unpardonable indiscretion of expressing his support of the Murray-Wagner-Dingell Bill in a magazine article and in a debate. The BSHM was thereupon investigated by the Council of the L. A. County Medical Assn., and was requested to effect the resignation of its secretary. This it refused to do. A suggestion was also made at this Council meeting that the FBI be called in to investigate the BSHM. Then, the Board of Trustees of the L. A. County Medical Assn. instructed the Medical Library of the Association to cease buying books from our member. Though annual transactions had amounted to substantial sums prior to that incident, the Library has since bought not a single book from him. This same individual's name was later proposed as a member of the observation group for Operation Crossroads at Bikini. His name was rejected by the War Department, for "reasons of security"; the Army refused to explain its insulting action. There are only two possible reasons for this rejection: espousal of health-insurance and activity as a progressive Democrat. Some of you may know the name of this individual—for genuine reasons of security, and for fear of further reprisals against the BSHM, we have been requested to withhold it.

In conclusion, we would like again to introduce some quotes from Wendell Berge, recently Assistant Attorney General of the United States and head of the Anti-trust Division of the Department of Justice. Mr. Berge was personally responsible for the cracking of numerous monopolies, especially in the pharmaceutical field. He talks from direct experience. Concerning monopolies he says:

> "When it might be to their advantage in maintaining or exploiting their monopoly position, they have adulterated their products to an extent and in a manner endangering the health, and even the lives, of consumers. Almost incredible as these assertions may be, they are not subject to contradiction—the incontrovertible facts are clearly set forth in Congressional investigations and in the evidence in anti-trust cases of the Department of Justice."

> "The fact is that they have retarded technological advance and the introduction of improved devices and products whenever such developments seemed to threaten their vested interests, despite the fact that thereby national security might be jeopardized."

> "In numerous instances, scientific research has been perverted and misused in order to strengthen monopoly restrictions illegally based on patents."

> ". . . patents have been used to discourage research by independent inventors and businessmen. What incentive is there to inventors to develop new products, or processes, when they may be, in effect, inventing themselves into a patent infringement suit?"

> "Few effects of monopoly have been more insidious than the consequences of cartel control over many areas in the drug and medical fields."

> "The fight against disease is a primary concern of society everywhere. Yet, the brilliance and the industry of modern scientists have all too often been perverted by the efforts of selfish groups to fasten the grip of monopoly on products essential to health and welfare."

All of these quotations are from Mr. Berge's book, *Cartels, Challenge to a Free World,* published in 1944. They require no additional comment.

DISCUSSION

The presentation of papers constituting this Panel was followed by extended discussion from the audience of various pertinent points, such as: the provisions for research contained in the Murray-Wagner-Dingell Bill; the effect of the Anti-Trust Law on the monopolies and cartels mentioned; the stand taken by the American Medical Association on the subject of socialized medicine.

A member of the audience brought out the point that the importance of the evening's discussion was reduced through the fact that the persons present were those who, in general, already knew what was going on. He therefore resolved, and the audience unanimously passed the resolution, that the Medical Division of the Hollywood Arts, Sciences and Professions Council, be instructed to prepare the material of the Panel in such form that it might be readily circulated to members of the profession and other interested individuals and organizations.

A further suggestion was the publication of a magazine addressed specifically to medical men, in which frank discussion of the problems covered here could be carried on.

On the subject of immediate medical care, attention was called to the need in Los Angeles for new hospitals. The "Hamilton Report", it was pointed out, called for two new hospitals: this has been before the Los Angeles Chamber of Commerce, which is absolutely opposed to the allocation of any government funds toward this end, on the grounds that this would constitute totalitarianism. There is now being formed a committee of businessmen to support the hospital projects: this committee will devote itself to educating the public and enlisting all possible official agencies toward the construction of these institutions. The speaker urged that all present become active and join in the fight to get Federal funds for these hospitals. This, he felt, was the one huge immediate task at hand.

Following this discussion, a series of resolutions were unanimously passed. They are:

265

RESOLUTIONS

1. *Resolved,* that the Medical Division of the Hollywood A. S. P., which is a part of the PCA, go on record as opposing the formation or the furtherance of the Tenney Committee, the Rankin Un-American Committee, and the Truman loyalty test.

2. *Resolved,* that the members of this Panel express themselves in opposition to all thought control in medical research by monopolies and private industry.

3. *Resolved,* that we call upon all professional organizations to cease and desist from discriminatory measures against those of their members who espouse the cause of compulsory health-insurance.

4. *Resolved,* that all professional schools be called upon to cease their practices of discriminating against members of minority-groups.

5. *Resolved,* that a publication be undertaken by the Medical Division and other sections of PCA, to afford an outlet for discussion of problems such as those studied here, and to be distributed without cost to members of the profession, financing to come from an advertising program to be worked out with local business interests.

science and education

Saturday, July 12, 1947, 2:00-4:30 P. M.

Dr. Harry Hoijer, Chairman

Speakers: Carl Epling, Morris Neiburger,
J. B. Ramsey, Harold Orr, Carroll Richardson

Papers presented in this Panel were prepared by the
authors with the cooperation of a group of Southern
California scientists and educators.

Carl Epling
Ph.D.; Professor of Bot-
any at UCLA

THE NEGATION OF SCIENCE

TIME was when the pursuit of science was largely the avocation of men who, for one reason or another, were blessed with leisure, and whose curiosity found satisfaction in the observation of natural phenomena. One of the great scientists of this period was Benjamin Franklin. Yet, for all his preoccupation with science, Franklin was no less a citizen, and you will recall that the Society which he founded, was founded for the purpose of increasing and disseminating useful knowledge.

The amazing increase of useful knowledge since Franklin's time has had as its direct consequence the rise of the industrial state. This extraordinarily complex social organization has become increasingly dependent upon the science that nurtured it. The position of the scientist in the industrial state has accordingly become one of crucial

267

importance. He has now become an indispensable part of the social fabric and, in effect, holds the keys to our industrial civilization. But the scientist is no less a citizen; indeed, he is more so, for he is brought more and more into contact with the problems which affect other citizens, problems which he in part has created. He has, therefore, an added moral obligation to scrutinize the conditions imposed upon his work and to ascertain the ends toward which his ideas are to be employed. He cannot wisely or properly dissociate his function as a citizen from that of a scientist.

The purpose of this discussion, as it seems to me, is, therefore, to inquire into the restrictions on scientific endeavor which may be placed upon the scientist, first, as a scientist and, second, as a citizen. To restrict one is necessarily to restrict the other.

Just what is science? Science is something more than test-tubes and microscopes. It is an examination and synthesis of ideas, ideas derived from the facts and events of personal experience. These ideas may be one's own, derived from one's own test-tubes, or of others from theirs, but they are ideas. Their social justification is the possibility that, once applied, they may permit man further to modify his environment in ways which enhance his social and economic security, which contribute to the satisfaction of his material and intellectual needs or, as Bacon has succinctly said, science "works for the relief of man's estate." Whether this release from the vicissitudes of nature, this mastery of the environment, is preferable in the long run may be debatable, but it appears to be the desire of most humans and is the peculiar characteristic of man amongst other animals. It is the end and purpose of his social organization and may be summed up in the words "peace and plenty."

The ideas of science have seldom, if ever, been conjured from the mind and experience of one individual. They have taken form in many minds of diverse experiences by a long process of cross-fertilization. The primary means of cross-fertilization rests upon publication: the free and complete dissemination of information for the benefit of whomsoever it may reach, wherever he may be, to be utilized, passed by, or rejected, as the experience and judgment of the reader may dictate. No individual can predict where in the complex terrain of present knowledge his own small observation is likely to lodge and bear fruit.

Of cardinal importance to science, therefore, is the requirement that all scientists shall be able to avail themselves of the experience and ideas of workers in relevant fields. Publication of scientific data is the great forum in which men are heard and their ideas evaluated. The growth of science has coincided with the rejection of secrecy: the secrecy of the medieval guild. To return to it is to return to another and sterile age: it is to undermine the social form which free interchange has made possible. For this essential of free dissemination of knowledge closely parallels the basic tenets of our government: of freedom of speech, of press and assembly, and of religious freedom, for science is also a faith. The scientific letters of Franklin to his contemporaries and those of the Committees of Correspondence were expressions of the same fundamental need. That need is enormously magnified in our complex industrial society.

The free dissemination of knowledge is threatened whenever it comes into conflict with the limited objectives of established interests. Restriction is often increased as a consequence of the increasing organization of these interests. I suggest that the mounting threat to scientific endeavor, and indirectly to our social form, comes from two sources: the expanding ventures of industrial organizations into scientific research and, second, the increasing concern of government in it. Under the conditions which exist, both represent established interests with which free dissemination of scientific data is often in conflict.

The tendency of some (but not all) industry to suppress or canalize the fruits of investigation which might accrue to the social good, but which jeopardize its economic position of the moment, has been repeatedly established. Because of the large sums invested in fixed assets, innovations, however desirable, may prove impossible under existing conditions. The matter has been expressed bluntly as follows: "Why should a corporation spend its earnings and deprive its stockholders of dividends to develop something which will upset its own market or junk all its present equipment?" Under conditions as they exist, one cannot expect any social group thus to commit economic suicide. But the free expression of the scientists employed is being curtailed or prevented and I suggest that, so far as industry suppresses the ideas it fosters, it is likely to stifle the goose which, lo, has laid these many golden eggs.

That the increasing concern of government in science should prove subversive of the public good may seem a paradox. Nevertheless, it may and sometimes does unnecessarily place a limitation upon the free exchange of scientific information. The causes are principally two:

269

the effect of organization itself and, infinitely more dangerous and subtle, the secrecy which is and may be imposed by government subvention or intervention, under the plea of national security.

The effect of any organization, governmental or industrial, is to create a hierarchy which consciously or unconsciously is likely to impose a restraint upon its lower ranks. In many government agencies concerned with scientific research, papers may be published only with the consent of the superior, sometimes only after considerable revision. The scientists concerned have both families and ambitions. Like others, they dwell partly in the future. Confronted with the contrary judgment of a superior, there are few who would not compromise with that future, if by silence they might remain secure and undisturbed in their work. Their ideas cannot always be freely expressed, particularly in the areas of disagreement where they are most needed.

Far more dangerous, however, is the restraint imposed by secrecy, for secrets, by their very nature, induce compartmentalization. In many government contracts, particularly those sponsored by the armed forces, knowledge of the objectives and purposes of a given investigation are restricted to the small group in charge, the remainder working blindly upon the parts parcelled out to them, sometimes forbidden discussion even among themselves. Investigations of profound importance to every citizen are now being cloaked in secrecy and through the cloak one may discern the shadows of suspicion and self-seeking, of the evasion of responsibility and the concealment of false judgments, of subterfuge and sharp practice, none of which can fail to corrode the integrity of the scientist and be subversive of the great democracy of science, which undertakes that the voice of each worker be heard, whatsoever his station and nationality, and that his words be assessed according to their usefulness to others. Apart from the fact that secrecy is the very negation of science, neither the citizen-at-large nor the scientist-citizen has voice in the direction which investigations, fraught with his own destiny, may take.

Finally, every encroachment upon the rights of any citizen to free expression and full discussion of his ideas, and to free assembly, which are the basic tenets of our government, are threats to the integrity of that science upon which our state is founded.

What I have said is nothing new; it has been said many times over, in different ways, by different men. Briefly, the concept is this: our society is the consequence of an attitude of mind. Any attempt to repress or restrict this attitude, however subtle it may be, any attempt to infringe upon it, to intimidate it, is subversive of the social form itself. The continued and jealous vigilance to protect academic freedom is not a whim of scholars, but their recognition of the historical relationship between the rights of religious belief, of political and economic democracy and the rise of science; it is the central premise of the scholar's faith. If scientists are alert to the ultimate effect upon science and society of attempts to restrict this freedom, I suggest that they will do well, now, everywhere, to require as the condition of their employment the full measure of discussion and publication. The spacious satisfactions of Franklin's time have all but disappeared.

Morris Neiburger

Asst. prof., meteorology, UCLA; Ph.
D., U. of Chicago; with U.S. Weather
Bureau, 1930-40; taught, Mass. Inst.
of Technology, 40-41

THOUGHT CONTROL
OF SCIENCE IN INDUSTRY

FIRST, I should like to make it clear that I have not had any direct connection with industry, so that everything I say today is either by observation from outside or by second-hand report. Nevertheless, I hope that my comments will contribute a certain amount of stimulus and direction to the discussion of this topic.

The importance of industry's effect on scientific research may be inferred from the fact that in 1940 industrial research expended $300,-000,000, or almost ten times the total spent by the government and universities combined. While much of this expenditure was for development-work of a nature that might be classed as engineering rather than science, a considerable portion went into investigations regarding fundamental processes and their applications, and the entire sum has influence on the progress of science and society.

There are two aspects to be considered in this question of thought control in the applications of science in industry; firstly, those pertaining to the individual scientist and, secondly, those affecting science and society at large.

The individual scientist who enters the industrial lair must and usually does expect the same treatment as any other employee, with respect to personal freedoms and motivations. His activities must be confined to the objectives of the firm for which he works; his loyalties to the ideals of discovery of truth and service to mankind must be subordinated to loyalties to the aggrandizement of the size and prestige of the corporation and the profits of the stockholders. He even yields, in most cases, all rights to discoveries he may make while in the firm's employ, even if those discoveries are made outside of working-hours and are unrelated to the firm's activities. He agrees to consign to the corporation patents to his inventions, usually for the munificent bonus of one dollar.

272

The scientist in industry finds that he is limited in his exchange of information with other scientists. To a large extent, progress of the individual as well as of science as a whole depends on the free interchange of ideas. The gratification of the scientist in his work comes in part from this exchange of ideas and from the recognition of his work by his colleagues, which ensues on publication of its results. The scientific worker in industry finds himself hampered on the one hand by the fact that he cannot learn what others working in industry on analogous problems are doing and, on the other, by his inability to publish his results and thus obtain the criticism of other scientists regarding their validity, as well as recognition for his accomplishment. Under these circumstances, the industrial scientist is relatively inefficient, and it is not surprising, therefore, that in spite of the much smaller budgets, most basic research and many of the important applications thereof still come from academic institutions.

In justice, it must be remarked in this connection that the field of industrial research at the outset was restricted to application of the fundamental discoveries of academic research to profitable enterprises. Subsequently, when it was found that these applications gave rise to questions which could not readily be answered without further fundamental research, the large corporations allowed their research staffs to branch out into various fundamental investigations, often without immediately discernible connections to the improvement of the companies' products or production-methods. In some cases, these corporations allow their employees limited rights of communication and publication. However, secrecy is the only means by which a company can "protect its interest" in fundamental discoveries, in advance of their application to patentable devices or processes. Thus, even under the most favorable conditions, restrictions are introduced at critical points in the work of the scientist in industry.

More serious to the scientist than this restraint in his freedom of expression, is the restriction of the subject of his investigation. To the true scientist, the search for truth comes first, and in this search his only guide can be his own mental processes, by which he evaluates the various problems, chooses among them that which is of most interest and promise, devises various methods of attack, and selects the one which appears most practicable. At every point, he must be on the lookout for clues to the path, and when he sees a completely new task he must make his decision, whether to abandon the work of months and follow it, perhaps to a great discovery, perhaps to a blind alley.

In industry, such an apparently haphazard procedure would not be tolerated. Firstly, the scientist has his problem defined in terms of a specific objective of interest to the manufacturer, *e.g.*, to design a device or synthesize a material. Accepting this task may be no hardship to him, unless he has a prior interest in another problem, for the proposed problem may involve as great a challenge to his ingenuity and be as interesting intrinsically as any problem he might set for himself. When, however, the investigator comes to choosing his path, and especially when some particularly promising aspect deviating from the immediate purpose turns up, he is constrained by his duties to his employer, and must set aside any lead, however encouraging, if it does not point toward the solution of the employer's problem. The freedom of choice of subject-matter and procedure, which is so precious to the scientist, is given up when he enters industrial research.

In view of these circumstances, the questions might be asked, "But does not the scientist have the choice of not entering industry, just as any other worker, if he wishes to follow his own whims? Why should industry or anyone else pay a man for riding his hobby, be it golf or stamp-collecting, or investigating nature?"

The answers to these questions are many. Firstly, from the purely utilitarian viewpoint, our experience through the past three centuries has shown that almost all discoveries regarding the "laws of nature" ultimately prove applicable in improving conditions of human life. Secondly, the problems to be dealt with are so complex, and the procedures of obtaining solutions so difficult, that only when a man pursues them with undivided energy, without conflict of desires, and with the strongest personal drives, is there hope of solution. Thus, at least so far as the basic problems of science are concerned, the scientist should be free to follow his bent and make his own decisions regarding the choice of problems and the methods he follows. Whether industry should provide positions with such freedom, may be a question. It is surely true that industry benefits greatly from all past research carried on in this fashion, and it might be considered payment of its debt to past science for it to do so.

The choice of the scientist to work for industry is no more free than that of any other worker: he can work or he can starve; and, while some few scientists have made the latter choice, most men are not quite that unwilling to compromise their ideals. Many of them choose positions at universities and colleges at much lower salaries but with somewhat more freedom than industry offers, but the field is limited and for many the choice is not between lower- and higher-paying jobs, but between the relative lack of freedom and no job at all. Since most positions for men trained as scientists are with industrial firms, most of these men must perforce work for industry and submit to the thought control involved therein. That this control is less tolerable to them than to other workers, is due to the nature of scientific work.

Even in the matter of hours, the structure of industrial employment is antagonistic to creative activity. At times, the scienist may be impelled to work day and night for weeks on end; at other times, even eight hours a day in the laboratory are fruitless and depressing, and would best be dispensed with. The creative energies cannot be turned on and off by punching clocks, and the scientific worker loses his zest for the work, when required to attempt to do so.

Finally, I shall refer briefly to the frustrating effect on the individual scientist of suppression of his socially-useful results, or diversion of his efforts into socially-harmful directions. When a useful discovery is suppressed or obstructed because it would be unprofitable to a private interest, the inventor is disheartened and is less likely to apply himself to further discoveries. Similarly, a research-worker assigned to the task of designing a material which will appear durable but wear out fast, so that it will need to be replaced, cannot receive much pleasure from the successful attainment of his objective. The joy of scientific work comes from the discovery of the beauties in the laws of nature, and the enhancement of human welfare through their application. To the extent that the industry requires the scientist to abandon these purposes, it deprives him of his principal motivation.

For the progress of science and society at large, the restrictions on scientific activity placed by industry may be more serious. Strong cases have been presented by many demonstrating that our patent-system, rather than stimulating invention and progress in the application of science to everyday living, serves to decrease it. In addition to such occasional practices as suppression of useful inventions, the existence of the patent monopoly discourages the independent inventor from experimenting in many fields where large corporations hold patents.

According to Dr. Comfort A. Adams, Professor Emeritus of Electrical Engineering at Harvard, "within one year after the expiration of the Tesla induction motor patent the costs and weights of induction motors were reduced by thirty percent, without any sacrifice of operating qualities." The delays in the introduction of fluorescent lighting and FM radio are recent examples of actions by large corporations more interested in protection of existing capital-investment than in the improvement of the products reaching the consumer.

I have already mentioned the diversion of the efforts of the scientist from socially-useful activities to those which preserve the market. In automobile design, for example, the efforts to produce engines with greater operating economy, durability, and ease of repair, have been diverted into a race for higher power, faster acceleration, higher top-speeds, and advertising campaigns have been conducted to convince the public that these are the features they want. I do not know whether any scientists are actually employed by the cigarette industry to measure the number of coughs per carload, but even short of this there is a huge economic waste in the utilization of our available research personnel.

The great corporations in general have tended to resist changes which render their capital equipment obsolete. The gas companies, instead of incorporating the electric-light into their businesses, fought its development and made necessary the solicitation of new capital. Similarly, the Western Union Telegraph Co. resisted the telephone, and the telegraph and telephone companies put obstacles in the way of the development of wireless telegraphy and radio. And in the past decade RCA has been resisting the development of FM transmission.

It is only since the First World War that industry has undertaken research to any great extent. It is certainly true that thousands of students who would not otherwise have selected science as their vocation have been attracted to it by the availability of positions in industry. But this great diversion of personnel from basic to applied science, and from socially-useful activities to those insuring the profits of the industrialist, constitutes a severe drain on the creative talent of this country and the world. Increasingly, the brilliant young scientist, faced with the choice between an academic position at low salary, or an industrial position at an adequate one, chooses the latter. As Thomas Midgely, Jr., late president of the American Chemical Society and vice-president of the Ethyl Corporation, put it:

> "It is quite true that scientists, as a group, are more willing to work for the sheer joy of satisfying their inquiring minds than are most people; but it is true also that scientists have wives who want new automobiles and fur coats, quite as physicians' and lawyers' and judges' wives do, and scientists have children, just as other folks do, and scientists like to feel that they can raise and educate these children, as other folks do, and to do it they are

deserving of an opportunity to obtain a financial reward that is somewhat proportional to the services they render society."

As industry draws men, and diverts them to its purposes, there may result a retardation both in the carrying on of basic research, and in the training of new scientific personnel. For, while industry draws many present and potential university professors and instructors to its research staffs, it must ultimately depend, as the rest of science, on the university for the training of the staffs of the future. Thus, in a sense, industry is tending to kill the goose which lays the golden eggs.

Unless there is developed some method by which a larger proportion of scientific personnel can afford to remain in the fields of relatively-unrestricted basic research and teaching which the universities offer, the future will see a gradual decline of the quality and ultimately of the quantity of research, both basic and applied, for lack of qualified personnel. There is already a great dilution in the quality of teaching at universities and colleges, and this will continue to have increasing effects on the products of education, our trained personnel, until adequate incentives are established to keep a sufficient number of scientists from leaving academic institutions. So far, the freedom from thought control has proved one such incentive. That it is not always sufficient, is indicated by the drift of personnel under economic compulsion into the higher-paying jobs of industry.

J. B. Ramsey

Ph.D.; professor of chemistry, UCLA

THE SCIENTIST AND HIS WORK

W HEN, as today, the basic institutions of science are being questioned and attacked, scientists may find it necessary to examine with care the need for freedom in science, and to state their case and defend it before the world. It may also help the world on its way to freedom, to make known how freedom operates in science and how closely intertwined it is with all other freedoms. The fact that the same forces which spearhead the attacks on racial minorities, for instance, also lead in the perennial attacks on science, is surely no accident.

A statement submitted by Dr. Enrico Fermi to the Senate Hearings on Science Legislation, defines the function of freedom in science as follows:

"Experience has indicated that the somewhat haphazard exploration of the field of knowledge that results from an intensive freedom of the individual scientific worker to choose his own subject is the only way to insure that no important line of attack is neglected."

We have here a plea for freedom in science on the ground of social efficiency. The discretionary powers which a system of freedom grants to scientists are regarded as the only effective machinery for co-ordinating the efforts of individual scientists to the joint purpose of the advancement of knowledge. Usually one thinks of co-ordination as a process imposing restraint on the discretionary powers of individuals. Co-ordination can be achieved in science, however, by the opposite method of releasing the individual to follow his own impulses. Let it be noted that scientific work may be unique among all human activities in this regard: the real social value of leaving the scientist free to follow his own curiosity does not imply a social value in leaving the farmer free to determine what crops he should plant or the manufacturer to decide what goods he should assemble.

The co-ordination which is absolutely essential in science is not one imposed from without, but that gained by the completely free com-

278

munication of the scientist with other workers in the field and with the outside world. Thus, the criticism of his colleagues, men whose judgment he can trust, will tend to keep the researcher from pursuing an intellectual will-o'-the-wisp. Similarly, the advice and stimulation of other scientists is invaluable to even the most gifted researcher. The popular notion of the solitary and unsociable "mad scientist" is quite without foundation in fact.

The co-ordination of science consists of the adjustment of each scientist's activities to the results achieved by the others. Since such mutual adjustment depends on the independent decisions of each, its operations require the complete freedom of all, both in action and communication. If we regard science as a vast jigsaw puzzle, the need for both free thought and free communication becomes obvious, for clearly if we gave the same puzzle to a dozen players who were forced to work in isolation they would not progress much faster than one man alone. Similarly, if the work on a jigsaw puzzle is too closely restricted, it may go slowly, for frequently when an impasse has been reached in one part of the puzzle, attention may fruitfully be turned to the fitting together of obscure pieces which seem at the moment to have no relationship to the part which has been worked on.

To regard science as the solution of a jigsaw puzzle is, however, an oversimplification, as it fails to take into account the characteristic vagueness of the task pursued by science. The pieces of a jigsaw puzzle are bought with the certainty that they will yield a solution. Science does not proceed toward such predefined ends. There is inherent, nevertheless, in each new claim to discovery the practical affirmation of a coherent system of truth which is capable of indefinite extension into yet-unexplored regions. This dedication of scientists to the advancement of an intellectual process beyond their control and to the upholding of values transmitted to them by tradition, represents the sense in which science does possess and pursue a coherent task. As the Prince of Philosophers, Newton, phrased it so modestly:

"I seemed so tall, and I could see so far because I stood on the shoulders of giants."

Modern science depends for its material existence on support from outside. In order to maintain coherence and freedom within science, therefore, outside authorities must allocate their support to different scientific purposes according to the guidance of scientific opinion. They would otherwise inevitably disrupt the coherence of science and undermine its freedom.

279

It is clear, then, that dangers to academic freedom arise wherever the responsibility for the expansion of scientific institutions falls to public authorities who are not sufficiently familiar with the nature of science. As guardians of the public interest, they may feel reluctant to leave to scientific opinion full control over public funds allocated to science. Dazzled perhaps by the achievements of applied science in wartime, they may fail to recognize clearly the different nature of the quieter pursuits of pure research and not realize that these can be maintained only in complete independence.

There are, of course, some public authorities whose seeming ignorance is so aggressive that it can be construed as purposeful. In order to illustrate the misconceptions and outright fabrications which have been propagated by presumably responsible political leaders (including the President), it may be useful to refer to some of the Senate hearings on the confirmation of the membership of the Atomic Energy Commission. The Senate Committee opened on January 27, 1947, hearings some questions from which I should like to give verbatim:

> *Senator McKellar (to Mr. Lilienthal)*: "Did it not seem to you to be remarkable that in connection with experiments that have been carried on since the days of Alexander the Great, when he had his Macedonian scientists trying to split the atom, the President of the United States would discharge General Groves, the discoverer of the greatest secret that the world has ever known, the greatest discovery, scientific discovery, that has ever been made, to turn the whole matter over to you, who never really knew, except from what you saw in the newspapers, that the government was even thinking about atomic energy?"

> *The Chairman*: "Let us have it quiet, please."

> *Senator McKellar*: "You are willing to admit, are you, that this secret, or the first history of it, dated from the time when Alexander the Great had his Macedonian scientists trying to make this discovery, and then Lucretius wrote a poem about it, about two thousand years ago? And everybody has been trying to discover it, or most scientists have been trying to discover it, ever since. And do you not really think that General Groves, for having discovered it, is entitled to some little credit for it?"

It is possible to see in these questions of Senator McKellar an atttempt to discredit scientists. One may note that Alexander the Great, a military man, is represented as the real driving force behind the research, whereas his scientists seem to have had the status of court jesters or stableboys. Similarly, in our own work, General Groves is represented as the outstanding genius of the Manhattan Project. One wonders if the Senator has ever heard of the magnificent contributions of Fermi, Bethe, Oppenheimer, Lawrence, Chadwick, Bohr, Einstein,

Oliphant, Condon, Urey, Pauli and scores of others just as notable. It can be seen in this list, written down at random, that atomic energy is *not* exactly an American invention, or even an Anglo-Saxon Protestant invention. For all we know, there may even be atheistic materialists among these men.

Further hearings on the Atomic Energy Commission have revealed disquieting attitudes by other political figures for whom excuses cannot be made on the grounds of senility. To quote from later hearings:

> *Senator Capehart:* "Why is it not a sensible program, in view of world conditions, to return atomic energy to the military forces?"
>
> *Senator Taft:* "I would favor returning it to a military commission. The Panama Canal was to be built by civilian engineers, but before we got through with it, we said to the Army, 'You build the Panama Canal,' and the Army built it. I think the Army is competent to handle a job that civilians are competent to handle."

There is, of course, a more encouraging aspect of our government, represented by such men as Senator Hickenlooper, who opposed the return of military rule of atomic energy in the following words:

> "There has been injected into the debate the ominous suggestion—and a drive for it seems to be beginning—that atomic energy should be placed in the hands of the military.
>
> "No, Mr. President; that must not be at this time. If the emergency of war should descend upon us, certainly our entire industrial and economic plant must again be put under the dictation of war controls, but I have heard no one say that the power plants, the railroads, the economy of this country should now be placed in the hands of the military merely because there are rumblings, merely because there is uncertainty in the world, and fears in high places.
>
> "There are great fears and apprehensions, and in fact there may be ground for the fear that tomorrow's war may be fought with germs, with blights, with biologicals, the horror and extent of which no man today can fully realize. If that be the case, should we put all our pharmceutical houses, all our laboratories, and all our scientific biological experimentation and development projects, under the military? The fallacy of that seems apparent, and I think it is applicable to the great science of atomic energy, just as it is to the science of biology, or the science of bacteriology, or any other science which may be used to destroy mankind if we do not solve the problem of keeping out of war."

As an example of the wanton vandalism that has been and may again be committed under the guise of military necessity, one may consider the destruction of the Japanese cyclotrons, an act which contains an implicit thought control over Japanese scientists. Their reaction to this vandalism may be clarified by quoting from a memorandum by Dr. Nishina, director of the cyclotron laboratories:

> "Even today we absolutely fail to understand the reason for ordering the destruction of the cyclotrons. We surmise that cyclotrons might be considered as indispensable for the study or manufacture of atomic bombs. This, however, we know to be a mere 'superstition' of uninformed laymen. A cyclotron may have been an important apparatus in the early studies on the creation of atomic bombs, but now that the atomic bomb has been invented, the manufacture of it no longer needs a cyclotron. It is only necessary to have sufficient uranium to produce any number of atomic bombs without the aid of a cyclotron, and conversely, however many cyclotrons one may have, no atomic bomb can be manufactured without the uranium material. This fact is clearly revealed by the statements of American scientists engaged in the production of atomic bombs. . . .
>
> "Our request to S.C.A.P. for the authorization to operate the cyclotrons was for the purpose of researches in biology and medicine, aiming at new discoveries which may greatly improve agriculture, forestry, animal husbandry, fishery and medical therapy. This has been the line of thought apparent even before the war, and we expected from such researches no inconsiderable contributions toward the stabilization of national living and improvement of national health in post-war Japan.
>
> "It was indeed for this reason that Dr. Compton, Head of the Scientific Intelligence Survey, GHQ, and other scientists associated with him, recommended to GHQ the authorization of the operation of the cyclotrons, and the authorization granted in the first place. That not only this authorization would be rescinded but also the cyclotrons would be destroyed without adequate notice was almost beyond the limits of our credulity."

Let it be clearly understood that the above destruction was *not* advised by any scientist. In fact, the Association of Oak Ridge Scientists declared the wrecking of the Japanese cyclotrons was "wanton and stupid to the point of constituting a crime against mankind", and was "as disreputable and ill-considered as would be the burning of Japanese libraries or the smashing of Japanese printing presses". They concluded that "men who cannot distinguish between the usefulness of a research machine and the military importance of a 16-inch gun have no place in positions of authority."

The present influence of the military in American science is considerably more subtle than the control exercised in Japan, but it has many ramifications. Who knows how it may grow, if unopposed? The method of extending military influence may be clarified by quoting from an article by Prof. Philip Morrison in the *Bulletin of the Atomic Scientists,* November 1, 1946:

> " . . . The Army is sending some of its officers to Princeton to enter the field. The Manhattan District is now operating four laboratories—

Brookhaven, Argonne, Berkeley, and Oak Ridge,—of which the smallest proposes to do more work than the largest laboratory in the country did before the war. At least half-a-dozen universities have plans which only California would have contemplated in '39.

"The money, and it is real money, well in the tens of millions a year, is coming today from two main sources. The Army, through the Manhattan District, working chiefly through the large laboratories just mentioned, is a major supporter. In principle, however, this support will come from a special agency, the Atomic Energy Commission, when that body shall begin to function. The other large source of funds is the Navy, through a new bureau called the Office of Naval Research. To indicate how much nuclear science owes to the services, a few examples will be useful. At the last Berkeley meeting of the American Physical Society, just half the delivered papers—mind you, perfectly open, published papers on problems of essentially academic interest—were supported in whole or in part by one of the services. Again, at Berkeley, there exists one of the best-supported and strongest physics departments in America. But for every dollar the University of California spends in physics at Berkeley, the Army spends seven. The Navy may be said almost without hyperbole to own all of nuclear physics which is not owned by the Manhattan District. About thirty colleges have Navy contracts in the field of nuclear physics alone. Some schools derive ninety percent of their research support from Navy funds."

The history of the past few years has clearly shown that the scientist must bear a certain responsibility not only for the consequences of his own work but for many other things going on around him. It is probably no accident that the policy of violent anti-Semitism which was released in Germany by the seizure of power by the Nazis struck first at the universities and research centers. Fortunately for us, this attack on the Jewish people came in such a way that many of the brilliant Jewish scientists of Germany were able to escape and to enrich the scientfic life of England and America. If these men had been better treated in Germany, undoubtedly many of them would have contributed to the atomic-bomb project there rather than here.

Similarly, in our own country, it is more than a coincidence that the same investigating committees which have so vigorously attacked trade unions and such organizations as the Joint Anti-Fascist Refugee Committee have now turned their attention to discrediting and repressing scientific men. Congressman J. Parnell Thomas, chairman of the House Committee on Un-American Activities, member of the Armed Forces Committee, and former member of the Joint Atomic Energy Committee, has published an article in the June 21, 1947, *Liberty* magazine, which distorts the facts so as to give the impression that the scientific men working on the atomic-bomb project are fools, or worse.

To quote Congressman Thomas' article:

"Besides the danger from sabotage or the physical penetration by actual Soviet agents, there is another danger which lies in the susceptibility of gullible American scientists employed by the Atomic Energy Commission, or the contractors who operate its plants and laboratories. Our scientists, it seems, are well schooled in their specialties but not in the history of Communist tactics and designs. They have a weakness for attending meetings, signing petitions, sponsoring committees and joining organizations labeled 'liberal' or 'progressive' but which are actually often Communist fronts.

"Thus the the dossiers that I examined at Oak Ridge showed memberships in many organizations which have been classified by various investigating bodies as Communist front. One is called the Southern Conference for Human Welfare. . . .

"Among the politically naive, one front leads to another, and finally to action. Communism is not a disease of the poor but an affliction of the academic and professional classes.

"Among the scientific societies at Oak Ridge there is much advocacy of free interchange of scientific information.

"One high government scientist — let us call him Dr. V. . . . — was preparing to fly to a Moscow congress of scientists, and the army was jittery about what he might say overseas. The Russian plane which was to take him to Moscow was serviced by American Army mechanics at New York. First it had engine trouble and then a military truck accidentally backed into it. But after word came that the scientist's passport had been canceled, the mechanics speedily had it ready for the take-off.

"Chapter 25 of the International Federation of Architects, Engineers, Chemists & Technicians, C. I. O., conducted a special membership campaign in the atomic-research laboratories of the University of California at Berkeley. A state legislative committee, after investigation, concluded that the F. A. E. C. T. and its West Coast Chapters were Communist organized. Minutes of 1943 meetings of Chapter 25's executive committee disclosed a surreptitious plan to obtain lists of the laboratory personnel, to infiltrate the entire project, and to propagandize and organize the scientists there, meanwhile avoiding detection by the F. B. I. Scientists engaged in atomic research at Berkeley were at the same time lecturing on scientific matters at the Communist California Labor School in San Francisco."

In Congressman Thomas' reference to the F. A. E. C. T. we can see a familiar pattern of witch-hunting; that is, that the organization is first denounced by one investigating body, in this case the Tenney Committee, and then that denunciation is quoted by another group as incontrovertible proof of its case. Similarly, his reference to the California Labor School as the Communist California Labor School is an old trick of Red-baiters. It might be worth mentioning that Robert Gordon Sproul, President of the University of California and Chairman of the State Republican Committee, was one of the several conservative sponsors of the school.

In regard to the activities of the F. A. E. C. T. at the Radiation Laboratory, they were never more than the time-honored organizational activities of a trade union. There was no attempt to propagandize or infiltrate the personnel more than is common or proper in organizing an industrial plant and there was no greater risk of an information leak than there would have been in the scientists joining a church. In spite of this, the men working at the Radiation Laboratory were coerced into staying out of the F. A. E. C. T. and some of the scientists most active in it were ousted from their jobs and hounded from the West Coast area. One was drafted into the infantry, in spite of his obvious value as a civilian scientist, and ended up on the Okinawa battlefield.

If we consider the actual situation in regard to scientific information, it becomes apparent that repressive measures against scientists and restriction of publication cannot be justified on the grounds of military security. Even at the beginning one would ask, "Where is the war?"

The Bulletin of the Atomic Scientists has made this statement:

"There is little doubt that the delay in the development of the American project, caused by the wrecking tactics of a Congressional minority, has been as valuable—if not more valuable—to the nations which are anxious to catch up with us, as would be the acceleration of their own effort by information from spies which they might succeed in planting in our factories or laboratories."

The Association of Oak Ridge Engineers and Scientists states:

"We believe that true scientific education and research can flourish only if they are conducted in the way hundreds of years of academic tradition have taught us, that is, free from profit motives and free from any restrictive security regulations."

The history of science is full of simultaneous discoveries in widely-separated parts of the world, indicating the futility of regarding scientific secrets from the same viewpoint as military secrets. You can keep secret from the whole world the contemplated date and hour of an invasion, and if anyone should guess the secret you can easily change the date, but you cannot keep secret the critical mass of a plutonium bomb or an appropriate method of detonation. C. F. Kettering has said: "When you lock the laboratory door, you lock out more than you lock in."

Foreign resentment of American secretiveness in regard to nuclear data may be exemplified by a speech made in the House of Commons by Mr. Blackburn, Labor representative from Birmingham:

"British scientists know all the details of bombs made of uranium 235. We do not know the details of the construction of an atomic bomb made from plutonium. The Nagasaki bomb was made from plutonium, and was, in fact, about four times as powerful as the uranium 235 bomb which was dropped on Hiroshima. The seriousness of that is this. Of the peaceful development of atomic energy 90% is associated with the plutonium process and only 10% with the separation of uranium 235. British scientists know perfectly well how to construct a bomb made out of uranium 235. Therefore, it is not logical for the United States of America, on the grounds of military security, to refrain from divulging to us information about the plutonium process, because we know how to make a bomb made of uranium 235. . . . . Therefore it seems to me to be a most serious matter that the United States of America should be failing to allow our scientists to visit, for instance, Hanford Engineering Works, where plutonium is manufactured which produced the bomb. As an illustration of how important the plutonium process is as compared with the uranium 235 process, it is from the plutonium process that one is able to extract in bulk the radioactive substances and radiations which are of such vital value in medical research and therapy. This is, in some respects, most ungenerous, when one considers that Britain was responsible for almost all the fundamental research on this subject. Our British scientists went over to the United States of America; our British scientists contributed every scrap of knowledge they had on this subject."

In closing, it seems appropriate to quote from *An Appeal To Reason,* by E. U. Condon, one of the truly great American scientists:

"What is going on? Prominent scientists are denied the privilege of traveling abroad. Physicists are not allowed to discuss certain areas of their science with each other, even as between individuals working on closely related phases of the same subject. They can only communicate through official channels, involving censorship of their communications by army officers without knowledge and so without competence. Information essential to understanding is being denied to students in our universities, so that, if this situation were to continue, young students will get from their professors only a watered-down army-approved version of the laws of nature. . . .

"I beg of you, cast in your lot with the people who believe there is a possibility that men throughout the world can live in freedom and justice, in love and good-will, that they can devote their full energies to constructive application of the rational thinking we call science to the arts of peace. In asking you to join with us, I make no promise of certain security, I only promise, hope and tell you that the other way leads to certain doom. If we try to establish the brotherhood of man on earth we may fail, but if we do not even try we shall surely fail, and what an unbearable load of guilt our consciences will then have to carry."

Harold Orr

Instructor, L. A. public
schools, 20 years;
President, Calif. Fed.
of Teachers, L.A. Fed.
of Teachers

EDUCATION FOR FREEDOM
OR FOR TYRANNY?

THOUGHT control in education in America is mostly in the realm of the intangible. In a great many cases, it is difficult to say where the intangible pressure is exerted and the actual threat of coercion is exercised.

The teacher in America has always been restricted in the exercising of academic, political and personal freedom. In practically all communities of this country, the teacher is regarded as a second-class citizen. Although the teacher is supposed to train the future leaders of this country, he or she is not supposed to exercise any of that leadership in a political, economic or social manner. In too many communities, the teacher is not to take part in political discussion or run for office, is not to discuss or take part in economic problems, and is usually treated socially like a chauffeur or housemaid. This attitude by most of the public has existed for over a hundred years. A teacher has been too long regarded as a neuter gender who is not to drink, smoke, dance or exercise any of the rights of a normal citizen of the community. Only in the large cities, has there been any progress in throwing off all these restrictions that have been placed on teachers by custom or actual edict.

In this Atomic Age, teachers are beginning to realize, as the scientists are doing, that we must have the right kind of leadership or all of humanity will be destroyed by military annihilation. If all the teachers in all the countries were allowed to teach nothing but the truth, there would be no danger of war in the future.

Not only has custom placed restriction on the teacher, but school boards and administrators have further done everything possible to keep the teacher from expressing any opinions or exercising any democratic rights. Those who dare to oppose the autocratic administration

287

are usually dismissed, transferred or persecuted until they are willing to become subservient and not exercise any of their rights as citizens. Teachers are supposed to teach Democracy, but are not allowed to practice it themselves.

As if it were not enough that the school boards, administrators and community customs should restrict the teacher in political, economic and social rights, we have the Dies, the Rankin, the Tenney and Field Committees to strike terror into the hearts of teachers who dare to exercise their rights as citizens.

Let us take, for example, the witch-hunting and smearing tactics of the Tenney Committee of our own state. The attempt of this committee to smear, browbeat and persecute the liberal members of the faculty of the University of California at Los Angeles and Provost Dykstra was something that I hoped I would never see in a democracy. As I watched this persecution, day after day, I could well picture Hermann Goering with the Gestapo torturing his helpless victims. Here was a committee before which any witness could tell the most preposterous lies and have legal immunity, before which the defendants could not be represented by attorney, could not reply or refute any charges made and could not speak the truth if the chairman did not want to hear it.

This was thought control and Fascism at its worst.

Then, again, the Tenney Committee struck at academic freedom when Tenney attacked the two Canoga Park teachers. Because a few reactionaries in this community did not like the liberal teachings of these teachers, they tried to smear them before the Tenney Committee as teaching Communism. If it had not been for the fact that so many organizations and individuals demanded that the Board of Education conduct an open hearing in the community, Tenney might have been successful in having these teachers dismissed or transferred. After four days of hearings, by a committee appointed by the Superintendent and Board of Education, and months of other testimony, the teachers were entirely vindicated and no cause for disciplinary action was found, nor any taken. If anything, these four days of hearings were one of the greatest testimonials to the courage and fairness with which these teachers taught that I have seen anywhere. The principal, the faculty, the students, the alumni, the P.T.A. and the townspeople all rallied to the defense of these teachers and the school. It was probably one of the greatest surprises Tenney ever had. The Teachers' Union mobilized, led and financed the successful defense of these teachers. No wonder Mr. Tenney does not like the Teachers' Union.

When we look into the field of unwarranted restriction on the students, we find a lot of restrictions, but some of them are very difficult to define as to origin. While obstensibly the student councils make the restrictions and decisions, usually there is someone or some group that furnishes the initiative for making the decisions that are made. Take, for instance, the barring of certain student-organizations from the campus. I do not believe that the students themselves would bar their fellow-students from democratic recognition, but surely there must be some pressure from the administration or outside organizations that would cause them to do this. The A. Y. D. is a good illustration of a student-organization that has been excluded from recognition by the student councils on many of the campuses. This is one of those intangibles that make it difficult to tell exactly where the pressure does come from.

In most of the schools below the college level, the student self-government is only a fable in which the students go through the gestures of self-government; but all of the decisions other than routine are made by the sponsor or administrative head of the school. Students receive good marks or privileges when they carry on the work of self-government, so they are usually careful to make the decisions that will bring them the best marks or the most privileges. Student self-government is a device to make the students believe that they are exercising rights of Democracy, when actually they do not make the major decisions.

In some of the colleges and universities, we find student councils which have enough independent and courageous students to dare to try to make their own decisions. Once in a while, we see the administration wishing to expel some or all the members of a student council. Whenever you read of such instances, you will know that the students are really trying to exercise rights of citizens in a Democracy. Most universities and colleges will not allow the students to engage in any extra-curricular political activities where the name of the institution is in any way involved. The private colleges must not in any way displease their wealthy donors, and the state universities have to worry about the Legislative Committees that control their appropriations in the Legislature. So, whether they are private or state colleges or universities, they must not allow the students to anger those who furnish the finances to keep the institutions going. Thought control is, then, exer-

289

cised over the students in institutions of higher learning by those who control the finances that keep these citadels of learning operating. You can see that the restrictions are not exercised directly, but indirectly by those outside the university or college.

Not long ago, the Field Committee attacked the University of California at Los Angeles because some of the students joined the picketlines of the striking Hollywood studio unions out at Burbank. Some of these students carried signs saying they were from the University. Of course, these students were not on the campus, were not parading as an organization from the campus, and did not say that they were representing the University. The Field Committee wanted the students who had picketed to be expelled from the University. These students were only doing what any citizen had a right to do, and Provost Dykstra stated that after the students leave the campus they have a right to do anything that any other citizen does. To quote Provost Dykstra:

> "The University does not restrict its enrollment by political creed, religious belief, color, or race, and therefore has the same cross section of society that the community has. We have Republicans, Democrats, Socialists and Communists as the community has; we have Catholics, Protestants and Jews, Negroes, whites and other races as the community has. The University is not responsible for the homes from which the students bring their beliefs and has no jurisdiction except on the campus of the University."

I believe this is one of the most forthright statements made by the president of any large university in the U. S. in behalf of freedom of action for students attending that university. Provost Dykstra is to be complimented in standing up against the Field and Tenney Committees.

There have been many restrictions on the material to be used for education. Let us take textbooks. Textbooks are usually passed upon by the State Board of Education, the State Superintendent and the local Boards of Education, so they usually are very inoffensive by the time they have run this gamut.

About five or six years ago, there was a national furore about the Rugg textbooks. The N. A. M. was carrying on a national campaign to have these books removed from all the schools where they were in use, because they were too liberal in discussion of social problems. The local Board of Education took all the books out of the schools and never would give a reason to the teachers.

About a year and a half ago, the Curriculum Department of the

L. A. Schools attempted to take out the *American Way of Life* used in the high-schools. The Teachers' Union and the publishers put so much heat on, the books were put back on the recommended list. When investigation was made as to who was responsible for having the books removed, we were told that the local Chamber of Commerce wanted to have the text removed because there were some things favorable to labor and the New Deal in the book. The N. A. M. and the Chamber of Commerce wish to censor all the books used in the schools.

The Tenney Committee has been attempting to have the *Building of America* series taken out of the schools: The Sons of the American Revolution are pushing the attack on these books. The State Superintendent, the State Board of Education, the state Curriculum Dept., the P.-T. A., the Federated Womens' Clubs, the League of Women Voters, the teacher-organizations, the Citizens' Committee for Better Education, and many other organizations, as well as superintendents throughout the state, have defended these books and their use. They find nothing wrong with the books and for once the conservatives and liberals are both fighting side by side for the same cause. Mr. Tenney's attack on education again has suffered a defeat. But the fear of further attack will undoubtedly be a restraining influence upon the adoption of further liberal books in the future.

Liberal publications and supplementary material are usually kept out of all the school-systems except a few in the large metropolitan centers. The school boards and superintendents are usually conservative and do not allow liberal publications to be used in the schools. The local Curriculum Division claims that the *L. A. Times* and *Daily News* give all the news-coverage necessary, and that the C. I. O. *Labor Herald* and the A. F. L. *Citizen* would be needless duplication.

This censorship of texts and material to be used in the schools is an avowed program of the N. A. M. in its attempt to control what is being taught in the schools.

More and more legislators such as Tenney are attempting to take education out of the hands of educators and place it under the control of the legislators. That is what happened in the countries which have had dictators. The state takes over education. Tenney had twelve bills dealing with curriculum-content in education that would change the whole course of study of education in the State of California. Among his bills were American Principles as Prerequisite to Problems Courses (1024); American History (1025); Sex Education (1026); Propaganda and Controversial Issues in Courses (1027); Textbooks (1031), and others. These will give you some idea of how the kinds of courses, their content and the material to be used, would be legislated for the educators instead of allowing them to choose the courses, content and material they feel best-suited for the students.

In the universities and colleges, more freedom is allowed in the choice of texts and materials. Very little restriction is placed upon the individual instructor by administration, and what little is exercised is usually by the department-head or the members of the faculty of the department. Of course, the instructor has always to think about the material he uses, or the text or discussion, because there máy be some stooge of Tenney or the like in the class who would be very glad to report to the Gestapo what is being taught or said. Again it is that indirect, intangible threat that places a restriction on the free discussion and interplay of ideas that may not be orthodox in their content or meaning.

There are many extra-governmental influences on education, some of which I have already named. The control exercised through finances by donors to private institutions and legislative appropriations to state universities, over instructors, materials and courses; the legislative branch of the state, in making curriculum courses, texts and materials; the attack by organizations on teachers, texts and materials; the restriction of educators in political, economic and social rights by school boards and the community; the constant interference by parents and taxpayers in the operation and functioning of the schools; and an administration in most schools unwilling to defend the teacher against this constant outside attack.

The intent of bills such as Tenney's is clear. Locally, their prolonged discussion in the press had adversely affected education long before enactment into law. Many teachers, fearful of the possibility of misrepresentation, have curtailed free discussion. At the very moment when the freest examination of all available data should prevail for the rebuilding of a war-torn world, education is being straightjacketed by those forces which oppose Democracy in its fullest application.

Another restriction in the educational field is the restriction of minorities from enrolling in certain courses such as medicine, dentistry, law, and other professional vocations. Many colleges and universities have quota-systems that limit the number of Jewish, Negro and other population-group students, who can take these professional courses. Most universities will deny that such a quota-system exists, although a few have admitted it. Yet, practically all have an unwritten tradition that operates very effectively.

What most all citizens, as well as educators, need is a new education in intercultural education and tolerance. It is difficult to stamp out these age-old conflicts of racial and cultural differences. All communities, as well as schools and universities, must adopt a courageous, aggressive program of intercultural education.

A recent ruling of the Supreme Court of California struck a blow at racial segregation in the public schools. This practice has existed too long in some communities. San Diego schools are to be congratulated, in that they are carrying on an aggressive program to foster racial and cultural tolerance and understanding in their schools. If the citizens in all the communities would insist, I am sure that more schools would follow the example of San Diego.

Most schools try to guide the colored races into vocational jobs that are menial or unskilled labor, even though many of these students are well-fitted to perform skilled or semi-professional work. This screening of minorities is becoming more pronounced every year, as the proponents of unrestricted Rugged Individualism and Free Enterprise rise in ascendency from their debacle of 1933. As after every war, it is easy for the vested interests to turn the hate engendered during World War II into hatred of labor unions, liberals and progressives. We are now passing through that period, and that is why it is important for every liberal in this country to join the counter-attack against thought control in education in these United States.

Carroll Richardson

Psychological researcher, Army Air
Corps, 1942-45; M. A., U.S.C.; now preparing Ph. D. in sociology

THE RECURRING
WITCH-HUNTS IN EDUCATION

FIRST, we must define what we mean by an academic witch. A witch is one who, dressed in black cap and gown, consorts with the devil in any of his many disguises: racial equality, Communism, unionism, free love, progressive education, and so on. The devil has so many disguises that only an expert witch-hunter can pierce them all.

The Salem witches were accused of souring the milk and bringing on storms; the modern academic witch is known to tamper with sacred cows and thunder against injustice.

The witch of yesterday attended conventions on lonely mountaintops; today's educated witch may be found guilty of going to meetings of a teachers' union or a labor school.

The broomstick is an accessory that no self-respecting witch would be seen without, and the modern witch can often be seen sweeping away cobwebs from old corners of social and economic institutions.

If one further resemblance is needed, take note of the ordeal by water. The Salem witch was immersed as a test of innocence. If he drowned, he was proven innocent. Either way, he was a lost cause. The academic witch today is grilled. If he denies his *subversive* connections, he is obviously lying and may be jailed for perjury. If he admits and defends his unorthodox views, he will promptly lose his job.

The witch-hunt disciplines the entire community of scholars. Seeing the immersion of one scholar, others dare not expound *dangerous* thoughts. Reaction to the danger is often a loud denial of belief in the ideas under scrutiny and a positive affirmation of the established credos of the elders. For safety's sake, in extreme peril, one's neighbor is denounced as a witch. Thus, the thinking person is throttled. In time, this conditioned attitude comes to be quite normal.

This paper will trace through our history as a nation some of the attacks on the freedom of teachers to teach and of students to learn—

294

and on the freedom of both to act on their beliefs.

Dr. Thomas Mann neatly summed up the meaning of freedom and the dangers it faces, when he said, in January, 1946:

"Academic freedom does not mean only the right of youth mentally to sow wild oats, or the freedom to learn, but also the freedom to teach, the freedom of research, and the independence of science. Where this freedom is chained by people who apply to it the improper and offensive standard of 'patriotic' or 'un-American,' their culture, the soul of the country itself, is in danger. The enemies of liberty are playing their seductive and corruptive game under various masks and even under the mask of freedom itself. . . ."

The term "thought control" was first used in militarist Japan to silence democratic thinking. The attitude that free thought is dangerous is not peculiar to Japan. It exists in the U. S. Some vested group in the community has always wished to stifle all *dangerous* thought and attitudes favorable to progress, which circulate in the schools.

Thomas Jefferson expressed his position in regard to educational freedom when, speaking at the founding of the University of Virginia, he said:

"This institution will be based upon the illimitable freedom of the human mind. For here we are not afraid to follow truth, wherever it may lead, nor to tolerate error as long as reason is left to combat it."

Academic freedom is never secure against attack so long as there exists some unpleasant social fact that an educator is indiscreet enough to turn up, or some disagreeable social problem that he is not tactful enough to ignore. But educational history shows plainly that in times of social and political crisis, in times when the shifts in locus of power loom ahead, opposition to free thought in the schools becomes open, rather than covert—intense, direct, and organized, rather than mildly disapproving.

It is during these periods that the term "radical" is slung around with abandon. And "radicalism" is a conveniently flexible term which can mean almost anything. It usually indicates that the teacher deals with social problems realistically, that he has a sense of justice, a sympathy for oppressed groups, or a social conscience. It probably means that he is an earnest person who takes himself and the society in which he lives seriously and is eager to make his community a better place in which to live. And nothing is more damaging to a teacher than to be called a "radical."

Before scholars at our formal institutions of education turned their attention to the "dangerous thoughts" of the social sciences, the enemies of intellectual freedom had begun their work.

In the 1790's Democratic Societies and Republican Clubs were formed to preserve the gains of the Revolution against attacks by the wealthy merchants, speculators, and aristocrats in the Federalist Party. These societies, looking to Jefferson for leadership, advanced the demand for popular education and directly aided the formation of colleges and academies. They relied on the people's press as a means of popular education for Democracy.

The Federalists attacked the Democratic Societies and Jeffersonian newspapers as agents of "Bloody French Jacobins," subsidized by Paris gold. Unable to destroy the societies through propaganda, they turned to legislation. The Sedition Act imposed a fine up to $2000 and a prison term of two years on "anyone who should write, print, or utter any false or malicious statements against the Government of the U.S., or either House of the Congress, or the President, with intent to bring them into contempt or disrepute." A mechanic in Dedham, Mass., printed a leaflet which read, "I never knew a government supported long after the confidence of the people was lost, for the people are the government." He was sentenced to a year and a half in jail and given a fine of $400.

Forty years later, the outstanding "controversial issue" was abolition of slavery, which had become firmly entrenched in the economy and ideology of the South. An open violation of academic freedom occurred when three Abolitionist professors were forced to resign from Western Reserve University.

After the Civil War, treatment of Negroes remained in some areas a "peculiar institution", not subject to free criticism. A New York State Legislative Committee on Seditious Activities set up after World War I listed as one of the dangerous activities: "Stimulating race hatred in our colored population and engendering class-consciousness in their ranks."

In 1941, the late Governor Talmadge of Georgia caused the Board of Regents to dismiss Dean Walter Cocking and Dr. Marvin S. Pittman from the State University system for the crime of trying to establish racial equality in the schools.

In the 1930's, the D.A.R. campaigned to force schools to drop Professor David Muzzey's history-text because it called slavery the chief cause of the Civil War. In 1940, 12 students were refused readmission to the University of Michigan for their undesirable activities. Two of them were Negroes who had requested service at an Ann Arbor restaurant and had been refused. The others were white students who had helped the Negroes press for their liberties under the civil-rights laws.

One of the Tenney Committee's charges against Mrs. Blanche Bettington, teacher at Canoga Park High School in Los Angeles county, was the recommending of Carey McWilliams' books to her students. Another outrage committed by Mrs. Bettington was to inform her classes that racial minorities are discriminated against in the United States.

During and immediately after World War I, the conformist spirit in education reached its height. Support of the prosecution of the war, and hostility to Bolshevism, became test issues for American teachers. All criticism of American political institutions, local, state, and Federal, all advocacy of economic and social change, became taboo. Joining a union, and concern with labor problems, became signs of an "undesirable personality" for the teaching profession. A program of "Americanizing" immigrants was undertaken to quench the fire of social criticism and turn them away from labor unions.

The Manufacturers' Association of Connecticut was enthusiastic about this program. In a letter to members, it pointed out that English-speaking foreigners walked out during strikes in a smaller percentage than non-English-speaking foreigners.

> "The highest type of foreigner stuck to his work. No one is more vitally concerned in Americanization than the manufacturers, as is apparent when we see to what a large degree agitation and propaganda among the foreign-born are responsible for industrial disturbances in this and other states."

The record of persecution and dismissals during this period is a long and impressive one.

Henry W. Dana was dismissed from Columbia because of pacifist activities; Professor Charles Beard withdrew, along with Henry R. Mussey, from the same institution. Four professors of economics were dismissed from as many different universities, including Scott Nearing of Pennsylvania. Four teachers in the New York City high schools were released; two teachers in the elementary schools. A teacher in Washington, D. C., and one in Poughkeepsie were removed. The charges in these episodes were cut from the same pattern: "Bolshevist or Socialist teachings or sentiments," or "Failure to exert positive influence in the classroom towards prosecution of the war." A loyalty pledge was required of teachers in the New York schools. Three teachers opposed to this requirement were dismissed from De Witt Clinton High School. One of their crimes was that their names appeared

297

in *The New Republic* as supporting conscientious objectors.

The New Republic itself was declared a culprit, when, with *The Nation,* it was banned from Los Angeles school libraries in 1921 because it "undermined the economic principles of America."

Economics was so full of dangerous thoughts that in 1923 Portland, Oregon, dropped economics from the school curriculum and forbade teachers to assign "Socialism" as a debate topic.

The Sedition Act which had protected the Federalists against criticism was simply revived in spirit by local boards, in this all-out drive to force conformity in teaching.

The Lusk Laws of 1921 in New York State were aimed in particular at the Rand School in New York City, but the authors were doubtless aiming at other targets, too. These laws were pronouncements against advocacy of radical social change. They prohibited attacks on the theory of private property. The truly "American" spirit of these laws can be observed in this quotation:

> "In entering the public school system the teacher assumes certain obligations and must of necessity surrender some of his intellectual freedom. If he does not approve of the present social system or the structure of our government, he must surrender his public office. The public school must not be allowed to spread the gospel of discontent among the people. No person who is not eager to combat theories of social change should be entrusted with the task of fitting young and old for the responsibilities of citizenship."

Equally forceful was the statement of U. S. Commissioner of Education John J. Tigert, in 1921:

> "It is my intention to crush out of the schools Communism, Socialism, and all persons who do not recognize the sanctity of private property and the right of genius to its just rewards."

However, when teachers of Lancaster, Pennsylvania, were refused an increase in their salaries in 1920 by the Board of School Directors, and affiliated with the American Federation of Teachers to secure what they thought were their "just rewards," the union teachers were not rehired and this action was upheld by the State Superintendent of Schools.

The "American" doctrine in the schools was also upheld by Governor Thomas Campbell of Arizona:

> "I can conceive of no greater service than teaching through our schools and colleges how absolute equality is granted in the United States. Those people rebelling against the possession of large fortunes do not seem to be able to realize that the wealth of these individuals proves the desirability

of our system. The man without wealth has been unwilling to pay the price in self-denial, effort, and thrift."

A 1919 bulletin used in Iowa schools explained that the Bolshevik doctrine means "live riotously on the savings forcibly taken from others." A 1921 Indiana school-manual told teachers to "instill a sense of the greatness of their state in their pupils. The right to revolution does not exist in America. We had a revolution 140 years ago which made it unnecessary to have any other revolution in this country." In 1922, the New York Branch of the DAR protested against Professor Muzzey's history-text because it gave "to military history insufficient emphasis to make good soldiers out of our children."

The decade of the '30's was an especially adverse one for the cause of academic freedom. The longest and most severe depression in our history forced serious thinkers to evaluate the whole social order and the processes of social change and reform. The Roosevelt program became a matter of vital interest in intellectual circles.

Teachers from kindergarten to university were hit hard by the depression. Salaries were lowered, promotions were delayed, tenure was not granted on schedule. In some cities, salaries were not paid at all. These experiences made teachers more interested in problems of labor, full employment, relief, and the general political and social scene. They saw how Fascism in Europe ended academic freedom. Many teachers became leaders in the fight against Fascism in the United States.

And the forces hostile to academic freedom got very busy. The hunt for witches inside the schools was stepped up.

A typical example of educational persecution occurred in Eureka, California, in 1934. Victor R. Jewitt, social science teacher, was put under fire for "Communist doctrines." He was charged with sneering at religion. He replied that he stood for actual application of Christian principles instead of verbal profession of them. He was accused of distributing Communistic literature, then refusing to let the pupils take it from the building. He explained he had recommended the library's one pamphlet, *Modern Economic Systems,* for class reading. He also used *The Nation* and *The New Republic* in connection with class-work. He was accused of drilling his pupils in the pronounciation of Russian names, the main one being the word "Nazi". Just before the next school-term started, he was quietly transferred from the social sciences to mathematics.

In the same year, 1934, Cecil Crews, a high-school history teacher at LeRoy, New York, was dismissed without a hearing. The students organized a protest strike. A hearing finally disclosed that Crews had said, in class, he would "give his very life for the cause of social justice". This, to the Board, was "the inoffensive way of saying Socialism." He was attacked because of his open-forum methods in the classroom and his modern methods of teaching, and the dismissal was sustained.

The year 1937 was a remarkable one for the witch-hunters. Dr. Jerome Davis lost his job at Yale Divinity School. Henry Klein was dismissed from Brooklyn College. Dr. Alan Sweezy and Dr. J. Raymond Walsh were informed by the Harvard Economics Department that their appointments would be terminated. Both men had been active in forming the Cambridge local of the Teachers' Union. Dr. Walsh had supported passage of the Child Labor Amendment by the Massachusetts Legislature. Beyond their very practical advocacy of labor's rights, both had fostered new ideas in economic theory and had effectively criticized conventional economics. Their academic competence was far beyond question and their popularity with students was well-known.

At Columbia, a student was expelled for leading a demonstration outside President Butler's home in protest against sending an official delegate to Heidelberg University. (Again, the educational authorities showed reluctance to have students know how to pronounce "Nazi.") Four union-minded cafeteria-workers were dismissed, and a faculty committee at Teachers' College sponsored an investigation of labor conditions. Dean Russell of Columbia invited faculty-members who disapproved of University labor policies to submit their resignations, so he could have them on file. Russell, soon after, announced the closing of New College on budgetary grounds. New College was a noted leader in progressive methods of education and realistic inquiry in the field of social sciences. This was shortly before Dean Russell's address before the State Convention of the American Legion, entitled, *How to Tell a Communist and How to Beat Him.*

In 1938, Mrs. Florence James, assistant professor of drama, and an outstanding progressive, was dismissed from the University of Washington after 8 years' service. The Instructors' Association at the University asked President Sieg for a review of the case, according to terms of an agreement with the University enacted shortly before. The request was denied.

In 1939, Dr. Moyer S. Fleisher, professor of bacteriology, was dismissed by St. Louis University after 25 years' service. His sin: he had sponsored a meeting in support of the Spanish Loyalists. Pressure on the University from the Archbishop and the Catholic Club of St. Louis helped bring about Dr. Fleisher's dismissal.

In 1940, Professor Philip Mankin was dismissed without charges from State Teachers' College, Murfreesboro, Tennessee. A whispering-campaign had called this professor of English a Red, an athiest, and an opponent of R.O.T.C. The State Board found Professor Mankin guilt-less of any charges, but upheld his dismissal.

The New York State Legislature, following the pattern of the Lusk days, set up in 1940 the Rapp-Coudert Committee to Investigate Communists in the New York City Schools. City College of New York was the focus of inquiry. A number of college-teachers were dis-missed, not for violation of the law but for "conduct unbecoming to a college instructor." Morris U. Schappes, Instructor in English, was sentenced to prison for 2 years for perjury.

The end of the decade of the '30's did not, unfortunately, bring with it the end of witch-hunts.

Limitations of space and focus prevent full discussion here of several interesting and vital phases of the attack on academic free-dom. Each phase could be the subject of a detailed analysis. One study could deal with the use of the free-love devil to censor such scholars as Bertrand Russell, to hold back education for marriage as an offer-ing in the secondary-schools and colleges, and to ban progressive writings such as Howard Fast's *Citizen Tom Paine* from the public schools. Another study could examine the subtle and open pressures which prevent the teaching of scientific facts about race and the economic and social facts about the causes, processes, and effects of discrimination.

A most important study could elaborate the hint at the beginning of this paper about the widespread self-imposed thought control on the part of teachers. This is the tendency to "play it safe", to persuade themselves that the truth really needn't all be told and maybe it isn't really all true.

Our concern with academic freedom is not based on protection of an ivory tower in the schools. Objectivity in method, and freedom from pressures when sifting out truth, are essential to science, both natural and social. As Bacon reminded us, knowledge is power. Our schools should both extend and refine our knowledge so that the people can use it to attain a better life.

This one fact is certain: those who fear the truth in our schools fear a free people and a democratic world.

DISCUSSION

The discussion included questions about further instances of repressive practices against teachers and students on local campuses. It was decided that this information should be presented to the PCA office as available, and be kept there at the disposal of interested parties. A committee, it was suggested, should be formed to centralize such material.

After some remarks about the sometimes deleterious effects of parent guidance and home environment upon students, and what could possibly be done about this, it was suggested that a Continuations Committee be formed by the A. S. P. Council to carry forward the work of the Panel, and look into these problems.

Following the discussion, two resolutions were passed:

RESOLUTIONS

1. *Resolved,* that all those present, members of the Panel and of the audience, denounce the actions of the Un-American Activities Committee, specifically condemning the disgraceful attacks upon such outstanding men as Drs. Shapley, Condon and their fellows.

2. *Resolved,* that this meeting adopt as a statement of its policy, the *Bill of Student Rights,* passed by the College Panel, National Youth Lobby, June 15, 1947, at Washington, D. C., the text of which reads:

"A democratic and vigorous educational system is indispensable for the progressive development of a democracy. There exist today certain conditions contrary to that objective, namely discrimination based on color, race, religion, national origin, political belief and economic circumstance.

"Discrimination in education today is established by admission quota-systems based on color, race, religion, national origin; exclusion because of political belief or affiliation, applying in particular to graduate and professional schools; and, specifically in the case of Negro students, segregation in Jim-Crow schools.

"The attack on academic freedom is materializing and growing in scope on college campuses throughout the nation. An outstanding example of this has taken place on the college and university campuses in Michigan, especially on the campus of Michigan State College.

"This attack on academic freedom, which now takes the shape of an offensive primarily against the rights of American Youth for Democracy, is aimed fundamentally not only against American Youth for Democracy and other student groups such as AVC, YPCA and independent organizations, nor only against the rights of students, but is ultimately directed against the fundamental freedoms of the American people as a whole. Harvard University has, by its resistance to pressure to abridge academic freedom, and by grantnig a charter to an American Youth for Democracy chapter, symbolized progressive American opinion, which views the defense of academic freedom in this perspective.

"These are aspects of the profound crisis gripping the American campus today. In this crisis, American students must unite to combat the forces which seek to restrict or to obliterate our democratic rights. We therefore resolve that the following constitute a Student Bill of Rights for which we must work. We propose the adoption of this Bill of Rights by student bodies throughout the nation.

"1. Academic ability and merit, with no reference to color, race, religion, national origin or political beliefs, shall be the only qualifications for admission to any school or college open to the public in the United States: this further applies to all campus appointments, graduate assistantships, scholastic recognition and promotion opportunities.

"2. Students shall have the right to assemble, speak, organize and publish their own opinions free from restrictions and censorship imposed through discrimination against color, race, religion or political beliefs.

"3. Each secondary school and college shall have a representative student government, recognized as such by the administration and empowered at its discretion to investigate, appraise and publish its own views and to take action on any issues affecting student welfare, free from coercion from any source.

"4. Student employment, housing and other campus facilities, and the right to participate in social and athletic activity, shall be made available to all students without discrimination or segregation.

"5. The functioning of educational institutions and the activities of students and professors at these institutions shall be free from coercion or intimidation by outside agencies."

THOUGHT CONTROL IN U.S.A.

● ● ● ● ● ● ● ●

No. **5**

the FILM

the ACTOR

THOUGHT CONTROL IN THE U. S. A.
The collected proceedings of the
Conference on the Subject of Thought Control in the U. S.,
called by the Hollywood Arts, Sciences & Professions Council, PCA,
July 9-13, 1947

Edited by Harold J. Salemson
Designed by Herbert D. Klynn
Published by Hollywood A. S. P. Council, P. C. A.,
1515 Crossroads of the World, Hollywood 28, Calif.

Printed in the U. S. A. by union labor
Aldine Printing Co., Los Angeles, Calif.

the film

Carey McWilliams
Noted journalist; author, *Factories in the Field, Southern California Country,* etc.

WITH WHOM IS THE ALLIANCE ALLIED?

ON February 5, 1944, the *Los Angeles Examiner,* in its most florid style, reported the formation of the Motion Picture Alliance for the Preservation of American Ideals, a portion of whose title was derived from the masthead of a Hearst publication. As originally stated, the Alliance was formed, as Mr. Sam Wood put it, to counter the impression that Hollywood was "a hotbed of sedition and subversion." Echoing this same motivation, the *Statement of Principles* expressed "resentment of the growing impression that this industry is made up of, and dominated by, Communists, radicals and crackpots." It is obvious, however, that this explanation masked another and quite different intention. If the impression was erroneous, as the Alliance implied, then logically the organization should have been dedicated to the demonstration of its falsity. But, almost from its inception, the

Alliance has contended that the impression was correct, although the evasive indirectness with which this thesis was originally stated indicated a marked reluctance to attack the leadership of the industry. For, if the industry had, in fact, become dominated by Communists, the ultimate responsibility for this state of affairs necessarily rested on the producers.

If the leaders of the Alliance were at first somewhat reluctant to state their real objectives, this reluctance was not shared by the Hearst press which, from the outset, showed a deep insight into the subsequent course that the Alliance was to take. In an editorial in the *Los Angeles Examiner* of February 8, 1944, a somewhat different explanation for the formation of the Alliance was given than that offered by Mr. Wood, its first President. With no evasiveness whatever, this editorial charged (a) that a subversive minority had contrived to make "a long succession of insidious and evil motion pictures"; (b) that in the making of these films, the same minority had disparaged American history and traditions, American heroes and institutions; and (c) that for this "deplorable state of affairs the managers and producers" were themselves largely to blame. This statement clearly foreshadowed a campaign to undermine the uncoerced status of motion pictures as a medium of mass entertainment. Whatever the original intention may have been, the part that the Alliance has played in the subsequent unfolding of this campaign leaves little doubt that its real allies have always been outside the motion picture industry itself.

The strategy of the campaign required the propagation of a myth, namely, that a subversive minority controlled or insidiously influenced the production of motion pictures. For the vulnerability of the producers to attack hinged upon the establishment of this thesis. And, since the charge is essentially incredible—given the ideology of the producers,—it had to be invested with an air of authenticity by having it arise out of what appeared to be a revolt within the industry. On this foundation of straw and sawdust, Mr. Rankin could then build a mansion of lies. Once voiced in Hollywood, the charge could then be officially taken up in Washington and the producers could, in turn, be relied upon to draw the necessary inference. This inference would be that unless the producers initiated a purge and ceased production of such "evil" films as *North Star, Casablanca,* and *Mission to Moscow,* a frontal attack could be expected. There were also, of course, some important minor objectives: 1944 was an election year; the unions in Hollywood could be effectively baited; and the current of progressivism in the industry might be arrested. Overshadowing these considerations, however, was the larger issue of censorship, of thought control. Had there not been a set of Quisling-like characters in Hollywood willing to go along with a movement like the Alliance, for whatever reasons, it would have been necessary to have invented the Alliance for the purpose of bringing off this larger campaign.

Underlying this triple play from Rankin to Hearst to the Alliance and back from the Alliance to Rankin and Hearst, were two important considerations. The motion picture industry represents, after all, private enterprise, and even J. Parnell Thomas must have some excuse for attacking so important—albeit so vulnerable—a segment of American industry. The second consideration had to do with the attitude of the producers. In all of its experience in fending off attacks from without, the motion picture industry had never had to contend, prior to the appearance of the Alliance, with a Trojan-horse conspiracy from within the industry. Largely for this reason, the industry had ignored the various earlier "passes" which had been made at it, from time to time, by the House Committee on Un-American Activities. That this apparent indifference had annoyed the committee is shown by a statement of its chariman on May 29, 1947, that "up until the present time, there has been no inclination on the part of the industry itself to cooperate with the committee in ferreting out these influences,"—a statement which carries the additional implication that there had also been too little cooperation in making the "right" kind of pictures. To bring about this desired cooperation, it was, therefore, necessary to jockey the producers into a position where capitulation would be accepted as the price to be paid for the removal of a label which had been pinned on the industry by its own Quislings and stooges.

The role played by the Alliance is best shown in relation to the failure of earlier attempts to force the industry into line. Early in 1941, Martin Dies paid a visit to Hollywood and, in an article in *Liberty* under the caption of *Reds In Hollywood,* had expressed considerable annoyance over the elaborate runaround which he had been given by the producers. Later, the same year, Senator Burton Wheeler needled the Senate Interstate Commerce Committee into making, or threatening to make, an inquiry into "war-mongering" on the part of the industry. That Wheeler, like Dies, was carefully feeling out the vulnerability of the industry, is shown in a speech which his colleague, Gerald Nye, made in St. Louis at a time when this investigation was still pending. After listing a number of picture executives with Jewish names, Nye had then suggested that "such men in time of world upset are susceptible to riotous and inflammable national and racial emotions." Under Wendell Willkie's able generalship, this particular attack petered out; but it was revived in midsummer, 1943, by a provocative series of articles in *The Chicago Tribune*, the first of which carried the caption *City of Magic, Fantasy and Filth—that's Hollywood.* Despite continuing talk, outside the industry, of Red-infiltration, etc., none of these earlier attacks or threats ripened into an all-out assault on the industry.

On March 7, 1944, shortly after the Alliance was formed, Senator Robert Rice Reynolds placed in the *Congressional Record* an interesting communication signed by "A Group of Your Friends in Hollywood." Urging an investigation of the industry, this communication had stated that

> "Because of the flagrant manner in which the motion picture industrialists of Hollywood have been coddling Communists and cooperating with the so-called intellectual superiors they have helped to import from Europe and Asia, there has been organized in Hollywood the Motion Picture Alliance."

When prodded by the guilds and unions in Hollywood, the Alliance had disclaimed responsibility for this communication, but the timing and the tenor of the document raised a strong inference that it had been written by members of the Alliance. Then, on April 21, 1944, Dies Committee sleuths appeared in Hollywood, according to *Variety,* in response to charges made by the Alliance. On this occasion, the Alliance did not disclaim responsibility. While concentrating their fire on the screen writers, spokesmen for the Alliance, about this time, began to broaden their smears while still maintaining an essential vagueness and a reluctance to name names, to identify subversive pictures by name, or to specify their objectives. In an effort to smoke out the Alliance, a thousand delegates from the Hollywood guilds and unions, representing approximately 22,000 of the 30,000 workers in the industry, held an open meeting on June 28, 1944, to which the officials of the Alliance were invited, but which they failed to attend. At this meeting the Alliance was denounced as "a violently partisan group under the leadership of notorious union-wreckers." The partisan character of the organization was, in fact, clearly revealed in November, 1944, when the Dewey-for-President movement was headed up in Hollywood by such active Alliance members as Cecil B. de Mille, James K. McGuinness, Howard Emmett Rogers, Sam Wood, Walt Disney, Victor Fleming, Rupert Hughes, Cedric Gibbons, Lela Rogers, King Vidor and Morrie Ryskind. Early in 1945, Rankin made a speech in the house in which, after the usual ranting about "alien-minded Communistic enemies of Christianity," he went on to say that "the old-time American producers, actors and writers" in Hollywood were behind his impending investigation and had furnished "evidence," so-called, to substantiate his charges. In Hollywood, the promised investigation was greeted with warm praise by spokesmen for the Alliance. This pattern-of-events indicates how the Alliance has consistently intrigued with forces outside the industry whose objective has been to control, and to exploit for their own ends, the propaganda potential of motion pictures.

By way of indicating that the Alliance has long been allied with forces outside the industry, one might point to the selection of Dr. John R. Lechner as Executive Director. For several decades, now, Dr. Lechner has been an active race-baiter and professional patriot in Los Angeles, whose record, as such, could not have been unknown to the Alliance. When the Japanese-Americans were evacuated from the West Coast, Dr. Lechner at first attempted to solicit business from a Japanese-language publication, and, when these feelers were rebuffed, proceeded to publish a recklessly defamatory race-baiting pamphlet about the Japanese, entitled *Playing With Dynamite*. Long posing as a spokesman for the American Legion, he was explicity repudiated by the Legion in an official statement published in the *California Legionnaire* of January 15, 1944.

On March 26, 1947, J. Edgar Hoover gave the Thomas-Rankin Committee in Washington a gruesome account of Red infiltration in the industry. He was followed on the witness-stand by State Senator Jack Tenney who presented the Committee with a 372-page document devoted to the familiar theme of Reds in Hollywood. Once this foundation was laid, Mr. Eric Johnston felt compelled "to welcome an investigation" on behalf of the industry and to promise "full cooperation." On the eve of the appearance of the committee in Los Angeles, the Alliance presented Mr. William Henry Chamberlin as part of an educational program which had previously included such experts on Communist-infiltration as Eugene Lyons and Sidney Hook. At this meeting, Dr. Lechner read a list of motion pictures which the Thomas-Rankin Committee allegedly had certified as containing "sizeable doses of Communist propaganda." Among the pictures thus proscribed were *The Best Years of Our Lives*, *Margie*, *The Strange Love of Martha Ivers*, *A Medal for Benny*, *The Searching Wind*, *Watch on the Rhine*, *North Star*, *Mission to Moscow*, and *Pride of the Marines*. It was following this carefully-timed show that J. Parnell Thomas and his associates arrived in Los Angeles to hear from a long list of Alliance spokesmen in closed hearings held at the Biltmore Hotel. Just as the Washington hearings, so-called, laid the foundation for the Los Angeles hearings, so the Los Angeles hearings have now prepared the way for the full-dress show scheduled for Washington in October.

Now that the collaborationist role of the Alliance has been exposed—now that its spokesmen have been photographed arm-in-arm with J. Parnell Thomas,—a question arises as to the "alliance," if any, between the producers and the M.P.A. While a few producers, Mr. David Selznick among them, were quick to repudiate the initial "smears" of the Alliance, the Motion Picture Producers' Association, as a unit, was conspicuously indifferent to the call-to-arms which the Screen Writers' Guild sounded in June, 1944. As long as the Alliance concentrated its fire on the writers, the producers were obviously unconcerned. Few of them were apparently farsighted enough to realize that the red-paint being used to smear the writers could also be used, and was intended to be used, to smear them, too. While no "industry position", as such, seems to have been taken in reference to the Alliance, individual executives have denounced its actions if not its program. For example, Walter Wanger has accused the Alliance of having "provided ammunition to the industry's chronic enemies", while *Variety,* in an editorial on March 15, 1944, levelled one of the most serious charges that can be made against an organization in Hollywood, when it denounced the Alliance for having "seen fit to carry an industry matter outside the trade." Recently, Mr. Samuel Goldwyn has spoken out sharply in criticism of the Alliance for having circulated the report that *The Best Years of Our Lives* is loaded with Communist propaganda and L. B. Mayer has expressed less than complete enthusiasm for Robert Taylor's charge that *Song of Russia,* produced at the M.G.M. Studios, is likewise larded with subversive notions.

Ambivalent as the attitude of the producers has been toward the Alliance, there is now every indication that some in the industry will acquiesce in the campaign to impose censorship, a campaign in which the Alliance has played such an important and thoroughly discreditable role.

Emphasizing this new orientation, Eric Johnston announced on March 21 that the industry must produce more pictures extolling the American way of life and glorifying the homespun virtues. While an executive of Paramount Pictures suggested, in his appearance before the Thomas-Rankin Committee, the formation of a joint Industry-

Congressional Committee which could in effect determine the propaganda content of pictures.

This knuckling-under process can well result in the whole industry being brought under the direct censorship of the Thomas-Rankin Committee. Nor should it be forgotten that the Committee is well aware of the techniques which can be used, if necessary, to whip the industry into line. Through a reconsideration of tax-exemption regulations, and of tax-deductions generally, it has already suggested that recalcitrant individuals and organizations can be made to realize the advantages of compliance with its thought control program. This end-result for which reaction has been intriguing since 1941 would not be so perilously near realization today if it had not been for the Alliance; nor could the Alliance have moved so near its goal of censorship, had it not been for its alliance with forces outside the industry. For, while not too much is known about the actual membership of the Alliance, it is safe to say that at best it speaks for only a small minority within the industry.

Thus, "preserving American ideals" has meant in practice that the Alliance has connived at bringing the motion picture industry under the direct censorship of a Congressional committee. While naturally reluctant to attack the leadership of the industry directly, the Alliance has cooperated with John Rankin, whose anti-Semitic tirades directed at this same leadership have certainly not been lacking in candor or bluntness. Repeating like so many trained seals that "there is no place for propaganda in films,"—"We are the makers of music," says Mr. McGuinness, "the weavers of dreams,"—the leaders of the Alliance would have the public believe that films devoid of ideas are also films devoid of propaganda. What they have been aiming at, from the outset, is a censorship of films controlled by those with whom they are in alliance. Some of their strictures on the subject of Communist-infiltrated propaganda are, incidentally, most interesting. "Just think over," said Mr. McGuinness in a recent speech, "the number of times you have seen industrialists portrayed on the screen as slave drivers." It will be interesting, indeed, to see what these apostles of "films as pure entertainment" will have to say about the heavily-weighted propaganda films now in production.

Foremost among the preoccupations of the Alliance has been its deep concern that "the right to fail" should be maintained unabridged and undefiled. People have been failing in America since Jamestown was founded and, so far as I know, this right have never been called in question. To safeguard the right, however, the Alliance announced in its first statement that it had "no new plan to offer" and that it was opposed to plans, new or otherwise, as a matter of principle. Implicit in this apotheosis of the right to fail is the notion that Social Security constitutes a diabolic interference with the right of homespun, upright, Godfearing Americans to go broke.

Listening to Mr. Rupert Hughes proclaim that "the four freedoms would rob the American people of the stimulus of fear and poverty," conjures up a vision of thousands of Americans, bilked by monopolistically-manipulated prices, swindled by fake stock-promotions, gouged by rigged market-operations, flimflammed by dishonest advertising, marching on Washington under banners proudly proclaiming their God-given, Constitutionally-sanctioned right to fail—their inalienable right to join the Legion of the Dispossessed. It takes real courage to launch a movement to defend a right so universally-conceded, so fresh in the memory of the 13,000,000 victims of the late Depression. It takes real imagination to invest a crusade to protect this right with the emotional overtones of Valley Forge and Cold Harbor, of the Argonne Woods and the Battle of the Bulge.

Avoiding the pitfalls of "this share-and-share-alike business", to which Mrs. Lela Rogers takes such violent exception, the leaders of the Alliance have invited J. Parnell Thomas and John Rankin to impose a Fascist censorship on the motion picture industry in the name of preserving American ideals. An absurd and revolting spectacle, indeed; but a dangerous one, also. For the Alliance itself is shot through and through with the self hatred, the blind mole-like fear of change, the deep-seated social envy and sense of personal inadequacy, the cheap cynicism and the pseudo-hardboiled know-nothing-ism of those who cannot imagine the existence of values really worth defending and who traduce, by their every act and statement, the basic American ideals.

Irving Pichel

Stage actor, director,
1915-30; since, screen actor, director; occasional
university instructor; author, several books, many
articles

AREAS OF SILENCE

IF we consider the screen in America as a vehicle for the evocation and transmission of thought, it labors under two disadvantages. One is the simple historical fact that it is Theatre. The other is a complex of factors stemming from the industrial organization of film production and exhibition.

To deal with these considerations in order, it is my belief that the theatre, from its very beginnings, rarely shapes the thinking of its audience, rarely changes an audience's mind or feelings about anything, and rarely ventures beyond a reflection of widely-held views and accepted tenets of social behavior. Its subject-matter has always been the fate of the man who deviates,—the nonconformist to codes of conduct, of belief, of law. When it calls into question the codes themselves, if it is in any sense a popular theatre, it gets shut down. The Greeks exiled playwrights and the Puritans suppressed the theatre entirely. The theatre functions successfully when it appeals to principles concerning which there is unity. It counts on spectators laughing about the same things, deploring the same actions, holding the same concepts of good and evil. It receives its sanction from the approved mores and values of the society in which it rises. Freedom of expression has existed in the theatre from the earliest times in a very limited sense of the word.

When the war came, America not only needed but experienced a greater unity than it had ever known before. We discovered the adaptability of the motion picture to uses to which it had never before been applied so consciously and with such concentration. It was used to convey public information, to accelerate the acquisition of new and urgently-needed skills, to foster and document viewpoints and to activate the responses necessary in the prosecution of the war. The motion picture served these ends and did it superbly. A considerable

313

number of the workers in Hollywood—writers, directors, actors, camera-men, cutters and technicians—experienced a new exhilaration. They made a contribution to the national purpose in terms of their prac-ticed skill, but more than that they were able to put the medium in which they worked to the most effective use it had ever in their experi-ence served. Today, these same workers cannot help but feel that they and the medium have been caponized. Certainly, we do not complain because there is no more grand-scale war. Nobody laments that there are no more buzzbombs and V-2's and burning cities and gaschambers for us to dramatize, but we must grant that the universal tragedy, from Warsaw to Nagasaki, while it was being enacted, gave America a unified morality which in turn gave films a mandate for reality and purpose.

This war, let us remember, was a dramatization of a conflict be-tween groups of nations divided by explosively antithetical moralities. The issues were not small ones. They had little to do with the un-satisfied romantic longings of young men and young women or with competitive struggles for individual sexual or property advantage. Today, we find ourselves functioning as though the curtain had fallen on the tragedy, as though millions of dead, maimed and homeless had re-solved the issues for which the war was fought. In reality, these great issues were left unresolved and their residue constitutes the most divisive factors in our social, economic and political life today. This is an elaborate way of saying that theories of racial superiority, or disguised or overt Fascism, of anti-democratic principles in our polit-ical expression, are active, possibly dominant, sources of conflict in our lives as individual citizens. We have the Columbians, Inc., the Ku Klux Klan, lynching, racial and religious discrimination in employ-ment, restrictive residential covenants, a successful and all but non-partisan attack on labor, and a host of other social strains which are not the aftermath of war but identical with the antecedents of war.

Let me appear to digress for a moment. I want to make a gen-eralization about the function of dramatic fiction. Drama deals with the strains to which human relationships are subject and the conflicts that result from them. These strains and conflicts spring from many forms of antagonism and aggression. For the control of these antagon-isms and aggressions, society has produced religions, philosophies, sys-tems of ethics, of government, of law, of political and economic con-trol. None of them so far has worked perfectly, or even well. Re-ligions and their ethical codes have not abolished sin. Legal codes and

314

their enforcement have not done away with disorder. And all the variety of economic systems have not produced universal security and justice.

The fact is that the aggressions and strains continue and are exacerbated by the religions, the laws, the philosophies, the systems, not only because these are at variance among themselves, but because they often oppose the deepest instinctual needs of human beings, even as they seek to guide them to fulfillment. And, unhappily, they have a faculty of generating great and belligerent loyalties—the kind that make bigots of the religious, nationalists of the patriotic, and lynchers of the racists.

An examination, analysis and criticism of the systems is a proper function of political thinking and activity.

An examination and depiction of the antagonisms, the aggressions, the strains and the conflicts that survive under the systems, is the proper function of the art of fiction, whether in the form of the epic narrative, the novel, the drama, or the dramatic film.

Today, however, we find ourselves limited in the use of our great medium for the depiction even in the most objective terms of those sources of strain and conflict which have the greatest contemporary interest for us. The screen remains a medium, but is not a voice. It does not speak for itself, but as though it were merely an accomplished actor memorizing and repeating words that have been applauded in other media, and have been pre-censored, sifted, filtered against deviation from the most commonly-accepted and widely-held social generalizations. The screen is asked to ignore the antagonisms most current among us, most productive of disruption in the contemporary scene, most dramatic in their threat to our social and political present and future, even though the story-resolutions of such conflicts might be in terms not of any partisan program or systematic thesis but in such terms as the personages of our story might find for themselves.

The unity of the war-years has vanished. The abstract principles of right and wrong, of justice, of humanitarian feeling, to which we subscribed during the war, under which we condemned the practices of a hideous enemy, have become blurred and inapplicable to domestic situations and strains concerning which not so long ago we were perfectly clear. A difference of opinion concerning the interpretation of events is inherent in a democratic society; we may debate about the application of principles; but the principles, themselves, the basic

315

considerations upon which America was founded, these we have thought beyond debate.

We have been heartened by the appearance of pictures like *The Best Years of Our Lives,* which stipulates an obligation to returned veterans of the war, or *The Farmer's Daughter,* in which simple honesty and common sense defeat a Fascistic political candidate, and we await *Crossfire,* in which anti-Semitism is made the motivation for a murder. Not one of these pictures seems to assume too much. Not long ago, it would have been all but treasonable to deny the rights of citizen-soldiers to everything a way-of-life they had fought to preserve might give them. Not long ago, Fascism abroad was teaching us to recognize and abhor evidences of the same poison at home. It was our greatest danger. And, not long ago, anti-Semitism was the motivation for six million murders, which shocked and horrified us.

It is pictures like these which are under attack today, just as some of the pictures of the war period, applauded in their time, are also being attacked—films like *Wilson, The Ox-Bow Incident, Tender Comrade, A Medal for Benny,* or *Pride of the Marines.* It is beside the point that the attacks are stupid and silly. It is even beside the point that *The Best Years of Our Lives* and *The Farmer's Daughter* are enormously successful at the box-office and make very good sense to the public which throngs to see them. The real point is that the public is being told, in effect, that it is being poisoned and subverted by these tales concerning which it does react with unanimity, which do subscribe to the most generally accepted and approved tenets of American democracy. The Thomas-Tenney-M.P.A. axis says to the American people that its morals are mistaken, that its principles are being misapplied, that its sense of democratic decency, it very traditions of equality and tolerance, are merely being appealed to in order to destroy their way of life. The attack is only incidentally against the limited freedom of the screen; it is basically directed against the fundamental freedom of the United States.

I spoke of a second set of factors that limit the screen as a medium for affecting the thinking of its audiences, arising from its industrial organization.

Motion pictures are a big business. Huge sums are invested in studios and theatres, in story properties and in talent contracts. The screen makes money so long as it pleases the public, it loses money when it fails to please or actively displeases the public. As in other businesses, its owners and managers strive to operate it profitably. This they do by setting out entertainment which the public will purchase in quantity. They seek conscientiously to safeguard the product from anything which might affect its acceptance by the widest possible audience. They compute the sensitivities of any groups which might take offense at anything in any story. They defer to the censorships of states and cities and clubs and churches. It is their proper business to keep from the screen anything which is divisive, which might shatter the unity of response of an audience, which might repel any considerable number of theatre-goers or, at worst, create active opposition to their product.

This has its difficulties, of course. Entertainment deals with intangibles, and it is not always possible to know in advance what will delight and what may offend. Mistakes are made occasionally. But, allowing for the subtle and often incalcuable values involved in entertainment, I know of no industry which expends greater effort to set up the standards and gauges by which its product can be measured. A steel plant has a testing laboratory; the motion picture industry has the Breen Office, the Audience Research Institute, expert "showmen" executives, and banks.

Everything intended for the screen is sifted, tested and checked, not once but from five to a dozen times. Nothing is produced by the sole decision of one man. And, during the entire process of production, scores of people are involved whose participation is not mechanical but intellectual—people with minds, feelings, opinions which must ultimately come into agreement. The fact that the screen is theatre, if you accept my generalization, limits its freedom in one sense. The fact that it is a highly organized business limits it from another direction to remaining successful theatre.

If then, ideas, incidents or statements subversive to the American way of life are "slipped into" pictures despite the vigilance of the censors, the financiers and the conscientious guardians of an important big business, it can only be because these men and institutions believe in all sincerity that the said incidents or statements reflect the generally-accepted thinking and feeling of the public. I intend this as a tribute to the sincere and aspiring executives, producers, writers and directors who have been under attack. I believe heartily both in their loyalty as Americans and their loyalty to the medium in which they are working. I believe they are the last people in the world who want to see audiences alienated by controversy or repelled by antipathetic distortions of the American scene. I believe the only offense with which they can be charged is their belief that the scene should be reflected truthfully and contemporaneously.

It is possible that film makers can, by repeated and indiscriminate attack, be frightened into an even greater reticence and evasion. But the greater danger is that the thoughts and feelings of the mass of American theatregoers will be fragmented in the hope of rewelding them by raising a new enemy into a new unity—a unity of apprehension, of suspicion, of fear, a unity which will be only a caricature of the characteristic hopefulness and love of freedom which have marked the growth of this country to its present power and influence. Should this calamity befall, American thought will be, indeed, under an iron control which will rigidly clamp itself upon every medium by which thought is communicated. The screen, utterly dependent upon popular response, will be the first to fall.

Howard Da Silva

Paramount star; appeared, *Lost Weekend, Unconquered;* original Broadway cast, *Oklahoma!, The Cradle Will Rock, Abe Lincoln in Illinois,* etc.

THE ACTOR'S RELATION TO CONTENT IN MOTION PICTURES

I WISH to speak to you in behalf of a persecuted minority. I hope that this will not be considered out of order, because what I have to say is in your interest, too, whether or not you are a member of this oppressed group. The persecuted minority I speak for . . . is that of the actor.

His plight is similar in many ways to that of other suffering peoples, such as the writer, the director . . . in fact, all artists.

Norman Corwin, in the opening session of this conference, quoted that notorious aesthete and arbiter of good taste, Mr. Westbrook Pegler:

> "The actor has forgotten the past out of which he came . . . he is speaking up to his betters . . ."

Now, we actors are in a very difficult and contradictory position . . . There's no denying that we are told what to do. For example, I am encouraged, that is, persuaded . . . well, forced to endorse a cola drink which I detest because it's too sweet and it keeps me awake . . . and I endorse a razor-blade that takes six for a clean shave or one for a throat-cut . . . and I say I wear a watch that's precise, though it keeps time as precisely as a calendar . . . Yes, I'm told what to tell others to do!

But may I endorse homes for veterans? May I endorse Peace? May I endorse my political candidate? May I endorse Democracy? Quiet, you're an actor!

An actor (they say) is the most important thing in the film. The actor is so important, he or she is so responsible to the public, to the studio and to the contract, exerts an influence so important to the impres-

319

sionable minds of the audience, that he or she is betraying a trust if he or she speaks publicly . . .

But that's not entirely true. I was never particularly interested in Mr. Robert Taylor as an actor, but last Sunday I read an article about him and I became fascinated by him as a citizen.

The writer commended him for his bravery in performing publicly for the Thomas Committee and, although I had never thought of it in that light before, I must say I became somewhat awed by Mr. Taylor's courage. I remembered a childhood contemporary of mine who was the only kid on the block brave enough to climb down a sewer and stick his hand in . . . The other fact I learned about Mr. Taylor is that he doesn't read. The article didn't say that he can't read; just said he doesn't like to. His wife was even quoted as saying that, although cooking is a hobby of his, he never even reads a recipe. "He just looks at the pictures and starts mixing."

Now this may be a perfectly sound method for making salad-dressing, but I suspect something more is required of a man to be an artist and a citizen.

Which brings me to Katharine Hepburn. And *Daily Variety*, front page, right column, which tells the young and timid actor that Leo McCarey has decided not to cast Katharine Hepburn in his next picture because of her speech at a meeting for Henry Wallace.

Taylor spoke behind the closed doors of the star-chamber in which Rankin and Thomas carry on their proceedings. And Katharine Hepburn talked publicly to 27,000 people.

Well, you get the point. It's not so much that the actor is not allowed to endorse . . . it's *what* he endorses. It's not that an actor cannot be a political citizen . . . it's which side his politics are on.

I think the actor is important. I think the actor is responsible to his audience, to his craft, to his fellow creative artists in the industry, and (although this is not often considered) to himself.

By now, it is well-known that the undershirt industry was thrown into panic when Clark Gable appeared in *It Happened One Night* without benefit of chest undercovering.

It is a fact both wonderful and frightening that the actor does exert such personal, immediate influence on the 57,000,000 people in America who attend a movie at least once every three weeks.

The great names of pictures supply a kind of touchstone to the dreams, frustrations, fears of the audience; the little orphaned Mary Pickford; the symbolic little man, now giant, Charles Chaplin; the working-girl, Joan Crawford; the rampant male extravert, Gable; or the shy introvert, Stewart; the happy home-life of Pidgeon and Garson.

Many people lead a life as close to, and intimate with, the world on the screen as they do with their own families.

So, I agree that the actor is responsible to the people. But I'll tell you what I think the responsibilities of the actor are: first, to speak out loudly, honestly, as a citizen, on the real and decisive problems which face his audience today—on war, on peace, on unemployment and depression, on living standards and the plight of the minorities; second, the actor is responsible to consider his craft, the parts he plays and how he plays them.

For good or bad, the actor exerts an exceedingly important influence on the content of motion pictures. In the case of the star, it seems obvious: the performance of Bogart in *The Maltese Falcon* gives rise to dozens of cliches in imitation. Writers, whose chief concern should be with reality, are asked to write another Bogart-type script. You will hear from Adrian Scott about the stars who encouraged the production of, and fought to be in, *Crossfire*. Well, then, stars, for good or bad, influence the content of motion pictures.

What about the featured and bit players? Well, it's not easy, when rehearsal-time is an exception, and begrudged, when you make ardent love to a closeup camera, when a moment of high emotional intensity is diluted by having to play the scene over and over again before you hear the words "print it"—it's not easy. The actor must face these, and many other, technical problems, but there are also the many technical properties of the motion picture medium which *facilitate* the actor's creation. These are the craft-tools of the actor's art. Some are instruments of great effectiveness, some are unwieldy and difficult to use well.

Actors must get together and talk about these tools, and especially about methods of making the difficult ones more efficient. But, first, we must know what we want to build. The actor, or any artist, who regards his work as something more important than lucrative whoring, directs his talent and his craft toward the objectives of achieving truth and reality. Only in these can he find the satisfaction, the exaltation which art can effect. When I speak of reality,

I mean, of course, much more than naturalism. Fantasy may project essential reality, while fidelity to realistic detail sometimes adds up to a vicious distortion of truth and reality.

And here the actor runs smack-up against the cliche role, the stereotype. Nor is the actor alone. The Golden Rule of Precedent has already enmeshed the writer and director.

"This type of character", the chorus chants to the actor, "has always been done, and who are we to tamper with tradition?" To the writer the lyric reads, "This kind of idea." To the director, "This style of treatment." But the music is the same, "We did it before and we will do it again."

What can an actor do, when called upon to give life to a character made of faded carbon-paper? There are times when his integrity will demand that he refuse to play the part. But there must be a consistent policy that he can follow and remain in the motion picture business.

He can slip into the cliche role as into a raincoat, and then shrug it off with a comment about the Hollywood climate. That is surrender. The actor *must struggle* to give meaning to every word he utters, every movement he makes. (Occasionally, an actor of real genius can take a line like "Share and share alike, that's Democracy," and make it mean a threat to the American Way of Life—it says here!)

No, there is no shortcut for the actor. He must tackle every part with all the knowledge, technique and talent at his command, to imbue it with a substance of life and reality. He will not always succeed in hurdling the obstacles to truth in film-acting, but he must never cease trying. When he does, he's dead as an artist, and when enough others give up the drive for reality, the motion picture is dead as an art.

Big actor and little actor, you've got to keep swinging. Whether you're a heavyweight or a lightweight, according to the studios' strange scale, you've got to throw your weight around and make every pound felt.

The stereotype is an old problem to the film-artist in Hollywood. But in this post-World War II era of atom-bombs, Thomas poisoning, and flying saucers, the drive against truth and reality has been intensified and the artist's problems increased.

Why have the lie-lovers included on their condemned list such pictures as *Margie, The Strange Love of Martha Ivers, Boomerang, The Best Years of Our Lives, Pride of the Marines*—Communist propaganda? Rankin should live so long. And it can't even be simply that these are good pictures, because they're not all that good.

No, these appreciators of outhouse art put their sticky thumbs down on these films because each of them, in one way or another (and some ever so slightly) touched on reality. And when you touch reality, you're stamping on their heartbeats—and they see Red!

And the way to evade reality and to distort truth is, of course, the way of the cliche, the stereotype. Stereotype. What a beautiful Bilbonic ring the word has!

A Frenchman: "Oh, la la!"

An Italian: "Mama mia!"

An Irishman: "Faith and begorra!"

But, best of all, the boys really like to hear, "Yessah, boss— nossah, boss." Insult the Negro people, twist the Negro, distort him, just don't, under any circumstances, present Negro life, and the Negro problem, with any trace of truth or reality.

If a man speaks with a foreign accent, that's funny . . . or menacing. If a man works with his hands, that's funny . . . or menacing.

These are the people into whom the actor must blow the breath of life. That—or *we* are dead.

Pegler said, "The actor has forgotten the past out of which he came."

We remember. Just as we remember Moliere, the actor-playwright, was buried in unconsecrated ground because he was an actor. We remember that Moliere died on the stage. We remember that his last words were, "The comedy is over."

Pegler said, the actor "is speaking up to his betters."

We're living in serious times. We actors *must* speak up to everyone—to our betters, as well as to the Peglers. The comedy *is* over.

Adrian Scott

Member, SWG; producer,
*Murder, My Sweet, Cornered, Crossfire, So Well
Remembered*

YOU CAN'T DO THAT

I'D like to talk about *Crossfire* for a few minutes. As many of you know, it is the first picture that has been made which deals frankly and openly with the subject of anti-Semitism. I would like to tell you a little of its history first, focusing on the behind-the-scenes problems and the pressures to which we—who made it—were subject.

The project was conceived some two years ago. A book, *The Brick Foxhole,* had been written by Richard Brooks, then in the uniform of the Marine Corps. *The Brick Foxhole* was melodrama. It was soldiers in wartime. It was an attack on native Fascism—or the prejudices which exist in the American people which when organized lead very simply to native Fascism. It was an angry book, written with passion rooted in war —"in a dislocated, neurotic moment in history." While it did not deal exclusively with anti-Semitism, it nevertheless gave an opportunity to focus simply on anti-Semitism. It was a subject we wanted to do something about, it was a subject that needed public airing. And it was melodrama.

We had made several melodramas and were generally dissatisfied with the emptiness of the format, which in many ways is the most highly-developed screen format. The screen had done melodramas well, but mainly they were concerned with violence in pursuit of a jade necklace, a bejeweled falcon. The core of melodrama usually concerned itself with an innocuous object, without concern for reality, although dressed in highly realistic trappings. Substituting a search for an anti-Semite instead of a jade necklace, at the same time investigating anti-Semitism, seemed to us to add dimension and meaning to melodrama, while lending an outlet for conviction.

This was all fine, theoretically. It was fine to talk about it, and it would be interesting to do; but, as you know, the working producer doesn't have the right or the power to make what he wants. Neither does a writer. Nor a director. The problem was the okay from the

Front Office—that civilized monster which has no other concern but to think up devious ways to make you unhappy, or so you think. As producer, it was my job to go to the front office, which I did. At the time, William Dozier was the executive in charge.

I outlined the scheme to him: to make this picture at a minimum cost; in a short period of time, 23 days; to use people that we had confidence in, who had never been given a chance; in brief, to make this highly controversial subject-matter an exciting picture and an honest gamble. Dozier commented that he was worried about anti-Semitism; and, though he had no sure way of knowing, he'd felt from his personal experiences that it had grown since Hitler's demise, rather than diminished. Dozier ordered an option taken on the material.

So far, so good. We did some more thinking about it. Virginia Wright of the *Los Angeles Daily News* announced the project in a column. People called me. They said it would be fine if we could do it, but there was a long way to go to get it in production. People called Edward Dmytryk, the director, and John Paxton, the writer, with the same sort of mournful note in their voices. Some said it was wrong to do it in a melodramatic format. Some said: Why do it? We were young. This picture could come later. We were sticking our necks out. It could be catastrophic. Not only did people say this to us—we said it to ourselves.

We left for England to make *So Well Remembered* and, on the estate of Sir Oswald Mosley—now turned into a boarding-house,— we thought about *The Brick Foxhole* some more. We *worried* more about it than we *thought* about it. We wondered if they would really let us make it. I got a sinus attack for which a Harley Street specialist could not find a reason. Clearly, he was a quack. Paxton had some stomach trouble which he attributed to the English food, although none of the rest of us had trouble at that time. Paxton and I continued to kick the project around—with Dmytryk when he was free from his chores,—and we managed (in these conferences which were to create *Crossfire*) to find a number of reasons why *Crossfire* couldn't be made.

1) It had never been done before. 2) They wouldn't let us do it. 3) Everybody says that pictures of this kind lose their shirts at the box-office. Besides, motion pictures decline social responsibility. They have one responsibility only: to stockholders, to make them rich or richer. Sure-fire stuff is rule-of-thumb; legs, torsos, bosoms, shapely and magnificent, with or without talent, are the vestiture and invest-

ment of films, beyond which only the fool goes. Why be a fool? 4) This was the wrong way to do this subject. 5) Actors would not risk their reputations. 6) A number of exhibitors would refuse to play the picture. 7) This picture would hurt somebody's feelings. Probably some nice anti-Semite's. 8) This was not an effective way to combat anti-Semitism. It was much better not to talk about it.

And, having exhausted that, we continued discussions on the most effective way of making it.

We returned home in November of last year. The studio had gone through a change of administration. Peter Rathvon was in temporary charge of production, negotiating, as we later found out, with a new production head.

I was home from England a few days, when I was told by the Story Department that there was a possibility that the option on *The Brick Foxhole* might be dropped.

About this time, I had a series of X-rays on my stomach. Clearly, I'd fallen victim to the old producer complaint—ulcers. I drank horrid white liquid and a man with lead gloves poked me in the stomach and the damn fool couldn't find anything wrong.

I felt I was the victim of a plot and I said to nobody at all that they couldn't do this to me.

I was ready to have it out with Peter Rathvon. Incidentally, Rathvon is quite a man to have things out with—he is not only president of the production company, he is President of RKO Theatres and also Chairman of the Board of Directors of RKO. He speaks with some authority.

I told him about the project, and he said it was very interesting and this was the first he'd heard of it. We all had been abroad. We had no opportunity to discuss it with him. Familiarizing himself with the lot, he'd run across *The Brick Foxhole*. He assumed that I would on my own drop the option, since it was about a moment in history which could be better analyzed several years hence. He had no objections to a picture on anti-Semitism. As a matter of fact, he thought it was a good idea. The sterility of general motion picture production was something which bothered him—here was a good, useful way of introducing a new subject-matter. He ordered the option to be renewed.

At about this time, my ulcerous condition mysteriously abated.

We started actual work on the screenplay when Dore Schary was made head of production. Schary's record is known to all of you.

It is a record generously-laden with progressive picture-making. But—now something else had to be considered. Schary was new. He had an extremely difficult job of reorganization facing him. Sure, he wanted to make pictures with a mature content. He was on record as saying this. But anti-Semitism was a different matter. This was an explosive subject. It would be highly embarrassing to present him with a decision of this nature a few weeks after arriving on the lot. Was it right to do it now? Maybe a few months from now? These were our nightmares.

The night after I sent John Paxton's magnificent script to him, two sleeping-pills didn't work. I arrived haggard the next morning—a little late. I learned that Mr. Schary had made an appointment with my secretary—I was due in his office in ten minutes. So I went up.

He said, "I think this will make a good picture. Let's go." Overnight, the lot was transformed into a unit for *Crossfire*. Every department swung into operation to meet the challenge of making an "A" picture on a "B" budget. Robert Young left Columbia at 12 o'clock, having finished one picture, and at 1 o'clock started *Crossfire*. Robert Mitchum cut short a vacation. Robert Ryan would have murdered anyone who prevented him from playing the part of the anti-Semite.

Conferences were held with Schary, who made suggestions which improved the script. This, of course, is revolution, when it is necessary to admit into the record that the contributions of a studio head were not only used but welcomed. The picture went into production on a 23-day schedule. The photography by Roy Hunt was painstakingly faithful to the script values. Dmytryk brought it in on schedule and, most important, achieved his finest direction to date.

That is the story and these were the pressures we were subject to.

I have gone into the history of *Crossfire* at this length, not for the purpose of examining *Crossfire* but to examine my colleagues and myself. For two years, we feared not that we would not make a good picture, but that we would not make a picture at all. Through all the long months before we started work, fear consumed us. Why does this fear occur? Where does this fear come from? It does not require complex medical opinion to discover the source.

It is a fear produced with a Hollywood trademark. Throughout its comparatively short history, Hollywood has been the victim of an infinite variety of lobbyists who claim the right to dictate what pictures shall be made and what the content of those pictures will be. As a result of these pressures, a complex and subtle system of thought has grown up around the industry. At times it is not so complex and not so subtle. And the newcomer, before he can successfully make his way, must not only become accustomed to this pattern, but must become a part of it. The producer's first consideration of any property is: "Can I get this by the production Code?" Notice the wording: "Can I get it by?" It is not a deliberate thought process, it is a reflex action—that automatic. Similarly function the writer and the director and the executive. And pity the poor cameraman who because of the famous cleavage controversy must now subvert the bosoms of American womanhood from two into one!

Incidentally, it is not my purpose here to estimate whether the individual or the industry is chiefly responsible for this fear among us. I am principally interested in the fact that it exists, in the fact that it does touch the individual, and transforms his work into something he does not want it to be.

My colleagues and I are guilty. We imposed a censorship on ourselves, in first considering a picture on anti-Semitism and during its preparation. There is nothing in the code of the Producers' Association which prevents the making of this picture. The Producers' Association, Mr. Breen in particular, applauded this picture. He felt it was a fine contribution, and went so far as to defend us against snide and ridiculous rumors. This fear—this self-imposed censorship resulting from fear—is not an isolated phenomenon confined to my colleagues and myself. It is a virus infecting all of us. It can cause creative senility, hackery and lousy pictures. It constitutes conservatism to the point of reaction. This creative reaction results in cliche thinking and cliche work and cliche pictures.

We are not, however, the cliche that we produce on the screen. We are not that hero—the strong American, rough, tender, witty, intelligent, unconquerable except by the little school-teacher from Boston. We are not the Clark Gable we write, direct and produce, who with his bare hands tears rich dynasties apart, with only Hedy Lamarr by his side. We are—rather—the wish-fulfillment of this creation. We are, in fact, cliches compounding further cliches.

The fear is a state of mind, and like a state of mind it is subject to change. It is not easy to change; it is sometimes not profitable; on the other hand, it is sometimes immensely profitable. The enormous success of pictures honestly dealing with their subjects is proof enough. But, I repeat, it is subject to change. It has changed in the past. Behind us, we have a record of picture-making which has dignity and courage.

I would like briefly to cite a few cases—pictures which were made in spite of the taboos:

The Story of Louis Pasteur, the great French scientist, was a realistic appraisal of the scientist. At the time it was held that you could not make a picture about a bug, about diseased cows, about hydrophobia and mad dogs and children suffering the ravages of the disease. Aspects of Pasteur was seized upon and made highly unattractive. The result we know—a biography of dignity, entertainingly telling the story of a man who in his day fought medical reaction.

Grapes of Wrath by John Steinbeck. I do not know whether Darryl Zanuck, who produced this, was subject to pressure. It is quite conceivable that he was. But the mere fact of making this picture made Mr. Zanuck take a stand—against the abuse of people. That it was attacked when it was released, is an established fact. That it was a fine picture, needs no elaboration.

There are others made in opposition to pressure: *Confessions of a Nazi Spy, Mission to Moscow* and the pictures which depicted the gangster era. The part the gangster pictures played in causing legislation against prohibition is well-known.

More recently *Boomerang* and *The Farmer's Daughter* have been attacked, and *The Best Years of Our Lives*—and to their everlasting credit, Samuel Goldwyn and Dore Schary have answered their attackers. During the preparation of *The Best Years,* it is conceivable that Mr. Goldwyn was told that he shouldn't make a picture about returning veterans—the people were tired of war, of soldiers in uniform, they wanted to forget, they wanted to think about something else, to be happy, joyful. If Mr. Goldwyn had listened, he would not only have done himself and the public a rare disservice, he also would not have had the biggest grosser of the year.

These pictures, all of them, did not ask for revolution. They merely asked for an extension of democracy. They treated humanity with compassion—and this today is becoming a crime. This crime is something which the American people want. Their support of *The Farmer's Daughter* and *The Best Years of Our Lives, Kingsblood Royal* and *Gentleman's Agreement,* I submit as evidence. I have it on my own personal record from two preview audiences of *Crossfire.*

We received the largest number of cards ever accorded an RKO picture in its two previews. Over 500 were received from the preview held at the RKO 86th Street Theatre in New York—on the fringe of Yorkville, the old Fritz Kuhn district. Over 500 were received at the RKO Hillstreet in Los Angeles. 95% of the cards heartily approved of *Crossfire*. An overwhelming majority liked those scenes best which directly came to grips with anti-Semitism. A great majority asked the screen to treat more subjects like this.

That tired, dreary ghost who has been haunting our halls, clanking his chains and moaning, "The people want only entertainment," can be laid to rest, once and for all. The American people have always wanted and more than ever want pictures which touch their lives, illuminate them, bring understanding. If we retreat now, because of our own doubts, not only do we do a great disservice to the American audience, but we do a most profound disservice to ourselves.

For, this Fear we've become accustomed to, this adjustment we have made to taboos, are the allies of the Thomas Committee, the Tenney Committee, and their stooges within and without the industry. Our Fear makes us beautiful targets—we are in the proper state of mind for the operation of these committees which in pretending to defend actually subvert our democratic way. We are magnificently adjusted to bans, and ripe for more bans, which inevitably will result if we allow it. There are supercilious cynics among us who conceivably could derive a singular pleasure from further bans on what we write, direct or produce. Further bans extend an already-flourishing martyr complex—more reason to sit by, substituting luxury and creative locomotor ataxia for honest creative effort.

I believe we have a job to do: to combat the controls which can lead only to more sterility in the motion picture and to more reaction generally. If we allow ourselves to be consumed by our fears, this can happen. While this marriage of reaction is going on, we've got to speak now—or we'll be forced to "forever hold our peace".

Richard Collins

Screen writer, credited with
films including *Song of Russia*, *As Thousands Cheer*,
Private Miss Jones, *Little
Giant*, etc.

THE SCREEN WRITER AND CENSORSHIP

LAST Spring, in a casual discussion, Thomas Mann said that what was wrong with American films was not lack of liberty, but lack of creativity. It is not hard to understand why the great German author, standing outside the industry, should feel thus.

It is true, thought control over this industry is not exercised by storm-troopers placed at the door of each office. But the many pressures—all subtler, all gentler—are nonetheless efficient. There are two immediately apparent reasons why creativity is being strangled in Hollywood today: the first is the objective censorship operated by such groups as the Breen Office, the Johnston Office, the Tenney Committee, the Thomas Committee, the Hearst press, Pegler and the M.P.A. Besides, there are the pressures from women's organizations, organized church groups and, finally, although often in contradiction to the others, the audience. The second, the self-censorship of writers and other creators in the industry who, as a result of the above pressures, tend themselves to limit their whole field of operation and to play safe.

What is thought control in films? How does it operate? Well, for example, the Breen Office does not permit mature sexual relations on the screen. I do not mean smut. Smut is permitted—witness *Duel in the Sun*. But I do mean, for example, the treatment of sex in marriage. Those of us who are familiar with the Breen Office, can imagine what would happen if a wife expressed one-tenth of the desire for her husband that Jennifer Jones expressed for Gregory Peck. Of course, the Breen Office takes care of this under the category heading 'Pure and Impure Love'. I mean, also, by mature sex relations, a recognition that marriages are often made in poolrooms and dancehalls, and not in heaven. There are, it is true, millions of Americans who believe the latter, and we most certainly respect their point of view. Catholic

331

morality comes out of Catholic religion and it is perfectly proper for a church to make films with its morality. But there is no reason why the entire motion picture business should accept any one religion or philosophic system as official. Jewish organizations are also responsible for the hush-hush policy concerning the presentation of Jews on the screen, which has prevailed until very recently.

Beside this religious pressure, we are now experiencing political thought control. We were never asked before that all of us should follow Roosevelt's policy, or Hoover's, or Coolidge's—but we have now been told by Eric Johnston to write films supporting the present American foreign policy. Now, if a writer believes in the Truman Doctrine, let him write about it. If this is truth for him—well and good. But if, on the other hand, he does not believe that a temporary political expedient can be accepted as either true or eternal, it is corrupt for him to write in support of it. What will this same writer do if tomorrow a deal is made which changes the Doctrine? What will he do if an opposite political philosophy dominates the American scene? Will he flop over to the new side? Or is it not a classic tenet of a free people and a free art that a writer should write as he believes, and not as he is told? There are other areas which are under attack as leftist and subversive. And these areas have been under attack for many years. The first anti-Nazi film, *Confessions of a Nazi Spy,* was labelled 'Communist' by Dies and his Committee, as was the strong anti-lynching film, *Fury.*

There are many areas of silence now. These areas have been accepted subjectively by the writers. Faced with objective censorship, we have tried to deal with it—because a writer not only writes for expression, but also to communicate. This means that he always exercises some censorship in relation to his audience. The writers, therefore, in trying to get around censorship, have either gone deeper and deeper into themselves or else have become extremely subtle in their approaches.

In some cases, the writer loses the very audience he is trying to reach. He hesitates to explore new areas because he has been taught for many years to try to make films to which no one will object. Obviously, the only way to do this is to stop films from reflecting any of the real conflicts and stresses of our society. Yet, in spite of this pressure, we have succeeded year after year in making memorable films. One has only to look at the Gassner-Nichols *Twenty Best Film Plays* to see the wide variety of subjects that the films have handled.

Most of these twenty plays met with success at the box-office. But the same subjects which were treated in these films now involve us in very controversial ground, both in American life and in our foreign policy.

We are vastly impressed with such a picture as *Brief Encounter*. This is a fine film, but should it really be astonishing to see a picture that admits there are many middle-class women, leading dreary, dull lives, who want romance even if they have a nice suburban husband and two children? And that they might perhaps even have a fast and unreasonable, and sometimes beautiful, relationship with another mar· ried man—and through all this they are neither wicked nor vile?

Our Production Code, as a matter of fact, flies in the face of science. Modern psychology and social science teach us that the vices of men come from society. The Code takes for granted that these vices are inherent in man's person. This excludes the dynamic of the inter-relation between society and character. Science, for example, says a man drinks to excess out of frustration, not out of weakness. The non-dynamic view makes the producer treat sex as a game, rather than explore the relations between characters. This non-dynamic, static view of human personality creates the gap between life and the screen. It is a very tidy world we have in the films. The Production Code guarantees this. Adultery is not permissible; all murderers are brought to justice; good triumphs over evil.

This is not a new problem for creators. Chekhov, in a letter to Kiselev, makes this clear:

> "To think that the task of literature is to gather the pure grain from the muck-heap is to reject literature itself. Artistic literature is called so just because it depicts life as it really is. Its aim is truth—unconditional, and honest. A litterateur is not a confectioner, not a dealer in cosmetics, not an entertainer. He is like any ordinary reporter. What would you say if a newspaper reporter, because of his fastidiousness, were to describe only honest mayors, high-minded ladies and virtuous railroad contractors? To a chemist nothing on earth is unclean. A writer must be as objective as a chemist."

Although he is speaking of literature, I believe this is equally valid for our own medium. I do not see why, what is good for the thousands who read books, can be bad for the millions who see films. I do not see that the reflection of life can do more harm than life itself—rather I believe that the reflection of life accurately will give useful experience to the audience, will enable them better to meet and conquer their day-to-day problems.

In the high-schools of the city of Los Angeles, there is a class called "Senior Problems". This class has its counterpart in cities all over the United States. It is a class which discusses the future of the senior high-school student. It covers world affairs, propaganda, divorce, marriage, love, personality conflicts, petting, venereal diseases, depressions and unemployment. The high-school students discuss these subjects openly, sharply and honestly. But there is virtually nothing that they are allowed to discuss that we are being allowed to put into films, including their discussions of the Negro and Jewish questions. Although we have managed to break anti-Semitism into the open with such pictures as *Crossfire* and the forthcoming *Gentleman's Agreement,* both of which take courage and strength from their makers, we have done the very reverse with the Negro question. We have solved the Negro problem in Hollywood by ignoring Negroes in pictures. This is the pattern of every problem. Is it any wonder that other countries now have the opportunity to take the lead in films?

In *Great Expectations,* there is sharp criticism of British legal procedure and the treatment of criminals in England's past. Yet, in the United States, exception is taken to a criticism of American Marines in Nicaragua in the film *Margie.* Are we to assume not only that the present Truman policy is above reproach, but also that everything that ever happened in the United States was right? This will be difficult. Following this line, slavery was undoubtedly correct until the day Lincoln signed the Emancipation Proclamation. On that day it became wrong. Or did it? I have an idea we had better leave this whole area alone. The film *Boomerang* apparently outrages the "one hundred percenters". Is this because they will not admit that injustice is ever possible? . . . What areas will be left?

For the screen writer faced with great and unprecedented unemployment, this question is not only aesthetic, but food and drink. He is called upon to write for sale; naturally, he exercises a great degree of self-censorship. The pressure on him to conform is very real. Yet, at the same time, the experience of unemployment and insecurity brings him into conflict with censorship.

But it is not only the screen writer who is thus affected, for, as the area of creative content shrinks, only one conclusion is possible: the policy of the M.P.A. and the Thomas Committee means ruin for this industry creatively and financially. Beyond that, is the less tangible but equally serious answer, that the creators of the pictures can ruin them because they are, so to speak, in the habit of ruin.

We, as writers, as often as not, impose self-censorship even where no open threat of censorship exists. We not only tax ourselves with the real difficulties of writing pictures which will be artistically and commercially successful, but we also impose hidden taxes on ourselves. It is not only in political areas that we as screen writers impose such hidden taxes on our realism. Hard as we try to write about marriage, love, infidelity, drunkenness and murder in an absolutely truthful and realistic manner, there is nevertheless a margin of aberration in our thinking which has been enforced upon us by a lifetime of thought control. The free film, on the other hand, pressures the writer into looking to new areas and forces him to meet competition with daring, imagination and vitality.

All that we should ask of a writer is that he write about objective reality the way it is. The writer should help audiences master reality, by imaginatively possessing it. If the screen is free, no police is necessary. As Chekhov has said in this same letter:

> "There is no police which we can consider competent in literary matters. I agree we must have curbs and whips, for knaves find their way even into literature. But think what you will, you cannot find a better police for literature than criticism and the author's own conscience. People have been trying to discover such a police since the creation of the world—but nothing better has been found."

Let the audience be the critics. Let them say to us, "Don't deal with reality and we won't buy tickets. Deal with reality and we will support you."

To achieve a free and adult screen, all of us here have a duty. It is for the audience, the P.C.A. nationally, to lift the pressures from the creators, to do away with the censorship committee, the political pressure-groups. And, with this help, the writers can then proceed to do their duty, which is to fight the objective censors and at the same time free themselves. This relation between writer and audience—in common struggle—will create the dynamic relation which in turn can create dynamic content for a free film.

DISCUSSION

The discussion following this Panel was of a general nature, high-lighted particularly by the lengthy statement by *dancer-actor Paul Draper*, essential passages of which follow:

"We are not yet through with *The Time of Your Life*, but I consider that I am fairly well-established in it by now, so I want to relate to you how some of the threats that have been levelled at the film industry, and some of the fears that certain members of the film industry have, have affected scripts.

"The first is a small point—not world-shaking,—but, so that you can see which way the wind blows, here it is: In this film, I play the part of Harry—a dancer and a somewhat mad fellow, besides. The original intent of the producers of this film—James and William Cagney—was to follow the original play as closely as it possibly could be followed. They in fact did not use a certain director who had a concept for the screen which was at variance with what Saroyan had written, and they wanted it word for word. When I was asked to read the part, we came to a place where I had to say, when trying to prove that I can be funny:

" 'Maybe the headline's about me. I take a quick look. No, the headline is not about me—it's about Hitler . . . 7,000 miles away . . . I'm here. Who is Hitler? Who's behind the 8-ball? I turn around—everybody is behind the 8-ball . . .'

"Since the play was written in 1939, I asked: 'Whom do I use for "Hitler" here?' The reply: 'Oh, say Stalin . . .'

"I had not yet signed the contract, so—somewhat softly—I suggested that perhaps this was not the best way to handle an awkward situation. I asked whether they were sure, and got the reply: 'I wish we could make it "Wallace" . . .'

"I didn't feel that I could press the point then. Four weeks later, I signed a contract for the picture and started to shoot it.

"But I kept thinking of that line. I hope to give shows some day and to dance in the Soviet Union and throughout the Balkans—naturally, I did not want to say it. And, even if this were not the case, I still would not like to: I like living, I like moving ahead, not away from the world . . .

"I talked to Jimmy about it . . . and to others, including some of the grips . . . Finally, after I just kept on with light pressures, I was told to 'make that "Stalin" line "Molotov" . . .'

"I did not feel that my problem had been wholly solved . . . So I finally had a long and quite serious discussion with the foreign representative of J. Arthur Rank, who said that I could indeed quote him on the fact that his organization would not distribute a film which had a line in it derogatory to the Soviet Union. I told this to Jimmy Cagney, and there was flashing action. Half-an-hour before this came up to be shot, the line changed. As an alternative, for those places which would not show the film with the derogatory line, it became:

"'No, the headline is not about me . . . It's about "Kilroy". "Kilroy" isn't here. I'm here . . . etc. . .'

"Now, I do really think that this is as good and swift and crea-tive a solution as you could conceivably find—it is, at least, non-committal. But I was told at that time not to go over the director's head; that we should do one version with 'Molotov'—and we did. I am not smart enough in film-making to realize that once they have it in the can, that's it, so I said it, and there exists this version of the speech. If any of you see it, you'll know that I do not honestly mean it . . .

"There is another item, but which did not concern me directly. It is in the lines spoken by McCarthy, a longshoreman, who is played beautifully by Ward Bond. They are:

"'A strong man with any sensibility has no choice in this world but to be a heel or a worker. I haven't the heart to be a heel, so I'm a worker.'

"This sentence has been deleted entirely from the script. I was not on the set when it was shot, but I got at least curious and asked why it had been omitted. It seemed to me to be a line which was a powerful development and expression of McCarthy's philosophy. I was assured it had been deleted because you couldn't mention the word 'worker' in the pictures made today, because of the Thomas Committee. The word 'worker' is absolute dynamite; we dare not use it. However, lines deleterious to labor unions have been kept in the script, which could have been taken out without in any way inter-fering with it.

"One final thing: Joe, who is the leading character of the film and is played magnificently by Jimmy Cagney, is the character who keeps what slight curious wonderful thread of the story there is, moving. He is asked by his friend and helper how he happens to have enough money all the time to be able to order champagne, etc. Joe answers:

> " 'Now don't be a fool, Tom—listen carefully. If anybody has got any money to hoard or to throw away you can be sure he stole it from other people—not from rich people who can spare it, but from poor people who can't . . . from their lives and from their dreams . . . And I'm no exception—I earned the money I throw away . . .'

"This was changed to:

> " 'Now don't be a fool, Tom—listen carefully. I'm no exception— I earned the money I throw away . . .'

"As I say, these things are not world-shattering, and the film is not going to be good or bad because of the commission or omission of these lines. It is, I think, a pretty fascinating film, anyhow. But I was asked to point these things out to you to give you a specific story on something that has already happened in a film to a script, directly as a result of the antics of a Thomas Committee . . . and Adolphe Menjou, Robert Taylor, Mrs. Rogers, et al.

"We all admit that they make fools of themselves and the Committee. This was a small example of the effect—and we cannot overcome their threat by speeches.

"We can perhaps overcome it by increasingly direct action. I hope that in the life of my relationship to the films, which I am so happily and proudly enjoying now, I can be of far more assistance in the future than I have been able to be this afternoon."

After this discussion, a set of resolutions were moved, seconded and unanimously carried by the Panel on The Film, as follows:

RESOLUTIONS

1. *Resolved,* that the Hollywood Arts, Sciences and Professions Council investigate the possibility of organizing audiences throughout the United States to support those motion pictures which, like *The Best Years of Our Lives,* promote a deeper understanding of the struggle of our citizens to gain peace and security. And that at the same time the ASP organize audiences to carry on a fight against pictures of a reactionary and non-progressive nature.

2. *Resolved,* that in view of the urgent need for such a service, there be set up through the ASP Council a sort of Mental Consumers' Union, to report, in whatever manner is deemed most practical, the status of thought control activities in the various media of mass communication and influencing of public opinion.

3. *Resolved,* that the PCA take leadership in calling upon labor and progressive organizations to get together and demand representation in the Breen Office, administering the Production Code and thereby determining the content of our films.

4. *Resolved,* that this body be constituted as the core of a Continuations Committee to be reconvened by the Panel speakers at another meeting in the near future, for further study of the problems discussed here today.

5. *Resolved,* that this Panel urge the Conference on the Subject of Thought Control, as a whole, to support the Civil Rights Congress in the case of Carl Aldo Marzani, and that the Conference go on record as asking the Attorney General to drop charges against Marzani.

the actor

Saturday, July 12, 1947, 8:00-10:30 P. M.

Vincent Price, Chairman

Speakers: Lee J. Cobb, Anne Revere, Howard Da Silva, Ludwig Donath, Selena Royle

Sketch by Ben Barzman and Stanley Prager

Participating in discussion: Morris Carnovsky, Sam Levene, Larry Parks, Shepperd Strudwick, Dorothy Tree, Phoebe Brand, Philip Loeb, Connie Stone, Art Smith and members of the audience

All papers in this Panel prepared under the direction of the Actors' Division, ASP, PCA.

Lee J. Cobb

Former Group Theatre
actor; stage, screen cre-
ator of father in *Golden
Boy;* recently, *Johnny
O'Clock, Captain from
Castile,* etc.

THE ACTOR'S HISTORICAL STRUGGLE FOR CITIZENSHIP

. . . To show the very age and body of the time his form and pressure.

BEFORE we proceed to a discussion of how actors today show—
or fail to show—the very age and body of our time its form and
pressure, let us skim through the many events of the past which have
built the traditions and heritage of our particular art.

Aristophanes was an actor in Athens some 2500 years ago. When
he wrote his first play, *The Knights,* an outspoken attack upon one
Cleon, a political demagogue, the local actors were intimidated and

340

none could be found to portray the part of the leading politician of the day. Aristophanes played the part himself, recklessly dispensing with the customary mask and, for make-up, squeezing the juice of a berry on his nose. Needless to say, the entire audience immediately recognized Cleon, a notorious lush.

Cleon instituted several law-suits in an effort to have Aristophanes deported out of Athens. Only native citizens of Athens could enter plays in the festivals and play-tournaments. But so popular were Aristophanes' plays with the audience of his day, that all efforts to brand him a "foreigner" were thrown out of court.

Thought control? Yes. And why? Not only because our outspoken Aristophanes satirized a political demagogue, but more importantly because he launched his sharp-witted attacks against the political ineptitudes and the imperialism of his day.

This little anecdote merely emphasizes that acting, like every art, has been, from its beginnings, a product of the historical period in which it flourished. Developments, national and international, economic and sociological, have left their mark on the actor; he, in turn, has left his mark on the society in which he lived.

Witnesss another actor, who also did a little writing on the side: William Shakespeare. History conspired to make the Golden Age of Elizabethan England a propitious time for his birth. England's agricultural-feudal system was crumbling. In its place, manufacture and trade flourished. The enriched nobility, in quest of pleasure for their new leisure, established acting-companies, and theatres to house them.

But not even the royal patrons could spare the Elizabethan actor from the wrath of the Puritans, who attacked the moral looseness of the Court through an anti-actor campaign. In the struggle for power between the anti-royalists, who used the Puritans as their spearhead, and the Court, the actor found himself in the middle.

This was only one of the factors contributing to the actor's instability. To add to his woes, his economic well-being varied with the caprice of the nobleman who was his patron. When he was in favor, the actor was a pampered soul, protected even from arrest by the insignia of his patron, which he wore on his sleeve. But when he fell out of favor, he had no choice but to become a strolling-player, wandering through the countryside. Here he was in danger of being branded a vagabond—a designation which brought with it heavy penalties.

For, in England, feudalism was breaking up so rapidly that thousands of serfs who had been thrown off the land had not yet been absorbed into the factories and mills. They were a huge floating population against whom the authorities leveled harsh restrictions.

Strolling actors were often victimized by these laws; they were imprisoned, whipped, had their ears cut off and their breasts branded with a V—for vagabond.

This interlude placed a brand of disrespectability upon actors which, in varying pitches of intensity, has clung through the years. It still crops up today when, though actors are idolized professionally, our fellow-citizens still raise skeptical eyebrows at the suggestion that we can function constructively in public life.

For all the hardships which many actors endured in the Elizabethan period, the theatre flourished past the death of Elizabeth and through the reign of James I. Then came the eclipse. The rising merchant-class, competing against the nobility for power, struck at one of royalty's best weapons for public sympathy—the actor. In 1642, Oliver Cromwell banished the actor from London. It was not until the restoration of the monarchy in 1660 that Charles II permitted the theatres to reopen.

The Restoration Period is notable for an outstanding development in the acting profession. Prior to this time, feminine roles, including the great Shakespearean women, had been played by men and boys.

The advent of the actress was heralded in typical fashion by Samuel Pepys of diary fame: "It being very well done, and here is the first time that I ever saw a woman come upon the stage." Some of the most popular personalities of the day were women—notably Nell Gwynn, a favorite comedienne, who manifested the identity of the actor with the new royalty by becoming the mistress of Charles II.

The period was also notable for the first actors' strike in history. In December, 1694, London's leading actors, led by Thomas Betterton, drew up a petition of their grievances against the managers who were cheating, duping, coercing and bullying them. Managers, for instance, kept actors in their debt by advancing them small sums against their share in the takings that, even in Shakespeare's time, were deposited in the "box" which became the "box-office." One manager, Henslow, boasted, "Should these fellows come out of my debt, I should have no rule over them."

Betterton's petition was presented to the Lord Chamberlain. Until the grievances were righted, the actors refused to act. In 1695, the strike was won. Actors were permitted to establish their own theatres, free from the economic domination of the theatre-owners and managers.

It was the beginning of a new era for England. In 1689, just a few years before the Betterton strike, the Bill of Rights had been established. Ahead, for England, was the growth of a great middle-class, and a new emphasis on the individual human being and his rights. This period marked the birth of the democratic tradition in England. The actor no longer belonged solely to the ruling-class. He was reaching out to a new audience—the people.

In America, we have records of actors here as early as 1703, when Anthony Aston, a strolling English player, wrote in his diary: "We arrived in Charles-Town, full of lice, poverty, nakedness, and hunger."

In America, actors soon faced the same intense anti-theatre preju-dices which had been virulent in England before the Restoration. Some of the prejudice was based on Puritan resistance to all forms of pleas-ure. Some of it was economic. Frugality was a necessary virtue; going to the theatre was gross extravagance.

In 1774, the Continental Congress banned the theatre altogether. Its resolution reflects the low esteem in which the theatre was held:

"We will discountenance and discourage every species of extravagance and dissipation, especially all horse-racing, and all kinds of games, cock-fighting, exhibitions of shows, plays and other expensive diversions and entertainment."

In the years following the Revolutionary War, American national consciousness burgeoned. America was throwing off the last vestiges of colonial economy and culture, and becoming a self-contained nation.

This new nationalistic feeling, an aftermath of the War of 1812 against Britain, manifested itself in the theatre through the appear-ance of plays written by Americans, dealing with the American scene, and through the development of native American actors.

The theatre idol of the day was Edwin Forrest, a native Phila-delphian and the first great native American actor. Here was an actor who was, indeed, a mirror of his times.

Whenever Forrest, in his role as Spartacus, delivered his diatribe against tyranny, in the popular play *The Gladiators,* it was invariably greeted with prolonged cheers—partly due to Forrest's eloquence, but also partly due to the democratic sentiments he articulated.

Paralleling this rising consciousness, of a national American culture, there was growing a resentment among actors of the conditions surrounding their profession. One chronicler of the times tells of an incident when supernumeraries (extras) revolted, just before a second-act curtain was to rise, because the manager was in arrears on their pay.

"The manager was resolved that the play should proceed; 'that anybody can be done without.' And the great scene in the Temple of the Sun was in its course produced. The original intention was to introduce a grand procession of the Peruvian chiefs and soldiers, whom Rolla addresses in his celebrated patriotic speech. Instead, however, of this numerous host, accompanied by a large train of virgins of the Sun and other characters, the concourse was represented by four little girls, Orano (a character in the piece), a flying messenger, an old blind man and his son. To the valor and patriotism of these eight persons—or seven and a half persons—did Rolla pour forth his stirring appeal and his assurance of their powers to resist the invading armies of Pizarro."

Not only the extras, but the stars, too, had their troubles. Joseph Jefferson, in his autobiography, tells us:

"In Springfield, Illinois, we hired a lot and built a theatre . . . then religious people got a heavy license imposed upon us—so heavy as to make opening impossible. A young lawyer called on the manager. He had heard of the injustice and offered to take the matter up—no fee. He handled the subject with tact, skill and humor, tracing the history of the drama from the time when Thespis acted in a cart to the stage of today. He illustrated his speech with a number of anecdotes and kept the Council in a roar of laughter. The tax was taken off. The young lawyer's name was Abraham Lincoln."

The country was growing up—and, with it, the theatre was growing up. Ahead lay the Civil War, the bitter days of the Reconstruction, a complex society to follow. The theatre kept pace with the country, reflecting the ever-changing American scene.

More than one company attempting to play *Uncle Tom's Cabin* in localities divided on the slavery question was put to flight in the middle of performances. The play's influence was tremendous during the last decade of slavery, and its part in the creation of anti-slave sentiment incalculable.

The great migration westward was soon reflected in the traveling stock-companies that toured the length and breadth and height of the land—the height of Leadville, Colorado, a miningtown, where the air was so rarefied, actors gasped through whole plays.

The upheavals created by World War I were reflected in the spontaneous rise of independent theatre movements, such as the Provincetown Playhouse, the Washington Square Players, later to become the Theatre Guild, and the Neighborhood Playhouse. This gave actors the opportunities for freer and more vital expression denied them by the limitations of the commercial theatre. This protest against the commercialism of the theatre had not only an artistic basis but also an economic one. With the theatres in the hands of syndicates, it became necessary for actors to band together to protect themselves from economic injustices.

Perhaps the single most significant achievement of the actor in his struggle for stability and recognition has been the headway made in the past few decades toward self-organization, chiefly through the unions which are now banded together in the 4A's.

The first of these actors' unions in America was the White Rats, in which the vaudeville artists banded together against the many evils besetting that profession. Back in 1898, they struck, but unsuccessfully. Some years later, they tried again, but again were defeated by the organized syndicate of theatre-managers and booking-agencies.

Then came Equity, through which the actors of the legitimate theatre sought redress of their grievances, such as rehearsing indefinite periods at no pay and often being dismissed the day after opening to give way to less expensive actors; or being stranded across the continent with no return fare and often with no salary.

Immediately, the Producing Managers' Association issued a tearful warning (August 7, 1919):

". . . this association will aid in protecting the actor of stage and screen from inequitable and unfair contracts and assure to the *employers* thereof a continuance of the privilege *to deal with them individually as artists*."

When the actors sought affiliation with the A. F. of L., the P.M.A. stated, "The actor cannot serve two masters—the theatre and unionism."

And when Equity had won the support of the A. F. of L. workers in the theatre and sought an Equity shop—a union shop,—the now-horrified P.M.A. cried: ". . . it will work enduring harm to the theatre, and it will be humiliating, unjust, and Un-American."

But the actors were not intimidated. One of them, Frank Bacon, was playing a star part on Broadway (in *Lightnin'*) for the first time, after years of obscurity and insecurity. Bacon said later that he had discussed the situation with his wife who told him simply: "We're with the actors, Frank. I've cooked our meals over a gas jet before. I can do it again."

Broadway was truly electrified the next day when buses filled with cheering actors drove through Times Square bearing streamers announcing, *"Lightnin' Has Struck!"*

As other shows followed suit, the producers hurried to court and got injunctions against their actors. The Shuberts sued Equity and its members for $500,000. A company-union was hurriedly formed, but only a handful of scabs joined it.

Monster benefits were given by the actors for their strike fund. The names on those bills were dazzling to behold. The Barrymores, Marie Dressler, Joe Sawyer and Joseph Santley, the entire Foy family, Eddie Cantor and the m.c.—W. C. Fields. Ed Wynn, at the first of such benefits, rose from his seat in the auditorium and said, "Ladies and Gentlemen, Justice Lydon has forbidden me to appear on the stage tonight. Of course, the orders of the court must be obeyed. If I had been able to appear tonght I had in mind telling you a story about—" and did his whole act from his seat.

Lest the producers manage to tie up their strike fund by securing a judgment against them, the money was deposited in a bank in the name of "Isaiah, 59:14", which reads: "And judgment is turned away backward, and justice standeth afar off: for truth is fallen in the street, and equity cannot enter."

Anne Revere

Actress; nearly 20 years
in theatre; last seven in
films; soon to be seen in
Gentleman's Agreement

THE ACTOR'S SEARCH
FOR A STAGE

There is a tide in the affairs of men . . .

*150 years ago, William Dunlap, American painter, playwright, producer
and historian, in the dawn of the American theatre, wrote:*

*"If, as we believe, the world is to be in the future a democratic world,
it is expedient that every source of knowledge be open to the governors,
the people. One great theatre in every city in the Union, supported and
guided by the state, would remedy every evil of our present playhouse
system."*

IT is very unfortunate that a depression was required to force
Congress into some recognition of the actor's plight in America. It
was the economic crisis of the 1930s that ushered in the most vital
and significant national cultural experiment in our history—the Federal Theatre. Here was a bold enterprise, which pushed outward the
boundaries of art and left behind an unprecedented spectacle: 12,000
theatre-workers in 31 states of our union; 63,000 performances, before
some 30,000,000 people at a 55-cent top. Here was the beginning
of an answer to our cultural heritage . . . and yet, this innovation of
amazing creativity that swept across our nation, the Federal Theatre,
was voted out of existence by the Congress of the United States of
America.

The story of the first subsidized theatre in America bears telling.
firstly, because it demonstrates that such a project can work; and,
secondly, because the connotations of its defeat in 1939 teach a
lesson we can well apply today. The mouthings of the present Un-
American Committee are reminiscent of the loud guffaws that filled
our halls of Congress not so many years ago.

Hallie Flanagan, Professor of Drama at Vassar College, who headed the Federal Theatre Project, gives a fascinating account of the
rise and fall of Federal Theatre in her book, *Arena*. It tells a tale of

the roles played by the Dies and Woodrum Committees, by members of these Committees and other legislators. It is the story of powerful anti-democratic forces at work within the law-making bodies of our country—that emulate the pattern employed so skillfully by Fascism in its bid for power,—and it is the story of forces which, without compunction, conspired to deny the people of America a cultural outlet. This is primarily the story of Federal Theatre.

Let's go back some years. How was the actor faring in the early Thirties? Miss Flanagan writes:

"The country was in the throes of depression, and Art in America being a luxury, the actors with other artists were the first to experience the effects of the crisis. In 1932-3 and -4, the people of the theatre—directors, actors, designers, costumers, stagehands—turned to any sort of job that could be found, however temporary, however poorly paid. They were willing to dig ditches and they did dig ditches, but unskilled labor was also unemployed and could dig better ditches. Try as they could, they could find no recourse except charity.

"The Works Progress Administration was set up by Congress in 1935 and the questions arose: 'Could a theatre have a place in this new conception of work for the unemployed? Could a nation-wide plan be devised for theatre activities?'

"Proposals poured in from all over the country when it was announced that the government was going into show business. Some were less dull than others. Here was a 'cosmic ray' drama which the author insisted if shown all over the country would end theatrical unemployment by a series of electrical discharges. Then there was the man who had written 48 songs about Franklin Roosevelt (whether pro or con was not disclosed) which, he said, if sung nightly from every stage in the land, with appropriately lavish royalties paid to the composer, would, and this is in his own lyric phrase, 'wipe out unemployment and set the whole world singing one Grand Sweet Song.'

"A broad plan had to be evolved encompassing the whole country. Because of the size of our country and because of the origins and aims of the project, the type of theatre needed could not be modeled on a government-operated enterprise of any other country. Government subsidy of the theatre brought the U. S. into the best historic theatre tradition and into the best contemporary theatre practice, but there the similarity ended. This was a distinctly American enterprise growing out of a people's economic need over a vast geographic area.

"The plan was finally laid out and the aims stated:

"To set up theatres which have possibilities of growing into social institutions in the communities in which they are located . . . and to lay the foundation for the development of a truly creative theatre in the U. S. with outstanding producing centres in each of those regions which have common interests as a result of geography, language origins, history, tradition, custom and occupations of the people."

And Harry Hopkins spoke of this new kind of theatre:

"I am asked whether a theatre subsidized by the government can be kept free from censorship. What we want is a free, adult, uncensored theatre."

And so the mammoth undertaking began. It set in motion powerful impulses . . . It created an audience of millions . . . It nurtured thousands of young artists, many of whom are in the forefront of cultural leadership today. It unleashed new forms of theatre—like the *Living Newspaper* with its presentation of *One-Third of A Nation* and *Power*. It gave us plays like *It Can't Happen Here,* which opened simultaneously in 21 theatres in 17 states in an amazing variety of methods,—English, Yiddish and Spanish,—in cities, towns and villages,—before audiences of every conceivable type. *It Can't Happen Here* played under Federal Theatre 260 weeks, or the equivalent of five years. Hundreds of thousands of people all over America crowded in to see a play which said that when dictatorship threatens a country it does not necessarily come by way of military invasion, that it may arrive in the form of a sudden silencing of free voices.

The *Hollywood Citizen-News* at the time reported:

"The Federal Theatre is stepping boldly into the limelight of a controversial issue . . . the project has been the target of criticism from sources holding that the play *It Can't Happen Here* will (*and get this—A.R.*) antagonize sympathizers of the Hitler and Mussolini regimes . . ."

The *Examiner* used epithets like "scabrous bad taste" and "propaganda, naked and unconcealed."

Similar criticism of plays such as *Prologue to Glory,* the story that dealt with Lincoln in his youth, were voiced. Mr. J. Parnell Thomas, a name familiar in our papers today, in a syndicated article appearing among other places in the *San Francisco Examiner,* September 4, 1938, under the headline, *REP. THOMAS BARES RED GRIP ON WPA THEATRE PROJECT,* said:

"The play *Prologue to Glory* portrays Lincoln battling with politicians. This is simply a propaganda play to prove that all politicians are crooked."

So amazing did this assertion seem to Miss Flanagan, that she mentioned it to Mr. Thomas one day when they happened to be on the same train coming from Washington to New York.

Mr. Thomas said:

"Do you remember the debate scene? It showed Lincoln criticizing the local assembly for debating the subject: Resolved, that bees are more valuable than ants. He urged them to discuss, instead, the need for damming the Sangamon River, and said, 'It seems to me that the subjects for debate before this forum ought to be alive—subjects for action, useful for living.' That is Communist talk."

Called to testify before the Un-American Committee, Miss Flanagan was asked an amazing variety of questions, amongst which was one (by now a classic) by Congressman Starnes. He referred to an article she had written for *Theatre Arts*, in which she had described some of the new theatres springing up as having "a certain Marlowesque madness."

"You are quoting from this Marlowe," observed Mr. Starnes. "Is he a Communist?"

The room rocked with laughter, but Hallie Flanagan tells us, she didn't laugh. 8,000 people might lose their jobs because a Congressional Committee had so prejudged them that even the classics were "Communistic." Miss Flanagan said, "I was quoting from Christopher Marlowe."

Mr. Starnes, a little ruffled, muttered, "Tell us who Marlowe is, so we can get the proper references, because that is all we want to do."

Hallie Flanagan replied very quietly, "Put in the record that he was the greatest dramatist in the period of Shakespeare, immediately preceding Shakespeare."

Mr. Starnes subsided.

Congressman J. Parnell Thomas then took over and attacked a Federal Theatre children's play called *The Revolt of the Beavers*. This play, after an audience-survey conducted by trained psychologists, brought only favorable reactions from children, such as "teaches us never to be selfish," "it is better to be good than bad"—how the children would want the whole world to be: nine years old and happy . . . This was labeled "Communistic."

Chairman Martin Dies, the great Democrat, elected by eight percent of his constituents, cried out, "Are you out to entertain your audiences or to instruct them?"

The *Congressional Record* quotes Miss Flanagan as saying, "The primary purpose of a play is to entertain, but it can also teach."

"Do you think," Dies asked, "the theatre should be used for the purpose of conveying ideas along social, economic or political lines?"

Miss Flanagan replied: "I would hesitate on the political."

Then, soothed Mr. Dies, "eliminate political; upon social and economic lines?"

"I think," replied Hallie Flanagan, "it is one logical, reasonable and I might say imperative thing for our theatre to do."

And so, with this kind of ignorance, prejudice and hatred, these Committee inquisitions were held. Reason, justifiable evidence, was either ignored or dismissed. The Committee, however, proceeded to its final deliberations—its theatre-going record still intact: officially, it never saw a production of the project under examination.

The Dies Committee Report, filed with the House of Representatives January 3, 1939, may in the future, says Miss Flanagan, be of as much interest to students of jurisprudence and government as of theatre. Six months of sensational charges tapered down to one short paragraph:

> "We are convinced that a rather large number of the employees on the Federal Theatre project are either members of the Communist Party or are sympathetic with the Communist Party . . ."

As the day for Congressional vote arrived, the Federal Theatre staff sat in the gallery of the House of Representatives and watched a scene, "which if dramatized on one of our stages, would have resulted in a charge that the Federal Theatre was libeling the legislative branch of the government of the U. S." Every mention of a so-called salacious title—and apparently every title that had the word love in it impressed them as salacious—was greeted with howls and catcalls. Some restraining voices were raised, but they were shouted down. The House in '39, like the House in '47, was in no mood to debate the issue. The speaker pounded his gavel, and a vote was called—192 to 56. Federal Theatre had lost its case in the House.

A tremendous tide of opinion arose to save the theatre and all the other arts. The commercial theatre itself continued to fight with and for Federal Theatre. Actors' Equity, the Four A's, Theatre Arts Committee, the League of New York Theatres, the Tri-Guilds in Hollywood, the Federation of Art Unions—all these organizations held mass meetings, thousands of telegrams poured into the Senate.

Tallulah Bankhead, sitting on a table in a manner probably rare in Senatorial offices, cried dramatically before her father, "But actors are people, aren't they? They're people!" Her voice broke and Senatorial handkerchiefs were out.

Orson Welles, who had escaped the censorship imposed on the Federal Theatre production of Blitzstein's *The Cradle Will Rock* by forming the Mercury Theatre and presenting the show under private auspices, lent his voice to the growing cry to save Federal Theatre. A broadcast over a national hookup from Hollywood, by the three guilds of the motion picture industry, was presented. Many actors participated, including Lionel Barrymore who said (characterizing himself not only as an old actor but an old citizen):

> "I think it is dangerous for a nation to start proving what a fine country it can be and then, right in the middle of doing it, let it slide back to the dark days of depression." He urged Congressmen to remember that "the American people have never let anything be taken away from them—permanently."

Writers filled columns for Federal Theatre—Heywood Broun, Olin Downes, Leonard Lyons, Eleanor Roosevelt, Walter Winchell, Johannes Steel. All of them and others protested the destruction of the Arts Project. But, despite all of this, the Federal Theatre was killed by an Act of Congress, June 30, 1939.

How was it possible, with such an overwhelming support and with a record of accomplishment so substantial, that Federal Theatre was nevertheless ended? No movement sponsored by the art-world ever received wider and more varied backing.

Hallie Flanagan said:

> "It was not ended as an economy move, though this was the ostensible reason given: the entire arts program, of which Federal Theatre was one of five projects, used less than three-fourths of one percent of the total W.P.A. appropriations; and that appropriation was not cut one cent by the ending of Federal Theatre.
>
> "It was ended because Congress, in spite of protests from many of its own members, treated the Federal Theatre, not as a human issue or a cultural issue, but as a political issue. It was ended because the powerful forces marshalled in its behalf came too late to combat other forces which apparently had been at work against the Federal Theatre for a long time. Through two Congressional Committees, these forces found a habitation and a name.
>
> "Were these forces afraid? Were they afraid of the Federal Theatre because it was educating people, the people of its vast new audiences to know more about government, and politics, and such vital issues as housing, power, agriculture and labor? True, these issues were dealt with only in a small fraction, less than ten percent, of Federal Theatre plays. Still I can see why certain powers would not want even 10 percent of the Federal Theatre plays to be the sort to make people in our democracy think. Such forces might well be afraid of thinking people."

Thus Federal Theatre ended as it had begun, with fearless presentation of problems touching American life.

> "If this first government theatre in our country had been less alive," says Hallie Flanagan, "it might have lived longer. But I do not believe anyone who worked on it regrets that it stood, from first to last, against reaction, against prejudice, against racial, religious and political intolerance. It strove for a more dramatic statement and a better understanding of the great forces of our life today. Creating for our citizens a medium

of free expression . . . and offering people access to the arts and tools of a civilization which they themselves are helping to make, such a theatre is at once an illustration and a bulwark of the democratic form of government."

"The greatest significance of Federal Theatre lies in its pointing to the future," says Miss Flanagan. "The ten thousand anonymous men and women, the et-ceteras and the and-so-forths who did the work, the nobodies who were everybody, the somebodies who believed it—their dreams and deeds were not the end. They were the beginnings of a people's theatre in a country whose greatest plays are yet to come."

But these plays will not come if the Un-American Committee is permitted to continue the task it has begun. The voice of Congressman J. Parnell Thomas, working for the Dies Committee in 1939, screamed "every play done by Federal Theatre is clear unadulterated propaganda" (and these plays included those of William Shakespeare, Moliere, Christopher Marlowe, Sinclair Lewis, George Bernard Shaw, Eugene O'Neill, Tolstoy, Charles Dickens, etc.). He is still on the rampage today, promoted for his good work to majordomo of the Un-American Committee—and charging that the films *Margie, Best Years, Pride of the Marines,* etc., were subversive and Communist-inspired. This vindictive hate for culture has merged today with Fascist intolerance and reaction, menacing all human freedom. The Thomas-Rankin Committee spearheads this drive.

This Committee and its predecessors were accused of lying, by Franklin Delano Roosevelt; of damaging U. S. morale as if "Mr. Dies were on the Hitler payroll", by Vice-President Wallace; of "undermining the democratic process", by Wendell Willkie.

We cannot tolerate Congressional Committees of this ilk in a democracy—Committees which may hold their hearings in public or private, as they see fit; may or may not hear witnesses, as they please; may cite for contempt witnesses who do not respond to their subpoena, but on the other hand may not be compelled to hear people who demand to testify. Operating as quasi-judicial bodies which are a law unto themselves, these Committees become dangerous—and the lesson of Federal Theatre has exposed their purposes and their methods. As actors and citizens, we must render impotent those who would control thought—so that the dreams and deeds of Federal Theatre did not end, but, as Hallie Flanagan says, "they were the beginnings of a people's theatre in a country whose greatest plays are yet to come."

This was followed by a sketch entitled It's a Picture!, *written by Ben Barzman and Stanley Prager and enacted by Mr. Prager*

353

and George Tyne. The skit lampoons Hollywood's alleged search for something new, always to end up with the same old formulae, within the framework of the intimidation of producers by the recent and current House Un-American Activities Committee investigations of the films. (This playlet is available in mimeographed form for organizations interested in presenting it in their struggle to defend freedom of thought. Address requests to Hollywood Arts, Sciences & Professions Council, PCA, 1515 Crossroads of the World, Hollywood 28, California.)

At this point, Mr. Howard Da Silva again delivered his paper entitled The Actor's Relation to Content in Motion Pictures, *text of which will be found beginning on P. 319, in the Film Panel of this volume.*

354

Ludwig Donath

State-Theatre, Berlin, to
1933; Zurich anti-Fascist cabaret *Le cornichon*, 1934; U.
S. films since 1941, *Counter-
attack*, *The Jolson Story*, etc.

THE ACTOR
UNDER FASCISM

The seeming truth which cunning time puts on . . .

I N the presence of writers, directors, producers—and even the public,—
it may seem a little presumptuous for an actor to speak about thought
control. The phrase itself presupposes that actors think. This proposi-
tion has yet to be generally accepted. I do not intend to defend my
profession; it needs no defense. We have been the step-children of
democratic institutions with respect to the favors of democracy, but we
have, nevertheless, not been favored with exception in the reign of
terror.

The members of my profession were killed, tortured, along with
the workers, the scientists, the hundreds of thousands of brave German
and Austrian people who resisted Hitler before 1939. And it is about
the resistance before the war and the fight against Hitler during the
war that I wish to speak. For we, along with the millions, were the
victims of thought control. For us, thought control is no metaphysical
expression. It is a weapon—a deadly weapon!

The theatre in Germany before Hitler was a flourishing institution.
It has, as most of you know, a long and honored tradition. Historically,
it occupied a very important position in the cultural life of the people.
The American theatre is principally concentrated along a few blocks
that run off Broadway. In Germany, there was hardly a town that
didn't have its own theatre, its own acting company, its own directors,
its own authors in some cases. For hundreds of years, theatre in Germany as in other countries had been subsidized by royalty of one kind
or another. Before the war there were no less than 300 theatres in
Germany alone, exclusive of German-speaking theatres in Switzerland, Austria, Czechoslovakia. When Hitler came to power, he immediately eliminated all liberal elements from the theatre. But Hitler,
always alert to propaganda advantage, arranged matters so that the

355

actors became a fixture of the Nazi court. That is, Aryan actors—for the actors of Germany were subjected to a pedigree test and, if you couldn't prove correct Aryan ancestry dating back to 1799, you were summarily kicked out of your job.

Actors found favor as never before in history; so did actresses. For a while, Leni Riefenstahl was quite a figure in Nazi film circles. Hitler and Goebbels went out of their way to woo, flatter, bribe and blackmail the 6,000 German actors, because they realized that these 6,000 could be used as personal ambassadors, as mouthpieces for Nazi propaganda. Goering went even further—he married an actress. Knowing the inherent German love for titles, Hitler created two categories for favored actors: *Staatsrat,* or Counsellor of the State, and *Staatsschauspieler,* or Actors of the State. These were awarded not on a basis of merit, but on a basis of usefulness. The first title was granted to a select few, the second was more general and also brought with it a yearly salary of 6,000 marks. The theatre was no longer a place of cultural education and entertainment, but a platform for Nazi ideology. And with the Stalingrad debacle, the theatre lost all its utility. Hitler just ordered all theatres closed, and actors, stage hands, treasurers—and even producers—became slave-laborers in Nazi armament-factories, or were sent to the front, to die in the name of the Hitler propaganda which they had been declaiming.

But, for the people of Germany, even during the darkest days of Nazi terror, the theatre, not unlike the church (with which it had once been so closely related), was a meeting-place, and there were incidents of protest. In Schiller's classical play, *Don Carlos,* one of the characters, Marquis Posa, demands of Philip of Spain, *"Geben Sie Gedankenfreiheit"* (Give us freedom of thought). This is a famous and popular quotation, dear to every German, to which Philip replies, by calling the Marquis "strange dreamer." But at one opening under the Nazis, Philip's answer was lost . . . Afer the line, "Give us freedom of thought," the entire audience at the *Deutsche Theatre* in Berlin rose in applause. For twenty almost unending minutes—with the actors standing petrified on the open stage,—the shouting and trampling could not be stopped. Goebbels at once, of course, ordered these lines deleted. But the demonstrations were repeated at subsequent performances with the result that the play was completely withdrawn.

One of the best-known and best-loved of German comedians, Karl Valentin, spent half of his time in prisons and the other half in theatres and cabarets. He had a series of gags that irritated the Nazis a lot. But his popularity was so tremendous and his personality so disarming, that each time he had to be released again. For example, you all know that the Hitler oak was a symbol of Nazi strength. All good Germans were supposed to plant oak-trees. Valentin did, too. One day he said, "A year ago I got myself a Hitler oak. A nice little strong tree. It grows like the devil. Do you know where it is now?" (With a gesture as of one slitting his throat.) "Up to here!" Another time, he came out on the stage with a salute, "Heil ... Heil ... God damn it, now I've forgotten the name!" The same night, he was arrested.

Wherever refugee actors meet, you will hear the name of Hans Otto. He was a leading-man, but first of all the most popular and beloved chairman of the local of the Actors' Union in Berlin. Hans Otto was an Aryan, though I don't think he would like to have been called that. When Hitler seized power, Otto was warned to leave Germany. He stayed. He was denounced, tortured and, when he persistently refused to reveal to the interrogating Gestapo officer any information, the inquisitor grew impatient and simply tossed him out of the fourth-floor window. On the anniversary of his death, the underground movement mailed thousands of Otto's photographs, bordered in black, to the actors of Germany who still stayed in the Nazi theatres. The effect was tremendous. Actors receiving this photograph nearly fainted.

I knew this man, and I know that if Hans Otto were alive and in this country he would be here today, to speak to his fellow-actors and tell them that they must take part in this struggle for intellectual and artistic freedom. I am shocked when I pick up the papers and find that the Nazi stoolpigeons and informers, the fingermen who were responsible for the death of Hans Otto and a hundred other actors, Jews or non-Jews, are now reinstated by the British and American authorities in the course of the so-called de-Nazification.

The bloody pattern of Fascist suppression, introduced in Italy and perfected in Nazi Germany, was either imposed by the Nazis on its conquered countries, as in Poland, or accepted by the Fascist satellites, as in Spain, Greece, etc. In Poland, before the war, there was hardly a town that didn't boast of some kind of theatre but, when the Nazis raced through Poland, the first edicts abolished the cultural and educational mediums—the press, the radio, the theatre, the schools. The Polish resistance carried on through the underground. The only public performances permitted by the Nazis were cabarets. The plays of

Shakespeare were banned. Most of the actors refused to appear in the cabarets; they took their place alongside the underground fighters. The few who did appear publicly did so only to be saved from death through starvation.

With the liberation of Poland, came the reopening of the theatres, despite the poverty of the country and the dearth of male actors on account of the high death-rate. Today in Poland, there are 62 theatres and 14 opera-houses, 3 large vanguard-theatres traveling throughout the country, and 40 schools for actors. Considering that the whole of Poland is smaller than California, this is quite a remarkable achievement.

As a cultural representative of Poland said, "He who works for the culture of his country, works for the culture of the world, and hence for the freedom of the world."

In Greece, the story was the same. The Metaxas dictatorship, collaborating with Hitler politically, also collaborated culturally with the Reich. Metaxas was educated in Potsdam. In 1936, the democratic theatre council, which had governed Greek theatre, was summarily abolished by Metaxas and a Thought Controller installed. He had his office in the theatre. His first act was to ban the performances of *Julius Caesar* because the speeches of Brutus and Casius were too inflammatory. *Antigone,* which had been performed regularly, was now cut so that it no longer made sense either to the actors or to the audience. When, in 1941, the Nazi Gauleiter Altenburg took over the theatres, the little that was left of Greek theatre in terms of Greek culture was immediately liquidated, and along with this many Greek actors who refused to conform were thrown into concentration-camps and killed. The popular comedian Iatrides was shot on the stage. A few escaped. A few stayed on and tried from time to time to continue the tradition of their country.

It is the same in Spain, too. There was no real theatre in Spain during the Monarchy, in the years before 1930, but shortly after the establishment of the Republic in 1931 certain figures began to work for the creation of a modern Spanish theatre. Garcia Lorca wrote at least five plays of his own. Together with his friend the composer DeFalla, well-known over the world, Lorca produced modern versions of many of Spain's traditional *Zarzuelas* (light operas), he founded the theatre which he called *La Baraca,* and he enlisted the enthusiasm and support of the Spanish students, the members of the *Federacion Universitaria Escolar* (FUE), to help write, act, direct and present plays throughout Spain.

The students carried on all during the war-years, 1936 to 1939, bringing their plays to the soldiers at the front, in the hospitals. Printing-presses blossomed throughout the Republic during those war-years, when the Loyalists fought their great tragic battle for survival against Fascism. Military units published books of poems, stories, first-person accounts by the soldiers. The Spanish war posters at times achieved the quality of great art, and are treasured as such today. The poets and playwrights and musicians had a new burst of creative energy—and the whole democratic world looked with wonder upon this miracle of a great national cultural renaissance in the midst of war and hunger.

But Franco put an end to that era, as ruthlessly as he put an end to the liberty of the people. Antonio Machado died fleeing across the Pyrenees in mid-winter from the advancing Fascist hordes. Garcia Lorca was assassinated in Granada in 1936, when he was 37 years old. Miguel De Unamuno, the philosopher, died a broken man, a virtual prisoner in Fascist-controlled Salamanca. Raphael Alberti is in exile in South America, Manuel DeFalla died in exile a year ago, and Pablo Casals, the world's greatest violoncellist, lives in France, refusing to return to Spain, refusing even to perform in the United States or in England, because he feels these two countries tacitly helped dig the grave of his beloved Spanish Republic.

J. B. Trend, the English historian, puts it this way in his book, *The Civilization of Spain*:

"This was the modern Spain that was dispersed in 1939. Very few of its distinguished men remain in their country . . . Spain had more to lose than a government."

It is true, Spain lost its cultural heart.

And today? Under Franco? A recent report in the *New York Times Book Review* says the Spaniards read "light escapist fiction, imitations of American westerns, translations of American and British mysteries—and the comics." And, the reporter adds, one of the best-selling novels in Spain today is a book called *Nada*. "Nada", in case you don't know, means "nothing."

The French actors took their place alongside the people in 1935 and 1936 during the initial stages of the Popular Front. The actors of the Opera-comique entertained from the balcony of the theatre during their own sitdown strike; Maurice Chevalier sang in the streets, and Jean Renoir produced and directed a picture, *La Marseillaise,* the money for which was subscribed by the people themselves, each one contributing one franc.

Between Munich and Vichy, France, like other countries, was in a state of reaction and inaction but, with the emergence of Petain and the Vichy collaborationists, the actors and artists took their place in the underground opposition. Others operated successfully, even under the Vichy censors and the Gestapo. Many paid with their lives. Harry-Baur, Robert Lynen, Sylvain Itkine were a few of the victims of Nazism. The heroism of the people of the arts in France has already been told in Hollywood by Pierre Blanchar, the leading French actor, on his trip here a short time ago.

Today, the actors in France are 100% unionized and are part of the C.G.T. (French Federation of Labor). And a great many of them are active in the political life of France. Jean-Louis Barrault, Madeleine Renaud, and the same Pierre Blanchar, took an active part in the campaign for the Constitution of France which, as you know, was adopted despite the opposition of the De Gaullist and Vichy elements in France.

I have cited briefly some of the story of the theatre during the past tragic period. The full story remains to be told. I have cited it not alone as a tribute to the brave and the dead, but, in the hope that from these experiences and this short history, we of the theatre may gather the strength to carry on the democratic traditions of this and other countries.

For myself, I must draw these conclusions, which I submit:

1. It is clear that under Fascism neither theatre nor actors can survive. Fascism and reaction must inevitably and ruthlessly suppress all forms of honest expression. Therefore, the actor in his own selfish interest must take his stand with the people. In a sense, this is the only means available to the actor to repay his audiences for their support, by using his talents in the best interests of his audience.

2. For all theatre people, actors, directors, producers and technicians, it is essential that a greater concentration be directed towards the establishment of audience contacts. The creation of audiences, it seems to me, is something that is entirely overlooked in the current theatrical situation in America. We had such an opportunity in Europe, and we never took full advantage of these possibilities. In other words, our contact with our audiences must extend long after the last fadeout in a picture, or the final curtain in a play. Actors have a tendency to huddle together, to live and breathe theatre and films twenty-four hours a day. I think that we must as individuals take time off and find out how people generally live.

It is demanded of us, when we appear on the stage or on the screen, to act realistically, to relate ourselves to other characters. That, as I see it, is also our job off-stage: to act realistically as citizens of this great country, and to relate ourselves to the people of this country. To help them and help ourselves in creating the one world of peace and security. For this ideal, many people of our profession have died. In their honor and in their memory, we can do no less.

Selena Royle

Actress, most recently in
Romance of Rosy Ridge,
Summer Holiday; first presi-
dent, Actors' Dinner Club,
N. Y.

THE ACTOR IS A CITIZEN

This above all, to thine own self be true . . .

ACTORS are people—some reports to the contrary notwithstanding,—
and as such they possess an inherent privilege: that of choice. They
can choose between being good citizens or bad citizens. It's quite
simple to be a bad citizen. All you have to do is to close your ears
and eyes. Refuse to listen or to talk. Overlook racial intolerance, forgive lynchings in the South, witch-hunting in the North. Remain untouched by anti-labor legislation, ignore starving nations abroad, and
hungry families at home. That's all. It's quite simple. It's harder to be
a good citizen. To look squarely at the injustices and inequalities of
our post-war world and know them for what they are.

Because actors are vocal, they are being told that to be good
citizens they should stick to their knitting, and keep their noses out
of politics. They don't tell that to the grocer or the butcher or the
haberdasher. But the very people who now tell us to stick to our
knitting are the ones who have made it impossible for us to accept
this decree. They have been the first to call loudly and long upon
the actor for every and all causes. From the day billboards were
changed from "Benefit Performance for Edwin Booth or McCready"
to read "Benefit Performance Tonight for Day Nursery, United
Jewish Appeal, Texas City Disaster Victims or The Crippled Children's
Home" or "Bond Drives and War Rallies, at which will appear Edward
G. Robinson, Katharine Hepburn, Gene Kelly," etc., etc., etc., the
actor climbed out of the category of "second-rate citizen," and became
a Number One, all-wool-and-a-yard-wide first-class citizen.

With the inauguration of President Roosevelt, the country got a
new deal and the actor his certificate of citizenship. For the first time
in our history we had a man in the White House who not only loved
actors as fellow human beings, but knew their worth.

362

The struggle seemed to be over, for the actors were not only invited but cordially urged to participate in the affairs of their country. And with enthusiasm they responded. They campaigned across the continent for the man who understood their problems as they felt he understood the problems of other diverse groups which make up this country.

At rallies, over the air, on caravans, they spoke, persuaded and inspired . . . Bette Davis, Orson Welles, Joan Bennett, Humphrey Bogart, Olivia de Havilland. Names too numerous to list in their entirety here. There were also those far-seeing ones who spoke for the Loyalists in Spain: Helen Gahagan, Melvyn Douglas, Gale Sondergaard. Understanding, as few did in that time, that there in Spain was the curtain-raiser for the Big Show that was to come.

When the Big Show did come, and the United States went to war, from the West Coast alone, 1,934 actors joined the armed forces. The following figures paint a true picture without benefit of flowery phrases: from October 22, 1941, through 1946, the U.S.O.-Camp Shows, Inc., gave over 400,000 performances here and abroad to an estimated audience of over 200,000,000. The Victory Committee of Hollywood arranged over 56,000 free appearances of 4,147 stars and feature players, traveling an aggregate of 5,000,000 miles. They sent 176 personalities on 122 tours; arranged 406 hospital and camp shows; over 2,000 one-night stands by variety troupes in Western military installations. 214 actors spoke at War Bond rallies. 264 broadcasts and transcriptions were made for the Treasury Department's War Bond Drives. 8,428 overseas broadcasts and transcriptions through the Armed Forces Radio Service. And top stars made 38 film shorts, while 390 broadcasts were made for war relief and war charities. The Hollywood Guild Canteen had 4,000 volunteers, all of the profession, and served 5,000,000 men. The Entertainment Committee of the American Red Cross Camp and Hospital Service sent out over 100 shows a month to the various hospitals in this area. We have no way of knowing how many actors gave their services through other organizations, such as the American Legion, the Navy Mothers, the Vacs, etc. As I say, these are figures for the West Coast alone.

I am not saying that we did more than any other profession or group. But we did do as much, and we'll do it longer. Because it has been discovered that what actors have to give is more than entertainment and a few moments of relaxation and fun. It's therapeutic. It helps to heal wounded minds and bodies.

The actor is still out at the hospitals and without reimbursement, because he takes his job in a democracy seriously. Therefore, the actor resents the assumption that what those men and women in Veteran or Navy hospitals fought for doesn't concern him. That the part America plays in reconstruction of war-torn countries doesn't concern him. That America's foreign policy doesn't concern him! We have as big a stake in the future of our country as the next man, and we have earned the right to be part and parcel of the America of the Future.

Realizing that they have this right and this duty, actors have responded in many ways and against many injustices. They rose strongly and eagerly against that prime example of unjust legislation, the Taft-Hartley Bill. They gave of their time and their talents, they broadcast from New York as well as from the West Coast. They spoke at meetings and signed petitions. And now, since this infamous bill was passed, they will find ways of rallying around, and saving, their own unions.

Sometimes, in their fight against injustice, they get hurt— they are threatened and called names. For instance, there is the Frank Fay Case.

It began one night in 1945. A group of actors working on Broadway went over to Madison Square Garden to speak on behalf of the Spanish Refugee Appeal. This group included Jeanne Darling, David Brooks, Luba Malina, Margo and Sono Osato. I can't quote from the speeches they made that night, but I remember the sense. They told the audience about the pitiful conditions in which the Spanish refugees were living. About starvation. About babies wrapped in newspapers to keep them warm. About veterans—men who fought Franco—who needed artificial limbs and medical attention. They urged the audience to contribute to the relief fund. They all made the same humanitarian appeal.

The following day, in the name of his God and his religion, Mr. Fay launched his attack. Shouting through the Hearst press, he claimed that the meeting at which these actors had spoken had been staged for the purpose of attacking the Catholic Church, attacking religion, and attacking God. He informed the papers that he was going to the Council of Equity to prefer charges against them.

Mr. Fay's hysterical accusations, plus vindictive and unfair editorials in Hearst's *Journal-American,* brought the bigots out in force. One evening, when Margo was going into the stage entrance of her show, she was stopped by a maniac who called her "Anti-Christ" and spat in her face.

For two days, Jeanne Darling received calls every half-hour from a man who threatened to kill her and her mother. In Sono Osato's case, people coming to see *On the Town* were approached in the lobby by hecklers who shouted that she was a "Jap-Communist." "No decent citizen," they screamed, "would enter a theatre in which a disgraceful, yellow Un-American was performing."

At the subsequent Equity Council hearing, Mr. Fay bleated that he was the victim of a "Bolshevik trial", and demanded that his case be taken to the membership. It was. The vote was roughly 460 to 50 against Mr. Fay. That ended the incident, but not the attack on the actors.

The minute an actor steps out of line, bop! he gets hit over the head with a column—like this one by Westbrook Pegler, for example:

"Canada Lee," says Mr. Pegler in a column about anti-Negro prejudice, "is said to be a rather good actor, which is little enough to say about anyone, for it is unimportant work, followed in the main, by vain, frivolous, self-important people who have got out of hand since our politicians discovered that they could draw crowds and adorn bad causes by presenting actors at their rallies."

Then there's a sports writer named Vincent X. Flaherty. He throws a curve at Paul Robeson, declaring that the treatment Robeson received in Peoria and Albany—when he was refused the right to appear—was well-deserved, that Robeson earned $5,000 a week and that he was a plutocrat. In Flaherty's words, "Robeson is a menace."

In both cases, while Negroes are singled out for attack and ridicule, the real target, obviously, is any and all actors who dare to step out and say something about political and economic conditions. Attacks have been leveled at Edward G. Robinson, Katharine Hepburn, John Garfield, Gene Kelly, Charles Chaplin. Fredric March and his wife Florence Eldridge—two of our finest actor-citizens—showed their contempt for these attacks by appearing recently as character-witnesses for Herman Shumlin, who was, with sixteen other members of the Joint Fascist Refugee Committee, on trial for courageously refusing to turn over the membership records of the organization to the Un-American Investigating Committee—for smearing purposes!

Last year, the *Joan of Lorraine* company made history by its appearance in Washington, D. C. Maxwell Anderson, Ingrid Bergman and Sam Wanamaker arrived in Washington prior to their opening, to learn that the Lisner Auditorium, in which they were to play, had just been refused to the American Veterans' Committee because, believe it or not, there were Negroes in this organization! (And this, in spite of the fact that the Auditorium is partially supported by government funds.)

The contract for the appearance of the *Joan of Lorraine* company was already signed, but they decided that some action was necessary. They contacted Bob Sherwood, who wrote a denunciation of discrimination which was published in the *Washington Post* and the *New York Times*. Miss Bergman issued a strong statement denouncing the management's stand. Maxwell Anderson stated that he would never have signed with the theatre-manager if he had known that such a policy existed, and would not do so again until the policy was reversed. Through The Playwrights' Company, he organized 33 important playwrights—now grown to 60—to support this position. At a company-meeting of *Lorraine* actors, they unanimously opposed discrimination and sent a wire to the Actors' Equity Council asking that action be taken so that an actor could refuse to play in a theatre where any minority group was denied admittance. They also sent a wire to the Washington management to reverse its position. The arguments used by the theatre management were: (1) that changing of the discriminatory policy would be against the tradition of the community; (2) it would cut down attendance if whites had to sit next to Negroes; (3) there would be riots.

The Washington Committee for Racial Democracy and the University Chapter of A.V.C. mimeographed hundreds of copies of the Bergman, Anderson and Sherwood statements and distributed them on the picketlines in front of the theatre. For participating in this just protest, four A.V.C. members from Washington University, who helped organize the picketlines at the theatre, were expelled—on the grounds that they were Communists.

The stand taken by the *Lorraine* company, the A.V.C., the Playwrights and Actors' Equity is a splendid testimonial of democracy, and one that should make every actor, every member of a union, proud.

In the *Equity Magazine* of June there appears the following:

"The joint report of those committees was read to the Council on April 22nd. It recommended that if discrimination against Negro patrons at the National Theatre, in Washington, or in any other legitimate theatre in that city, had not been ended by June 1st, 1948, Equity would withdraw the services of its members as of that date. The Council endorsed that recommendation.

"Some time this summer we shall sit down with the League to negotiate a new Basic Agreement and Contract to replace the current one which expires on September 1 of this year. Equity's first demand will be for a formal acknowledgment of its right to enforce this policy in Washington. If that is conceded the negotiations will proceed. If the League is not prepared to negotiate on that basis there will be no Basic Agreement. Equity's stand on this matter has been received with very general approval."

Not very many weeks ago, a slender figure stood up before 27,000 people and stated clearly and with conviction where she stood. It's no longer possible to be neutral. The history of what happened to neutrality is written in the history books for all to read. Some people may disagree with Miss Hepburn and the stand she took at that historic meeting for Henry Wallace in Gilmore Stadium, but no one can fail to admire her courage and the clean statement of her convictions. She received an ovation the following day in the commissary of her home-studio. And Dr. Lechner, ex-secretary of the Motion Picture Alliance, whom she castigated in no uncertain terms, resigned shortly after her speech. I would like to give you a quotation from that brilliant speech.

"The artist," Katharine Hepburn said, "since the beginning of recorded time, has always expressed the aspirations and dreams of his people. Silence the artist and you silence the most articulate voice the people have. Destroy culture and you destroy one of the strongest sources of inspiration from which a people can draw strength to fight for a better life."

I recently played in a movie called *The Romance of Rosy Ridge*, laid in the post-Civil War period, times very like ours, when hate and injustice rode side by side with the night-raiders. Sairy McBean was a simple country woman. She couldn't read or write, but she thought very clearly, and said, "Talkin' never yet shucked an ear of corn. Trouble is nobody's doin' nothin' 'bout it."

Nothing excites an actor like full houses, Standing Room Only. If you look about you, if you search, you will find an audience you never dreamed of.

DISCUSSION

Chairman Price opened the discussion with a question as to what might be the future of a Federal Theatre, and what we might do about it. What, he asked, is going on in America in the independent theatre movement today?

He called upon *Morris Carnovsky, celebrated actor of stage and screen,* to answer this. Mr. Carnovsky said in part:

"When I first arrived in Hollywood, I recall that the agent I had then brought me up with a start by remarking once, 'Oh, well—what do you care what you play or what you play in—after all, it's the money, etc., etc.' Instinctively, my unspoken comment was: Now, he's a member of a whole general conspiracy, a little here, a little there, to cut my talent and my individuality down to size—to undermine my integrity, to give me a new view of myself, with a proper respect for the overwhelming fact of The Industry in this town . . .

"Later, along with that, there were handed me certain cliches—attitudes of contempt, of denigration—all in effect a kind of subtle invitation to accept a philosophy of nihilism and philistinism. 'Well, you know, that's pictures—*they* have no comprehension of the true values—*they* don't give a damn about you as a human being . . . Forget about art, it's all business . . .' These and many more such attitudes were wafted toward me—intended, I believe, as a kind of inflation for my shrunken ego. And these are some of the things that tend to drive us inward on ourselves and away from our fellowmen, in this particular situation. Drawing away is one way of maintaining our so-called independence and, in spite of everything, no man relinquishes that without a struggle.

"The artist in his struggle to integrate what he believes and practices with society, comes into constant abrasive contact with attitudes similar to those I have indicated. Is this a species of thought control? I think so. Not so very subtle, but very powerful. In a million different ways, the artist is confronted with prohibitions and trammels, some of them even resembling rewards.

"I am thinking now not so much about the meaning of independent film as of independent theatre. Now, the theatre is an art-form, which is to say that it has a life and history and perpetuating body of its own. The print of its own time is indelibly upon it. It moves; it is sensitive to life; it changes. And the *unit* of the theatre is not the entrepreneur, not the money-changer—it is the worker in the theatre, the lover of the theatre, whether he be dramatist, scene-designer, actor. Of course, theatre is a collective affair, and I choose to believe that the actor is the most vibrant element in it; and as such it matters very much that the actor *thinks*. He thinks; *ergo, he is*. He is; therefore, he is alive! He is alive to the needs of his theatre—he sees that acting will be justified only so long as he provides it with the most progressive technique. He does his part. He works: he becomes a better actor. He is alive to his audience. He believes in them—they are sharers; he will not sell them short. He gives them spirit, courage; and they reward him with tears and laughter. Out of this experience arises more thought. So, he becomes alive to the world that he and his audience have in common. He regards it more profoundly; he perceives its tragedies, its iniquities; he appraises human decency, human obscenity, from a new point of view. He becomes a participant. His very actor's nature drives him to an understanding and abhorrence of poverty, of lynching, of racist dogmas, of all that would make man less than he should be. He may not know it, but he has become an independent actor, because he has become an independent man.

"For him, the theatre has become a continuation of life by artistic means. What more logical, then, than this desire—his need—for an independent theatre, a place where he may meet the audience in company with his creative partners? They are sensitive, gifted craftsmen, who have found their path just as he has, and who want to use themselves as conscious human beings, whose world is the theatre and whose theatre is the world.

"The artist is the enlightener of the human struggle, or he is nothing. There is the measure of the contribution of a Picasso or of a Charlie Chaplin. And that is the measure of any theatre worthy of the name. It is for us to be alive to the persisting influence of every independent theatre that ever existed in America—from the Province-town Players and Theatre Guild to the Federal Theatre, the Group Theatre, the Mercury, the Theatre Union, each in its own way a battle and a victory. Every time it happens, the old theatre breathes again—very much as our oppressive Hollywood breathed again at that wonderful moment in the theatre when Katharine Hepburn—an independent actress—got up, and thought, and spoke."

Sam Levene, actor, called upon all present to send wires of solidarity to the distinguished stage producer who was convicted of Contempt of Congress by the Thomas Committee, his crime being that he is an anti-Fascist.

The chairman then called upon *Shepperd Strudwick, actor,* who related some of the role of the American Veterans' Committee insofar as actors who are members of that organization are concerned. AVC, he said, had spearheaded the protest in Washington, D. C., against racial discrimination in the theatres of the capital, and it was the AVC Theatre Chapter which in New York staged the huge rally on the same subject.

Dorothy Tree, actress, read a passage from an interview by Earl Wilson, with Lena Horne, on this subject, from the daily press of Wednesday, July 2.

In answer to a question from the floor as to why there had been no discussion here of the locked-out studio workers of the Conference of Studio Unions, it was pointed out by *Selena Royle* that this Panel was concerned exclusively with the direct problems of actors, and that for that reason time limits had made it necessary to eliminate many questions originally scheduled for the agenda. Moreover, this Panel was not designed to discuss any other groups within the industry, but was restricted to the actors.

During the course of this discussion, and at its conclusion, a series of resolutions were moved, seconded and unanimously adopted by the Panel on the Actor. They are:

RESOLUTIONS

1. *Resolved,* that the Actors' Division of the ASP Council of PCA recommend to the parent body that its program call for such action as is necessary to abolish the Thomas-Rankin Committee, and that it take immediate steps to effect elimination of the Tenney Committee from the Legislature of this state.

2. *Resolved,* that a committee be established to investigate acts of discrimination in the theatre and the film industry, and that this be a permanent PCA committee to act as a clearing-house for such information and further that those present commend and support as a body the stand taken by Actors' Equity and The Playwrights' Co. against discrimination in the legitimate theatres of Washington, D. C.; and that this committee when formed support such a stand as it effects persons on both sides of the footlights.

3. *Resolved,* that the above committee consider to come within its purview equally the cases of those persons who are persecuted or discriminated against because politically they are liberals.

4. *Resolved,* that the actors of this community, in accordance with their desire to share in the responsibilities of the moment, and feeling a great need for topical material, both satirical and serious, do call upon the writers of ASP to do their utmost to provide them with such material.

5. *Resolved,* that the papers presented here tonight be published in printed form and sent to little theatre groups, neighborhood playhouses, and similar organizations, throughout the world.

6. *Resolved,* that we hereby establish a National Theatre Committee whose function shall be to continue the work of formulating and perfecting the present Federal Fine Arts Bill; that this committee discuss and make plans for the establishment of a government-subsidized theatre on national, state and local levels; and that it plan to present to Congress such a bill upon completion of its formulation; that this committee further investigate and report upon the work of the American National Theatre and Academy; and that it make regular progress reports of information secured and work accomplished, to future meetings of the Actors' Division.

7. *Resolved,* that in order to perpetuate and continue the work of this Conference, which we believe to be the guardian of free expression, and also the expansion of that freedom of expression which we now enjoy, a committee be established from this Conference, consisting of several writers, actors and directors in the film industry, who would have the responsibility of watching out for any abridgment of these freedoms and for any opportunity for extension of these freedoms, and report to this end to all other divisions in the cultural branch of PCA.

THOUGHT
CONTROL
IN U.S.A.

● ● ● ● ● ● ● ●

No. **6**

TOWARD FREEDOM
OF THOUGHT

the closing session
index to the proceedings
of the conference

THOUGHT CONTROL IN THE U. S. A.
The collected proceedings of the
Conference on the Subject of Thought Control in the U. S.,
called by the Hollywood Arts, Sciences & Professions Council, PCA,
July 9-13, 1947

Edited by Harold J. Salemson
Designed by Herbert D. Klynn
Published by Hollywood A. S. P. Council, P. C. A.,
1515 Crossroads of the World, Hollywood 28, Calif.

Printed in the U. S. A. by union labor
Aldine Printing Co., Los Angeles, Calif.

the closing session

Sunday, July 13, 1947, 8:00-10:30 P. M.

Hugh De Lacy, Chairman

Speakers: Donald Ogden Stewart, Harold Orr, Ben Margolis, Hugh De Lacy, Howard Koch, Robert W. Kenny

Speech-dance by Paul Draper

Sketch by Richard Collins

Donald Ogden Stewart

Playwright, novelist, screenwriter; most recent screenplays, Life With Father, Cass Timberlane; latest play, How I Wonder

PRELIMINARY SUMMATION

THE call to this conference noted a tendency in our national life, a tendency to restrict that freedom of individual expression which has always been the guarantee of our democratic culture.

The number and scope of the resolutions for action proposed from the various panels on the arts is an indication of the variety and scope of the infractions of cultural freedom. We won't be able to offer or even read all of these resolutions. Those referring to the separate fields of the arts will be referred to the Continuations Committees which were proposed from each of the panels. The proposals affecting all artists, scientists and professionals will be presented for your action later. In this summary, I am only going to show the shape of the pattern of thought control in the fields of the arts.

From the evidence offered, this control takes the form of a squeezeplay between political and economic pressures on the artist.

I begin with the political because—statistically speaking—the name most frequently mentioned in all of the panels was Thomas—J. Parnell Thomas, and the Committee which now bears his name. The activities of the Dies-Wood-Rankin-Thomas Un-American Committee were traced from its formation. The first major target of the Dies Committee was the Federal Theatre Project—at which time (as mentioned in both the Actors' and Literature Panels) the Committee pretty well established its intellectual level by asking whether the pre-Elizabethan playwright, Christopher Marlowe, was a Communist.

However, ignorance did not discourage the Committee from broadening its activities to cover every other field of the arts. Its familiar pattern of intimidation, innuendo and invective has recently been augmented by court action—a new form,—so that we find a novelist, a director, a magazine publisher, convicted of contempt of the Un-American Activities Committee and liable to imprisonment.

A second new aspect of the work of the Committee was pointed out by Carey McWilliams in the Film Panel—the extra-legal assistance of groups within the various fields of the arts. Carey McWilliams, in a carefully-documented paper, showed that the Motion Picture Alliance for the Preservation of American Ideals represented forces outside the motion picture industry—"a Quisling-like" group within Hollywood which has "invited J. Parnell Thomas and John Rankin to impose a Fascist censorship on the motion-picture industry in the name of preserving American ideals."

The Actors' Panel pointed to a similar instance in New York, in which Mr. Frank Fay cooperated with the Hearst *Journal-American* to smear a group of fellow-actors who dared to speak on behalf of Spanish Anti-Fascist refugees.

The Fine Arts Panel pointed to another such attack by the California Art Club upon the annual exhibition of fellow-artists at the Los Angeles County Museum as "radical art, containing subversive propaganda inimical to our form of government".

A third new aspect of the work of the Thomas Committee seems more important and more dangerous than any other. The government itself has stepped in to take a hand. On April 4, the *Los Angeles Examiner* announced that Secretary of State Marshall had halted an American art-exhibition touring abroad. Marshall was quoted as saying this was done "in the best interests of the State Department in view of controversial issues involved." And President Truman felt moved to comment on the nature of the artists and their work.

Only recently, the United States Embassy in Mexico refused a visa to Xavier Guerrero, a leading artist of Mexico, on the grounds that he was an enemy of the United States because of his political opinions.

The political motives which underlie the broadening scope of the very Un-American Committee's activities are all-too-obvious. As pointed out in the Actors' Panel, Franklin Roosevelt was a man great enough to encompass the democratic meaning of culture and the democratic determination of artists as a whole. Artists organized for progressive political action in the Thirties. Artists mobilized for the anti-Fascist war in the Forties. The outrageous political ends of the Thomas Committee, the reactionary aims of the Truman Doctrine, the economic disasters planned by the N.A.M., are not being met with silence by the artists of America. So silence must be imposed.

The other half of the squeezeplay on the free artist seems to be the increasing tendencies toward highly-centralized economic control in all fields of the arts.

The monopolistic nature of the major media of communication was abundantly documented within all the panels. The Press Panel quoted the Commission on Freedom of the Press in a report financed by Henry Luce and the *Encyclopedia Britannica*: "The Commission set out to answer the question, 'Is the freedom of the press in danger?' It's answer to that question was 'yes'." And the chief reason given by the Commission is the greatly decreased proportion of the people who can express their opinions and ideas through a press which has grown so tremendously as an instrument of mass-communication.

The Radio Panel asked: "Where in the Constitution does it say that 4 radio networks, or 20 advertising agencies, shall have the unrestricted right to broadcast to 140,000,000 people only that which those networks or agencies want the people to hear?"

But most alarming are indications that the well-known and commonly-accepted economic control in film, radio and press is reaching out to control the fields of the arts which have beten supposed to be comparatively free in the past.

Arnaud D'Usseau and Arthur Laurents indicated a growing tendency toward control on Broadway. If Hollywood has the Johnston Office, Broadway has a climate which quite effectively serves the same ends, not to mention narrowing sources of financial backing and increasing monopoly of theatres.

The Music Panel reports that "no performer, however talented, may be booked through any major circuit unless he is under contract to one or the other of the country's two largest concert agencies."

The Fine Arts Panel calls city-planning today "the law of the jungle". The only planning there is, is carried out by the major loan-companies. The censorship of the loan-companies, says Reginald Johnson, "is making it more and more impossible for the American people to live in houses which should, by all rights, represent the advanced scientific thinking of today."

Another tendency, closely related to the work of the Un-American Committees and their friends, is the increasing attention given the minorities by reaction. This inevitable by-product of political repression and economic imperialism has particularly disastrous results in the arts. The anti-Semitic overtones of the M.P.A. and the Thomas Committee were documented in the Film Panel. The larger cultural implications of this tendency, and in particular the narrowing role of the Negro in the cultural field—both as to employment and treatment,—were brilliantly analyzed by Phil Moore in a paper for the Fine Arts panel.

Beyond the indications of restriction, the panels discussed the results of these restrictions.

In the Film Panel, Irving Pichel and Richard Collins discussed the sterile, worthless cliches and stereotypes which remain outside of the proscribed "areas of silence".

Reuben Ship, in Radio, described the pitiful scramble to find real excitement or humor in the lives of people, when the stuff which makes the lives of people exciting and funny is forbidden.

The Fine Arts Panel commented that the Metropolitan Opera Company, which is now extending its hegemony to Los Angeles, has been willing enough to accept contributions from the American public, but has been singularly reluctant to spend any money in the performance of new American artists. The strictures imposed by the big businessmen of music offer little opportunity for original American composers.

The results of political and commercial censorship on the work of the individual artists need no further stressing. Their more obvious examples can be heard any morning over the radio, seen any evening at the neighborhood theatre, studied in the architecture of any city, or purchased on any magazine-stand.

But it is encouraging to notice that the panels also discussed the more subtle results of censorship. With wider and wider areas of reality denied the artist in all fields, with narrower craft-restrictions put on his work, the artist tends to a sterile search into himself, into his craft-form for form's sake—turning to the ivory tower, not out of any natural inclination on the part of artists to avoid life, but simply because he is not permitted to look at the real world outside of the tower.

It seems fitting, also, that each of the panels recalled the lessons of the complete degeneration of art under Fascism. When they heard the word culture, the masters of thought control reached for their guns . . . to silence those who could not be turned to the use of the war-lords. Donath, Tabori and others quite properly warned us of the end of the path which accepts intimidation. That end is the sterilization of art.

But they also told us of the proud majority of artists who would not be intimidated, of Mann, Aragon, Feuchtwanger, Hans Otto, Karl Valentin, Barrault, Peri, Lorca, DeFalla, Casals, Alberti, Brecht, Eisler . . .

It is an ironic commentary on our times that a victim of the master inquisitor of the age—the composer Hanns Eisler—is now again the victim of our own tawdry imitation of the Nazi culture-haters.

Finally—and fundamental to this Conference,—the critical need for action on the part of all artists was expressed in every panel:

To turn their prestige and talent to the defense of our democratic heritage and the proud fighting tradition of all artists everywhere;

To fulfill a full function as citizens—along with our fellow-citizen scientists and professionals, along with our fellow-citizen workers and trade-unionists and all people of good will;

To fulfill a full creative function—in the words of Albert Maltz' paper in the Literature Panel—as the conscience of the people;

To do this, to fulfill their function, each panel recognized the need for artists to find new ways of reaching people, new media

377

of communication outside of the control of commercial and political pressure.

Later, you will hear proposals of how this can be accomplished. To the support of these—I think I can speak for all the panels of the arts—we dedicate ourselves.

At this point, there was presented a sketch by Richard Collins, entitled Osubverso. *This playlet, enacted by Betsy Blair, Frances Cheney, Rose Hobart, Marilyn Moore, Howard Da Silva and David Sarvis, introduced a new machine, the "Osubverso", designed to ferret out radical propaganda slipped into films. Submitted as a sample was the famous scene from RKO's* Tender Comrade, *cited because of the line, "Share and share alike—that's democracy." The machine then rewrote the scene to be played as it would appear without its "subversive" overtones. (Mimeographed copies of the sketch are available from Hollywood Arts, Sciences & Professions Council, PCA, 1515 Crossroads of the World, Hollywood 28, Calif., for organizations interested in presenting it to further their fight against thought control. Cost of construction of the properties required for the "Osubverso" machine is estimated at $40.00.)*

Harold Orr

(Biographical note on
Dr. Orr will be found
on P. 287)

REPORT ON SCIENCE AND EDUCATION

IT is obviously impossible, within the limits of the time allotted for the report on science and education, to do justice to the material presented in five papers, three dealing with science, two covering problems in the field of education.

However, an over-all pattern emerged from the discussion, which both defines the issues in these fields and suggests their relationship to a larger pattern affecting the culture and social life of our time.

The scientist, as Dr. Epling pointed out, does not function ' in a social vacuum." The historic purpose of science, the key to its development and use, is to modify and master man's environment in order to "enhance his comfort and security" and "contribute to the satisfaction of his material and social needs."

The educator, even more directly and obviously, fulfills a clear and indispensable social function.

Yet, the scientist and educator face dangerous and increasing limitations upon the free research and communication which are the only means by which they can fulfill their function and perform the tasks to which their life and work are dedicated.

The Science Panel pointed out that the recent trend toward the militarization of science—with its accompanying repressive controls and interference with normal exchange of information and freedom of experiment—is not based upon any rational military necessity.

It cited the Senate hearings on the confirmation of the membership of the Atomic Energy Committee as indicative of what was described as "misconceptions and outright fabrications" propagated by presumably responsible political leaders in order to discredit

379

scientists and justify the extension of military authority over research. Senator McKellar insisted that General Groves was the real discoverer of the atom-bomb.

"One wonders", said the report, "whether the Senator has ever heard of the magnificent contributions of Fermi, Bethe, Oppenheimer, Lawrence, Chadwick, Bohr, Einstein, Oliphant, Condon, Urey, Pauli, and scores of others just as notable. It can be seen in this list, written down at random, that atomic energy is not exactly an American invention, or even an Anglo-Saxon Protestant invention."

The degree to which Congressional ignorance and disrespect for science can go, is illustrated by an article by J. Parnell Thomas, in *Liberty*, June 21, 1947, in which he points to the danger arising from

"the susceptibility of gullible American scientists employed by the Atomic Energy Commission. Our scientists, it seems, are well schooled in their specialties but not in the history of Communist tactics and designs. They have a weakness for attending meetings, signing petitions, sponsoring committees, and joining organizations labelled 'liberal' or 'progressive', but which are actually open Communist fronts."

To subject scientists to restrictions imposed by men of this mentality is obviously to destroy the creativeness of science and to make the scientist a lackey of the soldier or the politician.

The report cited the disgraceful vandalism involved in the destruction of the Japanese cyclotrons—by orders of men who apparently did not even know that the cyclotron is not necessary for the manufacture of atom-bombs, but is indispensable for researches in biology, medicine, agriculture and industry. The Association of Oak Ridge Scientists declared the wrecking of the Japanese cyclotrons constituted "a crime against mankind . . . as disreputable and ill-considered as would be the burning of Japanese libraries or the smashing of printing presses."

Dr. Neiburger's paper dealt with another aspect of repressive controls that limit the work of the scientist. In industrial employment, the scientist frequently (and, it is essential to note, increasingly) faces the "suppression of socially useful results", the concealment of inventions that would contribute to human welfare because their introduction would cost money and make existent equipment obsolete, and the downright fraud, in which the scientist is forced to participate, in devising salable objects which wear out quickly in order to create more demand.

The problem of the scientist is obviously related to the problem of the educator. Indeed, the Science Panel closed with a quotation from E. U. Condon:

"Information essential to understanding is being denied to students in our universities, so that, if this situation were to continue, young students will get from their professors only a watered-down, Army-approved version of the laws of nature. . .".

The historical review of recurring witch-hunts in education showed that every field of education, and especially the teaching of economics and the social sciences, is under attack by forces whose history reveals their purpose—the control of thought for political ends. Since knowledge is power, those who wish to wield power for selfish and predatory advantage are determined to prevent the objective and free dissemination of knowledge which is the aim of a democratic culture. Economic pressure, threats, dismissals are the means by which these enemies of democracy secure their control of the schools; the record of witch-hunts, from the Lusk Laws in New York State in 1921 to the Rapp-Coudert Investigation in N. Y. in 1940, and the current attempts of the Tenney Committee to establish political control over California's schools and colleges, leaves no doubt of the conclusion reached in this report: "Those who fear the truth in our schools fear a free education in a democratic world".

It is astonishing that the teacher, who performs such a vital social function, should be subject to restrictions in political, economic and social rights that no citizen should be compelled to endure. I noted, in the paper I presented, that "in practically all communities of this country, the teacher is regarded as a second-class citizen; he or she is not supposed to exercise any political or social leadership, and is usually treated as a chauffeur or a house-maid, socially".

This is part of the pattern of control — the degradation of culture that has been referred to in other panels, affecting the artist, writer, musician, as well as the educator and scientist.

Another aspect of the pattern of control is the restriction of opportunity for minorities, both in enrolling in courses and entering the teaching profession. Discrimination is not accidental— it is a political weapon of those who are consciously attempting to regiment science and straitjacket education.

During the discussion, a speaker from the floor introduced startling evidence of the degree to which the democratic rights of students are being curtailed. The speaker stated that certain institutions employ spies to enter as students and report on student activities; that parking-lot attendants at one college have admitted they are so employed as spies to note down conversations and report "dangerous thought". A girl student distributing leaflets was approached by one of these spies and asked for information; when she refused, he showed her that he had a gun. Six students were place on probation at U.S.C. for insisting on further investigation of the burning of a KKK cross on the campus. The speaker cited examples of dangerous attacks on student-rights in other parts of the country, especially at Syracuse and the University of Michigan, where students have been placed on probation and excluded from all activities simply because they were members of the American Youth for Democracy.

In view of the urgency of the problem that students face, one of the major decisions of the panel was the adoption of the Bill of Rights for Students adopted by the National Youth Lobby.

The panel also adopted resolutions condemning the Thomas-Rankin Committee and demanding that it be abolished, and strongly condemning recent attacks on such noted scientists as Dr. Harlow Shapley and Dr. E. U. Condon.

We believe that the action of the Conference should include these recommendations, and should inaugurate a powerful movement for the free and democratic development of science and education.

Ben Margolis

Attorney, specializing in
labor law; member, Galla-
gher, Margolis, McTernan
& Tyre; Exec. Board mem-
ber, PCA

REPORT ON PROFESSIONAL PANELS

MONG the professions, two conducted panels, doctors and lawyers, the former panel being prepared by the Medical Council of PCA, the latter by the Los Angeles and Hollywood chapters of the National Lawyers' Guild. Although these two panels were separately prepared with no effort to use a common theme, one factor dominated in both. We find that there is a direct relationship between the concentration of economic power in monopoly and its elimination of competition on the one hand and suppression of free thought on the other.

The domination of medical research by the representatives of Big Business imposes the same kind of restrictions on the freedom of thought as do a monopoly radio and press upon the freedom of communication. As a means of suppressing political heresy within the medical profession, the American Medical Association, with its monopoly ties with hospitals and the pharmaceutical industry, utilizes its great power to deprive non-conformists of access to medical facilities and to impugn their professional standing. The utilization of economic power by the A.M.A. may well be compared to the control wielded by private employers over their employees and by the Federal Government with its abominable loyalty-tests which threaten with destruction every Government employee who does not conform to the thought standards set by the administration.

In the paper on *Medical Care and Thought Control*, it was pointed out that organized-medicine has maintained a consistent attitude opposing change, only grudgingly giving in when it must, to prevent greater change. We learn that this opposition to change—which means support of our present inadequate standards of medical care—is effectuated through an alliance between the Medical Association, ostensibly serving the health of the nation, and the drug-manufacturing industry, which in utilizing its control to sell billions of dollars' worth of nostrums has become one of the major forces most responsible for people's ill-health. This combination exercises its pressure upon individuals in the profession through its complete domination of the medical field and through its control of hospital appointments, which are absolutely essential to the doctor who wishes to function effectively.

The concepts accepted by this combination are imposed upon the medical profession with the resultant denial to all the people of the benefits—including adequate medical care for all—which might otherwise be achieved.

The paper entitled *Medical Research For Whom?* demonstrated that the dead hand of monopoly keeps the lid down upon the tremendous gains which medical research could make towards health and longer life for all. Research requires expensive facilities, large staffs and long-term expenditures. That means big money, and big money in turn has meant Big Business or monopoly. Not only is research directed away from those channels, no matter how vital, in which success might endanger profits, but the actual results of completed research are often suppressed.

In many ways, the Legal Panel was able to come to grips with the heart of the problem of thought control. Thought control is exercised through the application or misapplication of laws—or through the failure of the law to conform with the necessities of our changing social-structure. The lawyers are concerned with questions such as how the law is being interpreted, how it is being applied, what development of law is necessary in order to give to the people of this country, under conditions existing in 1947, the freedom which was the object of the founders of this country.

Charles Katz in his paper, *Toward a Free Press,* quotes an anony-mouse wag in Fleet Street, during the reign of Queen Anne, as saying that the power of the press is the "suppress". At the time of the writing of our Constitution, the danger of suppression of a free press came from Government censorship. This danger was directly and successfully attacked by the First Amendment to the Constitution. Today, however, the threat to the free press no longer comes from the Government.

Today, the newspaper industry is Big Business. It should surprise no one that a press controlled by Big Business expresses only the ideas and policies of Big Business. Access to the press as a means of communication is no longer available to the common man. Mr. Katz stated in his paper that

"so few men have access to the vehicles of communication today, and so one-classed have the owners of the instruments of publication become, that for the great mass of our citizenry the phrase 'freedom of the press' has tragically retained little of its original meaning."

The question of a free press today has resolved itself into the question of freedom of access to the press. That the press is controlled by monopoly and is clothed with a public interest, very few would contest. The privilege of publishing a newspaper calls for responsibility to the people; in this day and age, that means throwing open certain sections of the newspapers as a means of communication for people who disagree with the publishers *and this on a free basis,* and, further, it means the sale of advertising-space to all, without discrimination.

Just as other monopolies and public utilities have been held subject to regulation, so it must now be recognized that the press is subject to regulation.

In a paper presented by Mr. Milton S. Tyre, the same principles are set down for the airwaves. Time does not permit the full and detailed discussion which this merits.

The subject of the Truman loyalty-tests, that domestic counterpart of the Truman Doctrine, was presented in a paper by Mr. Fred Okrand, pointing out that the American tradition is one that abhors the concept of loyalty-purges or test-oaths. In another day, many honored Americans have struck down similar measures—men who, like Alfred E. Smith, recognized that within the limits of the penal law every citizen may speak and teach what he believes and that the entire concept of loyalty-tests is in direct conflict with the freedom of thought protected by the first ten Amendments to the Constitution. These concepts are challenged by those for whom the prevention of change is more important than the right to free thought.

Full description of the procedural dangers inherent in the loyalty-tests would require far more time than is available here. Characteristic of that procedure, however, is the fact that the Attorney-General of the United States is given unlimited authority to designate organizations which according to his views are subversive or totalitarian. One man is thus given the power to define the permissible limitations of thought. That the standards of permissible thought so defined are actually those set by Big Business, becomes clear when the application of the term *subversive* is observed. The loyalty-tests serve the purpose of requiring Government employees to conform in their thinking first to the basic policies of the administration and second to those mores which the press and monopoly business would impose on the American people.

A paper presented by Mr. Sanford Carter dealt with *Discrimination in Employment*. The control by private employers of millions of employees who are dependent upon them for economic existence is here given consideration. Just as the courts have held that a private employer had no right, under the Wagner Act,—at least, before the enactment of the Taft-Hartley Law,—to discriminate because of union activity, so it must now be established that there may be no discrimination because of activities in the field of politics, culture, art, science, etc. To accept any other · principle is to give to private employers almost complete power of thought control. The existence of a California statute which protects employees against discrimination because of their political affiliations and activities is noted and its strict enforcement is urged. Furthermore, this principle must be broadened so that freedom of thought in all of its aspects will be protected.

Finally, Mr. Morris Cohn submitted a paper on the Un-American Activities Investigating Committees. In this paper, it is pointed out that the function of legislative committees should be limited to the fields in which Constitutional legislation may be enacted. He points out:

> "The immediate object of the Thomas Committee is the investigation of propaganda. The resolution asks for a study of un-American propaganda in the United States, and of the diffusion within the United States of subversive and un-American propaganda instigated from foreign countries.

> "There has yet to be submitted a bill suppressing propaganda which, except in time of war or imminent danger, is capable of becoming a law under the Constitution of the United States. Stripping the word propaganda of its emotional charge and looking at it as a court must do, the word propaganda means news, persuasion, literature, the articulate expression of ideas. It is perfectly plain that the subject-matter of investigation is precisely the ground occupied by the First Amendment, and while the First Amendment may not in all instances be invoked in order to prevent an inquiry, for example, an investigation to aid in the dissemination of news as by an investigation into the control

of press and radio, the Amendment is a sword against any attempt by the state or national government, in the absence of a clear and present danger, to stifle or to discourage the clash of opinion. No valid law can be passed suppressing propaganda."

Thus, it is clear that the Un-American Activities Committees not only have no basis for existence but that their very existence is a challenge to the Constitution that the Committees purport to support.

Many procedural guarantees in the law are necessary. Among them are the right to counsel, the right to present witnesses, the right to refuse to disclose opinions and political affiliations. We must acknowledge the battle being waged by those who have dared to challenge the Thomas-Rankin Committee in refusing to yield to its unconstitutional demands. All progressive organizations must come to the defense of all those who are charged with contempt of the House Committee—regardless of any differences in political opinion. Their defense is our own first line of defense.

Many legal aspects of thought control were not touched upon by any of the papers. However, albeit briefly, a few of them must be referred to here. The dangerous and growing trend toward refusal of meeting-places to organizations whose views conflict with those who control meeting-places must be observed with apprehension and must be followed by action. Here, again, the control of access to the means of communication is utilized as a means of thought control.

Not satisfied with controlling all major channels of communication, those who seek to control the thoughts of the American people have secured the enactment of the Taft-Hartley Bill, which attempts to deprive labor organizations of their right to communicate in any form with respect to basic political matters. Peaceful picketing and other forms of activity which have been labor's forms of communication are declared illegal by that same vicious law. That bill is unconstitutional and must be defeated in the courts and in the field of public opinion. Its repeal is a *must*, if democracy is to survive.

The professionals have attempted to outline a partial program of action. It is necessary and proper that they should do so. However, only the united action of all progressives seeking to discard the chains of thought control can achieve the objectives of such a program.

Hugh De Lacy

Former Congressman from
State of Washington; leading national progressive figure

THE PANEL
ON THE PRESS

FIVE studies of fields in which the American press exercises crushing control over the sources of the people's basic information and
their thinking on critical issues presented to our panel an array of
facts seldom before gathered in such useful focus.

Mr. Leo Lania told how Nazism was helped to power by a press,
even the liberal German press, which censored itself, which kept
critical facts from Germany, which sought, unavailingly as it turned
out, to buy immunity, by not telling the whole truth. Mr. Lania was
there, trying as a liberal journalist to bring to the people the moving
truth. He feels Hitlerism could have been kept from getting its mass
base in Germany, if the press had not conformed in advance to the
Nazi pattern. He now warns America against the *Gleichschaltung* of
our press. Noting the ominous disappearance even from the columns
of the greatest newspapers of our day of news-stories at variance with
editorial policy, he illuminated our desperate need for accounts of foreign and domestic events which would truthfully reveal how far the
Vandenberg-Truman coalition has taken us from one world of hope
and plenty.

Papers by Charlotta Bass, Darr Smith, Bob Joseph and Joe Weston
documented the repressive role of our papers in the fields of minorities, of labor, of world peace, and told how advertising influences
the millionaire press, confirms policies native to it as a substantial
part of Big Business itself, and how even bought and paid-for advertising-space is denied to all but approved groups and causes.

If there was any deficiency in our panel's rich treatment of these
known truths, freshly and brilliantly set forth in our stimulating papers,
it was that their very fulness did not leave enough time for those
attending the panel to contribute from their own experience and
deeply-felt needs.

388

Several sharp demands from the floor for a program of action were left dangling, inadequately answered.

We are particularly happy, therefore, to present to this concluding session suggestions for continuing an effective and, we hope, corrective interest in the subject we feel we have so promisingly opened.

1. We recommend to this concluding session that a statement be drafted to newspaper publishers, to the American Society of Editors, and to the Newspaper Guild, pointing to the press' shameful betrayal of living democracy, to the systematic poisoning of the American mind by playing up certain conforming facts and suppressing other vital facts. We propose a factual recital, a simple, eloquent appeal. We hope it might influence the lords of the press. Distributed in millions of copies to the readers of the press, we know it will help people keep their minds open and free.

2. We recommend that this concluding session concur in our panel's endorsement of the Buckley Bill, H.R. 2848. It would bar from the mails and prescribe $5000 fine and five years at hard labor for any person circulating race hatred or any form of bigotry against other Americans of diverse religions, colors, or national origin.

3. We urge the setting up of a Continuations Committee Against Thought Control in the Press. Under the sponsorship of artists, scientists, and professionals, and with their active interest and participation, we believe telling research could be carried on and challenging actions undertaken. In particular, we recommend that this committee, in cooperation with like-minded lawyers, should bring test-cases in court against newspapers refusing paid advertising to groups and causes with which they editorially disagree. As public services, the papers should not be immune from the same principle that applies, or must be made to apply, to places of public accommodation.

We urge, further, that the Continuations Committee undertake to publicize the shortcomings and offenses of papers which give race labels to crime news, distort labor news, inflame public thinking against other peoples and nations, endangering world peace. We suggest that delegations of citizens be organized to visit such offending papers to demand space in their letter-columns and an opportunity, through paid advertising, to bring out the true story. We suggest that the committee appeal for funds to center and carry on its work.

4. We recommend, finally, that our Continuations Committee launch a voice for the people, one they can look to as their own. We propose a Readers' Guide, a Mental Consumers' Guide, if you wish,

a monthly bulletin, bringing to thoughtful groups everywhere a documented analysis of propaganda methods by which the Big-Business press is seeking to regiment our thought.

We propose, secondly, the launching of a National News Review, a weekly magazine, to bring to millions what will at once be an example of free reportage and a stimulator of democratic action.

On behalf of our panel, I wish to move the adoption of this report and its several recommendations.

I request the chair to put them separately for consideration and action.

At this point, Paul Draper presented a speech-dance on the topic of thought control, not included in these proceedings because it was felt by the author that the text did not come through on its own and could be appreciated properly only in conjunction with his own interpretive presentation.

Howard Koch

Writer, screen, *Casablanca,
Mission to Moscow, Ser-
geant York,* etc., stage, *In
Time to Come* (with John
Huston), radio, Martian in-
vasion script for Orson
Welles

THE CHAIRMAN'S REPORT

FOR the past five days, we have participated in a unique event—
the first conference against the control of thought in the history of
the world. Mankind's oldest vice is meeting mankind's most progressive answer.

As chairman, may I commend each individual panel and each
speaker on the uniformly-high quality of their contributions and,
above all, on the spirit in which the subject was approached. We
asked for scientific objectivity, for documented fact—and we got
them. A note-worthy aspect was the scholarship of the papers—the
burrowing down to the historical roots of the problems in each field
and the dignified restraint with which even the most degrading instances of censorship and thought control were discussed.

I want particularly to commend the staff of the Arts, Sciences and
Professions Council—George Pepper, Joy Darwin, and Joan LaCour—
for their part in the success of the conference. Such devotion
as they exhibited cannot be bought for wages—it has to come from
a deep conviction of a national need for what we are all trying to do.

Finally, I want to commend our audiences for their responsive-
ness not only to contemporary political comment but to the profound
analyses of the bases of our problem . . . As to the size of our audiences, to put it in Hollywood terms, we "did well at the box-
office". On second thought, Hollywood wouldn't put it that mildly.
We believed this was going to be a small conference, a sort of intra-
mural discussion and comparing of notes on the part of people we
knew to be interested. We were looking for a spring and we tapped
an ocean. We all but took down the hotel-walls, but the management
was unwilling to cooperate to that extent.

Now this gives us a very comforting assurance—that we are not

391

a few lone Jeremiahs crying in the wilderness, that the alarm we feel and the aspiration we still hold, when articulated and spread abroad, will find an American chorus of a thousand protesting voices for each one of ours.

In case at this point you are gathering the impression that the conference was a diamond without flaws, I have here to disabuse you. We made mistakes. In the same objective spirit which pervaded the conference, I feel I should mention these mistakes so that we can learn from them and pass on the benefit of that knowledge to the National Conference Against Thought Control to be held in the East later this year.

When some of us on the committee discussed the problem of the length of panels and papers, we said, "What are we going to do about those lawyers? They're such verbose fellows. Get them started and they'll talk all night." Well, we found the lawyers were not unique in that respect. We all talked too long. I can only say in extenuation, we were not being paid by the minute—we were just sort of full of what we had to say.

But, in some of the panels, this tendency caused a serious loss— the loss of an adequate period of discussion on the floor. This is one of the things we most wanted. We tried to correct the situation in the later sessions, but we couldn't entirely overcome the initial mistake.

Also, we feel we could have improved the accumulated results of the conference in another respect—by the closer coordination of its various divisions. Had each of us known more of what the other was doing, we could have effected a closer integration of the whole. Actually, the ASP itself was in a sense being improvised along with the conference. I believe the conference has helped to define its character and functions. We realize the ASP still needs many things; most of all it needs you.

Now, what was the theme that emerged from the conference? What was the over-all motif that kept running through the sessions?

In the keynote speech, you remember, Norman Corwin quoted Archibald MacLeish to the effect that modern war must first be waged on the minds of men. As we meet at the close of the conference, I think we know beyond the shadow of a doubt that this undeclared war is already in progress, that the attack is highly-organized and efficiently-planned, that already it has penetrated deep into the mental life of our nation, that it is levelled against every area of human thought. As you know from the panels, and from the reports you have just heard, the conference has mostly concerned itself with the particular manifestations of this attack in the fields of the arts, sciences and professions—the area of our culture. However, let us remind ourselves, as the panel papers kept reminding us, that this is not a private war against us, or a limited war against any group such as labor, or even a national war, although it is often dressed to assume that form. This is, in essence, a war to control the people, in spite of the people and against the people.

These are the days when it is popular to talk about curtains— iron curtains, silken curtains, uranium curtains. But what impresses me most, on the basis of the evidence collected, is the wall of words that has slowly been erected around us. Printed words over thousands of robot presses, spoken words dinned over the captive air. Words that tell half-truths or no truths, words that half-explain or don't explain at all, brash words out of the vocabulary of a Goebbels, high-sounding words that have been distorted into caricatures of their once-precious meanings, words cunningly-contrived to confuse, words fashioned out of malice, fear and self-interest, words that have lost all connection with the real world—the world of fact, the world of sense, the world of peace.

The other side of the picture—if I read the evidence, correctly— is the repressive side: the words that *can't* be said except to small groups in a room like this. The words that have been denied the presses, the words that are unwelcome on the airwaves. The wall, you see, works two ways. It keeps in and it keeps out. And so, we watch the frantic efforts by the makers of anti-human policy to close the chinks in the wall, to cement the cracks, then to police the top of the wall with the watchdogs of reaction—the Rankins, the Thomases and the Tenneys. Many in high and eminently-respectable conservative circles often disclaim these lurid men, and sometimes even give them a vote of mild censure. But this is like keeping mad dogs on the loose, and then apologizing because they infect people with hydrophobia. They regret their crude habits, but they neglect to chain them up. Why? Because they want the wall guarded, even if it takes madness to do it.

In this fantastic, Alice-in-Wonderland atmosphere within the wall, we live and breathe. Fantasy, given enough of it, becomes a dangerously normal climate. We see so little of the other world beyond the wall—the real world, of reason and fact,—we almost forget it is there, until finally the inside climate becomes so oppressive we begin to suffocate under the weight of superimposed delusions. Then, we know we have to do something about it.

That, ladies and gentlemen, is the clear and insistent call of every panel in this conference. "Do something about it. We're not doing enough about it. We're moving too slowly. We must reach more people. We must do more things."

We *are* going to do something about it. And we are going to start it here in this room tonight. Later, you are going to hear suggestions and even plays for a P.C.A. national radio-program and newspaper—a political consumers' research, it has been called,—to print and broadcast factual information, to correct the distortion of news, to assess and evaluate events as objectively as such a research-group might analyze the ingredients of a packaged-food. Isn't it equally as important that we know the quality of what is poured into our minds as what we take into our bodies?

Moreover, we are going to hold meetings here and in other parts of the country, to bring the findings of this conference to the people as a whole.

Yes, we are going to make a hole in that wall large enough to drive J. Parnell Thomas through it. We're not just going to talk to each other—as pleasant as that is. Now, we're going to knock big holes in that wall. We're going to let in air and light and truth.

The American people are essentially a people of progress and good will. Once they have access to the facts, we can have faith in their conclusions. We can have faith in their actions. One thing we're certain of—they're not regarding with pride or pleasure the two worlds of the Truman Doctrine or whatever latest substitute the reactionaries have thought up. They want the One World that Franklin Roosevelt charted. We and millions like us are going to knock down that wall so that the people can see that One World again with their own eyes. They can think about it with their own thought. They can design it out of their own hearts. They can build it with their own hands.

Robert W. Kenny

Leading California lawyer; former
State Attorney General; National
Co-chairman, So. Cal. Chairman,
PCA

CONCLUSIONS
AND CHALLENGE

I⊤ is my first pleasure to bring to the artists, scientists, and professionals, and our friends assembled here tonight, the warm greetings of the National Board of the Progressive Citizens of America. I was proud of our state and its hundreds of thousands of progressive-minded citizens, and particularly proud of the splendid work of our own Hollywood Arts, Sciences, and Professions Council, when the motion unanimously carried at our Chicago National Board meeting, adopting as the major national fight for all progressive citizens everywhere the fight we began here in Hollywood, the fight this Conference has carried so many steps forward, our fight, the whole people's fight, to stop thought control in America.

There is no mistaking it. A war has been declared on culture. A war has been declared upon the creators and guardians of culture, upon the independence without which a great people's culture cannot be conceived, upon the freedom without which it cannot rise, upon the basic spiritual and economic security without which it cannot flourish.

As artists, scientists, and professionals, many of us are growing used to personal attacks in the columns of a Pegler or before the Thomas-Rankin or Tenney Committees. We are realizing that these attacks are not aimed at individuals alone. They are raising a canopy of fear. A kind of cultural gas-chamber. They are blackmailing and blackjacking every independent spirit in the cultural field, in a desperate effort to drive from the avenues of public communication the last idea, the final memory, the trembling hope that yet remains from the Roosevelt Era.

It is plain, too, that the attack in a Hearst newspaper against one of our distinguished, outspoken fellow-citizens in the cultural world cannot be separated from the demand in the same newspaper for passage of the Taft-Hartley Bill, for the ending of price controls, for a 15% rent increase, for the Truman Doctrine. The silencing of radio commentators, the suppression of labor news, the attempted intimidation of a whole great industry, cannot be separated from the shocking acquittal of 26 self-confessed lynchers in a South Carolina court.

They are all part of the heavy blanket which the *owners* of great wealth are trying to thrust down over the *creators* of wealth, the workers of skilled hand, of disciplined brain, of moving heart.

I am not suggesting that Fascism has come to America. I have grown a little weary of hearing every wrong, every reactionary measure called the first, the original step toward Fascism.

Of course, Truman's witch-hunt, the Taft-Hartley Bill, the Thomas-Rankin Committee, the refusal to pass a Federal bill to stop lynching, are of the quality of Fascism. But why? Not because they are Fascism, but because they whittle down American democracy, because they spread division and fear, because they reduce our capacity to protect ourselves against a dictatorship of the Right thrusting itself upon us in the wake of depression or war.

It is not that I dismiss lightly the very real terror of Fascism, how it could steal up on us, and what it would mean if we failed to stop it. I simply assert that we do not have Fascism as a governing system in Hollywood, in California, or in the nation as a whole.

How far reaction is getting ready to go, however, is shown in an ominous bill introduced into this session of the Pennsylvania Legislature.

It would impose fines up to $5000, and ten years in prison, for giving verbal or written support or praise to any organization loosely described as disloyal, or traitorous to the American form of government, or to any member of such an organization, or for even signing a petition or paper in its behalf.

It robs persons of "disloyal" outlook of all right to hold public office, public employment, or office in an all-inclusive list of organizations.

Whether this shocking abridgement of fundamental American rights, sending its stench forth across the nation, can be more fittingly described as coming from the very birthplace of American independence, or out of the economic needs of Pennsylvania's vast coal, steel, textile, and ship-building enterprises, is a question I will leave for your own deliberation.

I say that this many-sided attack upon freedom of thought in America has no small relationship to the enormous profits of $12,-500,000,000 realized in 1946 by an American business which was freed by action of Congress from the Excess-Profits Tax, freed by action of Congress from price-control, and producing for a market temporarily without limit.

I say that this many-sided attack upon freedom of thought and this rigid censorship over the materials of thought are related to the fact that all the highly-advertised wage-increases cost industry less than five percent of its last year's—highest of all years'—profits.

I say the issue they tremblingly hide is whether many shall have more or few shall have all.

I say that the Taft-Hartley Bill, the evil works of the Thomas-Rankin Committee, the war on culture, the censorship, are signs, not of the strength of reaction, but of its insensate fear of the people and of what they started to learn and to do under Roosevelt.

As Chairman of the National Lawyers' Guild, I want to tell these captains of reaction that America still has some rights left, the same old rights she has always used to pull her people painfully up the economic scale. There is still a Bill of Rights. There is still a United States Constitution. There are still jury trials. There is still the right of independent citizens to join together, to meet, to speak, to write, and to work for progress.

And I will say further that America's fighting lawyers, America's moving artists and scientists and professionals, are going to stand their ground, are going to prove again and again and again that those old liberties are still the meat and bread of American life.

That is our obligation. Thanks to our parents, thanks to our teachers, and thanks, too, to something in ourselves, we have developed skills and influence which recent events make us doubly firm in our intention to continue using for the benefit of the rich field in which we labor and for the wider benefit of ourselves and all our fellow-citizens.

The closer we come to the crucial political contests of 1948, the hotter the attack will grow. Let us in this room take care not to fall by the wayside. Let us feed every glowing spark, let us foster and develop every feeling for justice and humanity in our colleagues.

Let us reach out, together, joining strength to strength until the walls of the castle go down and the people at last inherit their earth.

I share the pride of tens of thousands in this city and state in the way our organization, the Progressive Citizens of America, is leading the way. We have a bold program for a time that only boldness can conquer. Our National Board of Directors, at its Chicago meeting just two weeks ago, issued a ringing challenge to the bigots of today, the hangmen of tomorrow. Our Board reaffirmed its "unqualified opposition to the very Un-American Activities Committee and the President's loyalty executive order and to all the little Dies Committees proposed by state and municipal legislatures."

Declaring that such actions lead to book-burning, to driving liberals off the radio, denying halls to great artists, prohibiting musicians from playing Russian music, banning all but officially-approved texts from classrooms, intimidating the movie industry and making it sterile, and to a hundred other forms of suppression, the Board's resolution warns that these actions can end only by depriving all America of its freedom.

> "We warn our public servants that the American people have always known how to deal with those who would deprive them of their basic freedoms. They repudiated the un-American Federalists in 1800 and, after the First World War, drove the infamous Palmer out of public life. So today they will know how to deal with these new advocates of an ancient bigotry.
>
> "We pledge the total resources of our national organization to sweep away every vestige of control over freedom of thought and freedom to create."

Those are the fighting words of PCA.

That is our first, great, national blow to defend the people's right to continue on to victory the great fight which Roosevelt led, which Henry Wallace carries on.

We view with sympathy and encouragement those in the Democratic and Republican Parties who stand for progress.

We believe, with them, that the answer to the hungry is bread; the answer to the homeless is a home; the answer to the jobless is a job; the answer to the sick is care; the answer to insecurity is all these things plus peace and a World Organization that encourages every other people on toward the goals of their free choice.

We say, without fear, that it is time to recognize where Free Enterprise is not working and to provide in these areas alternatives that *will* work for the people. We call for public ownership of the coal industry, of the railroads, and of all sources of electric and atomic power.

This is an American program for the American people. To those who think it can be achieved within the Democratic Party, we extend our hand in good will. To those who believe it can be achieved only through a new political party, we likewise extend our hand in good will, for it is the program, the program that meets the needs of America and of a world that must remain at peace, which first commands our loyalty.

If the Democratic Party fails to meet the challenge a people's program offers, it will not retain the people's support. The Democratic Party will go forward to victory in 1948 with a man like Wallace, under Wallace's banner, or it will ignominiously perish.

Our part in this fight is to grow strong combatting bigotry and suppression, to hold high the torch of hope, to build membership of good courage, to make our PCA clubs, in every neighborhood and every city, stand in the eyes of their communities where Henry Wallace stands in the heart of his countrymen.

RESOLUTIONS

ON A MENTAL CONSUMERS' GUIDE

The resolutions passed by all the panels at this Conference point to the necessity of aroused and organized public action, in order to prevent further restriction of opinion, to dissipate the poisonous propaganda that befouls the free air of our country, and to return to our traditional freedom of enquiry and communication.

We propose that the Arts, Sciences and Professions Council of PCA take immediate steps to establish a publication, to serve as a Mental Consumers' Guide. The periodical will utilize the best methods of scholarship to expose anti-social and repressive trends and to fight for unrestricted freedom of expression. Interference with thought, speech and assemblage, will be investigated and exposed. Anti-democratic trends in our schools and colleges will be analyzed, and appropriate protest called forth. The public will be informed concerning the reliability of the material which is offered to it as truth or art.

If children's minds are being poisoned by the propaganda of intolerance, parents should know the facts. If the parents themselves are being similarly poisoned by distortion and misrepresentation, the facts should be publicized.

We proclaim that the truth is the best and most creative answer to political censorship and monopoly control of communication.

The Mental Consumers' Guide will seek national support. Its only interest will be truth; its only bias will be democracy. It will be dedicated to the great purpose proclaimed by Jefferson—relentless opposition to every form of tyranny over the mind of man.

ON THE RIGHTS OF NATIONAL MINORITIES

American culture is seriously threatened by the growth of hatred and prejudice against Negroes, Jews, and other minority groups. The revival of the Ku Klux Klan, the lynching and terror in the South, the

400

burning of fiery crosses even on college campuses, are symptoms of the effectiveness of the false and destructive propaganda of prejudice. We, therefore, resolve that we will use all our talent, skill and collective effort as American artists, scientists and professionals, to fight against persecution or discrimination because of race, color, or creed.

We shall endeavor to bring to the American people the great truth proclaimed in our own Declaration of Independence that all men are created free and equal.

We demand a permanent FEPC.

We shall investigate and expose every case of job discrimination, prevention of equal educational opportunity, exclusion of minorities from professional training and occupations.

We especially point to the disgraceful stereotypes that malign the Negro people in film, radio, books, magazines and newspapers. We maintain that discrimination against the Negro as an actor on the stage, screen, or in radio presentations, is closely related to the fact that the Negro never has an opportunity to give an honest, straight-forward characterization and that the problem of presenting normal contact between peoples of different origin becomes so involved with ignorant prejudices that it seems better to exclude the Negro altogether.

This situation, which is most extreme in regard to the Negro, applies to all minority groups. It degrades American life, disunites our people and drains the vitality of our culture. We shall establish a special committee of the arts, sciences and professions which shall deal specifically with this aspect of thought control and the reactionary line of propaganda that accompanies it.

ON INTERNATIONAL COMMUNICATIONS

There is no area in which thought control functions more perniciously and oppressively than in the field of international communications. Lies and prejudice serve to create false and meaningless issues between nations and lead to the disruption of normal commercial and diplomatic contacts. The hysterical and unjustified war-propaganda that is now being developed in the United States is an example of the destructive substitution of misinformation for the fruitful contacts that can contribute to the welfare of all peoples and nations, and create one world in which peace and security again rule.

All scientists and scholars recognize that exchange of scientific information is the very lifeblood of culture. Without such exchange, scientific progress and invention are delayed and historical progress is obstructed. Cultural contacts between peoples serve to overcome antiquated prejudices. We all have a tremendous amount to learn from our neighbors across the world. There is no more excuse for hatred across oceans than there is for hatred across the lawns and streets of an American community.

We, therefore, propose that there be a renewed and strengthened development of cultural contacts among all nations, through international meetings of scientists, artists, and scholars, and especially through the building and full utilization of the United Nations Educational, Scientific and Cultural Organization. These channels of communication must be put to use, not only to establish scienfic and cultural interchange, but also to dissolve myths and expose lies, and to create a foundation for international friendship and good will.

FOR A FEDERAL ARTS BILL

The development of a free culture in the United States requires a fully-rounded and democratically-administered Federal Arts Program. The vast achievements of the Federal Arts Project were among the great social and cultural gains registered during the presidency of Franklin D. Roosevelt. Art, music, theatrical entertainment, were brought to millions of the culturally-underprivileged citizens of the United States.

Reactionary forces that destroyed the Federal Arts Program in 1939 are the same forces that are seeking to undermine the foundations of a free culture in the present crucial period.

Hatred of democracy motivated the Dies Committee's successful onslaught on the Federal Arts Project: to keep culture from the people is essential for those who wish to keep knowledge from the people.

We shall work for municipal and state aid to the arts. And we shall immediately begin a national movement for the establishment of a national cultural center. All groups and organizations in the field of the arts, sciences, and professions will be called upon to join in the campaign, and to participate in the formulation of the programs and policies of the Federal program.

ON FREEDOM OF COMMUNICATION

Freedom of speech and communication is a mockery if the channels of communication are controlled by one faction of political opinion, which bars from equal or partial use of these channels those with whom it does not agree. Our investigation of the facts with regard to communication has revealed that the much-vaunted American free press, free radio and free screen is in truth free only to those who oppose democracy and progressive political attitudes. Those forces have entered into a conspiracy to prevent those who believe in a growing, living, progressive democracy from reaching the majority of their fellow-counrtymen who wish to hear a fair, balanced, impartial presentation of both sides of an issue.

The trend toward restrictive control is manifested in other fields of creative activity—in science, education and the professions. In the development of our society, the vast expansion of the industrial machine has been accompanied by an enormous concentration of economic power in a few hands. This concentration has proceeded in the fields of the creative arts and sciences so that today we find the machine-production of culture on a scale never before achieved in history and at the same time the unprecedented harnessing of science to the end of the industrial machine, so that thought is monopolized.

This historic development requires the increasing vigilance of the people in maintaining their traditional free character and democratic discussion under these new conditions.

We propose that we undertake a campaign to guarantee access to the means of communication. The press and radio must be treated in law and in fact as monopolized industries which perform a public service, and must function with reasonable respect for the public interest. The law must provide access to these means of communication both to those who can pay and those who are unable to do so. This means that for the privilege of publishing a newspaper or operating a radio-station, the publisher and the operator must be required to throw open to all points of view, without charge, a portion of the press and of the air. The law must also provide that the sale of advertising-space in newspapers and advertising-time on the air be free from discrimination.

Furthermore, the tendency of those who control meeting-places to refuse to rent to persons or organizations with whose ideas they disagree, is another eminent danger to our Constitutional rights. Consideration must be given to the enactment of legislation guaranteeing access to meeting-places without discrimination. The public must be aroused to the seriousness of this danger and to facts proven in all history that destruction of free assemblage precedes the destruction of voting rights. Access to the meeting-hall is as essential to democracy as access to the polling-booth. A voter who is ignorant of the issues is a voter who has lost his vote.

We propose a mass campaign to arouse the public to fight all cases of violation of the right of speech and communication and to bring about the enactment of appropriate laws.

But that is a long-range objective.

We intend immediately and militantly to assert our right of communication. We hereby resolve immediately to undertake the publication of a national weekly newsletter, which we hope will as quickly as possible grow into a national newspaper reflecting the views of the Progressive Citizens of America and reaching a wide and growing audience.

We further pledge ourselves immediately to raise the money to institute a weekly national broadcast over all major networks, with a program produced, written and acted by members of the Arts, Sciences & Professions Council.

We believe that these two undertakings can be of decisive service to the American people in breaking the stranglehold at present exerted on communication, and in reasserting the inalienable rights guaranteed by the first 10 amendments to our Constitution.

A LETTER TO THE PRESIDENT

Dear Mr. President:

This conference of artists, scientists and professionals has conducted panels over a period of four days to investigate the problem of thought control in the United States. We find overwhelming evidence that there is a dangerous and increasing encroachment upon the traditional freedoms of speech, assemblage and communication which are guaranteed by the Constitution of the United States and which are the foundations upon which our democratic system is built. We believe that it is the duty of every American citizen to speak out against this undemocratic and illegal attack on the rights of citizenship. We are convinced that no public official can condone or support this attempt at political censorship without being derelict in his duty.

We call on you, Mr. President, to make a clear and unequivocal statement followed by appropriate executive action to halt this dangerous trend and ensure full protection of Constitutional rights of speech, communication and assemblage. The revocation of the loyalty-test which you yourself have instituted is a first step toward the re-establishment of our traditional American liberties. The vast number of government employees must not be converted into second-class citizens with the constant threat of economic reprisals and public abuse, if they dare to advocate views or belong to organizations which advocate views considered subversive by government officials.

We call to your attention the fact that Franklin D. Roosevelt characterized the procedures of the Dies Committee as sordid, and consistently opposed the Committee's encroachments upon civil rights. Today the procedure of the Thomas-Rankin Committee has reached a degree of sordidness and unconstitutionality that its predecessor never dared to attempt. The objectives of this so-called Un-American Activities Committee—and thus far it has been dangerously successful in accomplishing these objectives—are to subject those with whom it disagrees to the loss of jobs and to the penalty of the blacklist; the deprivation of the means of communication such as the radio and the press and the refusal of meeting-places. Persons who persist in asserting their traditional rights are further threatened with persecution, fines and imprisonment. This committee, this unconstitutional instrumentality of thought control, must be abolished. If the persecutions of any of those who have taken the lead in challenging the authority of

Thomas and Rankin succeed—and it is immaterial whether we agree with the views or politics of those being prosecuted,—no progressive citizen or organization is safe.

Accompanying this direct political persecution is an increasing use of economic power by private employers to demand conformity of opinion from their employees and intimidate with the threat of discharge all those holding views which are pro-labor or politically progressive.

This campaign of repression is accompanied by organized propaganda, through the press and radio and also emanating from government sources, designed to create an atmosphere of crisis and hysteria, clearly designed to interfere with the normal functioning of the democratic process and to stimulate an unreasoning fever for war. We know of no facts that justify this crisis atmosphere and believe it is evident that the American people are being systematically misled concerning the facts. Free and unrestricted discussion is the only way to ascertain facts and determine political action in a democracy.

The law may be utilized either as an instrument of thought control or as the guardian of the freedom of speech, press, assembly and religion, through which the democratic process functions. We ask you to take a clear stand, Mr. President, affirming the full power of the law for the protection of the people of our country, and not as an instrument of economic intimidation and political power.

We ask you specifically to take the following steps:

(1) To abolish the discriminatory and un-American loyalty-tests;

(2) To instruct the Attorney-General of the United States to dismiss the charges against all those who are today being prosecuted for alleged contempt of the Thomas-Rankin Committee;

(3) To join your illustrious predecessor in emphatic rejection of the Thomas-Rankin Committee's illegal methods and objectives;

(4) To speak out against those who are denying meeting-places and freedom of the press and the air to the people.

index

to the *proceedings of the Conference on the Subject of Thought Control, Beverly Hills, July 9-13, 1947.*

NAMES OF PANELS, OF PAPERS PRINTED AND OF THEIR AUTHORS ARE IN CAPITAL LETTERS.

Names of works referred to are in italics.

Names of individuals, groups and organizations referred to are in standard type.

Index compiled by Harold J. Salemson.

410

General Mills—260
General Motors—151, 263
Gentleman from Athens, The—39
Gentleman's Agreement—329, 334, 347
George III of England—180
Georgetown University—32
German-American Bund—161
Gestapo—288, 292, 357, 360
Get Aboard the Peace Train—226
Gettysburg—20
Gewehre auf Reisen—124
Gibbons, Cedric—308
G. I. Joe—179
Gilmore Stadium—367
Gladiators, The—343-4
Gleichschaltung—123, 388
Godwin, Earl—162
Goebbels—123, 200, 231, 356, 393
Goering—125, 288, 356
Goethe—14, 203
Goldberg, Navy Cdr.—159
Golden Age (of Elizabethan England)—341-2
Golden Boy—340
Goldwyn, Sam—32, 310, 329
Goodpasture, Ernest W.—258
Good Samaritan Hospital—235
Gordon, Elizabeth—153
Gorham, Mrs. Thelma Thurston—94
Gorky, Maxim—193
Gosch, Martin—39
Gospel According to St. Luke's, The—179
Gouled vs. U. S.—43
Government Printing Office—56
Gow, James—205
Graener, Paul—232
Grafton, Samuel—32-3
Grapes of Wrath, The—199, 329
Great Expectations—334
Great Gildersleeve, The—164
Great Lakes Broadcasting Co.—141
Green, Percy—93
Greene, Graham—199, 203
Greenleaf, Thomas—181
Grocery Manufacturers of America—165

Gropius—234
Grosse Point Broadcasting Corp.—153
Grosz, George—233
Group Health Assn.—250
Group Theatre—340, 369
Groves, Gen.—280, 380
Gruenewald—233
Guerrero, Xavier—241-2, 248, 375
Gwynn, Nell—342

H

Halsey, Margaret—156
Hamilton, Alexander (and Hamiltonians)—15-7, 26, 180-2
Hamiltonian Principles—15
Hamilton Report—265
Hand, Augustus—84
Hand, Learned—84
Hanford Engineering Works—286
Harding, Warren G.—23
Harriet—156
HARRIS, ROY—5-7, 3
Harris vs. U. S.—43
Harry-Baur—360
Hart, Merwin K.—161
Hartford Convention—18
Hartford Courant, The—81
Harvard Economics Dept.—300
Harvard University—40, 106, 275, 300, 303
Harvey—210
Hatch Act—58
Hay, John—20
Hay, Judge—85
Hayes, Edward A.—161
Hayes, Helen—133, 156
Hays Office—80, 205
Health in Handcuffs—262
Health Insurance—249-56, 262-3, 266
Hearst, Wm. R. (and papers)—22, 78, 103, 116-7, 155, 159, 166, 205-6, 212, 226-7, 241, 305-7, 331, 364, 374, 395
Heatter, Gabriel—158
Hecate County (Memoirs of)—212-3
Heidelberg University—300

S

Sacco and Vanzetti—27
Sacramento daily press—116
Sade, Marquis de—199
Sadducees—13
St. Louis University—300-1
St. Louis Woman—225
Sairy McBean—367
Salem—9, 294
Salemson, Harold J.—407
Salt, Waldo—179, 211
San Bernardino daily press—116
San Diego daily press—116
San Diego Schools—293
San Fernando Valley Times, The—117
San Francisco Chronicle, The—106
San Francisco Conference—161
San Francisco Examiner, The—349
San Francisco Medical Society—254-5
Sanity in Art—245
Santa Barbara daily press—116
Santa Fe R. R.—225
Santley, Joseph—346
Saroyan, William—336-8
Sarvis, David—378
Saturday Evening Post, The—34
Sawyer, Joe—346
S.C.A.P.—282
Schappes, Morris U.—301
Schary, Dore—32, 326-7, 329
Schering Corp.—259
Schiller—201, 356
Schlemmer—233
Schmitthenner—234
Schnabel, Arthur—231-2
Schneiderman, William—78
Schneiderman vs. U. S.—62-3
Schoenberg, Arnold—230-2
Schongaver—233
Schreker, Franz—231-2
Schuyler, George—94
Schwartz—93
Science—258
SCIENCE AND EDUCATION—267-304, 379-82
Scientific Intelligence Survey, GHQ—282

SCIENTIST AND HIS WORK, THE—278-86
SCOTT, ADRIAN—324-30, 305, 321
Scott, Hazel—224
Scourge of Aristocracy, The—184
Screen Story Analysts' Guild—110
SCREEN WRITER AND CENSOR-SHIP, THE—331-5
Screen Writers' Guild—310, 324
Scripps (newspapers)—120
Searching Wind, The—309
Sears, Roebuck & Co.—262
Secession—91
Section of Fine Arts, U. S.—240
Sedition Trials—161
Seldes, George—102, 118, 155
Selznick, David—310
Senate, U. S.—41, 45, 133, 143-4, 146, 168, 216, 219, 251-3, 259, 262-3, 278, 280, 307, 351, 379
Senate Bill 545—253
Senate Committee on Education and Labor—252-3
Senate Committee on Interstate Commerce—133, 147, 307
Senate Hearings on Science Legislation—278
Senate Investigating Committee (1943)—143
Senate Subcommittee Investigating Small Business—144
"Senior Problems"—333
Sergeant York—391
Sex Education (1026)—291
Shakespeare, William—210, 341-2, 350, 353, 357-8
Shapiro, Victor—130, 172
SHAPLEY, DR. HARLOW—8-9, 3, 303, 382
"Share and share alike"—312, 322, 378
Shaw, George Bernard—353
Shawn, Ben—247
Shelley, Percy Bysshe—201
Sherman, Maurice S.—81
Sherman Anti-Trust Act—80, 84, 265
Sherwood, Robert E.—32, 366
SHIP, REUBEN—130-8, 171, 376

427

432